WINNING
AT THE
RACES

COMPUTER DISCOVERIES
IN
THOROUGHBRED
HANDICAPPING

WINNING AT THE RACES

COMPUTER DISCOVERIES IN THOROUGHBRED HANDICAPPING

by William L. Quirin, Ph.D.

WILLIAM MORROW AND COMPANY, INC. NEW YORK 1979

DESIGNED BY A GOOD THING, INC.

Library of Congress Cataloging in Publication Data

Quirin, William L
  Winning at the races.

  1. Horse race betting. 2. Horse race betting—Data
processing. 3. Horse race betting—Statistical methods.
4. Multivariate analysis. I. Title.
SF331.Q57   798´.401   79-1271
ISBN 0-688-03400-4

Printed in the United States of America.

To my wife Diane,
the best winner I ever picked,

and to the Thoroughbreds.

ODE TO JIM J.
In the blueness of reality
Rests a taste of unknown wonder
As streaming down the backstretch
Just a glimpse of vile thunder
For the acts of the swift
Are the truths of today
While the motions of life
Are the moves of Jim J.
—P. ZIPSE

FOREWORD

This book is part of what its publisher and I are pleased to call the Tom Ainslie—Winner's Circle Series. To qualify for inclusion in the series, a work must be the successful product of original thought and original research. That is, it must advance the frontiers of knowledge in its particular field.

The field of the present work is Thoroughbred handicapping, a marvelously challenging intellectual pastime in which the frontiers of knowledge are entirely too cramped. Although claims of quasi-miraculous scientific discovery abound in the literature of the game, truly scientific research is virtually unheard of. Most of the literature collapses under scrutiny. Some of it is merely egomaniacal. Some is fraudulent. Some is both.

Here we have a notable exception. Its author, William L. Quirin, Ph.D., is Associate Professor of Mathematics (Computer Sciences) at Adelphi University. He is by no means the first computer expert to tackle handicapping, and far from the first to offer computer findings in that subject. On the other hand, he is to the best of my knowledge and belief the only such person who combines (a) thorough mathematical competence, (b) thorough handicapping competence and (c) un-compromising adherence to the rules of scientific inquiry. Those rules forbid the issuance of claims unsupported by proper evidence.

In these pages, Dr. Quirin presents the most comprehensive study of Thoroughbred performance patterns in the history of racing. Whatever is held important in the handicapping of Thoroughbred races is here subjected to the test of statistical analysis. The significance of each handicapping factor is examined separately. Those that prove most promising are then tested in combination with each other.

To observe that experienced handicappers are due for some exciting surprises is to state the case in the mildest terms.

Although I believe that enthusiasts of the game will want to read the work from beginning to end and will find it endlessly rewarding, I should like to call particular attention to some of its more important sections:

1.   A detailed study of speed handicapping which includes speed charts for 101 North American tracks.

2.   An extraordinary review of the role of breeding in turf racing, with an up-to-date list of the most successful sires and a list of other runners likely to become good turf sires.

3.   A profound inquiry into the importance of early speed, including a new way to predict which horses are most likely to produce early speed in the upcoming race.

4.   An investigation of current form, with a new concept which distinguishes the excusable poor race from the unforgivable.   Also included are solid discoveries about the performances of horses after freshening layoffs.

5.   Revelations about the actual importance of past earnings and past consistency, and the most effective ways to incorporate them into handicapping procedures.

Having tested every popular handicapping theory and technique (and some not so well known), Quirin concludes with some computer-designed selection procedures which have performed handsomely in actual practice.

As the reader may imagine, this book is the product of years of devoted study. I predict without hesitation that it will stand alone for years as the definitive work of its kind, and that it will delight its readers by ushering them toward more winners.

TOM AINSLIE

ACKNOWLEDGMENTS

The author would like to thank, first and foremost, his good friend Tom Ainslie, for his guidance as this book evolved over the years, and especially for reading the various stages of the manuscript and suggesting numerous improvements and revisions that have helped bring the book into its present form.

I would also like to thank my close friends and racetrack compatriots Phil Zipse (who introduced me to the fascinating challenge of handicapping), John McCausland, Anton Hemm, and Glenn Magnell, for sharing their thoughts on handicapping, many of which appear in these pages.

Thanks also to the staff of the Adelphi University Computing Center, in particular to Frank Ely, Gary Tobey, and John Southard for their untiring assistance keeping my programs running smoothly and efficiently, and to computer operators Paul Szachacz, Fred Drechsel, Mary Beiner, Mark Thomas, Larry Ryan, and Mike Abbene for service above and beyond the call of duty.

Finally, I would like to thank the following people for the roles they played in making this book possible: Herbert Alexander, John Schipani, Fred Davis, and Howard Rowe. And special thanks to Hall of Fame trainer Johnny Nerud and Margaret Dimitrijevic for their help in acquiring photographs of Dr. Fager.

Most of the excellent photographs in the book are the work of Bob Coglianese, the New York Racing Association's Eclipse Award-winning photographer, to whom I am deeply indebted.

The author also thanks the *Daily Racing Form* for its permission to illustrate these pages with many of their copyrighted past-performance records and result charts.

CONTENTS

INTRODUCTION

You can beat the races, but not the race. Or perhaps you have heard the opposite—that you can beat an individual race, but not the races.

The latter philosophy implies the existence of "sure things." Experienced handicappers know otherwise. They know that horses, like humans, have their good days and their bad days. They know that horses break down. That even the best jockeys make mistakes. That trainers race horses that are not physically at their best. And that the "sure losers" sometimes do not cooperate.

The one sure thing at the track is that the government and the racetrack will profit from the day's transactions. Because of the pari-mutuel tax (approximately 17 percent in most states), the racetrack audience is guaranteed to leave the track separated from more than 17 percent of the money it collectively has bet. This tax is what makes beating the races so difficult. The odds are stacked against the player much more heavily than in the gambling casinos of Las Vegas.

Most of the games at Las Vegas offer no advantage at all to an intelligent player. Blackjack is a notable exception. Several books have been written detailing systems their authors claim will beat that game.

Horse-race betting is something like blackjack. The knowledgeable player has an advantage. Many people play the races as they would play the roulette wheel—with a lot of rhyme and little reason. Their money—less taxes—ends up in the intelligent players' pockets. Were it not for the casual, uninformed players, intelligent players could not hope to remain solvent.

It is no simple task to pick the winner of a given race. Some races defy prediction. The results of others defy explanation.

Many different factors combine to produce a winner. The clever forecaster must weigh these factors carefully before making his selection. More often than not, even the best handicappers find their efforts were in vain.

Even though there is no such thing as a "sure thing," there definitely are "sure types." Certain characteristics in a horse's past-performance records combine to produce a good percentage of winners and reasonable profit over an extended period of time. Other characteristics portend disaster for the unwary investor.

The purpose of this book is to make the serious handicapper aware of the various types of horses that are worthwhile betting propositions, and to teach him to beware of those that can only mean financial disaster.

This is done by presenting the evidence—the results of statistical studies of considerable amounts of past-performance data. Most of these studies were carried out by computer.

The computer was used to test some of the prevailing assumptions, convictions, and confusions in thoroughbred handicapping.

Individual handicapping factors were isolated, and their importance in the total picture evaluated.

Various methods of fitting the different pieces of the puzzle back together were tested, with some interesting systems resulting.

This book, then, deals with factor analysis (Chapters 1–23) culminating in handicapping procedures and systems (Chapters 24–26).

○ FAVORITES ○

To introduce the statistical terms that will be used throughout the book, we present the results of a study of 4,800 betting favorites:

NH	NW	NP	NS	WPCT	MPCT	$NET	I.V.
4800	1567*	924	678	32.6%	66.0%	$1.81	2.99

NH: Number of horses. This tabulation and those on later pages study horses with one or another specific characteristic. In this example, we examine 4,800 horses which were the betting favorites in 4,800 races run (on dirt) at major East Coast tracks, from New York to Florida.

NW: Number of winners. Of the 4,800 favorites, 1,567 won.

NP: Number that placed. Of the 4,800 favorites, 924 ran second.

NS: Number that showed. Of the 4,800 favorites, 678 ran third.

WPCT: Winning percentage of the horses under study. The 1,567 winning favorites were 32.6 percent of the 4,800 favorites.

MPCT: Money percentage. The percentage of horses studied that finished in the money—first, second, or third. Our 4,800 favorites accomplished this 66.0 percent of the time.

$NET: Dollar net. A flat $2 bet on each of the 4,800 favorites would have netted a loss of 19 cents per average bet—a loss of 9.5 cents on the wagered dollar.

I.V.: Impact value. The 4,800 favorites represented only 10.9 percent of the starters in their races, yet accounted for 32.6 percent of the victories. That is, they won 2.99 times their share of the races. I.V. statistics are calculated by dividing the percentage of winners with a given characteristic (%W) by the percentage of starters with that characteristic (%H). An I.V. of 1.00 means that horses with a specific characteristic have won no more and no less than their fair share of the races. An I.V. of 2.99 is conspicuously high, but the related $NET figure points out that a high I.V. is useless when the winners pay low mutuel prices—as favorites usually do.

Although not appearing in the sample tabulation, the important statistic %W will be used frequently, especially when studying handicapping characteristics common to several horses in a race. When just one horse in a field can have a certain characteristic, such as being the favorite, %W will be the same as WPCT.

The impact value is preferable to the winning percentage because it takes into account the number of horses in each race. Favorites (and all other types of horses) win more frequently in six-horse fields than they do in twelve-horse fields, for obvious reasons: fewer opponents, less traffic. But favorites in small fields are backed more heavily than favorites in large fields. The net result is the same: a 9 to 10 percent loss for chalk players, regardless of field size.

The I.V. and $NET alone are not quite sufficient for our purposes. What they lack is a guarantee that what they represent will be repeated in future samples.

Statisticians understand that fluctuations above and below the norm are to be expected. They also have ways of determining when a deviation from the norm becomes so large that it can no longer be accepted as a reasonable fluctuation.

A .300 hitter in baseball may knock out 35 hits in 100 at bats, and a statistician will hardly bat an eye. He realizes that such a pace is a reasonable fluctuation for a .300 hitter. But should the same batter make 40 hits in 100 at bats, the statistician would tend to believe the man is better than a .300 hitter—perhaps a hot .333 hitter instead.

We must be aware of this in our studies of thoroughbred performance. We may have observed a .300 hitter during a hot streak, and we must be careful not to conclude that he is a .350 hitter. The sample we have taken may represent a peak or a valley for the handicapping characteristic being studied, and we must not jump to conclusions. One sample that produces a high I.V. and a net profit may be countered by another that produces a lower I.V. and a net loss, with the aggregate result being nothing of interest or significance.

Fortunately, statistical techniques tell us when we have solid evidence about a strong or weak handicapping characteristic. We can compare the number of winners in our sample with a norm, and determine if the difference is statistically significant.

Our norm is called the *expected number of winners* (EW). Its justification can be found in Appendix A, which the mathematically inclined reader might wish to read at this point. Basically, it is this: Studies indicate that horses win as often as their odds predict they should. 2-1 shots win as often as 2-1 shots should—about 27 percent of the time. And 10-1 shots win about 7.5 percent of the time, just as the odds say they should. We can therefore use the odds of each individual horse in a sample to calculate the number of horses in the sample that should have won.

Statistical tests are available that determine if the difference between the actual number of winners in the sample and the expected number of winners is large enough to qualify as a trend, rather than a fluctuation. A trend indicates that something inherent in the nature of the horses being studied causes them to win or lose much more often than their odds say they should. And this is exactly what we are hoping to find.

When we do find a group of horses with a shared handicapping characteristic that win significantly more often than expected, we will place an asterisk(*) after the NW, as we did in the case of betting favorites. The 1,567 winning favorites far exceeded the 1,420 winners expected. When the actual number of winners turns out to be significantly less than the expected number of winners, we will use a double asterisk(**) instead.

So, in the studies that follow, a high impact value, together with a net profit and a single asterisk, points out a type of horse that can be counted upon to win much more frequently than its average odds predict, and produce profits over any extended period of time. A low impact value (well below 1.00), together with a drastic net loss and a double asterisk, points out a type highly unlikely to do much right over any extended period of time

Absence of the asterisk (or double asterisk) warns that what appears to be a strong (or weak) handicapping factor may not continue to produce positive (or negative) results in the future.

Favorites fall into neither of these categories. Although they win, and will continue to win, far more frequently than their odds say they should, they will not win often enough to produce a profit. Nevertheless, they represent an improvement over the average horse, which costs its backers 18 cents per wagered dollar—the effect of the pari-mutuel tax plus breakage.

The *Daily Racing Form* indicates that a horse had been favored in a previous start by placing an asterisk in front of the horse's odds for that race. Reviewer, the sire of Ruffian, was a very popular horse in his day — he was favored in each of the first seven starts of his career, six times at odds-on.

```
Reviewer                        B. c (1966-Ky, by Bold Ruler—Broadway, by Hasty Road    122   1969  2  2  0   0  $36,074
                                O. Phipps   E. A. Neloy            (O. Phipps)                 1968  5  4  1   0  $122,680
22Mar69–7Aqu  fst 7f  .22¾ .45¾1.22¾ BayShore   3  5  2¹  2¹½ 13  13  RUssery    130 *0.40  87-19  Reviewer 130³ Hey Good Lookin 113ⁿᵒ I Found Gold 111⁵      Handily 6
10Mar69–7Aqu  fst 6f  .22¾ .46¾1.11  Swift       2  4  3¹  2ⁿ  11½ 16  BBaeza     126 *0.40  88-24  Reviewer 126⁴ Count Jopa 126ⁿᵏ Mr. Coincidence 126ʰ         Easily 8
24Aug68–6Sar  fst 6½f.23  .45¾1.16  Hopeful      1 11  2½  1¹  1ʰ  2²½ JLRotz    b 122 *0.70  95- 6  Top Knight 122²½ Reviewer 122⁴ Bushido 122¹½      Slow start, tired 11
14Aug68–7Sar  fst 6f  .22½ .45  1.10¾ Special     6  4  3²  3¹  2½  12½ BBaeza    b 122 *0.40  96- 9  Reviewer 122²½ Hey Good Lookin 114ⁿᵒ Buck Run 122ⁿᵒ       In hand 6
27Jly68–8Mth  fst 6f  .21¾ .44¾1.10¾ Sapling      8  4  6⁷  5⁶  5²½ 1²  BBaeza     122 *1.30  90-15  Reviewer 122² Night Invader 122ⁿᵒ Al Hattab 122ⁿᵏ           Drew out 10
20Jly 68–5Mth  fst 5½f.22¾ .46  1.05  Allowance    4  3  3³  3⁴½ 2½  13  JVasquez   116 *0.90  92-17  Reviewer 116³ Dol's Imp 120³ Al Hattab 118¹½      Won with authority 7
19Apr68–3Aqu  fst 5f  .22¾ .46¾ .58¾ Md Sp Wt    7  8  8⁴½ 5³½ 2½ 14  BBaeza     122 *0.80  92-14  Reviewer 122⁴ Shut Eye 122⁵ Swooch Swoon 122ⁿᵏ           Easily best 9
Nominated for Kentucky Derby, Preakness and Belmont Stakes.      Apr 3 Bel tr.t. 4f fst .47½ h       Mar 29 Bel tr.t. 5f fst 1.01 b       Mar 20 Bel tr.t. fst .48¾ b
```

Copyright © 1979, by DAILY RACING FORM, INC. Reprinted with permission of copyright owner.

Statistics have been kept for years on the performance of favorites. Year after year, the results have been approximately the same —one of every three favorites wins, and two of every three run in the money. (Current statistics for any meeting can be found in the *Daily Racing Form.*) Our sample of 4,800 favorites was right on target in this respect.

Note the significance of these statistics. One of every two favorites fails to place; one of every three fails to show. Consequently, the one in two that does place would have to average a $4.00 place payoff to allow the "favorite to place" bettor to break even. And the two of three that do show would have to average a $3.00 show payoff to allow the "favorite to show" bettor to break even. Unfortunately, the average favorite does not pay so well in the place and show positions.

○ SPRINT VS. ROUTE FAVORITES ○

It would seem logical that favorites win more frequently at route distances than at sprint distances. There are fewer horses in the average route, and more time for the favorite (or any other horse) to overcome trouble encountered during the running of the race. The statistics indicate, however, that there is really no difference:

DISTANCE	NH	NW	WPCT	MPCT	$NET	I.V.
SPRINTS	3409	1106*	32.4%	65.4%	$1.79	2.92
ROUTES	1391	461*	33.1%	67.7%	$1.83	3.16

○ ODDS-ON FAVORITES ○

An especially interesting type of favorite is the odds-on choice. The big spenders are usually quite fond of this type of horse, since they are the ones that make the animal odds-on. The $2 bettor, however, would probably rather bet something else at more attractive odds.

Anyone thinking of betting an odds-on horse must be convinced that the animal has better than a 50-50 chance of winning. Is it worth the bet? Exactly 384 of the 4,800 favorites studied were of the odds-on variety, and here is how they did:

NH	NW	WPCT	MPCT	$NET	I.V.
384	213*	55.5%	86.5%	$1.90	4.40

Not exactly a reliable source of income. But they cost their backers only half the usual cost for betting favorites—five cents on the wagered dollar, rather than ten cents.

So it would not make sense to bet arbitrarily against odds-on favorites. If odds are to be a betting criterion, odds-on horses come closest to helping the bettor break even.

Nevertheless, there are those who reason that the presence of an odds-on horse makes another horse in the race an overlay. That horse is certainly not the second choice in the betting, as the following figures prove:

NH	NW	NP	NS	WPCT	MPCT	$NET	I.V.
384	62	96	69	16.1%	59.1%	$1.49	1.29

A large share of the second place finishes here must have been behind the odds-on choice. And even though these horses run in the money more often than expected, so do the odds-on favorites, which diminishes the place and show prices on both types.

○ CONCLUSION ○

Although its odds are a fair reflection of a horse's chances of winning, successful thoroughbred handicapping must go far beyond the odds. Betting the favorite in every race is a slow death. Betting longshots indiscriminately is quick suicide.

Thoroughbred handicapping is an inexact science, a game of percentages. Although overall, horses win in accordance with their odds, certain types are overlays, and others underlays. The overlays will win a certain percentage of the time at good enough prices to produce profits over an extended period. Whether or not one will win a given race can only be forecast in terms of percentages or probabilities.

This book will help build your grasp of the basic handicapping factors, so that you will more readily recognize advantageous betting opportunities when they arise. Only after you have mastered these basics can you fully appreciate the art of selecting winners.

Photo Credit: Jim Raftery—Turfotos

The late Bold Ruler, shown with owner Ogden Phipps and jockey Eddie Arcaro after winning the 1957 Trenton Handicap at Garden State Park. Sire of Triple Crown winner Secretariat, Wajima, and numerous other top-class horses, Bold Ruler is certainly the most influential sire ever produced in this country. His son Reviewer was the sire of the magnificent filly Ruffian, and his grandson Bold Reasoning the sire of 1977 Triple Crown winner Seattle Slew.

I hope that, even if you are a knowledgeable horseplayer you will, after studying the contents of this book, have added a few weapons to your arsenal, enough to provide an edge in a difficult game.

AN IMPORTANT DEFINITION

We will often use the word "good" in reference to the performance of a particular horse in a given race. Exactly what do we mean by a "good race"?

A horse's performance in a race is termed "good" if it ran *either* in the money *or* close to the winner.

By "in the money" we mean a finish either first, second, or third.

And by "close to the winner" we mean a finish within *two* lengths of the winner of a *sprint* race, or within *three* lengths of the winner of a *route* race.

So sprint finishes like 1^2, 2^1, 3^5, and 4^2 are all considered "good." Likewise route finishes such as 1^3, 2^2, 3^7, and 5^3.

The past performances of Gordorigo contain a variety of examples of good races—only his race on December 27 was not "good."

Gordorigo * $11,500 B. g (1964–Md), by Amerigo—Improve, by Better Self
Laurelton Stable M. Padovani (Mrs. H. L. Wright) **115**

1970	7	2	1	2	$9,960
1969	24	4	4	4	$24,015

27Mar70–2Aqu	my	6f	.23⅘ .48 1.12⅘	Cl	8500	3	5	5^5	4^2	$1^{\frac{1}{2}}$	$1^{1\frac{1}{4}}$	LAdams	b 117	2.30	79–26	Gordorigo $117^{1\frac{1}{4}}$ Bump You 119^h Beaustone $121^{\frac{3}{4}}$	Drew clear	8
18Mar70–1Aqu	fst	6f	.22⅗ .45⅘1.11	Clm	7000	4	10	11^{12}	$6^{6\frac{1}{2}}$	4^8	$3^{3\frac{3}{4}}$	EBelmonte	b 119	*2.10	84–17	Reserve Case 117^{31} Merry Rogue 113^{nk} Gordorigo 119^h	Rallied	11
10Mar70–2Aqu	fst	6f	.23 .47 1.12⅕	Clm	6500	2	4	5^5	4^3	$2^{\frac{1}{2}}$	$1^{\frac{3}{4}}$	ACorderoJr	b 117	5.00	82–20	Gordorigo $117^{\frac{3}{4}}$ Winslow Homer 119^{nk} Verjo 114^{nk}	Hard drive	12
23Feb70–2Hia	fst	6f	.22⅗ .46 1.11⅖	Clm	7000	2	4	$5^{3\frac{1}{4}}$	5^5	$5^{5\frac{1}{2}}$	2^h	ACorderoJr	b 112	4.30	87–12	Boston's Pick [illegible] Gordorigo 112no Cohesian 111no	Missed	12
7Feb70–2Hia	fst	7f	.23⅕ .46⅖1.24⅘	Clm	7000	7	9	9^{10}	$7^{5\frac{3}{4}}$	3^{nk}	5^2	ACorderoJr	b 112	6.00	82–18	On The Tiles $116^{1\frac{1}{2}}$ Roman Liege 114^{nk} Sy Gee 111^h	Hung	11
15Jan70–5TrP	sly	1 1/16	.46⅖1.10⅖1.4[illegible]⅘	Clm	8000	6	6	6^{11}	$5^{6\frac{1}{2}}$	3^6	4^3	EBelmonte	b 114	4.60	81–13	RichardB.Good $121^{1\frac{1}{2}}$ Carry BackBoy $108^{\frac{3}{4}}$ ArielHiatus $114^{\frac{3}{4}}$	L'te f't	8
3Jan70–5TrP	fst	1⅛	.46⅘1.11⅖1.49	Hcp	5000s	5	4	$4^{5\frac{1}{2}}$	3^4	2^4	$3^{6\frac{1}{4}}$	EMaple	b 116	3.70	82– 9	Arturo's Pride 113^6 Transponder 114^{nk} Gordorigo 116^1	Tired	8
27Dec69–4TrP	fst	1 1/16	.46⅕1.10⅘1.42⅕	Clm	10500	1	6	7^7	5^4	$5^{2\frac{1}{4}}$	5^7	EMaple	b 110	11.10	84–12	In Conquest 108^2 Ship Lock 120^1 Comprador 113^3	No mishap	12
20Dec69–7TrP	fst	1 1/16	.47 1.11⅖1.43	Hcp	5000s	10	8	$9^{5\frac{1}{4}}$	$6^{4\frac{1}{4}}$	$4^{3\frac{1}{2}}$	$3^{2\frac{1}{2}}$	CMarquez	b 119	7.00	84–15	Lord Claudy 114^1 Middletown Billy $118^{1\frac{1}{2}}$ Gordorigo 119no	Rallied	11
13Dec69–3Aqu	fst	7f	.23⅗ .47 1.25	Cl	c-6500	6	4	2^2	$2^{\frac{1}{2}}$	2^h	2^2	LAdams	b 118	*1.90	74–21	Relajante 114^2 Gordorigo 118^h Gala Purple 111^h	Gamely	9
8Dec69–4Aqu	sly	7f	.23⅕ .46⅘1.24⅗	Cl	c-5000	6	2	$6^{8\frac{1}{2}}$	4^5	1^2	$1^{4\frac{1}{2}}$	ACorderoJr	b 121	*2.00	78–24	Gordorigo $121^{4\frac{1}{2}}$ Metairie Padre 121^3 Sea Fable $118^{\frac{1}{2}}$	Handily	7
1Dec69–8Aqu	fst	6f	.23⅖ .47⅗1.11⅗	Clm	5000	5	3	$6^{2\frac{3}{4}}$	$4^{1\frac{1}{2}}$	$1^{1\frac{1}{2}}$	$1^{\frac{3}{4}}$	ACorderoJr	b 118	4.90	85–23	Gordorigo $118^{\frac{3}{4}}$ Farmer Boy 118^4 Ole Ben 118^6	Under strong drive	10

RACE
CLASSIFICATIONS

Most thoroughbreds begin their careers in maiden races. Those whose owners value them enough not to risk losing them on a claim run in Maiden Special Weights (MSW) races—the Eastern term for a non-claiming maiden race, more simply designated in the West as a straight maiden race.

The typical maiden special winner starts next in a Non-Winners of One (NW1) allowance race—often described as "non-winners of a race other than maiden or claiming," or as "non-winners of two races."

After winning such a race, a horse usually progresses to a Non-Winners of Two (NW2) allowance—a race open to horses that have not yet won two races other than maiden or claiming races, or possibly three races lifetime.

The typical NW2 winner then moves up into Non-Winners of Three (NW3) company, and faces other horses yet to win three races other than maiden or claiming.

Once a horse has succeeded in winning its way through the restricted allowance ranks, and is no longer eligible for such races, it becomes a member of what is called the Classified Division. It then races in Classified (CLF) allowance races against other horses that have also graduated from the restricted allowance ranks—including top-notchers prepping for future stakes engagements.

Of course, some horses can go only so far up the allowance ladder before they find the competition too difficult. To earn their keep, such horses must then descend into the claiming ranks.

To help in determining whether a claiming horse is moving up or down in class, we assume that the claiming "ladder" has 17 steps:

1. $50,000–$40,000
2. $35,000–$30,000
3. $27,500–$23,000
4. $22,500–$19,000
5. $18,000–$15,000
6. $14,000–$12,000
7. $11,000–$ 9,500
8. $ 9,000–$ 8,000
9. $ 7,500–$ 7,000
10. $ 6,500–$ 5,750
11. $ 5,500–$ 4,500
12. $ 4,000–$ 3,500
13. $ 3,250–$ 3,000
14. $ 2,750–$ 2,250
15. $ 2,200–$ 1,800
16. $ 1,750–$ 1,500
17. $ 1,250–$ 1,000

The correct classification of a race depends on the top claiming price listed in the conditions for the race. A race for horses entered with price tags ranging from $25,000 to $20,000 is a "step" 3 race, because its top claiming price falls between $27,500 and $23,000.

If a horse from such a race starts next in a contest where the claiming prices range from $16,000 to $14,000, it would be dropping two classes, because the latter race qualifies as a "step" 5 race.

THE
SIGNIFICANCE
OF
EARLY
SPEED

An old racetrack adage states that the advantage in a race lies with those horses that have early speed. It is truer than most players realize. You might go so far as to say that it is the key to handicapping a race.

Certainly, it seems quite plausible. The speed horse is out in front, where his rivals cannot bump him, force him wide on a turn, block him when he makes his run, or kick dirt or mud in his face. Not to mention the possible psychological advantage of being in front. Many horses get "brave" when they reach the lead, perhaps more competitive than usual, and surprise everyone by staying in front.

But many people shy away from the speed horse, fearing that it will waste its energy fighting off another speed horse. Or that it will set such a brisk early pace that it will have no reserve energy to fight off challenges during the stretch run. Of course, this line of reasoning ignores the obstacles the come-from-behind horse will have to overcome to get into a challenging position, and the energy it will use in the process.

How many times have you seen a horse charge up from behind and practically catch the early leader, only to have its rally fall short by a head or neck? And how many times have you seen a horse come with an impressive late run, after circling wide on the turn, or coming out around a wall of horses, but never get near the early leader? It happens regularly.

Conventional wisdom dictates that an early speed horse's chances of winning are much better when the track is wet. Most horses do not like having dirt kicked in their face, but will tolerate it. But when it comes to having mud thrown at them, many lose their interest in racing very quickly.

All of this being common knowledge, I wondered if early speed horses were bet so heavily on wet days that nobody could make a long-term profit on them. Investigation revealed otherwise.

The following study shows how horses finished relative to their running positions (first, fifth, etc.) at the first call in 15,348 races run over all kinds of footing on all North American tracks for which the *Daily Racing Form* publishes first call position information in its Chart Books. For sprint races, the first call position (FCP) is recorded when the horses have raced ¼ of a mile, usually as the field approaches the turn. For routes, the first call position is recorded when the horses have raced ½ mile, after leaving the clubhouse turn for the backstretch.

FCP	NH	NW	WPCT	MPCT	$NET	I.V.	Ave. Odds
1	15348	4075*	26.6%	55.5%	$3.38	2.50	4.50-1
2	15348	2574*	16.8%	47.3%	$2.37	1.58	5.00-1
3	15348	2100*	13.7%	42.8%	$1.94	1.29	5.45-1
4	15348	1764	11.5%	37.9%	$1.46	1.08	5.80-1
5	15348	1475**	9.6%	33.8%	$1.28	0.90	6.25-1
6	15347	1165**	7.6%	28.2%	$1.11	0.71	6.90-1
7	14396	884**	6.1%	23.1%	$0.95	0.59	7.80-1
8	12576	619**	4.9%	19.0%	$0.71	0.49	8.90-1
9	9977	421**	4.2%	15.3%	$0.74	0.45	10.60-1
10	7807	173**	2.2%	11.0%	$0.46	0.24	12.75-1
11	4639	73**	1.6%	7.0%	$0.27	0.18	14.30-1
12	3040	25**	0.8%	5.0%	$0.23	0.10	17.20-1

(Note: The MPCT and $NET statistics here are based on 5339 of the 15,348 races studied.)

These figures could be grouped as follows:

FCP	NH	NW	WPCT	MPCT	$NET	%W	I.V.
1–3	46044	8749*	19.0%	47.9%	$2.56	57.0%	1.79
4–7	60439	5288**	8.8%	31.0%	$1.21	34.5%	0.82
8–12	38039	1311**	3.5%	14.4%	$0.56	8.5%	0.32

Or we could use the following grouping:

FCP	NH	NW	WPCT	MPCT	$NET	%W	I.V.
1–3	46044	8749*	19.0%	47.9%	$2.56	57.0%	1.79
Front Half	29067	2929**	10.1%	32.8%	$1.44	19.1%	0.95
Rear Half	69381	3670**	5.3%	21.3%	$0.76	23.9%	0.50

In the second tabulation, the category FRONT HALF includes all horses—other than those running first, second, or third at the first call—that led at least half their opponents at the first call. The category REAR HALF includes those that failed to lead half their opponents at the first call. For example, in a nine-horse field, the horses running fourth and fifth at the first call could be included in the FRONT HALF group, and those running sixth, seventh, eighth, and ninth at the first call would be included in the REAR HALF group.

No matter how you look at these statistics, the same conclusion must be reached: The closer a horse is during the early stages of a race, the closer it will be at the finish, and the more familiar its backers will be with the cashiers' windows. All the vital statistics become increasingly less favorable as we move down these tables, from the pacesetters, to the pace-prompters, to the come-from-behinders.

Most significantly, the %W column points out that the early leaders—the FCP 1–3 group—accounts for 57 percent of the victories—a rate slightly better than 5 races per 9 race card.

Notice that as a horse drops farther and farther back in the early stages, its average odds grow larger and larger. So the bettors, as a group, are aware to some extent that the advantage lies with those horses that possess some early foot. But, as the $2.56 average payoff for the FCP 1–3 group proves, early leaders are far from being overbet. Quite the contrary, they are lucrative overlays, in spite of the fact that they win almost twice their share of the races (I.V. = 1.79).

Horses that wind up at the rear of the pack in the early stages win and run in the money infrequently, returning their backers less than half their wager, on the average. Admittedly, many of these horses look hopeless on paper, and no sensible handicapper would even consider them. But approximately one third of them receive enough attention at the betting windows (odds below 10-1) to suggest that they have some chance of winning. But even these win at only a 7–8 percent rate, and return their backers only 75–80 cents per $2 bet.

A comparison of WPCT and MPCT figures reveals that the early speed horses are the "brides," while the come-from-behind horses are the "bridesmaids."

Piamem is a classic example of a "bridesmaid" type—three wins, but 14 seconds, in 45 starts over two years. Notice that Piamem can usually be found at the rear of the pack in the early stages of his races.

Ride the Curl, on the other hand, almost always sets the pace, and, like many front-runners, is a frequent winner.

When they run well, early speed types are more likely to win than place second or third. Come-from-behind types are more likely to settle

Piamem Dk. b. or br. h. 7, by Pia Star—Elle-Meme, by Grey Sovereign
Own.—Alfenzo M
Br.—Runnymede Farm (Ky)
Tr.—Barrera Lazaro S
117

Turf Record	St.	1st	2nd	3rd		St.	1st	2nd	3rd	Amt.
	4	0	0	0	1977	20	1	7	3	$77,098
					1976	25	2	7	1	$83,653

8Nov77- 7Aqu	sly 7f	:22⅗ :45⅖ 1:23⅖	3↑ Allowance	5 4 5^{15} 5^{13} 4^{7} $3^{4¾}$	Hernandez R	b 117	4.50	80-22	Jaipur's Gem 117¾ Patriot's Dream $115^{3½}$ Piamem $117^{7½}$	Rallied	5
31Oct77- 8Med	fst 6f	:22⅕ :45⅗ 1:11	3↑ Allowance	1 6 6^{13} 6^{11} 4^{11} $4^{8½}$	Cauthen S	b 117	3.50	81-22	Cojak 117^{nk} Marve $116^{4½}$ Jiva Coolit $122^{3¾}$	Outrun	6
25Oct77- 8Aqu	fst 6f	:22⅗ :45⅗ 1:09⅘	3↑ Allowance	5 3 $5^{8½}$ $4^{7½}$ $4^{6½}$ 4^{6}	Hernandez R	b 119	3.30	88-17	See The U. S. A. $122^{1¾}$ Yamanin 115^{nk} Jaipur'sGem 119^{4}	No threat	5
12Oct77- 8Bel	fst 6f	:22⅘ :45⅘ 1:10	3↑ Allowance	3 6 6^{13} 6^{7} $5^{4½}$ $5^{2¾}$	Cauthen S	b 117	2.40	89-17	Gitche Gumee 117no See The U. S. A. 122^{2} Helixiv 122^{nk}	No mishap	6
24Sep77- 7Bel	sly 6f	:22⅘ :46⅗ 1:12⅕	3↑ Allowance	6 7 7^{14} 7^{10} 7^{5} 2^{3}	Hernandez R	b 117	2.70	78-25	Sticky Situation 115^{3} Piamem 117¾ Port Authority 114^{nk}	Rallied	7
10Sep77- 7Bel	gd 6f	:23 :46 1:10⅕	3↑ Allowance	1 5 7^{7} $7^{6¾}$ $5^{5½}$ $5^{2¾}$	Hernandez R	b 119	*2.20	88-10	Gitche Gumee $115^{1¼}$ Father Hogan 115^{nk} DistantLand 115^{nk}	Outrun	8
3Sep77- 7Bel	my 6f	:23 :45⅗ 1:09⅗	3↑ Allowance	7 6 7^{6} 6^{5} $4^{2½}$ 2^{nk}	Hernandez R	b 117	3.80	94-14	It's Freezing 115^{nk} Piamem 117^{hd} Miami Sun $115^{1¾}$	Finished well	7
29Aug77- 8Bel	fst 6f	:22 :45⅖ 1:10	3↑ Fall Hi Wt H	5 12 $9^{9½}$ $7^{4½}$ $4^{2½}$ $3^{2½}$	Hernandez R	b 129	27.10	89-19	What ASummer 134^{2} BroadwayForli 123½ Piamem 129^{nk}	Good effort	12
23Aug77- 6Sar	fst 6f	:22⅗ :45 1:08⅖	3↑ Allowance	5 1 $5^{3¼}$ $5^{4½}$ $5^{6½}$ $5^{8¾}$	Velasquez J	b 117	3.70	89-13	John Bryn 117¾ Miami Sun $112^{3½}$ Great Above 117^{4}	No excuse	6
11Aug77- 8Sar	sly 6f	:21⅘ :44⅗ 1:09⅕	3↑ Allowance	5 3 5^{8} 4^{3} 1^{hd} $2^{3½}$	Velasquez J	b 117	3.00	90-12	Port Authority $115^{3½}$ Piamem 117^{1} DancingGloves $117^{1½}$	No match	6

LATEST WORKOUTS Oct 23 Bel 4f fst :52 b Oct 7 Bel tr.t 5f fst 1:03 b Sep 23 Bel tr.t 3f fst :37 b

Ride the Curl Dk. b. or br. g. 4, by Kauai King—Backseat Driver, by Traffic Judge
Own.—Tanenbaum A
$31,500
Br.—Happy Hill Farm (Ky)
Tr.—Martin J
114

Turf Record	St.	1st	2nd	3rd		St.	1st	2nd	3rd	Amt.
	1	0	0	0	1973	12	5	0	0	$28,220
					1972	10	1	0	1	$3,390

21Jun73- 4Aqu	fst 6f	:22⅗ :45⅗ 1:09⅘	3↑ Clm 22500	6 3 $1^{1½}$ 1^{hd} $1^{1½}$ 1^{2}	Cordero A Jr	121	2.40	94-12	Ride the Curl 121^{2} Fare You Well 124½ Bostons Boy 116¾	Driving	8
5Jun73- 8Bel	fst 6f	:22⅖ :45⅗ 1:10⅖	3↑ Clm 22500	1 4 1^{1} 1^{hd} 1½ 1¾	Cordero A Jr	116	3.20	92-08	Ride the Curl 116¾ Bold Skipper $117^{1¼}$ Rule the Past $107^{1½}$	Driving	7
4May73- 5Aqu	fst 1⅛	:45⅗ 1:11 1:49⅘	Clm 30000	4 2 $4^{1¾}$ $2^{1½}$ 3^{3} $4^{5¼}$	Cordero A Jr	118	*1.50	82-18	Waza Roman 109^{2} I Found Gold 116^{nk} Pollution 114^{3}	Speed, tired	6
28Apr73- 9Aqu	gd 1⅛	:46⅘ 1:11⅖ 1:50	Clm 42500	6 1 1^{1} 1½ 3^{2} 4^{7}	Cordero A Jr	114	*2.70	79-14	Trupan 112no Helio Rise 107^{4} Paraje 112^{3}	Tired badly	8
18Apr73- 6Aqu	fst 7f	:23⅕ :45⅘ 1:23⅕	Allowance	7 2 1^{2} 1^{hd} 1½ $1^{2½}$	Cordero A Jr	119	5.60	85-15	Ride the Curl $119^{2½}$ Stoney Battery 114¾ Prince Luck 114^{nk}	Mild drive	8
12Apr73- 7Aqu	fst 1⅛	:46⅗ 1:10⅘ 1:49⅕	Allowance	4 1 1^{5} 1^{2} $2^{1½}$ 5^{4}	Arellano J	113	7.80	86-15	Traffic Cop 119^{hd} Whitey II $113^{1½}$ Grenfall 113^{2}	Tired	7
27Mar73- 6Aqu	fst 1⅛	:47⅗ 1:12⅗ 1:50⅘	Allowance	4 1 $1^{1½}$ 1^{1} 1^{3} 1^{3}	Cordero A Jr	122	6.80	82-20	Ride the Curl 122^{3} Tu Dan's Image 112½ Cupid's Comet 122½	Ridden out	7
19Mar73- 9Aqu	fst 1⅛	:47⅗ 1:12⅖ 1:51⅗	Clm 16000	4 1 1^{1} 1½ 1^{3} $1^{5½}$	Cordero A Jr	116	3.70	78-23	Ride the Curl $116^{5½}$ Overide 118^{2} Nota 116¾	Ridden out	7
7Mar73- 7Aqu	gd 1⅛	:46⅘ 1:11⅗ 1:50⅕	3↑ Allowance	3 1 1^{2} 1^{hd} 3^{4} $5^{7¾}$	Amy J^{7}	108	38.80	77-17	Prince Luck 115^{1} Paternity $108^{4½}$ Twice A Prince 112¾	Tired	7
17Feb73- 5Hia	fst 1⅛	:46 1:10⅗ 1:49⅖	Clm 20000	10 1 1^{hd} 2^{1} 8^{14} 8^{16}	Cordero A Jr	117	10.40	72-14	Prince Luck 108^{2} Nota $117^{1½}$ Trupan 117½	Tired	10

LATEST WORKOUTS Jun 15 Bel tr.t 4f fst :47⅘ h ● Jun 1 Bel tr.t 5f fst 1:01 h May 27 Bel tr.t 6f my 1:17 h May 20 Bel tr.t 4f fst :48⅕ h

for secondary honors, even when they rally strongly. Among those first, second, or third at the first call that hang on to finish in the money, almost 40 percent win. Among ralliers that "get up" to finish in the money, less than 25 percent win.

As mentioned above, our 15,348 race sample was nationwide. It included races run at all types of racetracks, at all distances, and over all kinds of racing surfaces. It included races for horses of all classes, from New York stakes horses to $1,500 claimers, ridden by jockeys of varying skills at rating a horse. Nevertheless, it appears that what we have discovered about early speed horses is a universal constant, as the following table of impact values proves:

	FCP 1	*FCP 1-3*	*Front Half*	*Rear Half*
Mile Tracks	2.48	1.76	0.98	0.51
Bullrings	3.10	1.92	0.92	0.44

None of the statistics presented thus far reflects the distances of the races involved. The following study of 5,339 races does that:

SHORT SPRINTS—5–6 FURLONGS

FCP	*NH*	*NW*	*WPCT*	*MPCT*	*$NET*	*%W*	*I.V.*
1	2831	834*	29.5%	58.8%	$3.77	29.5%	2.85
1–3	8493	1772*	20.9%	50.6%	$2.75	62.6%	2.02
Front Half	5752	534**	9.3%	32.6%	$1.36	18.9%	0.90
Rear Half	13127	525**	4.0%	17.7%	$0.64	18.5%	0.39

LONG SPRINTS—6½–7 FURLONGS

FCP	NH	NW	WPCT	MPCT	$NET	%W	I.V.
1	881	189*	21.5%	48.9%	$2.79	21.5%	2.04
1–3	2643	468*	17.7%	44.3%	$2.38	53.1%	1.69
Front Half	1727	181	10.5%	32.0%	$1.54	20.5%	1.00
Rear Half	4026	232**	5.8%	22.8%	$0.94	26.3%	0.55

ROUTES—1–1¼ MILES

FCP	NH	NW	WPCT	MPCT	$NET	%W	I.V.
1	1627	404*	24.8%	53.3%	$3.03	24.8%	2.17
1–3	4881	893*	18.3%	47.1%	$2.34	54.9%	1.60
Front Half	2585	296	11.5%	35.4%	$1.57	18.2%	1.00
Rear Half	6778	438**	6.5%	24.6%	$0.88	26.9%	0.57

(Note: most of the races in the first category were at 6 furlongs, and only a small number in the last category were at 1¾16 miles or 1¼ miles.)

Not surprisingly, early speed horses perform best in short sprints, but do nicely at all other distances. Come-from-behind horses (the REAR HALF category) are in difficulty regardless of how much time they have to catch up.

In three special situations, early speed is not quite so powerful. They are:

(1) The one-turn route races at Aqueduct, Belmont, and Arlington.

(2) The mile races at Laurel, which start from a special chute and proceed around 1¼ turns.

(3) The mile races at Ellis Park, which also start from a special chute, this one perpendicular to the backstretch (similar to the old Wilson chute at Saratoga), and cover 1½ turns.

Here are the I.V.'s for first call positions in these cases:

	FCP 1	FCP 1-3	Front Half	Rear Half
1-turn routes	1.09	1.23	1.05	0.81
Laurel chute	1.32	1.42	1.25	0.63
Ellis chute	1.64	1.20	0.90	0.90

Notice that the I.V. swing from 1.23 (for the FCP 1-3 group) to 0.81 (for the REAR HALF group) for one-turn routes is quite small compared to the usual swing from 1.60 to 0.57 for routes in general.

Although it may seem illogical, early speed horses at Aqueduct hang on much better at 1⅛ miles than at the shorter 1-mile distance (which is run around just one turn). The reason appears to be the clubhouse turn. That first turn in a two-turn route appears a big advantage for the speed horse that can quickly grab the rail and save ground. Many of the slower, come-from-behind types find it more difficult getting into stride around a turn than they would were the early part of the race run on a straightaway. For that matter, early speed types do not get into full gear until they reach the backstretch, thereby conserving energy they might have burned up more quickly if allowed to run freely on a straight course.

Early speed is not as productive as usual when the horses (the front-runners in particular) must buck a strong wind on the backstretch. Come-from-behinders have "cover," to use a trotting term, sitting in behind the early leaders, not having to bear the full brunt of the wind. When the field fans out for the stretch run, everybody benefits from the tailwind. Unfortunately, the front-runners may be exhausted, having fought the wind and their rivals for the early lead.

Due perhaps to the texture of the racing strip or the prevailing direction of the wind, some tracks are more or less favorable than average to early speed horses. In the table on page 18, we give the I.V. for the FCP 1–3 group at each track listed. (If a certain track does not appear on this list, it is because *Daily Racing Form* Chart Books do not provide information concerning first call position at that track.) The statistics for all major and most minor tracks are based on individual samples of at least 300 races (in most cases, many more). At a few minor league tracks, we used samples of only 50 to 100 races. In general, it is safe to say that any track showing an I.V. between 1.60 and 2.00 is average with respect to early speed.

○ CLEAR EARLY LEADS ○

Since early leaders do so well, it stands to reason that a horse able to get a clear lead of at least one length in the early stages of a race would have a decided advantage. Of course, some rank horses insist on setting the pace, regardless of how fast they must run. These horses usually surrender abjectly when challenged later in the race. But if a horse is able to gain a clear lead without extreme effort, it is often able to take a breather down the backstretch or around the turn and control the pace of the race, to slow down the early fractions. When such a horse reaches the stretch, it usually has a lot of run left. In effect, it has reduced the race to a two-furlong sprint.

Here are the astonishing results of a study of 2,728 horses (run-

Track	I.V.	Track	I.V.
Ak-Sar-Ben	2.10	Jefferson Downs	2.03
Albuquerque	1.45	Keeneland	2.01
Aqueduct (Inner)	1.78	Keystone	1.50
Aqueduct (Main)	1.83	Latonia	2.23
Arlington	1.70	Laurel	1.84
Assiniboia Downs	1.82	Lincoln Downs	2.22
Atlantic City	1.90	Longacres	1.55
Bay Meadows	1.63	Louisiana Downs	1.58
Belmont	1.42	Meadowlands	1.83
Beulah	2.31	Monmouth	1.94
Bowie	1.63	Narragansett	1.65
Cahokia	1.80	Oaklawn	1.70
Calder	1.43	Penn National	1.51
Centennial	1.65	Pimlico	1.80
Churchill Downs	1.87	Pleasanton	1.63
Delaware	1.70	Pomona	1.98
Del Mar	1.88	River Downs	1.66
Detroit	1.98	Rockingham	1.69
Ellis	1.48	Sacramento	1.20
Exhibition	1.67	Santa Anita	1.72
Fair Grounds	1.77	Santa Rosa	2.18
Fairmount	2.13	Saratoga	1.99
Fonner	2.42	Solano	1.44
Fort Erie	1.68	Sportsmans	1.86
Fresno	1.93	Stockton	1.53
Garden State	2.13	Suffolk Downs	1.83
Golden Gate	1.60	Sunland	1.70
Greenwood	2.20	Thistledown (Inner)	1.96
Gulfstream	1.87	Thistledown (Main)	1.81
Hawthorne	1.82	Timonium	1.83
Hazel	1.75	Turf Paradise	1.75
Hialeah	2.12	Woodbine	2.04
Hollywood	1.73		

ning at major East Coast tracks) that had a clear lead at the first call:

	NH	NW	WPCT	MPCT	$NET	I.V.
Totals	2728	814*	29.8%	59.8%	$3.60	2.68
Low Odds	1977	718*	36.3%	68.3%	$3.25	3.27

Those bet below 10-1 (LOW ODDS) won and ran in the money more often than favorites do while producing better than a 60 percent profit. This group probably included few of the rank speedballs mentioned above.

While it might have been expected that these horses would do well, the size of their average payoff—$3.60—seems unbelievably high.

One would expect that a horse likely to set the early pace by itself would be bet off the board. But this is not the case—these horses escaped at average odds of $4.20 to 1. Of course, it is not always possible to predict that a certain horse will steal the early lead. The fact that one horse is alone on the lead is often the result of another speed horse having its troubles at the break, or simply not running at all.

Our study of horses able to get a clear early lead of at least one length breaks down as follows, according to distance:

Distance	NH	NW	WPCT	MPCT	$NET	I.V.
5–6 Fur.	1319	435*	33.0%	62.5%	$3.87	2.97
6½–7 Fur.	331	61	18.4%	49.2%	$2.30	1.66
1–1¼ M.	1078	318*	29.5%	59.6%	$3.66	2.36

The long sprint category stands out here. A horse with a clear early lead in a route race is often able to set a slow enough pace to conserve energy for the stretch run. But there is probably no such thing as a leisurely pace in a sprint. The horse out there by itself on the early lead has probably expended considerable energy to get there. If asked to go beyond six furlongs, it may very well get tired. So tired that it will win "only" 18.4 percent of its races, and return its backers an average profit of "only" 30 cents per $2 bet.

The conclusion is obvious, regardless of distance: if a fit horse appears capable of setting the pace by itself, it is an outstanding bet. *Any horse in such a situation is worth considering.*

Pace Makes The Race I: The Rabbit

The 1967 Woodward Stakes was hailed as the "Race of the Century," and rightly so. Competing were Buckpasser, Damascus, and Dr. Fager—each would retire from racing with earnings in excess of $1,000,000 and a ticket into racing's Hall of Fame.

Dr. Fager's vaunted early speed was the talk of the backstretch the week before the race. Damascus and Buckpasser both liked to run from well back, and their connections feared they would never catch a Dr. Fager running loose on the front end. Nobody expected the speedy Handsome Boy, Buckpasser's major rival of the summer, to compromise his chances by engaging Dr. Fager in a head-to-head confrontation for the early lead.

Enter the rabbits. Frank Whiteley (Damascus's trainer) dropped the name of Hedevar, an accomplished miler, into the entry box. Ed Neloy (Buckpasser) entered the noted sprinter Great Power. Mission: to run Dr. Fager off his feet in the early stages of the race.

Poor sportsmanship, perhaps, but clever horsemanship. At least for Damascus, as Hedevar accomplished his mission and Damascus roared past Dr. Fager at the head of the stretch. Great Power was unable to keep up with Dr. Fager and Hedevar in the early stages, while an ailing Buckpasser, running the last race of his career, could barely catch a weary Dr. Fager late in the stretch.

Dr. Fager and Damascus met again in the 1968 Suburban Handicap, with Hedevar on the sidelines this time. Damascus (under 133 pounds) was forced to take matters into his own hands, and challenged Dr. Fager's lead early on the backstretch, seldom a successful tactic for a come-from-behind horse. Dr. Fager (carrying 132 pounds), more accustomed to pacesetting tactics, pulled away from Damascus through the stretch.

A few weeks later, Hedevar was ready and Damascus (130 pounds) was able to turn the tables on Dr. Fager, who had to carry 135 pounds and chase Hedevar through early fractions of :45.4 and 1:09.2 (compared to the :48.2, 1:11 pace of the Suburban).

Photo credit: Bob Coglianese

Damascus wins the "Race of the Century"

The greatness of these two horses was underlined by the times they ran—Dr. Fager equaled the track record in the Suburban, Damascus set a new record (that still stands) in the Brooklyn—under staggering weights. It is sad that their rivalry was marred by the presence of Hedevar, a horse entered with no hope or intention of winning.

Lesson: When one of the contenders also happens to be the only speed horse in its field, its come-from-behind rivals are in deep trouble. Very few claiming or allowance horses have personal "rabbits" that can be entered, when needed, to insure an honest pace. Unless one of the stretch runners prompts the early pace, the speed horse will coast along on an easy lead, and probably never look back. But what of the stretch runner forced to play the role of pace-prompter? Chances are the animal will tire from running too fast at a time when it usually is just trying to catch its best stride. It probably won't be able to run fast enough to force the speed horse to an unrealistic pace, and therefore will have little effect on the speed horse's chances of winning.

Photo credit: Bob Coglianese

Dr. Fager's revenge in the Suburban.

○ SPEED DUELS ○

Many handicappers hesitate to support a speed horse in a race against another animal with the same front-running style. They fear a speed duel, in which the two will exhaust each other and clear the way for a come-from-behinder.

Yet the presence of two or more speed horses in a race does not make a speed duel inevitable. One horse may simply have more early speed, and leave the others behind. Another speed horse may drop a couple of lengths off the pace and wait. Still others may break poorly and be unable to use their early speed to best advantage.

Even if a speed duel develops, the participants should not be counted out. Here is a study of 1,705 races at major East Coast tracks. In each, two horses engaged in a speed duel, running within half a length of each other and at least one full length ahead of the rest of the field at the first call.

Photo credit: Bob Coglianese

Jaipur (in blinkers) defeats Ridan (right) in the 1962 Travers after one of the greatest "speed duels" in racing history—the two horses had been at each other's throats for the entire 1¼ miles.

NH	NW	WPCT	MPCT	$NET	%W	I.V.
3410	686*	20.1%	49.9%	$2.65	40.2%	1.81

Very promising—better than 40 percent of the 1,705 races studied were won by one of the two horses involved in the speed duel. A $2 bet on both produced an average return of $5.30 for the $4 investment, a profit of more than 30 percent.

Studying the distances of these races leads to the obvious conclusion—the longer a horse must fight off a challenge, or the farther it must run after fighting off a challenge, the less likely it is to enter the winner's circle after the race.

Distance	NH	NW	WPCT	MPCT	$NET	%W	I.V.
5–6 Fur.	1794	422*	23.5%	54.2%	$3.04	47.0%	2.12
6½–7 Fur.	602	105	17.4%	45.5%	$2.16	34.9%	1.57
1–1¼ M.	1014	159	15.7%	45.1%	$2.24	31.4%	1.25

The potential profits are still there, at the longer distances, but nowhere near as large as at six furlongs.

Does the inside horse have an edge because it will save ground on the rail around the turn (or turns)? Apparently not.

	NH	NW	WPCT	MPCT	$NET	I.V.
Inner Post	1705	325*	19.1%	47.7%	$2.43	1.72
Outer Post	1705	361*	21.2%	52.2%	$2.86	1.91

These figures combine both sprint and route races. However, the same pattern was evident for both sprints (one-turn races) and routes (two-turn races). Clearly, inside speed horses in routes do not have the advantage handicappers have long accorded them.

Actually, the advantage favoring the outside horse seems to have been built up over wet or damp tracks. Many tracks are deeper along the rail. Some are slanted slightly toward the rail. Therefore, they will dry out faster toward the center of the track. When such a track is wet or drying out, the most difficult place for a horse to run is along the rail.

However, even on fast tracks, the inside horse really has no advantage. To save ground on the inside is often to suffer the discomfort of racing between horses (or between a horse and the rail). Many horses prefer the freedom on the outside.

How often does the collective wisdom of the crowd pick the better of the two speed horses? The figures indicate that the "preferred" (or more heavily bet) of the two wins twice as often, but that the other wins often enough at higher odds to return far better profits.

	NH	NW	WPCT	MPCT	$NET	I.V.
Preferred	1705	477*	28.0%	60.5%	$2.37	2.52
Not Preferred	1705	209*	12.3%	39.4%	$2.93	1.10

Pace Makes The Race II: The Duel

The 1976 Triple Crown races presented a situation completely different from the Dr. Fager–Damascus rivalry of the 1960s. There were two major contenders: Honest Pleasure, the favorite, and Bold Forbes. Both were intense front-runners that seemed to resent any attempts at rating. Everybody knew that the two might cook each other in a suicidal duel for the early lead, setting the race up for a less talented horse with stamina.

Realizing this, jockey Braulio Baeza tried to rate Honest Pleasure behind Bold Forbes in the Derby. His tactics failed—Bold Forbes was able to relax and set a reasonable pace, and had enough left to hold off Honest Pleasure's repeated challenges in the stretch.

It was a different story in the Preakness. Baeza changed tactics, and pushed Honest Pleasure into the speed duel expected in Kentucky. After running the fastest six furlongs in Preakness history, both horses paid the price, and Elocutionist roared past them in the stretch.

Having tried it both ways, and failed, Honest Pleasure skipped the Belmont, leaving Bold Forbes as the only speed horse in the field. Running uncontested in the early stages, the little grandson of Bold Ruler opened a long lead. He would need every inch of it. Although tiring badly in the stretch, the game Bold Forbes managed to hold off the late charges of Great Contractor and MacKenzie Bridge, and win at a distance probably beyond his capabilities under normal circumstances.

Lesson: Just because two horses figure on paper to hook up in a speed duel does not mean that a speed duel will materialize, nor that the two horses should be dismissed as possible bets. Search the two horses' records looking for answers to the following two questions:

1. Can the horse win after engaging in a speed duel? Or does the horse win only when allowed to set its own pace?
2. Can the horse rate behind a fast pace, and then come on to win?

If the answers to these two questions are both "yes," the horse can be bet regardless of its competition for the early lead.

Dearly Precious was an example of such a horse. Her record indicates several races where she battled for the lead for a half mile, then drew out to victory. And other races where she allowed a couple of rivals to battle for the lead, caught them at the head of the stretch, and pulled away to win.

Judgable had just the opposite reputation. When allowed to set his own pace, he was able to win major stakes races. But when forced to battle for the lead, he was hard to find at the finish.

Dearly Precious — B. f. 2, by Dr Fager—Imsodear, by Chieftain
Own.—Bailey R E — Br.—Pancoast Jean R (Fla) — Tr.—DiMauro S

	St.	1st	2nd	3rd	Amt.
1975	9	8	0	0	$250,989

6Sep75- 8AP	fst	6f	:22	:45⅕	1:11⅕	ⒻArl WashLas	10	1	32½	12	13½	14	Hole M	119	*.40	87-21 Dearly Precious 1194 Free Journey 1192 Head Spy 119no	Easily	12
22Aug75- 8Sar	fst	6f	:23⅗	:45⅘	1:10⅗	ⒻSpinaway	4	4	1½	12	12	11	Hole M	120	*.50	87-17 DerlyPrecious1201OptimisticGl12010¾QuintsVicki120½	Ridden out	6
26Jly75- 8Mth	fst	6f	:22⅕	:45⅖	1:10⅖	ⒻSorority	2	2	2hd	1½	11	12¼	Hole M	119	*1.10	88-17 DearlyPrecious1192¼OptimisticGl1197TotieFields1193½	Drew clear	6
13Jly75- 8Bel	sly	5½f	:22⅖	:45⅖	1:04⅕	ⒻAstoria	3	1	1hd	1hd	11½	12¾	Hole M	118	*1.00	94-15 Dearly Precious 1182¾ Old Goat115½FreeJourney115no	Ridden out	7
28Jun75- 8Mth	fst	5½f	:22	:45⅕	1:04⅕	ⒻColleen	1	4	33½	3nk	11½	14	Hole M	121	1.40	96-18 Dearly Precious 1214 Old Goat 1174 Bells and Blades1177	Driving	7
15Jun75- 8Bel	fst	5½f	:22⅖	:45⅘	1:05⅖	ⒻFashion	6	3	1½	1½	11½	12¼	Hole M	117	*.90	88-13 Dearly Precious1172¼HoneyPot117nkQuintasVicki1172	Ridden out	8
25May75- 8Del	fst	5½f	:22⅘	:47⅗	1:06⅘	ⒻP Drummond	4	3	21	12	11	13	Hole M	115	1.70	84-26 Dearly Precious 1153 Hay Patcher1152½MimiRose1152	Ridden out	5
22Apr75- 4Aqu	fst	5f	:22⅗	:45⅖	:57⅗	ⒻMd Sp Wt	1	1	11½	11½	16	19½	Hole M	115	11.80	97-13 DerlyPrecious1159½Angel'sCommnd115½Htton'sRos1102½	Handily	6
15Apr75- 4Aqu	fst	5f	:22⅕	:46	:59	ⒻMd Sp Wt	5	5	512	512	513	58¾	Baeza B	115	6.40	82-16 PleasntTune1151½XlpSunrise1151½ArtfulWomn1101¾	Broke slowly	5

Judgable * — Dk. b. or br. c (1967-Ky), by Delta Judge—One Quest, by One-Eyed King — **116**
S. Nadler — H. Nadler — (Thompson Bros.)

1971	8	2	1	0	$103,360
1970	24	5	5	4	$173,100

24Apr71-7Aqu	fst 1⅛	.48⅘	1.13⅕	1.49⅗	GreyLagH	5	1	12	1½	11½	11½	RTurcotte	b 112	5.40	88-14 Judgable 1121½ Never Bow 124h Knight In Armor 1122	Driving	10
10Apr71-7Aqu	fst 1⅛	.45⅘	1.11⅕	1.50⅘	Excels'r H	2	2	1h	1h	65	713	RTurcotte	b 115	13.60	69-23 Loud 1161½ Personality 126no Knight In Armor 1103	Speed, tired	9
5Apr71-7Aqu	fst 1⅛	.47⅕	1.11⅖	1.50	Allowance	6	2	2h	36½	613	613	RWoodhouse	b 120	3.60	73-24 Paraje 118no Tunex 1162 Twogundan 1161½	Tired	8
20Mar71-9GP	fst 1¼	.45⅕	1.09⅖	1.59⅖	GulfParkH	1	1	1h	815	717	823	WBlum	b 116	8.40	79- 7 FastHilarious116no ThePruner1132 SnowSporting1191	Swerved	8
6Mar71-9GP	fst 1⅛	.46⅕	1.09⅘	1.47	DonnH	4	1	14	12	1½	1no	WBlum	b 113	30.60	99- 9 Judgable 113no Snow Sporting 1191¾ The Pruner 1141½	Came again	10
20Feb71-8Hia	fst 1¼	.46⅗	1.11	2.03⅘	WidenerH	12	2	2½	54	914	1110	WBlum	b 116	32.60	69-26 True North 114¾ Twogundan 115h Sunny Tim 1151½	Tired badly	13
6Feb71-8Hia	fst 1⅛	.46⅘	1.10⅘	1.49⅘	SeminoleH	4	4	54½	1112	1116	1116	BBaeza	b 119	6.10	70-19 True North 1102 Native Royalty 1111 Twogundan 1153	Tired	12
15Jan71-9TrP	fst 1⅛	.46⅕	1.10	1.47⅗	TropicalH	2	1	12	2h	2h	23	JVasquez	b 123	5.40	92-19 Al Hattab 1223 Judgable 1232½ Dorileo 1171	Drifted out	12
5Dec70-7Aqu	fst 2	.48⅗	1.14	3.21⅕	DisplayH	6	1	1h	725	738	741	BBaeza	b 115	7.30	49-19 Hitchcock 117nk Chompion 1152½ Up II 1164	Stopped to walk	7
21Nov70-7Aqu	fst 1⅝	.47⅕	1.12⅕	2.41⅗	Gal'tFoxH	7	1	110	1½	68	715	LPincayJr	b 118	8.00	82-15 Hitchock 1121¾ Chompion 1133 Romanesco 1064½	Gave way	11
14Nov70-7Aqu	my 1⅛	.47	1.11⅘	1.50	QunsCntyH	1	1	1h	11½	1½	3½	EBelmonte	b 119	*2.90	85-22 Best Turn 118½ Irurzun 112h Judgable 119nk	Held gamely	12
7Nov70-7Aqu	fst 1 3/16	.46⅕	1.10⅕	1.55¹	RoamerH	6	1	11½	1h	1h	21	JVasquez	b 125	10.10	97-12 Protanto 1151 Judgable 125h Buzkashi 1153	Gamely	10

LATEST WORKOUTS Apr 30 Bel tr.t. 3f fst .36⅕ b — Apr 21 Bel 6f fst 1.14 b — Mar 31 Bel 4f fst .47⅖ h

Photo credit: Lexington Herald-Leader

Bold Forbes beats Honest Pleasure in the 1976 Kentucky Derby

○ FAVORITES AND EARLY SPEED ○

The first call position statistics presented in this chapter have indicated very clearly that the horse leading at the first call is the most likely to win the race. In other words, when the field reaches the first call, the horse on the lead has taken over the role of favorite.

Our study of 4,800 betting favorites discussed in the Introduction reveals in no uncertain terms that a horse should be favored (or backed when favored) only if it appears capable of gaining a position among the early leaders.

FCP	NH	NW	WPCT	MPCT	$NET	I.V.
1–3	2466	1006*	40.8%	74.8%	$2.20	3.67
4–7	1850	477**	25.8%	60.3%	$1.44	2.32
8–12	484	84**	17.4%	43.2%	$1.10	1.57

Slightly more than half of these 4,800 favorites were, in fact, able to secure a position among the first three by the first call. They won more than 40 percent of their races, and returned their backers a 10 percent profit, rather than the customary 10 percent loss produced by favorites. Although constituting only 50 percent of the 4,800 favorites, this group produced almost two thirds of the winning favorites.

The other half, those favorites that were not able to gain a position among the early leaders, fell far short of the 33 percent winners expected of favorites. They left their backers in a far worse position than the pari-mutuel tax had already placed them.

Favorites that figure capable of showing early speed are good bets. Any other favorite also provides a betting opportunity—they are prime targets for upset defeats. From what we have learned in this chapter, the logical horse to pull such an upset is one with early speed.

In the following tabulation, we study that horse, among the first three at the first call, that received the most support at the betting windows.

NH	NW	WPCT	MPCT	$NET	I.V.
4800	1567*	32.6%	66.1%	$2.39	2.94

Slightly more than half these horses were the actual betting favorites, and they won better than 40 percent of their races, producing a 10 percent profit. The other half, who were not favored, won 24 percent of their races and produced a 30 percent profit:

NH	NW	WPCT	MPCT	$NET	I.V.
2334	561*	24.0%	56.9%	$2.59	2.16

Notice that our group of "early speed favorites" win and run in the money as often as favorites do. But instead of producing a 10 percent loss, they reward their backers with a profit of almost 20 percent.

Among our 4,800 favorites were 384 at odds-on. All but 122 of these were among the first three at the first call. Playing the "early speed favorite" against those 122 odds-on choices with little or no early foot produced 28 winners and a 50 percent profit.

Pace Makes The Race III: The Paceless Race

The fall turf "foursome"—the Man O'War Stakes, the Canadian and D.C. Internationals, and the new Aqueduct Turf Classic, all at weight-for-age—were supposed to determine the 1977 grass champion. The situation that developed left doubts that the best horse had emerged on top.

Regarded as "most likely to succeed" were two stretch runners, Majestic Light and Exceller. The experts looked good when Majestic Light escaped a traffic jam to storm to a 4½-length victory over a poorly ridden Exceller in the Man O'War—and when Exceller reversed that decision at Woodbine, catching Majestic Light in the last furlong.

But when the scene shifted to Laurel, something was missing—the pacesetters. None of the contestants were front-running types, and everybody knew it. Trainer John Russell (Majestic Light) joked that he would instruct his jockey (Sandy Hawley) to take the lead immediately. Hawley, however, had one thing on his mind—Exceller. And Angel Cordero on Exceller kept one eye on Majestic Light, ignoring the slow pace being set by Crow and Johnny D. (who had been third in the previous two races, coming from eighth and fifth in the early going). By the time Majestic Light got into gear (Exceller never did) Steve Cauthen, sensing the slow pace, had sent Johnny D. out to an insurmountable lead.

Jockeys seldom make the same mistake twice in succession. Especially when their blunder gets a good deal of publicity. But sometimes they overcompensate. Two weeks later at Aqueduct, first Lester Piggott (who had replaced Cordero on Exceller), and then Hawley, challenged Cauthen's early lead. Advantage: Johnny D. More accustomed to making one run late in the race, both Exceller and Majestic Light tired from their early efforts. Johnny D., ordinarily a pace-

27

prompter, was the strong horse in the stretch, being more comfortable in the pacesetting role.

　　Lesson: Stretch runners are usually one-run horses whose move must be perfectly timed. If they start their run too early, or if they run too close to the early lead, they will not have their usual punch in the stretch. Even when their move is timed correctly, they still need some cooperation up front—a strong pace contested by at least two horses.

Photo credit: Bob Coglianese

Majestic Light beats Exceller (inside) and Johnny D. (outside) in the 1977 Man O'War

○ THE TRUE TRACK BIAS ○

　　Andy Beyer coined a popular phrase when he devoted an entire chapter of his book *Picking Winners* (Houghton Mifflin, 1975) to the subject of "track biases." Certainly, it is a big plus to be able to supplement the past performances with the information that a horse's chances in a particular race were aided or diminished because of the weather or the condition of the racing surface.

In this chapter we have discovered the universal track bias—that almost every racetrack, under normal conditions, favors horses with early speed. A wise handicapper will always be on the lookout for a trend in the other direction, but unless solid evidence presents itself, will confine his bets to horses with at least a reasonable amount of early speed.

IDENTIFYING
THE
PACESETTERS

It is interesting to know that the horses contesting the early fractions have the advantage. Such information is worthless, however, unless it can be predicted *before the race* which horses are most likely to be the early leaders. Everything you have read in Chapter 1 was of an "after the fact" nature, showing what happened to horses that *did* (or *did not)* show early speed.

In the past, handicappers have used an analysis of past early fractions to separate the early speed horses in a race. Their reasoning might have gone something like this: "Since horse A set fractions of :21.4 and :45.1 in its last race, while horse B could only run :22.2 and :46 early fractions, horse A is faster than horse B and will outrun that rival by a few lengths in the early stages today."

Unfortunately, it is not that easy. Horse A's last race might have been at Monmouth, where such blazing fractions are commonplace. And horse B's last race may have come at much slower Belmont, and the animal may have been running every bit as fast as horse A.

In other words, pace analysis requires some way of comparing early fractions at different tracks, just as speed handicapping (see Chapters 16–19) requires a method for comparing final times at different tracks.

In addition, the condition of the racing surface, and the strength and direction of the wind, all affect how fast the early fractions will be run on a given day of racing. Unless they are all taken into account, a pace analysis can be very misleading. A superficial pace analysis will often fail to identify the true early speed in a race.

To further complicate matters, a computer study of some 45,000 lines of past performances has indicated that the early speed tendencies of horses vary from race to race. Considering the hectic scramble for position at the start of each race, this is understandable. The loss of a few steps at the break can mean the difference between being among the leaders or in the middle of the pack during the early stages of the race.

The table below summarizes the results of that study. It indicates how often a horse is able to repeat an early speed performance from one race to the next.

The table is in two parts—one for sprints, the other for routes. Each part contains two tabulations, one for horses that had sprinted in their last starts, the other for horses that had routed.

Sprinting Today

LAST RACE A SPRINT

	FCP 1–3	CLOSE
FCP 1	70.7%	71.2%
FCP 1–2	65.0%	66.2%
FCP 1–3	59.6%	60.9%
On Lead	68.1%	68.7%
Close	58.5%	60.2%

LAST RACE A ROUTE

	FCP 1–3	CLOSE
FCP 1	39.9%	40.2%
FCP 1–3	29.8%	32.5%
On Lead	36.1%	38.6%
Within 1 Length	34.4%	36.5%

Routing Today

LAST RACE A SPRINT

	FCP 1–3	CLOSE
FCP 1	81.6%	79.1%
FCP 1–3	73.4%	74.8%
Front Half	66.2%	65.3%
On Lead	80.5%	80.9%
Within 3 Lengths	69.5%	70.9%
Within 6 Lengths	60.4%	62.7%

LAST RACE A ROUTE

	FCP 1–3	CLOSE
FCP 1	73.0%	73.0%
FCP 1–2	65.8%	66.2%
FCP 1–3	59.3%	60.3%
On Lead	69.8%	70.9%
Close	57.6%	58.9%

The horse's early speed performance in its last start is indicated in the left-hand column of the tabulations. The category ON LEAD includes all horses that were leading, or within a neck of the lead, at the first call. The category FRONT HALF includes all horses that led at least half their opponents at the first call. And the category CLOSE includes all horses that were within 2 lengths of the lead in a sprint, or within 3 lengths of the lead in a route.

The study indicates that among horses not changing distances radically (from a sprint to a route, or from a route to a sprint), only three of every five that were among the early leaders (FCP 1–3) last out were able to contest the early lead again in their next start. Just slightly more than seven of every ten that led their field at the first call in their last start were able to come back and race with the early leaders next out.

The odds are stacked against a horse dropping back from a route to a sprint and being able to contend for the early lead. Only two of every five that set the pace in a route (FCP 1) were able to be close or among the first three in a subsequent sprint.

Early speed is most predictable when a horse is stretching out from a sprint to a route. Four of every five that were on the lead in a sprint will be among the early leaders in a subsequent route. As a matter of fact, horses within six lengths of the early lead in a sprint are more likely to contest the early lead in a subsequent route than are horses among the leaders or close to the lead in a route last out.

Along these same lines, the results of a study of the early fractions in over 1,000 sprints and routes reveals that the average first quarter in two-turn routes of $1\frac{1}{16}$ to $1\frac{1}{8}$ miles is approximately 1.3 seconds slower than the average first quarter in 6–$6\frac{1}{2}$ furlong sprints. At the same time, the average first quarter in one-turn routes of 1 to $1\frac{1}{8}$ miles is only $\frac{3}{5}$ slower than in the average sprint. This suggests a "natural" slowing down of approximately $\frac{7}{10}$ of a second to negotiate the clubhouse turn in two-turn routes. Other than that, there is apparently only a $\frac{3}{5}$ of a second difference between the early pace in sprints and routes.

This implies that a horse capable of running within six lengths of the early lead in a sprint figures to be able to run within three lengths of the early lead in a route. And a horse able to set the pace in a route is capable of running within three lengths of the early lead in a sprint, if not much closer.

○ SPEED POINTS ○

Since we have not met with overwhelming success trying to predict early speed solely on the basis of a horse's most recent race, it would seem wise instead to base this prediction on a few recent races. Several different approaches to this problem have been studied and compared. The one described below, devised by the author, appears to be the most effective.

Each horse in a race will be credited with a certain number of "speed points" for each of three recent races. We will start with the most recent race and work backward, never going back farther than five races in the horse's record, to find *three* "ratable" races. The horse's speed point total for these three races will represent a consensus of its recent ability to flash early speed at the distance it will be racing today.

Here is how it works. Each horse in the race starts with one speed point credited to its account.

32

For a horse entered in a sprint today, additional speed points are awarded as follows:

1 point for any sprint in which the horse was 1-2-3 at the first call.

    AND/OR (with an exception for seven-furlong races)

1 point for any sprint in which the horse was close (within two lengths) at the first call.

0 points for any other sprint performance.

0 points for any route performance, *unless* the horse was within one length of the early lead, in which case the race is passed (receives a bye).

So a horse may receive from zero to two speed points for each of three races. For a sprint, only past sprints can contribute to the to-tal—all routes receive no points, or a bye.

For past races at seven furlongs, a horse is eligible for 2 points only if it led at the first call. If the horse had been second or third, or within two lengths (*or both*) at the first call, it receives only 1 point. This special rule accounts for the fact that the pacesetters in the average seven-furlong race are not quite as quick as their counterparts in the average six-furlong race.

Timeless Moment, for example, earned 4 additional speed points, for a total of 5. He earned 1 point for running third (or within two lengths) at the first call at seven furlongs on both April 22 and March 19, and 2 points for running third *and* within two lengths at six furlongs on December 12. The latter race was used because the route race on April 6 received a bye—Timeless Moment raced within one length of the early lead on that occasion.

Little Miracle, on the other hand, earned only two additional points, for a total of 3—one for running within two lengths of the early lead October 4, the other for running third at the first call September 23. His early efforts on August 23 earned him no additional points.

Mr. Sad earned only one additional point, for running within two lengths of the early leader August 25, giving him a total of 2 speed points.

Little Miracle — Ch. c. 4, by Native Heritage—Won't Tell You, by Crafty Admiral
Own.—Sommer S — $25,000 — Br.—Harbor View Farm (Fla) — Tr.—Martin Frank — 113

	St.	1st	2nd	3rd	Amt.
1977	20	8	6	1	$51,870
1976	2	1	0	0	$3,600

4Oct77- 1Bel	fst	6f	:23⅖	:47	1:11⅘	3↑Clm c-17000	4	2	4^{2}	2½	1^{hd}	1½	Maple E	b	120	8.70	83-20	Little Miracle 120½ Cast In Bronze $117^{1\frac{1}{4}}$PassenMood117^{2}		Driving	7
23Sep77- 2Bel	fst	6f	:22⅗	:46⅗	1:11⅗	3↑Clm 15000	3	2	3^{7}	3^{4}	1^{hd}	1^{nk}	Samyn J L^{5}	b	112	*1.90	84-17	LittleMiracle112^{nk}Larry'sDogoon$119^{7\frac{1}{2}}$Don'tBelieveIt117¾		Driving	8
23Aug77- 4Sar	fst	6f	:22⅖	:45⅖	1:10⅗	3↑Clm 18000	8	1	4^{3}	$7^{3\frac{3}{4}}$	$5^{4\frac{1}{2}}$	5^{3}	Cauthen S	b	117	4.40	84-13	Street Ruler117^{no}Critic'sCircle113½RestlessBomb117½		No mishap	8
8Aug77- 2Sar	my	6f	:22⅖	:45⅘	1:10⅗	3↑Clm 16000	3	3	2^{hd}	2^{hd}	2½	2^{5}	Cauthen S	b	113	6.20	82-13	Jig Away 113^{5} Little Miracle $113^{2\frac{1}{2}}$ Cast In Bronze 119¾		2nd best	8
19Jly77- 5Bel	fst	6f	:23⅕	:47	1:11⅖	3↑Clm 15000	5	3	6^{4}	4^{nk}	1^{1}	2no	Cauthen S	b	117	*1.70	85-18	RestlessBomb117^{no}LittleMircle117^{3}Mggie'sPrid$115^{2\frac{1}{2}}$		Just missed	7
23Jun77- 2Bel	fst	6f	:22⅖	:46⅕	1:11⅕	3↑Clm 14000	1	2	$4^{4\frac{1}{2}}$	4^{2}	1½	$1^{1\frac{1}{4}}$	Cauthen S^{5}	b	115	3.10	86-19	Little Miracle $115^{1\frac{1}{4}}$Pilot'sSon117½SplitInfinitive113^{nk}		Drew clear	10
4Jun77- 1Bel	fst	6f	:23	:46⅘	1:11⅖	Clm 13000	6	9	3^{5}	$3^{1\frac{1}{2}}$	1^{hd}	2^{hd}	Graell A	b	115	*1.80	85-18	[D]Ad Alley 110^{hd} Little Miracle $115^{3\frac{1}{4}}$SyrianRhythm$115^{1\frac{1}{4}}$		Bumped	9
4Jun77-Placed first through disqualification																					
28May77- 9Bel	fst	6f	:22⅗	:46⅗	1:11⅗	Clm 12500	5	6	4^{5}	$3^{2\frac{1}{2}}$	$1^{1\frac{1}{2}}$	$2^{1\frac{1}{2}}$	Graell A	b	117	*2.80	82-22	Judge Power $117^{1\frac{1}{2}}$ Little Miracle $117^{2\frac{1}{2}}$ RiverRunner108¾		Gamely	11
10May77- 3Aqu	my	6f	:22⅗	:46	1:11⅗	Clm c-10000	4	8	$4^{4\frac{1}{2}}$	2^{5}	2^{2}	2^{hd}	Turcotte R	b	117	*3.60	85-18	Name O'Fortune 117^{hd} Little Miracle117^{no}Fortune112^{2}		Lugged in	9
30Apr77- 3Aqu	fst	6f	:22⅗	:46⅕	1:11	Clm 12500	7	3	2^{hd}	2^{hd}	2½	$4^{2\frac{3}{4}}$	Turcotte R	b	117	6.00	85-13	Dorage 113^{hd} Sproull D. 114^{hd} Don't Believe It $117^{2\frac{1}{2}}$		Weakened	12

LATEST WORKOUTS Oct 17 Bel tr.t 3f gd :37 b Sep 8 Bel tr.t 4f fst :51⅗ b Aug 20 Sar tr.t 4f fst :49⅗ b

Mr. Sad *— B. c. 2, by Bupers—Dry Dock, by Misty Flight
Own.—Morgan Mrs C D — Br.—Morgan C D (Va) — Tr.—Barrera L S — 113

	St.	1st	2nd	3rd	Amt.
1973	6	2	2	0	$14,850

13Sep73- 5Bel	fst	6½f	:22⅗	:45⅘	1:17⅖	Allowance	4	1	$6^{7\frac{1}{2}}$	5^{6}	$3^{1\frac{1}{2}}$	$4^{3\frac{1}{2}}$	Rivera M A	116	2.20e	86-14	Ham 115^{nk} Green Gambados 116½ Sea Dee $116^{2\frac{1}{2}}$	Weakened	7
25Aug73- 3Sar	fst	6f	:22⅖	:45⅘	1:11	Allowance	4	2	4^{2}	$4^{2\frac{1}{2}}$	1^{hd}	1½	Maple E	118	2.40	85-08	Mr. Sad 118½ Cannonade 120^{nk} B. J.'S Boy $118^{3\frac{1}{2}}$	Driving	6
16Aug73- 5Sar	fst	6½f	:22	:45⅖	1:18⅗	Allowance	2	4	6^{6}	6^{4}	2^{3}	2¾	Maple E	119	3.20e	85-14	Sea Dee 119¾ Mr. Sad 119^{1} Please Succeed $119^{1\frac{1}{2}}$	Altered course	7
10Aug73- 2Sar	fst	6f	:22⅗	:46⅕	1:11⅘	Md 35000	9	1	2½	1^{hd}	$1^{1\frac{1}{2}}$	1^{2}	Castaneda M	119	*2.30	81-11	Mr. Sad 119^{2} Cycle Guard 119^{nk} Canto 117^{hd}	Driving	12
3Aug73- 2Sar	sly	6f	:22⅗	:46⅗	1:11⅖	Md 25000	3	4	1½	1½	2^{hd}	2^{nk}	Castaneda M	119	13.70	83-14	Mid Jay 119^{nk} Mr. Sad $119^{6\frac{1}{2}}$ Write a Ticket $113^{2\frac{1}{2}}$	Just missed	11
19Jly73- 2Aqu	fst	5½f	:22⅖	:45⅗	1:05⅕	Md 25000	8	6	5^{6}	4^{9}	5^{11}	4^{8}	Castaneda M	118	32.50	79-15	Lethal Call 118½ Dr. Zegarelli 118^{7} Stonewalk 118½	Evenly	9

LATEST WORKOUTS Sep 21 Bel tr.t 4f fst :48 h Sep 11 Bel tr.t 4f fst :49⅗ b Sep 4 Bel tr.t 3f fst :36⅘ h Aug 9 Sar 3f fst :37 bg

Petrograd *— B. g. 7, by Petare—Ruling, by Nasrullah
Own.—Walsh Mrs T M — Br.—Marriott P M (Fla) — Tr.—Walsh T M — 118

Turf Record St.	1st	2nd	3rd		St.	1st	2nd	3rd	Amt.
1	0	0	0	1975	9	5	3	0	$67,629
				1974	3	2	1	0	$26,295

22Dec75- 6Aqu	fst	1	:47⅕	1:11⅗	1:35⅗	3↑Allowance	2	2	2^{1}	2^{hd}	2^{hd}	2no	Turcotte R	b	122	2.60	88-16	Rushing Man 119no Petrograd $122^{1\frac{3}{4}}$ Canvasser $109^{2\frac{1}{2}}$	Nosed	6
17Dec75- 8Aqu	fst	7f	:22⅖	:44⅖	1:21⅖	3↑Tom Fool H	6	6	$6^{6\frac{1}{2}}$	$6^{5\frac{1}{2}}$	5^{7}	$6^{4\frac{1}{2}}$	Turcotte R		119	*1.40	89-12	Kinsman Hope $116^{1\frac{1}{2}}$ Lonetree 125^{nk} Right Mind 113^{nk}	No excuse	9
3Dec75- 8Aqu	fst	6f	:22⅗	:45⅖	1:09⅖	3↑Sport Page H	7	3	$7^{4\frac{1}{2}}$	$5^{6\frac{1}{2}}$	2^{5}	2¾	Turcotte R	b	119	3.10	95-23	Lonetree 122¾ Petrograd 119^{4} Piamem 114no	Reaching winner	8
17Nov75- 6Aqu	fst	1	:45⅘	1:09⅗	1:34⅗	3↑Allowance	1	2	$2^{2\frac{1}{2}}$	$2^{1\frac{1}{2}}$	2^{1}	1^{nk}	Turcotte R	b	115	2.10	93-12	Petrograd 115^{nk} Dashboard 117no No Bias 122½	Driving	7
4Nov75- 7Bel	fst	6f	:23⅕	:46⅕	1:10⅕	3↑Allowance	6	6	$5^{3\frac{1}{2}}$	3^{3}	2^{hd}	1½	Turcotte R	b	118	*1.40	91-18	Petrograd 118½ Lord Rebeau 118^{6} Dashboard $116^{2\frac{3}{4}}$	Hard drive	8
29Oct75- 4Bel	fst	6f	:22⅘	:45⅘	1:09⅘	3↑Clm 45000	2	5	$6^{3\frac{3}{4}}$	4^{3}	2½	1^{nk}	Turcotte R		118	*.60	93-15	Petrograd 118^{nk} Delta Champ 118^{2} Straight ToParis$118^{2\frac{1}{4}}$	Driving	7
12Oct75- 6Bel	fst	6f	:22⅗	:46⅖	1:10⅖	3↑Clm 31500	1	4	$7^{5\frac{3}{4}}$	3^{1}	1^{3}	1^{3}	Turcotte R	b	116	*1.50	90-11	Petrograd 116^{3} El Espanoleto 115¾ GoldenGuinea116¾	Drew clear	8
10Jly75- 8Bel	fst	6f	:22⅗	:45⅖	1:09	Allowance	5	3	$4^{2\frac{1}{2}}$	3½	1^{hd}	1^{nk}	Maple E	b	114	*.90	98-12	Petrograd 114^{nk} See TheU.S.A.$114^{1\frac{3}{4}}$NativeBlend114^{10}	Hard drive	6
4Jly75- 7Mth	fst	6f	:21⅗	:44⅕	1:08⅗	Allowance	4	3	2^{6}	2^{6}	2^{5}	$2^{3\frac{3}{4}}$	Maple E	b	119	*1.00	93-18	Jo Jo Tex $117^{3\frac{3}{4}}$ Petrograd $119^{1\frac{1}{4}}$ Kettle River 113^{7}	Gamely	8
20Apr74- 8GS	fst	6f	:22	:44⅖	1:08⅗	3↑Whirlaway H	1	6	3^{4}	3^{4}	2^{3}	2^{4}	Barrera C	b	118	1.30	97-22	Mr. Prospector 120^{4} Petrograd 118^{8} Game Lad115^{hd}	Second best	8

Petrograd earned no additional speed points. He showed sufficient speed at one mile December 22 to have that race passed, but such was not the case November 17. And the two sprints in between netted him no speed points.

At this stage, a horse will have anywhere from 1 to 7 speed points. The final step is to decide if the horse qualifies for the special bonus point, or is so slow from the gate that it must be penalized one point.

A bonus point is awarded any horse already having 7 points that was on the lead (first, or within a neck of the leader) at the first call in *each* of its *three* "ratable" races (all of which, of course, must have been sprints).

Dainty Dotsie is the typical 8-point horse—always on the lead at the first call (to say nothing of the finish).

Mr. Prospector is not as obvious, but his route performance last out qualifies for a bye. Since he led at the first call in each of his last three sprints, he qualifies for the bonus point.

Any horse in the 1 category that was in the rear half of its field at the first call in each of its rated sprints must be penalized one point, giving the animal a new total of 0 speed points. Likewise for the horse with

Dainty Dotsie — B. f. 3, by Olden Times—Mitomite, by Mito
Own.—Cowden J R — Br.—Cowden J R (Ky) — Tr.—Cowden James R Jr — **119**

	St.	1st	2nd	3rd	Amt.
1977	8	7	0	0	$105,328
1976	2	2	0	0	$6,420

•17Sep77- 6Med	my	6f	:21⅘	:45	1:10⅗	3↑ⒻEgret H	4	2	11½	11	1½	11	Perret C	120	*1.00	——	Dainty Dotsie 1201 Cast The Die 1201¾ My Fair Maid111½	Driving 8
3Sep77- 8Key	fst	6f	:22	:44⅘	1:10⅗	ⒻTrevose	6	4	11	12	13	13½	Perret C	121	*.40	89-20	Dainty Dotsie 1213½ Northern Sea 1213 Bed Pan 114½	Easily 7
13Aug77- 7Pen	sly	6f	:21⅗	:44⅕	1:08⅘	Allowance	1	2	12	14	16	14	Perret C	115	*.90	102-14	Dainty Dotsie 1154 Quicker Than Lite 1156½ IronDerby112½	Easily 7
23Apr77- 7Kee	sly	*7f			1:26⅘	ⒻAshland	4	1	12½	11½	33	514	Phelps B	116	*1.10	75-19	Sound of Summer 1184½ Mrs. Warren 1214OurMims1183	Bore out 9
13Apr77- 7Kee	fst	6f	:22	:45	1:09⅖	ⒻAllowance	10	2	13	14	15	14½	Phelps B	121	*1.30	95-13	Dainty Dotsie 1214½ Mrs. Warren 121hd Sans Arc 1181½	Easily 11
5Feb77- 8Bow	fst	6f	:22⅖	:46	1:12	ⒻVa. Belle	2	1	11	12	13	14½	Phelps B	118	*.40	80-30	Dainty Dotsie 1184½ George's Gift 1155 Runette 1184	Easy score 5
15Jan77- 8Key	gd	6f	:22⅘	:45⅖	1:10⅘	ⒻNew Hope	5	1	15	13	13	16	Phelps B	115	*.30	88-25	Dainty Dotsie 1156 Avilion 1125 George's Gift 1128	Handily 6
5Jan77- 8Key	fst	6f	:22	:45⅖	1:10⅖	ⒻAllowance	4	1	13	12	14	15	Phelps B	115	*.70	90-19	Dainty Dotsie 1155 Avilion 10712 Bold Scheme 1132	Handily 5
17Dec76- 8Key	fst	6f	:22⅖	:46⅕	1:12	ⒻAllowance	5	1	13	16	16	19	Phelps B	115	*.50	82-30	Dainty Dotsie 1159 Morning High 115¾ Favorite Rebel 1134	Easily 5
7Dec76- 5Key	sly	6f	:22⅗	:47⅕	1:13⅖	ⒻMd Sp Wt	1	3	16	15	18	117	Phelps B	120	2.70	75-33	Dainty Dotsie 12017 Grey Beard 1201½ Selari's Choice115hd	Easily 11

LATEST WORKOUTS •Sep 28 Key 5f gd 1:00 b •Sep 10 Key 5f gd :59⅕ b •Aug 31 Key 5f gd :59⅕ b •Aug 26 Key 4f fst :48 b

Mr. Prospector * — B. c. 4, by Raise a Native—Gold Digger, by Nashua
Own.—Aisco Stable — Br.—Combs L II (Ky) — Tr.—Croll W A Jr — **124**

Turf Record	St.	1st	2nd	3rd		St.	1st	2nd	3rd	Amt.
	1	0	0	0	1974	7	3	2	1	$60,486
					1973	5	3	1	1	$17,725

•7Jun74- 6Bel	fm	1$\frac{1}{16}$ Ⓣ		1:10	1:42	3↑Allowance	1	2	21	11	45½	411	Blum W	114	2.00	80-10	Shelter Bay 116½ New Alibhai 1131½ GoldenEagleII1139	Speed, tired 6
18May74- 8Bel	fst	7f	:22⅕	:45	1:22⅕	3↑Carter H	1	2	11½	11½	21½	22¼	Blum W	124	4.50	89-13	Forego 1292¼ Mr. Prospector 1241 Timeless Moment 1132¾	Gamely 8
9May74- 8Aqu	fst	6f	:22⅕	:44⅘	1:09	Allowance	4	2	11½	11½	12	13	Blum W	120	*.30	98-17	Mr.Prospector1203 PensionPlan112nk StrightToPris1157	Ridden out 6
20Apr74- 8GS	fst	6f	:22	:44⅖	1:08⅗	3↑Whirlaway H	6	2	11	13	13	14	Blum W	120	*1.20	101-22	Mr. Prospector 1204 Petrograd 1188 Game Lad 115hd	Ridden out 8
5Mar74- 9Hia	fst	7f	:22⅖	:44⅖	1:21	3↑Poinciana H	2	2	22	21½	23	22¼	Blum W	120	*.70	100-09	Lonetree1212¼ Mr.Prospector120no GovrnorMx1133½	Held for place 8
25Feb74- 8Aqu	fst	6f	:22⅕	:45⅗	1:09⅗	3↑Paumonok H.	7	3	2hd	1½	11½	33	Blum W	121	*.50	92-12	Torsion 1121½ Infuriator 1141½ Mr. Prospector 121nk	Weakened 8
13Feb74- 8GP	fst	6f	:21⅖	:43⅗	1:08⅕	Allowance	4	3	11	14	15	15	Blum W	113	*.40	98-14	Mr. Prospector 1135 Close Watch112¾ DashingPleasure1171	Driving 8
1May73- 8CD	sly	1	:46⅘	1:11⅕	1:37	Derby Trial	3	4	11	1hd	1½	21¼	Blum W	116	*.60	83-20	Settecento 1161¼ Mr.Prospector1166 I'mGuaranteed1193	Slow start 5
17Apr73- 6Kee	fst	1$\frac{1}{16}$	:46⅘	1:10⅘	1:42⅘	Allowance	4	1	12½	12	2hd	33¾	Blum W	115	*.40	88-19	ⒹStarkers 120nk Our Native 1233½ Mr. Prospector 1151	Speed, tired 5
31Mar73-10GP	fst	6f	:21⅗	:43⅖	1:07⅘	Allowance	2	6	1½	15	16	19½	Blum W	119	*.30	103-06	Mr. Prospector 1199½ Son Of Glut 1131 Cades Cove 1124	Handily 10

LATEST WORKOUTS •Jun 18 Mth 3f fst :33⅗ h •Jun 13 Mth 4f fst :45⅗ h •Jun 6 Mth 3f fst :35 b •May 31 Mth 5f fst 1:00 b

Copyright © 1979, by DAILY RACING FORM, INC. Reprinted with permission of copyright owner.

1 speed point whose last five races all were routes, with none of the last three resulting in a bye.

Honorable Miss is a classic example of a 0-speed-point horse—never close in the early stages of her races.

Highbinder, on the other hand, was close enough September 1—fourth of seven—to avoid the penalty, even though none of his three most recent efforts was quick enough to earn any additional speed points. His final total is 1 point.

Petrograd (discussed above) must be penalized because he failed to run in the front half of his field in either of his two recent sprints.

Paul's Hero (when entered November 26) earned no additional speed points because his last five races all were routes. However, he did not suffer the penalty because two of his last three routes qualified for the bye—he led at the first call November 5 and October 31.

Honorable Miss — B. m. 5, by Damascus—Court Circuit, by Royal Vale
Own.—Pen-Y-Bryn Farm — Br.—Bancroft Mrs T (Ky) — Tr.—Whiteley F Y Jr — **119**

Turf Record	St.	1st	2nd	3rd		St.	1st	2nd	3rd	Amt.
	2	0	0	0	1975	8	5	0	0	$96,595
					1974	12	4	3	2	$73,297

29Jly75- 8Key	fst	6f	:22⅖	:45⅘	1:10⅘	3↑ⒻLiberation H	1	11	1112	67	44½	1½	Vasquez J	b 124	*.70	88-22	Honorable Miss 124½ Foxy J. G.118noRingmistress1184	Hard drive 11
6Jly75- 7Bel	fst	7f	:22⅖	:44⅖	1:21⅗	3↑Nassau Co. H	3	7	713	612	65	64½	Vasquez J	b 126	*.60	90-10	QueenCityLad1091¾ProperBostonian121½Piamem115nk	No excuse 7
22Jun75- 8Bel	fst	6f	:23	:46⅖	1:10	3↑Gravesend H	3	7	66¾	62¾	2hd	12¾	Vasquez J	b 123	*.80	93-14	Honorable Miss1232¾QueenCityLad1112½Piamem118no	Ridden out 7
12May75- 8Aqu	fst	7f	:23⅕	:45⅘	1:22⅕	3↑ⒻVagrancy H	8	2	712	76½	2hd	11¾	Vasquez J	b 120	*1.00	90-12	Honorable Miss 1201¾VivaLaVivi126nkCoraggioso1212¼	Hand ride 8
7May75- 8Aqu	fst	6f	:22⅖	:45	1:09	3↑Toboggan H	6	5	68½	55¼	31½	11¼	Vasquez J	b 117	*1.30	98-13	HonorableMiss1171¼FrankieAdams1162Strthemp121no	Drew clear 6
23Apr75- 8Aqu	fst	6f	:22⅕	:45⅕	1:09	Allowance	3	6	68½	32	1½	13½	Vasquez J	b 112	2.80	98-13	HonorbleMiss1123½RelSupreme1162ElEspnoleto116nk	Ridden out 7
22Jan75- 6SA	fm	1⅛ Ⓣ	:47	1:11⅕	1:48⅕	ⒻAllowance	1	6	66¼	66	64	52	Vasquez J	b 120	*2.60	86-12	Joli Vert 113½ Maid In Waiting 116no Pricelyn 116¾	No mishap 7
4Jan75- 8SA	fm	*6½f Ⓣ	:21⅗	:44	1:13⅘	S'ra Madre H	6	10	1019	1015	1012	99½	Howard R	b 110	32.60	80-10	Century'sEnvoy1165½BahiKey1171AginstTheSnow115hd	No factor 10
14Nov74- 7Aqu	fst	1	:46⅘	1:10⅗	1:35⅗	3↑ⒻAllowance	4	5	510	57	56	43½	Vasquez J	b 119	*1.00	84-15	Batucada 1132 Flightoletti 114¾ Clear Copy 113¾	Belated rally 5
2Nov74- 4Aqu	fst	1	:47	1:11⅗	1:35⅘	3↑ⒻAllowance	5	4	48½	2hd	1½	2no	Vasquez J	b 119	*1.00	87-13	JvMoon114noHonorbleMiss1193YoungndFoolish1191½	Just missed 6

LATEST WORKOUTS Aug 30 Bel 5f fst :59⅘ b •Aug 20 Bel 4f fst :48 b •Aug 15 Bel tr.t 4f fst :48⅗ b Aug 9 Bel 3f fst :36 b

Highbinder * — B. h. 5, by Rough'n Tumble—Aspidistra, by Better Self
Own.—Tartan Stable — Br.—Tartan Farms Corp (Fla) — Tr.—Neruc J A — **122**

	St.	1st	2nd	3rd	Amt.
1973	5	2	1	1	$24,420
1972	6	2	1	2	$29,793

24Sep73- 7Bel	fst	6f	:21⅘	:44⅕	1:09⅕	3↑Allowance	5	5	49	49	34	3½	Woodhouse R	112	*1.10	96-13	Tap The Tree 113nk Champagne Charlie 111nk Highbinder 1122½	No excuse 6
11Sep73- 7Bel	fst	7f	:22⅘	:45⅘	1:22⅗	3↑Allowance	9	1	66¼	53	[illegible]½	12	Pincay L Jr	121	2.50	89-10	Highbinder 1212 New Hope 121nk Tap The Tree 1121¼	Drew clear 9
1Sep73- 6Bel	fst	6f	:22⅕	:45	1:09⅘	3↑Allowance	4	1	43	44½	32½	1hd	Woodhouse R	115	3.50	94-10	Highbinder 115hd Prove Out 1153 Busted 115½	Driving 7
23Mar73- 5Aqu	fst	7f	:23⅗	:47	1:23	Allowance	3	4	56¼	34	37	413	Woodhouse R	112	*1.50	73-25	Onion 1128½ Forage 1193 Favorecidian 119hd	Mild bid 6
12Mar73- 7Aqu	gd	6f	:22⅘	:45⅖	1:09⅗	Allowance	1	3	24	25	22	2¾	Woodhouse R	112	*1.70	94-14	Suitor 113¾ Highbinder 1127 Blessing Angelica 1154	Gamely 5
5Jun72- 7Bel	fst	7f	:22⅕	:44⅘	1:21⅗	3↑Allowance	4	3	46½	45½	33½	33¾	Woodhouse R	121	*1.90	95-08	Eastern Fleet 1183½ Towzie Tyke 121nk Highbinder 1212	Bid, weakened 7
10May72- 7Aqu	sly	6f	:22⅖	:45⅕	1:09⅖	3↑Tobag'gan H	4	4	43½	43½	31½	32	Woodhouse R	113	1.80	94-17	Leematt 1152 Invested Power 117no Highbinder 1139	Hung 4
27Apr72- 7Aqu	fst	7f	:23⅖	:47	1:23	Allowance	3	4	43½	21	11	1¾	Vasquez J	113	2.20	86-21	Highbinder 113¾ Tunex 1188½ ⒹI Found Gold 112hd	Driving 6
13Apr72- 7Aqu	sly	1	:46⅕	1:10⅖	1:35⅕	Allowance	3	4	51¼	22	2½	22	Vasquez J	116	2.10	89-19	Hitchcock 1132 Highbinder 1163 Tunex 116hd	Willingly 6
1Apr72- 7Aqu	fst	1	:44⅖	1:08⅗	1:34⅕	3↑Westchstr H	9	5	57	33	2hd	43½	Woodhouse R	114	3.80	93-15	Autobiography 119½ Tunex 1192 Native Royalty 118nk	In close 11

LATEST WORKOUTS Oct 3 Bel 4f fst :49 b Sep 20 Bel 4f fst :47⅘ b Sep 9 Bel 4f fst :48 b Aug 29 Bel 5f fst :59⅘ b

Paul's Hero — Own.—Beau Heart Stable — $25,000 — Dk. b. or br. c. 4, by Steward—Brookbridge, by Ambehaving — Br.—Hellman N (Fla) — Tr.—Schwizer Albert — 119

Turf Record	St.	1st	2nd	3rd
	1	0	0	0

	St.	1st	2nd	3rd	Amt.
1977	23	7	5	2	$59,999
1976	6	1	0	0	$5,700

26Nov77- 5Aqu	sly	7f	:22⅗	:45⅗	1:23⅕	3↑Clm 25000	3	4	$2^{1\frac{1}{2}}$	$2^{\frac{1}{2}}$	2^{1}	$1^{1\frac{1}{2}}$	Turcotte R	b 122	*.90	85-13	Paul's Hero $122^{1\frac{1}{2}}$ Future Planning 117^{hd} Ship Trial $115^{1\frac{1}{2}}$	Driving 7
19Nov77- 2Aqu	fst	1⅛	:47⅘	1:12	1:51⅕	3↑Clm 25000	3	3	3^{2}	2^{1}	1^{1}	$1^{1\frac{1}{2}}$	Day P	b 119	2.30	79-18	Paul's Hero $119^{1\frac{1}{2}}$ Imasmash $110^{1\frac{1}{2}}$ Our Reward $122^{1\frac{1}{2}}$	Drew clear 9
5Nov77- 2Aqu	fst	1⅛	:47⅗	1:12⅕	1:50⅘	3↑Clm 40000	2	1	1^{hd}	1^{2}	2^{5}	$5^{9\frac{1}{2}}$	Day P	b 119	*2.30	73-14	Silver Bullet $115^{7\frac{3}{4}}$ Brown Cat 113^{hd} ReallyCooking$119^{1\frac{1}{2}}$	Used up 7
31Oct77- 6Aqu	fm	1⅛	Ⓣ:48	1:13⅕	1:50⅘	3↑Clm 45000	7	2	$1^{1\frac{1}{2}}$	1^{1}	$2^{\frac{1}{2}}$	$5^{1\frac{1}{2}}$	Turcotte R	b 115	4.90	90-08	Secret Visit 112^{nk} Latrobe $115^{\frac{3}{4}}$ Kanawha River $110^{\frac{1}{2}}$	Weakened 8
20Oct77- 6Aqu	sly	1⅛	:48⅗	1:13⅘	1:51⅗	3↑Clm 45000	2	2	2^{1}	$1^{\frac{1}{2}}$	1^{2}	$1^{1\frac{1}{4}}$	Turcotte R	b 114	*.80	77-21	Paul's Hero$114^{1\frac{1}{4}}$TropicMonkey$113^{4\frac{1}{2}}$SecretVisit$114^{1\frac{1}{2}}$	Ridden out 5
10Oct77- 2Bel	my	1$\frac{1}{16}$	:46⅗	1:11⅗	1:42⅗	3↑Clm 25000	4	1	$1^{1\frac{1}{2}}$	$1^{\frac{1}{2}}$	1^{3}	1^{6}	Turcotte R	b 119	*1.40	89-16	Paul's Hero 119^{6} Sunderance 115no Hostile Planet $117^{4\frac{3}{4}}$	Easily 8
28Sep77- 4Bel	sly	1$\frac{1}{16}$	:46⅗	1:10⅗	1:42⅕	3↑Clm 20000	5	1	1^{5}	1^{10}	1^{9}	$1^{8\frac{1}{2}}$	Turcotte R	b 117	2.90	91-15	Paul's Hero $117^{8\frac{1}{2}}$ Brown Cat 112^{10} Canrith 115^{2}	Easily 7
6Sep77- 6Bel	fst	1$\frac{1}{16}$	:46⅗	1:10⅘	1:43⅘	3↑Clm 22500	3	1	$1^{\frac{1}{2}}$	2^{1}	2^{1}	2^{nk}	Turcotte R	b 115	10.90	83-18	Full Catch 112^{nk} Paul's Hero 115^{hd} Hostile Planet $117^{1\frac{1}{2}}$	Sharp 9
28Aug77- 3Sar	fst	6f	:22⅗	:45⅕	1:10⅗	3↑Clm 22500	5	9	$8^{6\frac{1}{2}}$	$9^{9\frac{1}{4}}$	$8^{9\frac{1}{2}}$	$8^{8\frac{3}{4}}$	Turcotte R	115	6.60	79-10	Click Off 113^{1} Bold and Stormy 117no Bold Legion $117^{\frac{1}{2}}$	Outrun 10
8Aug77- 2Sar	my	6f	:22⅗	:45⅘	1:10⅗	3↑Clm c-18000	8	6	$7^{5\frac{3}{4}}$	7^{5}	6^{5}	$4^{8\frac{1}{4}}$	Maple E	b 119	4.70	79-13	Jig Away 113^{5} Little Miracle $113^{2\frac{1}{2}}$ Cast In Bronze $119^{\frac{3}{4}}$	Wide 8

Photo credit: Bob Coglianese

The brilliantly fast Duck Dance, shown winning the 1971 Vosburgh Handicap at Aqueduct. Beaten just once in a sprint during his career (as a two-year-old), Duck Dance was seldom headed at any stage of a race—only two horses ever outran him for the early lead.

For a horse entered in a route, additional speed points are awarded as follows:

1 point	for any route in which the horse was 1-2-3 at the first call.
AND/OR	
1 point	for any route in which the horse was close (within three lengths) at the first call.
0 points	for any other route performance.
1 point	for any sprint in which the horse was 1-2-3 or within three lengths of the lead at the first call.
AND/OR	

1 point	for any sprint in which the horse was within 6 lengths of the lead at the first call.

Any sprint in which the horse was neither 1-2-3 nor within six lengths of the lead at the first call is passed (given a bye), and the handicapper refers back to the next most recent race, never going back more than five races.

Tentam, for example, earned 2 additional points for his early efforts in both the Governor and Baruch—2-3 and within three lengths of the leader—but none for laying a bit farther back in the United Nations. His final total is 5 points.

Paternity earned one additional speed point in each of his last three starts—for running within three lengths of the early lead (although not 1-2-3) June 9, and for running third (although not within three lengths) May 12 and May 24. His final total is 4 points.

Snappy Chatter's last three races were sprints, in which he demonstrated varying amounts of early foot. His dull effort May 28 received a bye. He earned 2 points for setting the pace May 18, and just 1 point for being within six lengths (but no closer) April 30. Because of the bye, his April 23 route is rated, adding another 2 points to his account, for a final total of 6 points.

Tentam * — Dk. b. or br. c. 4, by Intentionally—Tamerett, by Tim Tam
Own.—Windfields Farm — Br.—Gedney Farms, Breeding Inc (Fla) — Tr.—Miller M — **126**

Turf Record	St.	1st	2nd	3rd		Year	St.	1st	2nd	3rd	Amt.
	5	3	0	2		1973	8	6	1	1	$287,115
						1972	18	4	4	5	$137,802

27Sep73- 8Atl	fm	1 3/16 Ⓣ	1:11⅕ 1:54⅗	3↑U. Nations H	5	6	$6^{3/4}$	$4^{1\frac{1}{4}}$	2^{hd}	1^{4}	Velasquez J	b 123	*1.60	97-08	Tentam 123^{4} Star Envoy $116^{1\frac{1}{4}}$ Return To Reality 113^{hd}	Drew out	12
8Sep73- 7Bel	fst	1⅛	:45⅖ 1:09 1:46⅘	3↑Governor	8	4	3^{1}	1^{hd}	1^{3}	1^{2}	Velasquez J	b 115	*2.50	97-10	Tentam 115^{2} Rule by Reason 112^{nk} True Knight 115^{hd}	Driving	8
10Aug73- 7Sar	fm	1⅛ Ⓣ	1:08⅘ 1:45⅖	3↑B Baruch H	1	2	2^{3}	2^{1}	1^{3}	1^{2}	Velasquez J	b 118	*1.40	104-02	Tentam 118^{2} Scrimshaw 111^{nk} Astray 114^{1}	Driving	10
10Aug73-First Division																	
14Jly73- 8Mth	fst	1¼	:46⅘ 1:10⅘ 2:01⅕	3↑Haskell H	2	3	3^{1}	1^{hd}	2^{hd}	$2^{4\frac{1}{2}}$	Velasquez J	b 118	*1.90	91-12	West Coast Scout $114^{4\frac{1}{2}}$ Tentam $118^{4\frac{1}{2}}$ Windtex $113\frac{1}{2}$	Second best	11
4Jly73- 7Aqu	fst	1 3/16	:46⅗ 1:09⅗ 1:52⅖	3↑Brooklyn H	1	1	$1\frac{1}{2}$	1^{hd}	2^{hd}	3^{2}	Velasquez J	b 119	3.20e	108-07	Riva Ridge 127^{hd} True Knight 117^{2} Tentam $119^{3\frac{1}{2}}$	Weakened	7
28May73- 7Bel	sly	1	:44⅘ 1:09⅕ 1:35	3↑Metropltan H	7	2	2^{1}	$1\frac{1}{2}$	1^{1}	$1^{1\frac{1}{4}}$	Velasquez J	b 116	7.30	97-16	Tentam $116^{1\frac{1}{4}}$ Key To The Mint 127^{hd} King's Bishop 118^{6}	Driving	8
9May73- 7Aqu	sly	6f	:22⅖ :45⅕ 1:09⅖	3↑Toboggan H	6	5	$3^{1\frac{1}{2}}$	$2\frac{1}{2}$	$1\frac{1}{2}$	$1\frac{1}{2}$	Velasquez J	b 122	*2.10	96-13	Tentam $122\frac{1}{2}$ Spanish Riddle 115^{nk} Tap The Tree 118^{2}	Driving	7
17Apr73- 7Aqu	fst	6f	:22⅕ :44⅘ 1:09⅕	Allowance	6	1	$2\frac{1}{2}$	$1\frac{1}{2}$	1^{4}	1^{6}	Velasquez J	b 115	*2.00	97-15	Tentam 115^{6} Tarboosh 121^{1} Cathy's Prince 121^{hd}	Handily	6
18Nov72- 7Aqu	fst	1 3/16	:47 1:10⅖ 1:54⅖	3↑Queens Cy H	12	5	$4^{1\frac{3}{4}}$	$4^{2\frac{1}{2}}$	$4^{5\frac{1}{2}}$	5^{5}	Velasquez J	b 111	*3.50	97-12	Sunny And Mild $109\frac{1}{2}$ Chartered Course 111^{2} Rule byReason $112^{2\frac{1}{2}}$	Hung	12
7Nov72- 7Aqu	fst	1	:45 1:08⅘ 1:34	3↑Stuyvesant H	5	2	2^{hd}	$2\frac{1}{2}$	$3^{1\frac{1}{2}}$	$3^{2\frac{3}{4}}$	Velasquez J	b 114	4.50	94-13	Icecapade $119^{1\frac{1}{2}}$ Sunny And Mild $108^{1\frac{1}{2}}$ Tentam $114^{1\frac{1}{2}}$	Weakened	12

LATEST WORKOUTS — Oct 5 Bel Ⓣ 5f fm :58⅘ h — Sep 25 Bel tr.t 4f fst :50 b — ●Sep 21 Bel Ⓣ 6f sf 1:14 b — Sep 17 Bel tr.t 4f fst :49 b

Paternity * — Dk. b. or br. c. 3, by Dr Fager—Expectancy, by Intentionally
Own.—Tartan Stable — Br.—Tartan Farms Corp (Fla) — Tr.—Nerud J A — **109**

Year	St.	1st	2nd	3rd	Amt.
1973	9	2	5	1	$22,510
1972	4	1	1	0	$7,740

9Jun73- 7Bel	fst	1 1/16	:46 1:10⅕ 1:40⅘	Allowance	1	4	$4^{2\frac{1}{4}}$	$5^{4\frac{1}{2}}$	4^{9}	5^{9}	Woodhouse R	114	5.80	90-05	Forego 111^{9} Adaptive Ace 114no Illberightback 114no	Evenly	10
24May73- 8Bel	sly	1	:45⅗ 1:10⅕ 1:35⅕	3↑Allowance	3	3	$3^{3\frac{1}{2}}$	1^{1}	1	1^{6}	Woodhouse R	109	*.70	96-10	Paternity 109^{6} Amerikingdom 112^{5} Portentous $108^{1\frac{1}{4}}$	Easily	6
12May73- 6Aqu	fst	1	:46⅘ 1:11 1:35	3↑Allowance	7	3	$3^{3\frac{1}{2}}$	$2\frac{1}{2}$	$1^{1\frac{1}{2}}$	2no	Woodhouse R	b 110	5.10	92-09	New Hope 120no Paternity 110^{2} Tree of Knowledge 112^{2}	Gamely	8
13Apr73- 7Aqu	fst	1	:46 1:10⅖ 1:36	3↑Allowance	3	1	1^{2}	$1^{1\frac{1}{2}}$	1^{2}	2^{nk}	Woodhouse R	b 114	1.60	87-20	New Hope 113^{nk} Paternity $114^{1\frac{1}{2}}$ Plastic Surgeon 114^{5}	Just missed	7
31Mar73- 6Aqu	fst	1⅛	:47⅗ 1:11⅕ 1:48	3↑Allowance	5	2	$2^{1\frac{1}{2}}$	2^{1}	2^{1}	2^{nk}	Woodhouse R	b 112	*1.00	96-10	Harrison Kid 108^{nk} Paternity $112\frac{1}{2}$ New Hope 113^{3}	Gamely	7
17Mar73- 4Aqu	sly	1⅛	:47⅗ 1:11⅗ 1:50⅘	3↑Allowance	5	1	$1^{1\frac{1}{2}}$	1^{4}	1^{12}	1^{17}	Woodhouse R	b 111	*1.30	82-17	Paternity 111^{17} Flush $114^{1\frac{1}{2}}$ Christobal $122\frac{1}{2}$	Handily	7
7Mar73- 7Aqu	gd	1⅛	:46⅘ 1:11⅗ 1:50⅕	3↑Allowance	2	2	2^{2}	2^{hd}	2^{1}	2^{1}	Woodhouse R	b 108	2.40	84-17	Prince Luck 115^{1} Paternity $108^{4\frac{1}{2}}$ Twice A Prince $112\frac{3}{4}$	Best others	7
10Feb73- 4Hia	fst	6f	:21⅘ :45⅖ 1:09⅘	Allowance	7	5	3^{4}	$2\frac{1}{2}$	2^{1}	3^{5}	Woodhouse R	b 117	4.20	90-18	Forego $122^{2\frac{1}{2}}$ Borage $115^{2\frac{1}{2}}$ Paternity 117^{4}	Weakened	8
3Feb73- 4Hia	sly	6f	:22 :45⅖ 1:10⅖	Allowance	1	6	2^{hd}	2^{3}	2^{7}	2^{7}	Woodhouse R	b 117	4.20	85-19	Reverend Rose 115^{7} Paternity 117^{2} Swift Courier 117^{1}	2nd best	9
9Dec72- 3Aqu	my	1	:45 1:10⅕ 1:36⅗	Allowance	7	3	$3^{2\frac{1}{2}}$	$2^{2\frac{1}{2}}$	2^{hd}	2^{3}	Woodhouse R	b 121	3.00	81-16	Just De Duc 119^{3} Paternity 121no Cup Bearer 117^{3}	Bore in	8

LATEST WORKOUTS — Jun 27 Bel 4f fst :48⅘ b — Jun 21 Bel 4f fst :49 b — ●Jun 17 Bel 5f fst :59 h — Jun 6 Bel 5f fst 1:02 b

Snappy Chatter — B. g. 5, by Rock Talk—Frolic and Fun, by Jester
Own.—Heard D J — Br.—Walker Mrs J Jr (Md) — Tr.—King W Preston — **114**[5]

Year	St.	1st	2nd	3rd	Amt.
1977	7	2	2	0	$26,290
1976	20	5	5	3	$40,595

28May77- 8Atl	fst	7f	:21⅘ :43⅘ 1:21⅕	3↑Handicap	2	5	6^{11}	$5^{6\frac{1}{2}}$	5^{6}	$5^{3\frac{1}{2}}$	Intelisano GP Jr	b 111	21.20	92-20	SilverHope$121\frac{3}{4}$GyJitterbug121^{nk}Whtsyourplsur119^{2}	Showed little	6
18May77- 4Aqu	fst	7f	:23 :45⅗ 1:23⅗	Clm 37500	3	5	1^{hd}	1^{hd}	$2\frac{1}{2}$	$8^{6\frac{1}{4}}$	Cotto E5	b 115	6.90	77-22	Port Authority $113\frac{1}{2}$ Bonge $118^{1\frac{3}{4}}$ Bold Needle 122^{nk}	Lost whip	9
30Apr77- 7Aqu	fst	6f	:22⅖ :45 1:09⅗	Allowance	5	3	$5^{5\frac{1}{4}}$	4^{4}	4^{3}	1^{hd}	Gonzalez B5	b 110	10.50	95-13	Snappy Chatter 110^{hd} Sir Lister $115\frac{3}{4}$ John Bryn 115no	Just up	7
23Apr77- 3Aqu	fst	1⅛	⊡:47 1:12 1:50⅗	Clm 32500	8	1	1^{hd}	1^{hd}	3^{nk}	$7^{5\frac{1}{2}}$	Gonzalez B5	b 110	6.80	93-05	FrmptonDelight$112\frac{1}{2}$CompnyCommndr$117\frac{1}{2}$PnutVndor118^{nk}	Tired	9
13Apr77- 2Aqu	fst	6f	⊡:22⅕ :45⅖ 1:10	Clm 35000	7	5	$6^{2\frac{1}{2}}$	$6^{4\frac{1}{2}}$	5^{6}	2^{3}	Gonzalez B5	b 108	11.40	96-13	Raise A King 115^{3} Snappy Chatter 108^{nk} Vanistorio $117^{1\frac{1}{4}}$	Gaining	9
4Apr77- 6Aqu	fst	6f	⊡:22⅖ :45⅖ 1:10⅖	Clm c-25000	2	4	$4^{2\frac{1}{4}}$	$3^{5\frac{1}{2}}$	3^{5}	$2^{5\frac{1}{2}}$	Amy J	b 122	*1.80	91-14	Larry's Dogoon $112^{5\frac{1}{2}}$SnappyChatter122^{1}Paul'sHero117^{nk}	Bore in	7
26Mar77- 5Aqu	fst	6f	⊡:22⅗ :46⅗ 1:11⅕	Clm 20000	2	4	$3^{1\frac{1}{2}}$	$3^{1\frac{1}{2}}$	1^{hd}	$1^{2\frac{1}{4}}$	Amy J	b 117	3.00	93-13	SnappyChatter$117^{2\frac{1}{4}}$FreshNative$119^{1\frac{3}{4}}$FastandStrong115^{1}	Handily	7
18Dec76- 2Aqu	fst	6f	⊡:23⅕ :47 1:11⅘	3↑Clm 25000	4	3	$4^{1\frac{1}{4}}$	2^{2}	$2\frac{1}{2}$	$2^{3\frac{1}{2}}$	Velasquez J	b 117	*1.50	— —	Susurro $119^{3\frac{1}{2}}$ Snappy Chatter $117^{2\frac{1}{4}}$ Split Infinitive 115^{2}	Gamely	7
9Dec76- 2Aqu	fst	6f	⊡:22⅗ :46 1:11⅕	3↑Clm 25000	5	5	3^{2}	4^{5}	3^{4}	$3^{3\frac{3}{4}}$	Velasquez J	b 117	4.20	— —	Gabilan $119^{3\frac{1}{2}}$ Desert Outlaw 114^{nk} Snappy Chatter $117\frac{1}{2}$	Evenly	8
27Nov76- 2Aqu	fst	6f	:22 :45 1:10	3↑Clm 25000	8	5	6^{5}	4^{6}	$2^{2\frac{1}{2}}$	$2^{1\frac{1}{2}}$	Velasquez J	b 117	3.50	91-14	Gabilan $117^{1\frac{1}{2}}$ Snappy Chatter 117^{3} Susurro $122^{1\frac{3}{4}}$	Gamely	13

LATEST WORKOUTS — Jun 8 Bel 4f fst :46⅕ h — May 16 Bel 1 fst 1:44⅖ b

Bubbling earned two additional points for her performance October 27, another point for running within three lengths (but not 1-2-3) of the early lead at $1\frac{1}{16}$ miles September 14, and one more point for running within 6 lengths (but not within three lengths, or 1-2-3) of the early lead at seven furlongs September 4, for a total of 5 speed points.

Dr. Eyego, when entered at one mile April 12, had just two "ratable" races among his last six starts (the race in the fog was ignored). His sprint performances of February 1, March 31, and April 7 all received byes. He earned one point for running within 6 lengths of the early lead at 7 furlongs March 10, but no points for his route performance March 3. Dr. Eyego's final total is 2 speed points.

Bubbling — Ch. f. 4, by Stage Door Johnny—Sparkling, by Bold Ruler
Br.—Phipps O (Ky)
Own.—Hedgelawn Farm
Tr.—Johnson P G
116

	Turf Record	St.	1st	2nd	3rd		Amt.
	St. 1st 2nd 3rd					1975 11 6 1 2	$63,780
	6 5 0 1					1974 2 M 1 0	$2,420

Dr. Eyego ✱ — B. c. 3, by Niksar—Li'l Punkie, by Mr Turf
$21,500
Br.—Burns S (Md)
Own.—Fink L R
Tr.—Marcus A B
114

	St.	1st	2nd	3rd		Amt.
					1973 10 4 1 0	$15,300
					1972 10 M 1 1	$2,060

Copyright © 1979, by DAILY RACING FORM, INC. Reprinted with permission of copyright owner.

Photo credit: Bob Coglianese.

In one of the great come-from-behind performances in racing history, Forego (#10), carrying 136 pounds including Bill Shoemaker, catches Honest Pleasure right on the wire in the 1976 Marlboro Cup.

For routes, the bonus point is awarded any horse in the 7 category that was on the lead, or within one length of the lead, in each of its rated routes and/or on the lead, or within three lengths of the lead in each of its rated sprints.

Pearl Necklace qualifies for the bonus point—she set the pace in her last two starts, after being within one length early (from post 10) in the Boiling Springs.

Snappy Chatter (discussed above), when entered in the April 23 route, qualified for the bonus point for having run within three lengths of the early lead in each of his three sprints preceding that route.

L'Alezane, on the other hand, missed the bonus point by one-half length. Although she had run within three lengths of the early lead in the seven-furlong Alcibiades, and within one length in the mile-and-a-sixteenth Natalma, she had dropped back a little too far in the early stages of the Princess Elizabeth.

A router in the 1 category loses that point if it had failed to lead at least half its opponents at the first call in each of its rated routes. A horse entered in a route after five (or more) consecutive sprints is not subject to the penalty.

Copyright © 1979, by DAILY RACING FORM, INC. Reprinted with permission of copyright owner.

Sir Omni, for example, rallied from far back in all his starts, never appearing in the front half of his field at the first call. His speed point total is 0.

Baitman, on the other hand, ran much closer to the lead than Sir Omni. Although not earning additional speed points for any of his recent efforts, he escaped the penalty point for having run in the front half of his field at the first call August 22. Baitman's speed point total is 1.

Horses that have raced but once or twice in their careers must be given special consideration—their speed point total must be "projected" over three races. The table below indicates how to make such projections. Career starts are indicated in the left-hand column, and speed points earned in that many starts are listed across the top of the table. "Projected" speed points (in addition to the one point all horses start with) are found in the body of the table.

	0	1	2	3	4
1 start	0	3	5	x	x
2 starts	0	1	3	4	5

Luck Penny, for example, earned two speed points in her debut. The table says that this is equivalent to having earned 5 points over three starts. So Luck Penny has a final total of 6 speed points.

Soy Numero Uno earned 3 speed points in his two starts, which projects to 4 points over three starts—for a final total of 5 speed points.

Finally, Staunch Avenger's speed point total is 6—the 4 points he earned in his two starts project to (just) 5 over three starts. Consequently he is not eligible for the bonus point.

40

○ THE SPEED POINTS AS PREDICTORS ○

Two questions must be answered regarding the usefulness of the speed points. They are:

1. How well, or how accurately, do the speed points predict early speed?

2. Are the speed points useful in predicting the outcome of races?

The table below answers the first question. It indicates, by speed point total (SPT), the percentage of horses able to gain a position among the first three by the first call. The figures are based on a sample of 700 races which included 400 sprints and 300 routes. The overall pattern was evident for both sprints and routes.

SPT	%FCP 1–3
0	9.2%
1	19.8%
2	22.6%
3	31.6%
4	42.4%
5	56.7%
6	66.4%
7	70.4%
8	86.1%

These percentages appear reasonable. A horse with 3 speed points, for example, probably showed early speed in one of its three "rated" races, and so a percentage of 31.6 is quite plausible. Notice that horses with 0 or 1 speed point jump up every so often and show early speed, even though their recent record shows no such speed. And horses with 6, 7, or 8 speed points, that had shown early speed in each of their three "rated" races, at times will not show this speed.

The percentages in the table can be used to estimate a horse's probability of being among the early leaders. Such a probability, of course, must reflect the early speed potentialities of every other horse in the race as well.

To calculate these probabilities, simply add the percentages corresponding to the speed point totals for each horse in the race, and divide the sum into the percentage for the horse in question. Multiply by three, since there are three early leaders (FCP 1-3), and you have the probability the given horse will be among the first three at the first call.

For example, suppose the contestants in a nine-horse field each has a different speed point total: 0, 1, 2, 3, 4, 5, 6, 7, and 8. The total of the percentages for the race is

Su Page 41   .092 + .198 + .226 + .316 + .424 + .567 + .664 + .704 + .861

which equals 4.052. In this field, the horse with speed point total 8 has a comparatively low probability of being among the first three at the first call:

$$3 \times \frac{.861}{4.052} = .637$$

In other words, this horse has approximately a two out of three chance to be among the early leaders. But remember, the race was loaded with speedballs—the horses with speed point totals 6 and 7 had shown speed in each of their last three races, and those with totals 4 and 5 in two of their last three races.

Horses accorded a 75 percent or better chance of being among the early leaders stand an excellent chance of finishing among the leaders, as the following figures, based on a sample of 1,549 races, prove.

NH	NW	WPCT	MPCT	$NET	I.V.
806	167	20.7%	50.4%	$1.97	1.81

A study of 2,031 races reveals a direct correlation between a horse's chances of winning and its speed point total (SPT).

SPT	NH	NW	WPCT	MPCT	$NET	%W	I.V.
0	3915	292**	7.5%	26.5%	$1.12	14.4%	0.65
1	2215	230	10.4%	31.6%	$1.84	11.3%	0.83
2	1980	210	10.6%	33.7%	$1.45	10.4%	0.93
3	2699	297	11.0%	34.2%	$1.44	14.6%	0.96
4	1755	211	12.0%	36.2%	$1.48	10.4%	1.05
5	2200	292	13.3%	37.3%	$1.69	14.4%	1.16
6	1200	182	15.2%	42.5%	$1.64	9.0%	1.33
7	866	146	16.9%	43.6%	$1.72	7.2%	1.48
8	948	171*	18.0%	43.9%	$1.93	8.4%	1.58

Clearly, horses with 0 speed points should be avoided, especially in sprints. They win less than ⅔ their share of the races, costing their backers 44 cents per wagered dollar.

Unfortunately, the large mutuels so evident in Chapter 1 are nowhere to be found. In light of what we learned then, we might have expected long-run profits from horses whose speed point total was 5 or higher. But this is not the case. Yet our sample of 2,031 races does not differ from previous samples. The problem apparently is that many horses are capable of flashing early speed every other race, or every third race, or maybe just once in a while. When these horses do run early, they also seem to run late. Performances of that kind account for the large profits produced by early speed types.

The trick, of course, is spotting the signs that one of these erratic speedballs is going to have a good day. Looking at the horse's early speed performance in its last race, or over its last three races, does not necessarily give the clue.

Wopeedah, for example, showed unexpected speed on August 16, and won for the first time in at least 11 starts. Perhaps the tip-off that the old gelding would show more than his usual early foot was the jockey chosen for the occasion—Wally Blum, a noted speed rider.

Wopeedah Own.—Ellis Mrs J — $4,500 — dk. b. or br. g. 8, by Revoked—Level Sands, by Mahmoud; Br.—Dotter R L (Ky); Tr.—Dotter R L — 115 — Turf Record: St. 2, 1st 0, 2nd 0, 3rd 0

	St.	1st	2nd	3rd	Amt.
1972	11	1	2	1	$5,375
1971	25	3	3	3	$14,377

16Aug72- 2Mth	fst	6f	22⅕	.45⅗	1.11⅗	3↑Clm 3500	1	6	$3^{3\frac{1}{2}}$	2^{hd}	$1^{\frac{1}{2}}$	$1^{1\frac{1}{4}}$	Blum W	113	4.20	84–20	Wopeedah $113^{1\frac{1}{4}}$ Bossy 108^{4} Winds At War 114no	Driving 12
29Jly72- 2Aqu	fst	6f	22⅖	.45⅗	1.11⅗	3↑Clm 4500	10	1	10^{11}	10^{11}	$7^{4\frac{1}{4}}$	$5^{1\frac{3}{4}}$	Velasquez J	112	5.40	83–12	Aloha King 110^{nk} Rock Sun $116^{\frac{3}{4}}$ Weigh Anchor 121^{nk}	Stride late 10
13Jly72- 1Aqu	sly	6f	22⅕	.45⅖	1.11⅗	3↑Clm 5000	7	2	$4^{4\frac{1}{2}}$	4^{7}	$5^{6\frac{1}{2}}$	$5^{4\frac{1}{2}}$	Velasquez J	116	9.00	80–15	Weigh Anchor $120^{\frac{1}{2}}$ AGallantMoment $116^{\frac{3}{4}}$ DoubleGee $116^{\frac{3}{4}}$	No Mishap 12
26Jun72- 8Aqu	sly	6f	22	.45⅘	1.11⅖	3↑Clm 4500	8	6	$7^{6\frac{3}{4}}$	$6^{8\frac{1}{2}}$	5^{6}	$3^{2\frac{1}{2}}$	Velasquez J	116	7.40	83–15	Weigh Anchor $119^{\frac{1}{2}}$ Madison Street 114^{2} Wopeedah 116^{nk}	Rallied 11
3Jun72- 1Bel	fst	6f	22⅕	.45⅘	1.11⅖	3↑Clm 5000	3	3	$4^{4\frac{1}{2}}$	$3^{4\frac{1}{2}}$	$3^{4\frac{1}{2}}$	$4^{2\frac{1}{2}}$	Velasquez J	118	5.00	84–12	Wicked Man $118^{\frac{3}{4}}$ Gottogo 118^{1} Kayrang $116^{\frac{3}{4}}$	Lacked rally 11
23May72- 2Bel	fst	6f	22⅘	.45⅘	1.11⅕	3↑Clm 3750	7	5	$6^{7\frac{3}{4}}$	5^{7}	4^{2}	$2^{\frac{3}{4}}$	Velasquez J	116	6.90	87–17	Lesbob $118^{\frac{3}{4}}$ Wopeedah $116^{1\frac{1}{4}}$ Words and Music 109^{hd}	Gamely 13
28Apr72- 4Aqu	fst	6f	22⅕	.45⅖	1.11⅗	Clm 4500	4	6	11^{15}	11^{18}	10^{12}	8^{8}	Velasquez J	116	8.80	77–19	Ripple Mark 116no Tranquility 116no Gottogo $116^{\frac{3}{4}}$	No speed 11
17Apr72- 1Aqu	fst	7f	23⅕	.46⅕	1.24	Clm c-3500	6	8	9^{8}	$10^{9\frac{1}{2}}$	8^{12}	9^{14}	Turcotte R	113	*2.30	67–19	Lovin Bee 114^{4} Kayrang 112^{2} Slightly Misty 112^{3}	No speed 14
10Apr72- 1Aqu	fst	6f	22⅘	.46⅗	1.12⅕	Clm 3500	4	9	10^{8}	$10^{9\frac{1}{2}}$	$5^{7\frac{1}{2}}$	$2^{3\frac{1}{2}}$	Turcotte R	114	5.40	78–18	Big Impostor $112^{3\frac{1}{2}}$ Wopeedah $114^{\frac{1}{2}}$ Dom Swear 112^{nk}	Closed fast 14
18Feb72- 2GP	sly	7f	23	.45⅘	1.25⅕	Clm 5000	11	10	7^{7}	7^{12}	7^{14}	6^{9}	Castaneda M	116	7.40	69–21	GraphOCanic $108^{2\frac{3}{4}}$ MasterSteve $109^{3\frac{3}{4}}$ KurlashKid $116^{2\frac{1}{4}}$	Bumped start 12

LATEST WORKOUTS Aug 15 Mth 3f fst .37⅗ b Aug 10 Mth 6f fst 1.18 b Aug 7 Sar 3f fst .35⅗ h Jly 26 Bel 3f fst .37 b

In the tabulation below, we study only those horses in a 700 race sample (400 sprints and 300 routes) that *did* show early speed—horses that did run first, second, or third at the first call in their race. Each horse is classified according to its speed point total as calculated before the race.

SPT	NH	NW	WPCT	MPCT	$NET	I.V.
0	114	24*	21.1%	48.2%	$2.47	1.79
1	129	29*	22.5%	55.0%	$3.16	1.92
2	161	38*	23.6%	63.4%	$3.16	2.01
3	256	52*	20.3%	50.8%	$2.35	1.73
4	278	56*	20.1%	47.5%	$2.13	1.72
5	416	77*	18.5%	48.8%	$2.57	1.58
6	300	54	18.0%	49.0%	$2.06	1.53
7	174	35	20.1%	50.6%	$1.98	1.71
8	272	57	21.0%	52.2%	$2.21	1.79

In these 700 races, the three early leaders combined to win 422 times, for a win percentage of 20.1 percent and an impact value of 1.67. They returned their backers an average payoff of $2.39, nearly a 20 percent profit. But, as the tabulation indicates, the bulk of this profit can be attributed to horses that showed surprise early speed—horses in the 0, 1, and 2 speed point categories.

○ SPEED POINT PERCENTAGE ○

A speed point total of 8 suggests a horse with reliable early speed that most likely will be out there battling for the early lead, if not setting the pace alone. Such a horse's chances of winning are highest when it has little competition for the lead. If another horse in the race also has a high speed point total, there is the chance the two will fight each other for the early lead, possibly to the detriment of both late in the stretch run.

Accordingly, a horse's speed point total must be viewed in light of the speed point totals of all other horses in the race. To do this, simply add the speed points for the entire field, and then determine each horse's percentage of the total.

For example, if the contestants in a nine-horse race each have a different speed point total, the grand total for the race is $0 + 1 + 2 + 3 + 4 + 5 + 6 + 7 + 8 = 36$. The horse with 8 points has 22.2 percent ($\frac{8}{36}$)of the total.

On the other hand, in a field of six horses where one has 8 points and the other five each have 2 points, the total for the race is $8 + 2 + 2 + 2 + 2 + 2 = 18$, and the horse with 8 points has 44.4% ($\frac{8}{18}$) of the total.

The speed point percentage always makes the horse with the highest speed point total look strongest in its field. But it makes that horse look stronger in a field relatively light in early speed types, and less formidable when opposing several other speedballs. This is all reasonable, and in accord with our findings in Chapter 1.

Here is how the speed point percentage worked out for our sample of 2,031 races:

Percent	NH	NW	WPCT	MPCT	$NET	%W	I.V.
0%	3915	292**	7.5%	26.5%	$1.12	14.4%	0.65
1–9%	4714	458	9.7%	29.9%	$1.59	22.6%	0.85
10–19%	5719	694	12.1%	36.0%	$1.55	34.2%	1.06
20–29%	2590	416	16.1%	44.2%	$1.76	20.5%	1.41
30% up	840	171	20.4%	51.8%	$1.82	8.4%	1.78

Although the impact values work out nicely, there are no profits to be seen. Obviously, astute handicappers are well aware when a horse figures to dominate the early pace, as those in the 30 percent up category do.

○ THE SPEED POINT LEADER ○

As we have seen, the speed points do an effective job of identifying the early speed horses. Those with the higher speed point totals are most likely to be among the first three at the first call. The horse with the highest speed point total is most likely to be the early leader.

In almost three of every four races, one horse stands alone with the highest speed point total in its field. In a study of 1,549 races, we found 1,139 such horses, each with at least 4 speed points, to guarantee a certain amount of early speed dependability. Here is how they performed:

NH	NW	WPCT	MPCT	$NET	I.V.
1139	220*	19.3%	47.1%	$2.08	1.69

Not only did these horses return their followers a slight profit, but they did a fairly good job of producing the early speed promised by their high speed point totals. More than 76 percent were among the early leaders (FCP 1–3), and almost 46 percent actually led at the first call.

Since the speed point leaders ran so well, those with an advantage of at least 2 points over their nearest rival should do even better. They are serious threats to open clear leads in the early stages of their races.

Our study found 618 such horses, each with at least 4 speed points and an advantage of at least 2 points over their nearest rivals. Here is how they ran:

NH	NW	WPCT	MPCT	$NET	I.V.
618	125*	20.2%	47.9%	$2.21	1.77

The profit has grown to more than 10 percent, the winning percentage over 20 percent, and the power of early speed is even greater than before. More than 85 percent of these horses ran among the first three at the first call, with more than 55 percent leading at that position.

These two groups of horses, one a subset of the other, provide interesting spot-play systems based on this single handicapping factor—early speed. We shall see in Chapter 24 that, when early speed is combined with other handicapping factors, profits increase.

○ CONCLUSION ○

If you could bet on races after watching just the first quarter-mile (half-mile in routes), you could make a substantial living at the track.

You merely would bet on the horse with the early lead. You would not need the past performances, or any expertise in handicapping.

But you must bet before the race begins. And the past performances are necessary reading. But if you can visualize what is likely to happen in the first part of the race, you are well on the way to predicting what will happen later. The first step in the handicapping process should be an analysis of the early speed tendencies of each starter.

But handicapping should be somewhat more comprehensive than betting on a horse simply because it has early speed. In spite of the great advantage that early speed provides, remember that only five of the nine races on the average program are won by early speed types. The other four races fall to horses that come from behind.

The important lesson is this: if your handicapping has narrowed a field down to two horses, one a speed horse and the other a rallier, over the long run the speed horse will prove to be the better bet.

TRACK CONDITIONS

A wet track is a wet track is a wet track.

Not true. Racing surfaces are individuals.

During prolonged rain, most tracks become sloppy, which favors horses with early speed. Horses that race on the front end get no mud kicked in their faces, a tremendous advantage over come-from-behind rivals that must weave their way between horses and flying mud.

But anything can happen when the rain stops and the track begins to dry out, passing through the stages termed "muddy," "slow," and "good." The prevailing belief has been that speed horses tire more rapidly on a drying out track, an advantage to come-from-behind types. Statistics show that this is no longer true, if it ever was.

The table on page 48 contains the results of our first call position study of 5,399 races under various track conditions.

The lesson is clear: The more early speed a horse shows, the better are its chances of winning, regardless of track conditions. Early speed types do best over sloppy surfaces, but retain an advantage on drying tracks. Obviously, a tiring track affects horses other than speedballs.

Of course, there is no such thing as an "average" drying-out track. Some favor speed types, others make it almost impossible for them to hold on.

For that matter, not every sloppy track will favor the front-runners. The storm system that brought the rain may also feature high winds. Speed types find it difficult hanging on after bucking a strong wind on the backstretch. On the other hand, the combination of a wet track and a tail wind on the backstretch often produces a steady stream of front-running victories.

Interestingly, racetrack audiences seem to bet early speed types regardless of track conditions. The average odds for horses in the FCP 1–3 category showed little change for the different types of track conditions studied.

Fast Tracks

FCP	NH	NW	WPCT	MPCT	$NET	%W	I.V.
1	3903	1024*	26.2%	54.4%	$3.34	26.2%	2.48
1–3	11709	2281*	19.5%	48.0%	$2.59	58.4%	1.84
Front Half	7545	755**	10.0%	33.5%	$1.47	19.3%	0.95
Rear Half	17678	867**	4.9%	20.1%	$0.75	22.2%	0.46

Good Tracks

FCP	NH	NW	WPCT	MPCT	$NET	%W	I.V.
1	441	99*	22.5%	53.5%	$2.94	22.5%	2.08
1–3	1323	248*	18.8%	47.8%	$2.53	56.2%	1.73
Front Half	802	84	10.5%	34.0%	$1.44	19.0%	0.97
Rear Half	1954	109**	5.6%	21.4%	$0.84	24.7%	0.52

Slow Tracks

FCP	NH	NW	WPCT	MPCT	$NET	%W	I.V.
1	179	59*	33.0%	62.0%	$4.95	33.0%	3.03
1–3	537	108*	20.1%	49.7%	$3.12	60.3%	1.85
Front Half	329	35	10.6%	29.8%	$1.99	19.6%	0.98
Rear Half	781	36**	4.6%	22.0%	$0.56	20.1%	0.42

Sloppy Tracks

FCP	NH	NW	WPCT	MPCT	$NET	%W	I.V.
1	485	164*	32.8%	63.7%	$4.07	32.8%	3.05
1–3	1455	308*	21.2%	52.4%	$2.59	63.5%	1.91
Front Half	822	77*	9.4%	31.4%	$1.22	15.9%	0.84
Rear Half	2091	100**	4.8%	20.8%	$0.68	20.6%	0.43

Muddy Tracks

FCP	NH	NW	WPCT	MPCT	$NET	%W	I.V.
1	331	81*	24.5%	55.3%	$2.59	24.5%	2.21
1–3	993	188*	18.9%	49.2%	$2.00	56.8%	1.71
Front Half	566	60	10.6%	32.7%	$1.16	18.1%	0.96
Rear Half	1427	83**	5.8%	22.4%	$0.90	25.1%	0.52

○ THE RAIL ○

Many tracks drain toward the inside rail, and consequently dry out faster in the middle. When this happens, horses that race along the inside will flounder. Most of the winners will come charging down the middle of the track.

When a track is wet or drying out, the situation along the rail must be appraised, lest money be lost on misguided selections. Here are a few questions to ask while watching the first few races. The answers will provide all the necessary information.

1. Are the early speed horses with inside post positions actually contending for the early lead?
2. Who wins the speed duels, the inside horse or the outside horse? If the outside horse, how quickly does the inside horse fall back?
3. Are the speed horses able to hold on all the way? If not, are the first horses to pass them holding on to the wire? Or are they being overtaken in the late stages?
4. Over which part of the track are the winners running? Are they all coming down the middle of the track? Or are some sneaking through along the inside?
5. When the horses enter the stretch, are the jockeys swinging wide to avoid the rail?

The answers reveal not only the condition along the rail, but the importance of early speed on the particular day. This information must be obtained before serious bets can be made.

If remembered, this information can prove valuable at a later date. Horses trapped on a deep rail can be forgiven a resulting poor performance. Horses failing to rally on a sloppy track heavily favoring speed types may catch their strides next time. And pacesetters that quit badly on a heavy track favoring late runners will probably hold on better in their next starts if given more favorable footing.

Lefty, for example, was forced to race along Belmont's deep rail almost the entire trip on September 14. That he stopped badly in the last eighth was to be expected, and was not an indication that he lacked the stamina to stay one mile—as his race on September 28 proved.

Lefty — Ch. c. 2, by Prince John—Kushka, by First Landing
Br.—Meadow Stable (Va)
Own.—Meadow Stable
Tr.—Laurin L
122

	St.	1st	2nd	3rd	Amt.
1974	6	2	0	2	$13,320

28Sep74- 3Bel	fst	1	:47	1:11⅕	1:36⅘	Allowance	6	1	1^{hd}	2^{hd}	1^{hd}	1^{hd}	Velasquez J	b	119	4.40	85–13 Lefty 119^{hd} Cuchulain 121no Rueful 117^{4}	Driving	7
14Sep74- 1Bel	sly	1	:46⅖	1:11⅗	1:37⅕	Allowance	3	1	$1^{½}$	2^{hd}	1^{hd}	$3^{5¼}$	Velasquez J	b	121	*2.20	77–12 Harvard Man 121^{3} Sylvan Place $121^{2¼}$ Lefty 121^{4}	Weakened	8
2Sep74- 3Bel	sly	6f	:22⅗	:45⅘	1:10⅖	Md Sp Wt	6	1	2^{hd}	2^{hd}	1^{hd}	1^{4}	Velasquez J	b	121	3.10	91–13 Lefty 121^{4} Co Host 121no Shredder 121^{7}	Ridden out	7
24Aug74- 2Sar	fst	7f	:22⅖	:45⅕	1:24⅘	Md Sp Wt	10	2	$4^{1½}$	$3^{½}$	6^{1}	$6^{5¼}$	Feliciano B M	b	119	11.50	76–13 Guards Up $119^{1½}$ [D]Cuchulain $119^{1½}$ [D]Singh 119^{hd}	Lacked room	12
24Aug74-Placed fifth through disqualification																			
16Jly74- 3Aqu	fst	6f	:23⅖	:47⅕	1:12⅕	Md Sp Wt	5	2	$3^{2½}$	3^{5}	5^{10}	6^{11}	Maple E		118	4.50	71–16 Tuff'nRumble118^{1} Fleetsmok$115^{3¾}$ DuDilignc$118^{3¼}$	Unruly pre-race	9
4Jly74- 1Aqu	fst	5½f	:22⅘	:46⅗	1:05⅘	Md Sp Wt	1	3	2^{hd}	$4^{2½}$	$4^{5½}$	$3^{3½}$	Maple E		118	2.50	81–14 Century Gold $118^{2½}$ Guards Up $118^{¾}$ Lefty 118^{nk}	Finished well	8

LATEST WORKOUTS Sep 26 Bel 3f sly :38 b Sep 21 Bel 5f fst :59⅘ h Sep 8 Bel 3f sly :37 b Aug 30 Bel 3f sly :36 b

Copyright © 1979, by DAILY RACING FORM, INC. Reprinted with permission of copyright owner.

○ FAVORITES ○

Here is another look at the 4,800 favorites studied in the Introduction, this time as they performed on various types of footing.

	NH	NW	WPCT	MPCT	$NET	I.V.
Fast	3542	1156*	32.6%	66.1%	$1.80	3.08
Good	413	127	30.8%	63.9%	$1.71	2.85
Slow	112	29	25.9%	63.4%	$1.49	2.38
Sloppy	466	157	33.7%	64.4%	$1.94	3.04
Muddy	267	98	36.7%	72.3%	$2.00	3.31

The lesson is clear: Favorites are more reliable on fast or wet tracks than on drying-out tracks. Upsets are more likely on drying-out tracks because of uncertainties about the importance of early speed and the footing along the rail. The favorite may be the best horse in the race, but if it is a front runner on a come-from-behind track, or if it tries to make its run along a deep rail, it is going to lose, no matter how much of an advantage it might seem to have.

○ CONFORMATION ○

Horses, too, are individuals when it comes to inclement weather and poor track conditions. Some handle wet tracks easily, others are able to run well over drying-out surfaces. Many, however, prefer to hear their feet rattle on a dry strip.

Part of the reason for this is conformation. Forego, for example, was a large, long-striding horse. Great as he was, he could not handle a sloppy track. Many long-striding horses have difficulty getting into gear on wet footing.

Riva Ridge, on the other hand, was not a large horse, yet inability to run well on wet tracks was his Achilles heel. He lost the Preakness, and with it a Triple Crown, because he could not handle a sloppy surface at Pimlico. According to trainer Lucien Laurin, Riva Ridge could not stand up on a wet track, a fact Laurin attributed to the horse's small feet.

Actually, very few horses improve in off-going. Rather, the many that do not try make it appear that others actually relish the wet. When the going gets tough, the tough keep going, but the weak-hearted head back for the barn.

○ BREEDING ○

There is good reason to believe that breeding also enters into the explanation of why some horses race well over off tracks, and others do not. Certain sire lines seem to move up when the going gets wet. Notable current examples are the Graustark's, the In Reality's, and the Native Charger's.

Some attribute Prove Out's stunning upset of Secretariat in the wet 1973 Woodward to the fact that Prove Out was a son of Graustark. Another of Graustark's outstanding sons, Key To The Mint, scored his major victory over arch-rival Riva Ridge in the wet 1972 Woodward. Key To The Mint's son Sauce Boat, one of 1977's outstanding two-year-olds, seemed to have inherited his father's ability to handle wet going when he scored his first stakes success in the wet Arlington-Washington Futurity.

Photo credit: Bob Coglianese

Key To The Mint wins the 1972 Woodward, with Riva Ridge (checkered blinkers) fading to fourth. Flying on the far outside is the Native Charger filly Summer Guest, a stablemate of the winner.

51

Prove Out upsets Secretariat in the 1973 Woodward.

The great filly Desert Vixen, a daughter of In Reality, skipped over a sloppy racing surface like a rabbit. Her full brother Valid Appeal, while far from a champion, upset Wajima in the sloppy 1974 Dwyer. And sloppy conditions were probably a factor in Believe It's upset of Alydar in the 1977 Remsen Stakes. These are just three examples of the get of In Reality that seem to handle sloppy tracks with ease.

Interestingly, Bold Ruler's last two great sons (perhaps his greatest), Secretariat and Wajima, were victims of upsets in the slop. Both did run second, however, and the Bold Ruler's in general are more than able to hold their own in the slop. Current slop sensation Cinteelo is a grandson of Bold Ruler, to give one prominent example.

Finally, what better way is there to explain High Echelon's victory in the muddy 1971 Belmont than to mention that High Echelon was just another of the mud-loving Native Charger's?

The great Desert Vixen splashes to an easy victory in the 1973 Alabama. In a month's time, she would do the same thing to an outstanding field of older fillies and mares in the Beldame.

○ MUD MARKS ○

In the past, the *Daily Racing Form* would place an asterisk (*) to the right of the name of any horse that had demonstrated ability to run well on a wet track. These asterisks were called "mud marks."

Nowadays, the mud marks are no longer being assigned, at least not with regularity or consistency.

Consequently, unless evidence of mud-running ability appears in a horse's past performances, the handicapper must rely on his own good memory of the horse, or else be completely in the dark. Look for evidence of mud-running ability at the appropriate distance—a horse that has won a route wire-to-wire in the slop may not show the same fondness for the off-going when asked to come from arrears in a sprint.

The absence of mud-marks or proven mud-running ability adds one more problem to be faced when handicapping races to be run over an off track. The best solution, obviously, is to avoid off tracks whenever possible. But then, a sloppy track heavily favoring speed types can make for a pleasant day at the races, if you don't mind getting a little wet yourself.

POST
POSITION

How great an effect has post position on the outcome of a race? We have already found (in Chapter 3) that the seeming advantage of being on the inside, and thereby saving ground, may be outweighed at times by other considerations. The horse on the rail may be racing over the deepest part of the racing strip. Or a horse may be of such temperament that it will not give its best when forced to race inside, or between, rivals.

Before proceeding to a more detailed discussion of the relative merits of different post positions, let's review some elementary arithmetic. The turns of a racetrack—the clubhouse turn and the stretch turn—are semicircular and have (about) the same radius, say r feet. A horse hugging the rail around one of these turns must travel πr feet (the value of π is approximately 3.14). Assuming that the average horse and rider occupy 3 feet in width, we discover that a horse racing outside one horse around a turn must travel $\pi(r + 3) = \pi r + 3\pi$ feet, which is 3π feet more than the rail horse. Likewise, a horse racing three-wide around a turn must travel 3π feet more than the horse to its left, and 6π feet more than the rail horse.

Now 3π is approximately 9.42, and since a length is generally regarded as being from 8 to 9 feet, we discover that a horse loses slightly more than one length to an opponent racing immediately inside it around a turn. A horse racing three-wide loses approximately two lengths to the rail horse.

If the outside horse does not lose ground around a turn, it is burning up more energy to keep up. That, or it is a much better horse than its more advantageously situated rival.

With these preliminary remarks out of the way, we will now make a more detailed study of post position. We will study both sprints and routes, at both the mile tracks and the shorter "bullrings."

○ SIX FURLONGS ○

We begin with a study of 2,516 six-furlong races run at tracks which are one mile in circumference.

Post	NH	NW	WPCT	$NET	I.V.
1	2516	304*	12.1%	$2.15	1.22
2	2516	267	10.6%	$1.60	1.07
3	2516	279	11.1%	$1.46	1.12
4	2516	276	11.0%	$1.42	1.11
5	2516	249	9.9%	$1.26	1.00
6	2481	271	10.9%	$1.77	1.11
7	2375	220	9.3%	$1.42	0.96
8	2208	204	9.2%	$1.58	0.98
9	2025	164	8.1%	$1.88	0.88
10	1886	140	7.4%	$1.04	0.81
11	1107	91	8.2%	$1.43	0.96
12	727	51	7.0%	$0.42	0.84
Outside	2516	184	7.2%	$1.06	0.74

Note: $NET figures are based on 910 of the 2,516 races.

The category OUTSIDE refers to those horses that broke from the outside posts in their fields—the seventh horse from the rail in a seven-horse field, or the eleventh horse in an eleven-horse field, for example.

Horses breaking from the inner half of the gate enjoy a slight advantage—they accounted for 65.4 percent of the races and had a combined impact value of 1.10. But the only significant advantage lies with horses breaking from post 1. These horses won significantly more races than their odds predicted they would and returned their backers a small 7½ percent profit.

These results, together with the known hazards of post 1, prompted further study. Here are the results of a study of 1,522 horses breaking from the rail at six furlongs at the three New York tracks, Aqueduct, Belmont, and Saratoga.

Track	NH	NW	WPCT	MPCT	$NET	I.V.
Combined	1522	208	13.7%	38.9%	$1.81	1.21
Aqueduct	693	122*	17.6%	42.7%	$2.24	1.59
Bel-Sar	829	86	10.4%	35.7%	$1.46	0.94

Photo credit: Lexington Herald-Leader

Seattle Slew (#3, on the inside), shortly after the start of the 1977 Kentucky Derby. This picture demonstrates the problems a speed horse faces when it breaks tardily from an inside post position—a wall of horses in front, vying for the early lead, and others to the outside, scrambling for position.

The racing surfaces at both Belmont and Saratoga are known to be deeper along the rail. When these tracks are wet or drying out, post position 1 is regarded as the kiss of death. The statistics bear this out—the usual advantage of post 1 is not evident at either of these tracks. Contrast with Aqueduct, which really seems to favor the rail horse.

Whether an inside post is particularly advantageous, or an outside post particularly disadvantageous, is determined in great part by the distance of the starting gate from the first turn. The critical element is the amount of time outside horses have in which to gain a ground-saving position before reaching that turn. The inside horses have quite an advantage when the start is near a turn: Many horses from the outer part of the gate will be forced to take the turn wide. But when the start is a

57

considerable distance from a turn, the outside horses have a chance to overcome the luck of the draw for posts.

At a typical mile track, six-furlong races start at least two furlongs from the only turn. At Belmont, which is $1\frac{1}{2}$ miles in circumference, the distance from start to turn at six furlongs is only about $1\frac{1}{4}$ furlongs. In other words, as far as post position is concerned, six-furlong races at Belmont are equivalent to five-furlong races elsewhere.

The following tabulation compares horses breaking from posts 10 through 14 in 342 six-furlong races at Aqueduct and 292 such races at Belmont. The point of the study is not only the difference between these two tracks, but also the difference between five and six furlongs.

Track	NH	NW	WPCT	MPCT	$NET	I.V.
Aqueduct	924	81	8.8%	27.6%	$1.91	1.03
Belmont	888	63	7.1%	21.1%	$1.26	0.85

New York audiences apparently shy away from horses breaking from posts 10–14 at six furlongs, and rightly so at Belmont. At Aqueduct, and probably at most mile tracks, these horses are able to hold their own, and probably are underbet.

The statistical technique called linear regression (see Appendix B for more details) was used on a sample of some 45,000 past performance lines to determine the value, in lengths, of a post position at the six-furlong distance. Here are the results:

1. At the finish, the average horse breaking from post 12 finds itself one length behind the average horse breaking from post 1.
2. At the first call, the average horse breaking from post 12 finds itself one half length behind the average horse breaking from post 1.

Actually, horses breaking from inner posts are more likely to get good position early. Those that do not, however, tend to get pinched back by horses from the outside scrambling for position. This explains the small difference of just one half length between the inside and the far outside by the first turn.

Our studies reveal, therefore, that there is very little difference from one post to the next at the standard six-furlong distance at mile tracks.

○ **STANDARD ROUTES** ○

We turn now to a study of races at distances from one mile to $1\frac{1}{8}$ miles over tracks which are at least one mile in circumference. The most popular and frequently used route distance at such tracks is $1\frac{1}{16}$ miles. At the mile tracks, such a race features a run of approximately one furlong, or 660 feet, from the starting gate to the clubhouse turn. At some tracks, the distance from gate to turn may be considerably shorter or longer than 660 feet. At Aqueduct, which is $1\frac{1}{8}$ miles in circumference, there is a run of only 330 feet from gate to turn for races at $1\frac{1}{8}$ miles.

Since the outside horses figure to lose ground around the clubhouse turn in these races, and since the amount of ground lost depends on the distance from gate to turn (the closer the gate to the turn, the more ground outside horses lose), it is important to know the measurements of each track. This information can be found in the *American Racing Manual*, an annual publication of the *Daily Racing Form*.

The start of the 1975 Wood Memorial, a mile-and-an-eighth test for three-year-olds at Aqueduct two weeks before the Kentucky Derby. Foolish Pleasure (far left), the heavy favorite and eventual winner, broke from post 15, but overcame the inconvenience, catching Bombay Duck in the last few strides.

A study of 2,233 of these route races proved the expected: The closer a horse breaks to the rail, the better its chances of winning or running in the money. I.V. statistics decrease fairly steadily as post position increases. Here are the results of that study:

Post	NH	NW	WPCT	$NET	I.V.
1	2233	359*	16.1%	$2.09	1.44
2	2233	285	12.8%	$1.66	1.15
3	2233	297	13.3%	$1.79	1.20
4	2233	263	11.8%	$1.44	1.06
5	2228	241	10.8%	$1.31	0.97
6	2207	232	10.5%	$1.29	0.95
7	2070	178	8.6%	$1.25	0.79
8	1860	178	9.6%	$1.46	0.91
9	1264	102	8.1%	$1.55	0.82
10	829	59	7.1%	$1.37	0.77
11	415	21	5.1%	$0.88	0.59
12	261	18	6.9%	$1.86	0.83

Note: $NET figures here are based on 757 of the 2233 races.

Aside from the first three posts, especially post 1, there is little to recommend here. Once again, horses breaking from the rail had by far the highest impact value, and produced a slight profit for their backers.

The use of linear regression on 45,000 past performance lines revealed that the outside horses in standard route races at mile tracks suffered a much worse fate than did their counterparts in sprints. Here are the findings:

1. The average horse breaking from post 12 winds up $2\frac{1}{2}$ lengths behind the average horse breaking from post 1 at the end of the standard $1\frac{1}{16}$ mile route race. That is, a one-post advantage is worth approximately $\frac{1}{4}$ length.

2. The average horse breaking from post 12 loses $1\frac{1}{2}$ lengths to the average horse breaking from post 1 in the run around the clubhouse turn to the first call position.

3. A much higher percentage of horses breaking from inner posts gain a position among the first three at the first call. This percentage ranges from 47 percent for post 1, to 40 percent for posts 2-3, 33 percent for posts 4–9, and down to 25 percent for posts 10–12.

At mile-and-an-eighth Aqueduct, where $1\frac{1}{8}$-mile races start half as far from the turn as do $1\frac{1}{16}$-mile races at mile tracks, the horse breaking from post 12 will lose approximately $2\frac{1}{2}$ lengths to the rail horse on the clubhouse turn alone, and $3\frac{1}{2}$ lengths to that rival over the full distance of the race. At the first turn alone, this is almost twice the penalty the twelve horse must pay at $1\frac{1}{16}$ miles, with twice as long a run to the turn.

○ ONE TURN ROUTES ○

At Aqueduct, Belmont, and Arlington, races at one mile, and up to $1\frac{1}{4}$ miles at Belmont, are run around just one turn, the starting gate being placed in a chute extending from the backstretch. Such races feature a long run of at least four furlongs to the only turn, which would seem to negate any effect post position might have. A study of 382 of these races verifies this hypothesis.

Post	NH	NW	WPCT	I.V.
1	382	47	12.3%	1.11
2	382	43	11.3%	1.01
3	382	48	12.6%	1.13
4	382	45	11.8%	1.06
5	382	39	10.2%	0.92
6	382	52	13.6%	1.23
7	382	39	10.2%	0.92
8	318	31	9.8%	0.92
9	213	16	7.5%	0.76
10	123	13	10.6%	1.16
11	73	8	11.0%	1.27
12	45	1	2.2%	0.27
Outside	382	35	9.2%	0.83

ONE TURN ROUTES

This pattern appears valid at all three tracks. The outer posts seem only at a slight disadvantage, and post 1 does not appear as powerful as usual.

○ LAUREL'S CHUTE ○

At Laurel, races at one mile start from a special chute halfway around the clubhouse turn. Here are the results of a study of 262 such races.

Post	NH	NW	WPCT	I.V.
1	262	29	11.1%	0.97
2	262	34	13.0%	1.14
3	262	26	9.9%	0.87
4	262	24	9.2%	0.80
5	262	26	9.9%	0.87

LAUREL CHUTE

6	254	35	13.8%	1.22
7	228	29	12.7%	1.17
8	180	18	10.0%	0.98
9	131	13	9.9%	1.04
10	95	14	14.7%	1.62
11	60	9	15.0%	1.74
12	34	5	14.7%	1.76
Outside	262	43	16.4%	1.44

Apparently, horses from the outer part of the gate have a better "angle" on the backstretch. By far the best place to have started in such a race was on the far outside. Yet, horses breaking from the outside post did not produce a profit for their backers.

○ ELLIS PARK'S CHUTE ○

Ellis Park in Kentucky, one of the few mile-and-an-eighth tracks in the country, starts its mile races from a chute perpendicular to the backstretch (similar to the old Wilson chute at Saratoga). Unlike Laurel, where the angle of the chute seems to favor the outside horses, Ellis's chute appears to favor inside horses.

ELLIS CHUTE

Post	NH	NW	WPCT	I.V.
1	82	17	20.7%	1.85
2	82	13	15.9%	1.42
3	82	6	7.3%	0.65
4	82	6	7.3%	0.65
5	82	10	12.2%	1.09
6	82	9	11.0%	0.98
7	82	8	9.8%	0.87
8	72	7	9.7%	0.90
9	43	2	4.7%	0.47
10	23	2	8.7%	0.95
11	14	2	14.3%	1.64
12	7	0	0.0%	0.00

○ THE BULLRINGS ○

A "bullring" is a track anywhere from four to seven furlongs in circumference. The bullrings are noted for sharp turns and minor league racing, although Sportsmans Park in Chicago and Pomona outside Los Angeles offer purses of major-league caliber.

Most bullrings card short sprint races (three to five furlongs) around just one turn. Here are the results of a study of 601 such races.

Post	NH	NW	WPCT	I.V.
1	601	76	12.7%	1.24
2	601	54	9.0%	0.88
3	601	82	13.6%	1.34
4	601	71	11.8%	1.16
5	601	61	10.2%	1.00
6	601	56	9.3%	0.91
7	601	50	8.3%	0.82
8	601	62	10.3%	1.01
9	548	51	9.3%	0.93
10	474	30	6.3%	0.64
11	45	4	8.9%	1.03
12	25	4	16.0%	1.92
Outside	601	52	8.7%	0.85

Many of these races had a reasonable run to the turn, but still, the inner four posts seem to have a definite advantage—their combined impact value was 1.16. A great majority of these races were won by early speed types, so it would appear that the logical horse to play in such a race is a speedball breaking from the inside.

The standard two-turn race at a bullring is run at distances from $5\frac{1}{2}$ to $7\frac{1}{2}$ furlongs. A study of 1,048 of these races indicated that the advantage lies with the inner five posts, as might be expected.

Post	NH	NW	WPCT	I.V.
1	1048	133	12.7%	1.24
2	1048	113	10.8%	1.05
3	1048	112	10.7%	1.04
4	1048	120	11.5%	1.12
5	1048	126	12.0%	1.17
6	1048	98	9.4%	0.91
7	1048	101	9.6%	0.94
8	1048	92	8.8%	0.86
9	907	65	7.2%	0.72
10	817	73	8.9%	0.91
11	76	9	11.8%	1.39
12	54	6	11.1%	1.33
Outside	1048	94	9.0%	0.88

Horses breaking from the inner five posts combined for an impact value of 1.13.

Route races at the bullrings generally are run around three turns. Here are the results of 748 of them.

Post	NH	NW	WPCT	I.V.
1	748	107	14.3%	1.29
2	748	91	12.2%	1.09
3	748	88	11.8%	1.06
4	748	82	11.0%	0.98
5	748	81	10.8%	0.97
6	748	81	10.8%	0.97
7	748	87	11.6%	1.04
8	728	71	9.8%	0.88
9	438	35	8.0%	0.78
10	286	23	8.0%	0.81
11	19	1	5.3%	0.61
12	13	1	7.7%	0.92
Outside	748	66	8.8%	0.79

The rail horse obviously has an advantage. But after all the strategy and maneuvers that take place in a long race around three turns, posts 2 through 7 apparently are equals. The outer posts, however, appear to be at a disadvantage.

THE
DISTANCE
FACTOR

After reading the first four chapters, one could jump to the conclusion that any horse with early speed must be considered a contender, unless its chances are severely compromised by post position or track conditions.

Perhaps a more reasonable conclusion would be that horses with no early speed are unlikely contenders unless track conditions are making it almost impossible for speed types to hold on.

Although early speed is a wise place to start, a successful handicapping procedure must be more comprehensive. Other aspects of a horse's record must be considered.

Some speed horses seldom (if ever) win. Others win only when given the proper set of circumstances. These horses must be recognized for what they are: poor bets. This is done by getting a complete picture of the horse, not just what is revealed in the early speed column of its past performances.

In this chapter, we will look at the first of these factors, the distance of the race. Whether a horse is able to race successfully in routes, or is merely a sprinter, depends on its breeding, training, temperament, conformation, age, and physical condition. We shall not even attempt to study any of these influences, but will attempt to answer two basic questions about the distance factor:

(1) At how great a disadvantage (if any) is a horse that has yet to prove itself at approximately today's distance?

(2) How does a switch in distances affect a horse's chances of winning?

○ SUCCESS AT THE DISTANCE ○

To answer (1) above, the computer was asked the following question: "Does the horse's record show a good race at approximately today's distance?" The term "good race" was defined on page 9. By "approximately today's distance" we mean a race within one half furlong of today's distance, if entered in a sprint, or a route from 1 mile to 1⅛ miles, if entered in a route of similar distance.

Here is how a sample of 686 sprints answers this question:

	NH	NW	WPCT	MPCT	$NET	%W	I.V.
Yes	4809	609	12.7%	34.7%	$1.61	88.8%	1.10
No	1146	77**	6.7%	15.1%	$1.25	11.2%	0.58

And a sample of 422 routes:

	NH	NW	WPCT	MPCT	$NET	%W	I.V.
Yes	2613	350	13.4%	38.6%	$1.47	82.9%	1.05
No	706	72	10.2%	29.5%	$1.33	17.1%	0.80

Most races are won by horses that had previously run well at approximately the same distance. But the vast majority of the starters in these races shared this characteristic. Only in sprint races do horses lacking previous success at the distance appear to be at a serious disadvantage. The figures for the NO category in routes are nowhere near as bad.

Horses with little experience routing apparently are at only a slight disadvantage in routes, but are bet as if they had little chance of winning. One sample of 300 routes revealed that horses whose past performances showed at most two route races were able to hold their own, winning often enough at good odds to keep their followers in the black.

#Routes	NH	NW	WPCT	MPCT	$NET	%W	I.V.
None	94	13	13.8%	37.2%	$2.11	4.3%	1.14
1–2	261	29	11.1%	34.9%	$2.03	9.7%	0.90
3–10	2064	258	12.5%	37.5%	$1.37	86.0%	1.01

Horses with little route experience are at no disadvantage. With their early speed sharpened in sprints, many are able to take command immediately in routes, and enough stay there all the way.

○ STRETCHING OUT ○

Horses stretching out from a sprint to a route are almost able to hold their own. Here is a study of 453 route races, with the contestants classified according to the distance of their most recent race.

	NH	NW	WPCT	MPCT	$NET	%W	I.V.
Sprint	915	103	11.3%	34.5%	$1.55	22.7%	0.92
Route	2778	350	12.6%	38.0%	$1.44	77.3%	1.03

Of course, the vast majority (77 percent) of route races are won by horses with at least one recent route under their saddle. But horses coming out of sprints constitute 25 percent of the average route field, and do well enough to warrant further study.

What kind of performance in a sprint race points out a horse as likely to succeed when switched to a route distance? A good race in the sprint is a good sign, but it attracts heavy betting. A search of 45,000 past performance lines turned up 1,687 horses stretching out after a good race in a sprint, with the following statistics:

NH	NW	WPCT	MPCT	$NET	I.V.
1687	236	14.0%	43.2%	$1.66	1.14

The importance of a stretch gain in a sprint is overrated, and can be misleading. The horse with the big rally at six furlongs may have no kick at all in a route. As a matter of fact, it may set the pace in the route. After running three furlongs in a sprint, the horse may still be full of run and able to launch an impressive late charge. But after traveling six furlongs in a route, the same horse might not have the strength left to make its move, or maintain its lead. The fact that a horse is able to rally in sprints is no guarantee it will be able to race successfully at longer distances.

In the following tabulation (based on a search of 45,000 past performance lines), we study horses that rallied—passed horses *and* gained ground, for a total of at least three horses and/or lengths, from the stretch call to the wire—while finishing in the front half of their field and within five lengths of the winner in their recent sprint outing.

NH	NW	WPCT	MPCT	$NET	I.V.
718	111	15.5%	37.7%	$1.67	1.27

The stretch rally in a sprint often indicates the horse is in decent form, as attested to by the 1.27 impact value. But rallying sprinters, as a rule, are overbet when entered in routes.

Horses entered in routes after flashing early speed in a sprint do not fare as well as might be expected. The next tabulation studies horses that had run first, second, or third at the first call in a sprint race immediately preceding a route engagement. The statistics are the result of a study of 45,000 past performance lines.

NH	NW	WPCT	MPCT	$NET	I.V.
778	76	9.8%	27.1%	$1.32	0.80

Obviously, many of these horses met strong competition for the early lead, probably from another sprint type. And some of them, of course, were simply not capable of lasting the route distance.

But when a route race features just one horse with sprint speed, that horse is dangerous. Even if it tires badly in sprints, it may be able to go all the way at $1\frac{1}{16}$ miles. It may have been run off its feet in the early stages of the sprint, but when given a chance to settle down to a more leisurely pace in the route, it may become an entirely different animal able to continue strongly through the stretch.

One thing is certain—it will be able to outrun the typical route speed type for the early lead.

○ DROPPING BACK TO A SPRINT ○

A horse moving from a sprint to a route has a dangerous weapon—its early speed at the route distance. Horses dropping back from a route to a sprint find themselves in just the opposite position. Their early speed has probably been dulled because they have been routing, and they will most likely find themselves well behind in the early stages when they try to sprint.

A study of 777 sprint races indicates how serious this disadvantage is. Once again, the horses have been grouped according to the distance of their most recent race.

	NH	NW	WPCT	MPCT	$NET	%W	I.V.
Sprint	5688	700	12.3%	35.3%	$1.64	90.1%	1.10
Route	1226	77*	6.3%	26.2%	$1.11	9.9%	0.56

Horses dropping back from a route to a sprint constitute only 18 percent of the runners in sprint fields, but barely manage to win half their share of these sprints.

Only if a router contested the early lead (within one length at the first call) should it be given any consideration in a subsequent sprint. Although such a horse will not necessarily set the pace in the sprint, it may have enough speed to obtain a good position early, and enough stamina (from routing) to remain strong in the stretch.

Rocky Mount provides an excellent example of a router likely to drop back to a sprint successfully—particularly if the sprint is at the longer seven-furlong distance. Notice his sharp early speed in his two 1972 starts, and his ability to reach contention early at the slightly longer one-mile distance. (Rocky Mount easily won a seven-furlong grass race at Belmont on May 29.)

Here is how the 1,226 routers in our 777-sprint sample performed, when classified as having contested the early lead, or not, in their most recent races (all were routes).

	NH	NW	WPCT	MPCT	$NET	I.V.
Did	357	36	10.1%	33.6%	$1.69	0.90
Did not	869	41**	4.7%	23.1%	$0.86	0.42

Obviously, a horse unable to keep up in the early stages of a route race has little chance of winning a subsequent sprint race, and can be eliminated from consideration as a possible contender in such a race. It has probably been entered in the sprint for the purpose of sharpening its speed for a future route.

○ CONCLUSIONS ○

Summarizing our results, we have found two types of horses that can probably be eliminated as possible contenders. Both types are found in sprint races. One is the horse that has never (according to its past performances) run a good race at a distance within one half furlong of today's distance. The other is the horse whose last race was a route in which it failed to run within one length of the lead at the first call.

At times, other factors conspire to allow one of these horses to win. But over the long run, they prove to be highly unprofitable betting propositions.

According to our study, nothing pertaining to distance allows us to eliminate a horse as a possible contender in a route race.

FOREGO

It is a rare horse, indeed, that can compete successfully at any distance. It is all the more remarkable when that horse has a pronounced come-from-behind style.

But Forego was no ordinary horse, and he proved that conclusively late in his four-year-old season. Within the span of five weeks, he was able to change distances twice, and beat the best horses in training in three major stakes races.

On September 28, he took on the best routers in the country and beat them in the 1½-mile Woodward stakes. Three weeks later, he took on the best sprinters in the East, and beat them easily in the Vosburgh Handicap. And then, two weeks after that, he won America's greatest endurance test, the two-mile Jockey Club Gold Cup.

Photo credit: Bob Coglianese

"The Woodward"

"The Vosburgh"

"The Gold Cup"

Forego B. g. 4, by Forli—Lady Golconda, by Hasty Road

Br.—Lazy F Ranch (Ky)

Own.—Lazy F Ranch Tr.—Ward S W

	St.	1st	2nd	3rd	Amt.
1974	13	8	2	2	$545,086
1973	18	9	3	3	$188,909

9Nov74- 8Aqu	fst	2	:49⅗	1:14⅖	3:21⅕	3 ↑ J C Gold Cup	2	8	$4^{2\frac{1}{2}}$	1^{hd}	$1^{2\frac{1}{2}}$	$1^{2\frac{1}{2}}$	Gustines H	124	*.70	90–15 Forego $124^{2\frac{1}{2}}$ Copte $124^{\frac{3}{4}}$ Group Plan $124^{3\frac{1}{2}}$	Ridden out	8
19Oct74- 8Aqu	fst	7f	:22⅗	:45⅗	1:21⅗	3 ↑ Vosburgh H	4	10	$9^{9\frac{3}{4}}$	$7^{7\frac{1}{2}}$	2^{1}	$1^{3\frac{1}{2}}$	Gustines H	131	*2.20	93–10 Forego $131^{3\frac{1}{2}}$ Stop TheMusic118^{no}PrinceDantan$119^{1\frac{3}{4}}$	Ridden out	12
28Sep74- 8Bel	fst	1½	:49	1:13⅗	2:27⅗	3 ↑ Woodward	5	10	10^{17}	$8^{4\frac{1}{2}}$	4^{2}	1^{nk}	Gustines H	126	*2.30	83–13 Forego 126^{nk} Arbees Boy $126^{1\frac{3}{4}}$ Group Plan $126^{2\frac{1}{2}}$	Driving	11
14Sep74- 8Bel	sly	1⅛	:46	1:10⅗	1:46⅗	3 ↑ Marlboro H	2	9	8^{10}	$7^{2\frac{3}{4}}$	$3^{4\frac{1}{2}}$	3^{4}	Gustines H	126	2.70	90–12 Big Spruce $120^{2\frac{3}{4}}$ Arbees Boy $119^{1\frac{1}{2}}$ Forego $126^{\frac{1}{2}}$	No final rally	10
2Sep74- 8Bel	fst	1⅛	:45⅗	1:09⅗	1:46⅕	3 ↑ Governor	10	8	8^{12}	6^{5}	5^{7}	$4^{5\frac{1}{2}}$	Gustines H	128	*1.60	91–09 Big Spruce $118^{2\frac{1}{2}}$ Arbees Boy $121^{1\frac{1}{2}}$ Plunk $121^{1\frac{1}{2}}$	Wide	10
20Jly74- 8Aqu	fst	1¼	:47⅖	1:11⅕	2:01⅗	3 ↑ Suburban H	6	6	5^{12}	$4^{6\frac{1}{2}}$	$4^{4\frac{1}{2}}$	$3^{1\frac{1}{2}}$	Gustines H	131	*1.40	87–12 True Knight $127^{1\frac{1}{2}}$ Plunk 114^{hd} Forego $131^{2\frac{1}{2}}$	Rallied	10
4Jly74- 8Aqu	fst	$1\frac{3}{16}$	:46⅗	1:10⅖	1:54⅘	3 ↑ Brooklyn H	6	6	6^{15}	4^{8}	2^{hd}	$1^{\frac{3}{4}}$	Gustines H	129	*.40	88–14 Forego $129^{\frac{3}{4}}$ Billy Come Lately 114^{2} Arbees Boy 116^{6}	Ridden out	7
26Jun74- 8Aqu	fst	7f	:22⅗	:44⅘	1:21⅕	3 ↑ Nassau Co H	2	6	6^{12}	6^{12}	$5^{6\frac{1}{2}}$	$2^{\frac{1}{2}}$	Gustines H	132	*.70	94–10 Timeless Moment $112^{\frac{1}{2}}$ Forego $132^{\frac{1}{2}}$ North Sea $114^{2\frac{1}{2}}$	Fast finish	6
27May74- 8Bel	fst	1	:44⅗	1:09	1:34⅖	3 ↑ Metropol'n H	2	6	$4^{7\frac{1}{2}}$	2^{hd}	$1^{1\frac{1}{2}}$	2^{2}	Gustines H	134	*1.30	94–11 Arbees Boy 112^{2} Forego $134^{\frac{1}{2}}$ Timeless Moment 109^{hd}	Gamely	8
18May74- 8Bel	fst	7f	:22⅕	:45	1:22⅕	3 ↑ Carter H	7	8	8^{9}	$6^{3\frac{1}{2}}$	$1^{1\frac{1}{2}}$	$1^{2\frac{1}{4}}$	Gustines H	129	*1.40	91–13 Forego $129^{2\frac{1}{4}}$ Mr. Prospector 124^{1} Timeless Moment $113^{2\frac{3}{4}}$	Easily	8
23Mar74- 9Hia	fst	1¼	:47⅕	1:11	2:01⅕	3 ↑ Widener H	5	5	$5^{8\frac{1}{2}}$	$1^{\frac{1}{2}}$	$1^{1\frac{1}{2}}$	1^{1}	Gustines H	129	*.80	92–12 Forego 129^{1} True Knight 124^{2} Play the Field 114no	Driving	7
23Feb74- 9GP	fst	1¼	:46⅘	1:10⅘	1:59⅘	3 ↑ Gulf Park H	2	4	4^{13}	2^{2}	1^{hd}	$1^{\frac{1}{2}}$	Gustines H	127	1.40	98–14 Forego $127^{\frac{1}{2}}$ True Knight 123^{6} Golden Don 118^{3}	Ridden out	6
9Feb74- 9GP	fst	1⅛	:47⅕	1:11⅗	1:48⅗	3 ↑ Donn Hcp	2	4	3^{5}	$3^{2\frac{1}{2}}$	2^{1}	1no	Gustines H	125	*.70	91–19 Forego 125no True Knight $123^{\frac{1}{2}}$ Proud and Bold 122^{nk}	Just up	5

FORM:
FINISH
LAST RACE

Of all handicapping factors, present form is the most difficult. Horses have their ups and downs—some are on the improve, others are the worse for the wear.

Many a horse races as if its past-performance record is a forgery. The horse that looks so good on paper may have gone sour in training, not run a lick, and infuriate its backers.

With excellent performances in its last two starts, a horse might appear outstanding. But the effort expended in those races may have left the animal with little in reserve for today's race.

On the other hand, a horse may show dull form in its recent races, perhaps because it was racing at unsuitable distances, or against far superior rivals. The trainer, sensing that the horse has come to hand, has now placed it in the kind of race it can win. Some trainers do their best to disguise a horse's form, hoping to increase the odds the day they are really trying to win.

In the next few chapters, we study how a horse's chances of winning might be affected by its recent form, good or bad. We will look for dependable signs that a horse is ready for a good effort, or that its best efforts have already been given.

○ FINISH IN LAST RACE ○

In this chapter, we will focus on where the horse finished in its most recent race.

Here are the results of a study of 1,842 races, with the horses grouped according to their most recent finishes.

Finish	NH	NW	WPCT	MPCT	$NET	%W	I.V.
First	2278	387	17.0%	42.9%	$1.77	21.0%	1.52
Second	1869	329	17.6%	46.9%	$1.77	17.9%	1.58
Third	1845	240	13.0%	39.7%	$1.48	13.0%	1.17
Front half	2863	293	10.2%	35.5%	$1.45	15.9%	0.92
Rear half	7671	593	7.7%	25.1%	$1.43	32.2%	0.69

The FRONT HALF category here refers to horses, other than those finishing first, second, or third, that managed to beat half their opponents to the wire. The REAR HALF category refers to horses that finished behind at least half their opponents.

Horses that had beaten at least half their opponents in their last race—those that finished first, second, third, and the rest—combined for the following figures.

NH	NW	WPCT	MPCT	$NET	%W	I.V.
8855	1249	14.1%	40.7%	$1.61	67.8%	1.27

Obviously, horses that have run well in their most recent start are the most likely to run well in their next start. Notice the curious fact that horses that finish second win their next races somewhat more often than winners do. This probably relates to the fact that most winners are either forced up in class (this is especially true of many allowance winners), or required to carry more weight as a penalty for winning. Horses that run second (or worse) can race again in the same company without picking up extra poundage.

Running in the money appears to be a decent indicator of future success—52 percent of the sampled races were won by horses that ran in the money in their most recent attempts. Actually, finishing third is no longer as significant as it was in the past. Perhaps this is because so many races have small fields nowadays.

Almost two thirds of the starters in an average race had run out of the money in their last start. Some of these, no doubt, were too ambitiously placed, while others were probably running at unfavorable distances.

In any case, a poor performance (REAR HALF) last out is definitely a bad sign, regardless of circumstances. Even when the horse was outclassed, a poor performance cannot be totally ignored. Claiming horses dropping in class, or horses dropping into claiming races from allowance company, after running in the rear half of their fields last out, had the following record (based on a sample of 1,239 races):

NH	NW	WPCT	MPCT	$NET	I.V.
2529	261	10.3%	32.4%	$1.48	0.90

○ GOOD RACE LAST OUT ○

In the tabulation below, each of the contestants in 1,549 races has been classified as to whether or not it ran a "good race" in its last start. Remember (see page 9), a good race means either a finish in the money (first, second, or third), or a finish within two lengths of the winner in a sprint, or within three lengths of the winner in a route.

	NH	NW	WPCT	MPCT	$NET	%W	I.V.
Good	5290	822	15.5%	42.4%	$1.65	53.1%	1.41
Others	8787	727	8.3%	27.3%	$1.43	46.9%	0.75

Horses that had run a good race in their most recent start were able to come back and win almost twice as often as those that had not. The latter formed the vast majority of the starters, yet won just 75 percent of their share of these races. The former won far more than their share, but were so heavily overbet that they could barely improve upon the pari-mutuel average of $1.64.

The preceding tabulation will prove to be one of the keys in our study of thoroughbred form. It should be used as a point of reference. In the chapters that follow, we will study these horses—those that had run a good race last out—in various situations. Some will prove beneficial, improving the overall statistics. Others will not.

The net result will be the identification of situations in which recent good form is a strong positive sign pointing out a good betting opportunity, and situations in which apparent good form can be misleading and the horse is not likely to run as advertised.

○ THE RECENT WINNER ○

Horses coming off a victory in their latest start prove an abundant source of winners, and so warrant further study. Here are the results of a study of every horse aged three or older that raced again after winning a non-maiden race during an entire New York racing season.

NH	NW	WPCT	MPCT	$NET	I.V.
1412	257	18.2%	49.0%	$1.72	1.64

Although the impact value is higher than in the first tabulation of this chapter, the astuteness of the New York betting public is reflected in the lower average payoff.

Those winners that returned at the same distance (sprint or route) as their victory perform slightly better than the group as a whole, as the following figures prove:

NH	NW	WPCT	MPCT	$NET	I.V.
1137	221	19.4%	49.4%	$1.83	1.75

Of particular significance, as far as impact values are concerned, is the margin of victory. Horses that won by three lengths or more were more successful in their next start than the group as a whole, although they were also the most heavily bet.

NH	NW	WPCT	MPCT	$NET	I.V.
370	84	22.7%	53.0%	$1.76	2.05

Even more successful, but less obvious to the betting public, were those that won in exceptionally quick times. In the next tabulation, we study horses that won in time at least four lengths faster than the par time for the race in which they are now entered (par times and speed figures will be discussed in Chapters 16 and 17).

NH	NW	WPCT	MPCT	$NET	I.V.
92	24	26.1%	53.3%	$2.19	2.35

Allowance and stakes horses are of higher quality than claiming horses, and consequently hold their winning form longer:

	NH	NW	WPCT	MPCT	$NET	I.V.
Allow-Stakes	612	127	20.8%	51.8%	$1.89	1.87
Claiming	800	130	16.2%	46.9%	$1.59	1.46

○ THE RECENT MAIDEN GRADUATE ○

Of a completely different color is the recent maiden graduate making its first start outside the maiden ranks. A study of the next performance of each maiden winner aged three or older during two full New York seasons produced the following results:

NH	NW	WPCT	MPCT	$NET	I.V.
529	76	14.4%	34.6%	$1.44	1.30

Maiden graduates "move up" in their next starts, if only in the sense that they must face tougher opposition—other winners, rather than maidens. It is quite a testimony to the importance of current form that in spite of this, recent maiden winners are more than able to hold their own, as attested to by a 1.30 impact value.

Many maiden special winners, especially those that win by big margins or in fast time, become betting favorites in their next starts, which usually come in NW1 races. Although they win half again their share of these races, it is obvious that they usually are overbet:

NH	NW	WPCT	MPCT	$NET	I.V.
293	49	16.7%	38.6%	$1.38	1.50

The typical maiden claiming winner faces a more difficult assignment—many are moved up in price, and some race next in allowance races. Overall, their figures fall far short of those for the maiden special winners:

NH	NW	WPCT	MPCT	$NET	I.V.
236	27	11.4%	29.7%	$1.52	1.03

Surprisingly, it was the ones entered next in an NW1 allowance race that accounted for the higher $NET.

	NH	NW	WPCT	MPCT	$NET	I.V.
Allowance	60	9	15.0%	33.3%	$2.29	1.35
Up in price	104	10	9.6%	29.8%	$1.25	0.87
Not up in price	72	8	11.1%	27.7%	$1.25	1.00

It should be mentioned that seven of the nine that went on to win an allowance race had broken their maidens in time at least as fast as par time for maiden special races.

A maiden winner's chance of repeating in its next start is directly proportional to its margin of victory in the maiden race. Those that won by three lengths or more had the following record in their next starts:

NH	NW	WPCT	MPCT	$NET	I.V.
180	37	20.6%	42.8%	$1.98	1.86

Once again, accurate speed figures prove the most reliable barometer. Horses that break their maidens in time at least two lengths faster than par time for the race in which they run next prove the best bets:

NH	NW	WPCT	MPCT	$NET	I.V.
72	25	34.7%	52.8%	$3.08	2.42

The racing style of a maiden winner also seems important. Those that show some early speed in their maiden victories repeat more often than others do. Horses that come from behind usually depend on the speed horses tiring and coming back to them. But there is quite a difference between the horses they catch in their maiden wins and the ones they must catch in open company.

On the other hand, maiden winners that set or prompt the pace (FCP 1–3) in their maiden victories win more than their share of their next starts:

NH	NW	WPCT	MPCT	$NET	I.V.
310	50	16.1%	38.0%	$1.67	1.45

One final factor of importance is the previous racing experience of the maiden victor. A horse good enough to break its maiden in the first, second, or third start of its career is usually more capable of winning again in its next start than is a horse that had to try several times before winning. A talented horse does not spend too much time escaping the maiden ranks. The following 128 horses all broke their maidens after three or fewer attempts:

NH	NW	WPCT	MPCT	$NET	I.V.
128	26	20.3%	36.7%	$1.76	1.83

The horse that breaks its maiden in the first race of its career poses a difficult problem in its next start. Although approximately 25 percent of them win, they are heavily overbet. Those that win their debuts without serious opposition for the early lead are especially prone to failures at low odds. They have displayed their speed, but have yet to demonstrate that they have any class or courage. Many fall apart when challenged by a more experienced speed horse in open competition.

○ **DISTANCE** ○

The statistical patterns presented in this chapter appear independent of distance. Good form is as significant in sprints as it is in routes.

The brilliant filly Gallant Bloom defeats arch-rival Shuvee (second left) in the 1969 Gazelle at Belmont, clinching honors as the year's champion three-year-old filly.

FORM:
RECENT
ACTION

Certain trainers are known for their ability to prepare a horse for an important race on workouts alone. In Europe this is the rule rather than the exception. American horses, however, race far more frequently than their European cousins. Claiming horses in particular are usually conditioned through actual competition.

Consequently, a horse returning from a layoff is noticeable by contrast. In an era when too many tracks operate simultaneously, and too many horses race too often, many of them on drugs, does the fresh horse have an advantage? Or does it require a race or two to reach top form, like the freshened horse of the past?

A study of 2,021 races indicates that horses away from the races for more than 30 days are at a disadvantage in their first race back. The tabulation below groups horses according to the number of days since their most recent start.

Days	NH	NW	WPCT	MPCT	$NET	%W	I.V.
1–5	558	72	12.9%	38.9%	$1.65	3.6%	1.13
6–10	6086	806	13.2%	39.3%	$1.61	39.9%	1.16
11–14	3787	420	11.1%	34.2%	$1.45	20.8%	0.97
15–21	3292	377	11.5%	33.6%	$1.61	18.7%	1.00
22–30	1565	157	10.0%	31.0%	$1.49	7.8%	0.88
31–90	1584	137**	8.6%	25.9%	$1.59	6.8%	0.76
91 up	836	52**	6.2%	19.1%	$1.39	2.6%	0.55

This sample included both allowance and claiming races, sprints and routes. The findings indicated that the negative factor of "no race in

30 days" applies mostly to claiming sprints, and is of lesser significance in allowance races and routes, at least as far as the horse's chances of winning are concerned.

Here, for example, is the breakdown according to distance:

	NH	NW	WPCT	MPCT	$NET	I.V.
Sprints	2189	162**	7.4%	20.9%	$1.54	0.67
Routes	231	27	11.7%	30.0%	$1.33	0.99

Approximately one of every five starters in a claiming sprint has not seen action in the past month. These horses are able to win not even 70 percent of their share of the races. Of course, a good percentage of these horses are routers returning to the races in a sprint.

In one sample of 646 claiming sprints, we found 824 horses that had been away from the races for at least 31 days. Most (706) of these horses were capable of sprinting successfully—their past performances contained evidence of at least one good race at a sprint distance within one-half furlong of today's distance. The other 118 had no record of such success. Here is the breakdown:

	NH	NW	WPCT	MPCT	$NET	I.V.
Yes	706	52	7.4%	23.2%	$1.54	0.69
No	118	2	1.7%	9.3%	$0.83	0.16

In that same sample, 166 of the 824 horses were "routers" in the sense that at least half the races in their past performances were routes. The other 658 were "sprinters." Here is the breakdown:

	NH	NW	WPCT	MPCT	$NET	I.V.
Sprinters	658	49	7.4%	23.4%	$1.53	0.70
Routers	166	5	3.0%	12.7%	$1.08	0.28

Clearly, a "route type" can be eliminated from consideration as a possible contender when returning from a layoff in a claiming sprint.

For that matter, "sprint types" are no bargains when returning from a layoff in a claiming sprint. A detailed study of these horses disclosed nothing that might turn this generally negative situation to the advantage of the bettor.

Running style, as reflected in speed points, proved insignificant. Horses that tend to show early speed seldom are able to go all the way in their first race back, especially if they face strong contention for the early lead. Those that come from behind do not perform better simply because they have been rested.

Movements up or down the claiming ladder also proved insignificant. Those that are moved up when returned to the races are probably being raced into condition at a level where they are unlikely to be claimed. Those dropping down, before being given a chance to run back to their previous form, are probably claim bait. There was probably some reason other than fatigue for the recent vacation, and the trainer is probably trying to get rid of the horse.

○ DAYS SINCE LAST RACE AT THE DISTANCE ○

We can strengthen the negative category "no race in 30 days" in sprints if we ask instead the question "how many days since the horse last raced in a sprint?" Here is how a sample of 645 sprints answered this question:

Days	NH	NW	WPCT	MPCT	$NET	%W	I.V.
1–30	4537	567	12.5%	36.5%	$1.60	87.9%	1.12
31 up	1255	78**	6.2%	22.1%	$1.38	12.1%	0.56

A higher percentage of starters (21.7 percent) have this negative characteristic ("no sprint in 30 days") than the previous one ("no race in 30 days"). And the larger group has the lower impact value, making it clearly the stronger of these two elimination factors.

If we were to ask the corresponding question of the starters in a route race—"how many days since the horse last raced in a route?"—we would find little to choose between the two groups. Here are the results of a study of 295 routes:

Days	NH	NW	WPCT	MPCT	$NET	%W	I.V.
1–30	1854	233	12.6%	38.0%	$1.48	79.0%	1.02
31 up	529	62	11.7%	34.2%	$1.43	21.0%	0.95

As we learned in Chapter 5, a horse entered in a route race is at no great disadvantage because of the absence of (recent) form at route distances. Nor is it at any disadvantage because of lack of recent activity at route distances.

Interestingly, 45 of the horses in the first category (1–30 days) were racing again within five days of their most recent race, which also was a route. None of the 45 won. Clearly, a horse needs a few days rest after (before?) engaging in a route race.

○ DAYS SINCE LAST GOOD RACE ○

Both of the studies above produced a category of horses whose prospects for winning seem very remote. But neither study revealed anything of a positive nature. True, horses that have raced within the past month win slightly more than their share of the races. But this information does nothing for the bettor.

However, if we ask the question "how many days since the horse's last good race?" we will find some positive signs, as well as a much larger (and equally strong) negative category.

In the following tabulation, we have classified the horses in 945 races according to the number of days since their last good race.

Days	NH	NW	WPCT	MPCT	$NET	%W	I.V.
1–5	67	10	14.9%	56.7%	$1.67	1.1%	1.30
6–10	1290	248	19.2%	49.5%	$1.83	26.2%	1.67
11–14	836	125	15.0%	40.8%	$1.43	13.2%	1.30
15–21	1090	153	14.0%	40.6%	$1.81	16.2%	1.22
22–30	887	109	12.3%	37.7%	$1.48	11.5%	1.07
31 up	4038	300**	7.4%	25.9%	$1.39	31.7%	0.65

Almost half the starters in these races had failed to run a good race within the past 30 days, and they were the big losers. We have an ideal situation here: The typical field splits into two halves, those that have run a good race within 30 days, and those that have not. Since the latter group exhibits strong negative characteristics, the former must show positive signs.

In sprints, it is an extremely positive sign to be coming back within ten days of a good race. If a sharp horse waits longer than ten days to race again, there is no guarantee that it has retained its edge. The only guarantee is that the bettors, as a group, will presume that it has retained its sharpness.

In the following tabulation, we focus on horses entered in sprint races that had run a good race in their last start. These horses have been classified according to the number of days since that race (we ignore those idle more than a month).

Days	NH	NW	WPCT	MPCT	$NET	I.V.
1–10	1536	291*	18.9%	49.5%	$1.96	1.74
11–30	2551	337	13.2%	38.7%	$1.47	1.24

The situation is completely different in routes, however. A study of 300 route races turned up 950 horses coming back within 30 days of a good race. Here is how that sample divided according to the number of days away:

Days	NH	NW	WPCT	MPCT	$NET	I.V.
1–14	717	125	17.4%	44.8%	$1.55	1.41
15–31	233	41	17.6%	44.2%	$2.02	1.43

The very least that we can conclude here is that a 2–3 week layoff after a good race does not hurt a router, and apparently has the side effect of forcing the odds up higher than they would be were the horse coming back sooner.

Sprinters seem to need that razor-sharp edge; routers do not.

○ CONCLUSION ○

The fact that a horse made a good effort in its last race loses its significance when it is learned that the race came several months ago.

"What have you done lately?" is a valid question in thoroughbred handicapping.

A horse that has been idle for over one month is a poor risk. A horse that has failed to run a good race in over one month is an even worse risk.

Among horses that have raced (raced well) within the month, the exact number of "days since" does not seem to matter, with one exception. Sprinters coming back within 10 days of a good race do very well—almost well enough to allow their backers to break even, without considering any of the other parts of the handicapping picture.

FORM:
FRESHENED
HORSES

The fresh horse returning from a layoff of more than 30 days is not worth a bet, under any circumstances. If entered in a claiming sprint, it should be eliminated from consideration as a possible contender.

But what of the horse that had been rested, but has now had a race or two since returning? Does it have an advantage over rivals that are leg-weary from prolonged campaigns?

The answer is a definite "YES." Such horses do have an advantage, and they can be very rewarding from a betting standpoint. Particularly in sprints.

○ SPRINTS: SECOND RACE AFTER A LAYOFF ○

For a sprinter, one decent race after a layoff may be all the horse needs to return to winning ways.

In our first tabulation, we study horses entered in sprints that had raced but once following a layoff of at least one month. The statistics are based on a sample of 1,249 sprints.

NH	NW	WPCT	MPCT	$NET	%W	I.V.
1405	149	10.6%	31.2%	$1.47	11.9%	1.00

Although these figures, as they stand, are hardly exciting, they become quite interesting when confined to horses that gave a decent account of themselves in their first races after layoffs.

First of all, here is how this sample of 1,405 horses divides when we ask whether or not the horse ran a good race (see definition on page 9) in its first start back.

	NH	NW	WPCT	MPCT	$NET	I.V.
Good race	465	77	16.6%	45.4%	$1.85	1.57
Others	940	72	7.7%	24.1%	$1.28	0.73

And here is how the same sample splits when we ask whether or not the horse finished in the front half of its field in its first race back.

	NH	NW	WPCT	MPCT	$NET	I.V.
Front half	639	98	15.3%	41.8%	$1.85	1.43
Rear half	766	51	6.7%	22.3%	$1.16	0.65

Quite a difference, in both tabulations. Obviously, the horse that has been freshened, and then shown some effort in its first race back, has an advantage over its opponents, many of whom have been over-raced. Just as obvious is the fact that a horse that shows little, if anything, on its return to the races should not be expected to improve suddenly and dramatically without further racing.

When an old warhorse like Delta Traffic returns from a layoff, it usually takes just one race to return to top form. Notice that Delta Traffic showed good early speed upon his return from a six-week layoff, was still in contention at the stretch call, only to weaken slightly in the final eighth—all good signs that a winning effort is soon forthcoming.

Apparently, a good tightener is all a horse needs to become eligible to return to its top form in its second race back. However, too good a tightener in that first race back can do a horse more harm than good. By "too good" we mean a driving finish from the stretch call to the wire in which the horse was always within one length of the leader, if not the hard-pressed leader itself. Or a front-running type that had a clear lead at the stretch call, but was all-out at the wire to win or lose in a photo finish. Only 80 of the 465 that turned in good efforts in their returns fell into this category, and they had the following record:

NH	NW	WPCT	MPCT	$NET	I.V.
80	12	15.0%	45.0%	$1.32	1.40

Not really bad figures, aside from the fact that these horses were heavily overbet. This small group includes many beaten favorites —horses expected to improve after bang-up efforts in their first race back. Obviously, for many of these horses, the extra effort in that race was a case of too much, too soon.

Head Table, for example, returned from a six-week layoff with an all-out effort on September 20. He returned just seven days later against the same kind of horse he had beaten three times during the summer, reached even terms for the lead in midstretch, but weakened under pressure to finish third as the favorite. That first effort back had knocked this game horse out to the extent that he was able to race but once during the next two months, before starting another successful campaign—this time with a not-so-taxing effort in his first race back.

Eliminate these 80 suspect underlays from the sample, and the figures become even more impressive:

	NH	NW	WPCT	MPCT	$NET	I.V.
Good race	385	65	16.9%	45.5%	$1.96	1.69
Front half	559	86	15.4%	41.3%	$1.92	1.52

Obviously, it is to a horse's advantage not to be severely tested in its first race after a layoff, while at the same time turning in a reasonably good effort. Listen to what leading trainer Laz Barrera had to say to *Daily Racing Form* columnist Herb Goldstein about the return to action of Kentucky Derby-Belmont winner Bold Forbes in the fall of 1976:

If you rush things with a muscular horse, especially one who has been away this long, he will give you everything he has quickly, and then his muscles get all knotted. Then it takes weeks to get him over the soreness. I might get one good race out of him that way, but he'd be out for the rest of the season. He'd be so stiff after one real tough breeze or race, he'd be knocked out.

Photo credit: Bob Coglianese

The Governor: The 1975 Governor Stakes at Belmont—that's Wajima on the outside catching Foolish Pleasure in the last strides, after Foolish Pleasure had battled furiously to hold the short lead he had gained earlier in the stretch. It was Foolish Pleasure's first start since the ill-fated match race with Ruffian in July.

Obviously, it takes a certain amount of skill and patience to bring a horse back to the races properly. The horse's workouts must give it some bottom, a foundation upon which to build. If this foundation is not solid when the horse returns, an all-out effort in that first race may crack whatever foundation there is, and the horse may never run back to that promising first effort. Either that, or the horse may race dismally for

The Marlboro: *A few weeks later, and the picture looks the same. Except that's Forego, not Foolish Pleasure, losing a tight decision to Wajima in the Marlboro Cup. Foolish Pleasure finished a well-beaten fifth, apparently knocked out by his efforts in the Governor. Forego also had returned from a layoff in the Governor, but was not forced to give an all-out effort that day—his mild rally gained fourth position, about three lengths behind Wajima.*

a few races, building the foundation through racing rather than work-outs.

Once a horse has been returned to the races, it does not seem to matter how quickly it comes back for its second try. Here is how our sample of 1,405 sprinters divides with respect to the number of days between the horses' first and second starts after layoffs:

Days	NH	NW	WPCT	MPCT	$NET	I.V.
1–14	926	100	10.8%	33.5%	$1.47	1.02
15–30	479	49	10.2%	26.7%	$1.48	0.96

○ SPRINTERS: THIRD AND FOURTH STARTS
AFTER A LAYOFF ○

A horse reaches its peak in its third and fourth starts after a layoff.

A computer study of the records of 3,091 horses revealed that the average horse records its highest speed figures (we used a modified *Daily Racing Form* speed rating + track variant, which will be explained in Chapter 17) in its third or fourth starts after a rest of at least one month. The table below indicates the average difference (in lengths) between the speed figure recorded in a horse's first start after a layoff and those recorded in subsequent starts.

Start	Difference
2	+.09
3	+.75
4	+.74
5	+.64
6 up	+.39

Although the average differences are slight, the graph does have the "right shape," rising to a peak for starts 3 and 4, and then dropping off.

This same study also offered a possible explanation as to why horses eventually tail off. Instead of following a horse from the end of one layoff to the beginning of another, the computer was asked to follow the horse only as long as it continued to race at the same distance (sprint or route) at which it had returned to the races. For example, if a horse had returned in a sprint, it would only be followed as long as it sprinted.

Here is how that study worked out. The numbers in the second column have the same meaning as above.

Start	Difference
2	+0.37
3	+1.12
4	+1.37
5	+1.10
6–11	+1.62
12 up	+0.79

In other words, it appears that changes in distance have an effect on how long a horse is able to hold its form.

Horses in their third and fourth starts after a layoff also provide the most lucrative betting opportunities. Here are the results of a study of 1,249 sprints, in which 2,188 horses were racing for the third or fourth times after a layoff:

NH	NW	WPCT	MPCT	$NET	%W	I.V.
2188	273	12.5%	33.9%	$1.80	21.9%	1.18

The $1.80 average payoff at this stage is much higher than at any other time during a horse's campaign.

And it can be improved. If one of these freshened horses ran a good race, or at least beat half of its opponents, in its last start, all the vital statistics get better.

	NH	NW	WPCT	MPCT	$NET	I.V.
Good race	812	145	17.9%	45.1%	$1.92	1.66
Front half	1118	180	16.1%	42.5%	$1.83	1.50

Add a requirement that the horse race within 10 days of its preceding start, and a profit can be realized, although the number of betting opportunities decreases rather sharply.

	NH	NW	WPCT	MPCT	$NET	I.V.
Good race	310	64	20.6%	48.7%	$2.30	1.93
Front half	421	75	17.8%	45.4%	$2.02	1.65

Ahira shows all the signs of a freshened horse ready to win— some early speed and considerable support at the betting windows in his first start after a six-month layoff, and then a much improved effort second time out. Eight days later, on the heels of a sharp blowout, Ahira was ready. He won, and paid a generous $10.20.

It is interesting to see how the "GOOD RACE LAST" statistics "come alive" when supplemented by a sign suggesting that the horse is likely to run well again. Later in a campaign, one more all-out effort might be all that is required to tap a horse's energy reserves. But early in a campaign there is always the promise of more.

We should point out that a similar study failed to produce positive results for horses that had raced more than four times since their most recent layoffs.

○ THE FRESHENED ROUTER ○

The picture is quite different in route races. Unless a horse fits a certain pattern, its chances of success in its first few races after a layoff are dim and, apparently, good form is of little significance.

The ideal pattern for a router after a layoff is to race twice in sprints before attempting a route. In the tabulation below, we study such horses in their third, fourth, and fifth races (first, second, and third routes) after a layoff.

NH	NW	WPCT	MPCT	$NET	I.V.
125	23	18.4%	39.2%	$2.61	1.48

Each of the races studied was a route. Once these horses started routing (in their third race after a layoff), they continued in routes, and continued to meet with success for three races. Those that raced well in preceding starts did even better:

	NH	NW	WPCT	MPCT	$NET	I.V.
Good race	52	14	26.9%	55.8%	$4.00	2.17
Front half	70	17	24.3%	48.6%	$3.36	1.96

Aglimmer presents the ideal picture for a router returning from a layoff: two sprints, the second slightly longer than the first and resulting in an improved effort. With her speed honed and her conditioning completed, she went on to win two grass allowances before placing second to Lie Low in the Firenze Handicap.

On the other side of the coin is the horse entered in its first post-layoff route after inadequate preparation.

We have already seen that horses are able to return from layoffs in routes and just about hold their own (although their backers suffer a much worse fate). But apparently, the strain of returning to the races in a route has a lastingly ill effect.

The following tabulation studies horses that returned from layoffs in routes and continued in such races for four more starts. Here is how they performed in these four attempts (their second, third, fourth, and fifth races after the layoff).

NH	NW	WPCT	MPCT	$NET	I.V.
292	35	12.0%	39.4%	$1.33	0.97

Many of the members of this group that did well were surprises to form followers—a good race last out seemed to be of little significance.

Similarly, bringing a recently laid-off horse back to a route after only one sprint appears to be a case of "too long, too soon," adversely affecting the horse for several subsequent races. The following tabulation studies horses that returned to the races in a sprint, then routed for their next four starts. Here is how they performed in those four routes:

NH	NW	WPCT	MPCT	$NET	I.V.
194	13	6.7%	29.9%	$0.63	0.54

FORM:
SOME
POSITIVE
SIGNS

It is often difficult to determine when a horse is about to come into form, or go off form. Some horses give everything race after race. Others make an effort only once in a while, usually without forewarning.

Horses often serve notice of improving form, or continued good form, by the manner in which they race, and not necessarily where they finish. A sharp move at any stage of a race may be the only tipoff a wise player needs to be in on a "good thing" next time the horse runs.

In this chapter, we will define and study several of these "moves," at times finding results in disagreement with traditional handicapping tenets.

○ THE TAXING STRETCH DRIVE ○

Traditional handicappers suppose that a horse involved in an all-out drive from the stretch call to the wire may come up empty when asked for a strong run in its next start. But statistics show that the opposite is true.

In the first tabulation below, we study horses that were within one length of the lead, or leading themselves, but by no more than one length, at both the stretch call and the finish; or horses that had a clear lead at the stretch call, only to falter and finish in a photo, winning or losing by no more than a neck.

Dot's Imp, for example, was involved in such a drive on November 9, November 30, January 9, and February 28, but not on March 8, when he finished more than one length ahead of his nearest pursuer.

Dot's Imp ✱ B. rig. 9, by Big Pete—Ebbie's Girl, by Murane
Br.—Dot-Ed Farm (Fla)
Own.—Marietta Stable Tr.—Leatherbury K T **122**

Turf Record	St.	1st	2nd	3rd		St.	1st	2nd	3rd	Amt.
	6	2	2	0	1975	4	2	1	0	$10,980
					1974	10	5	2	0	$18,280

8Mar75- 2Bow	fst	6f	:23	:46⅕	1:11⅗	Clm c-13500	7	1	1½	1hd	1hd	11¼	McCarron C J	b	119	*.70	85-15	Dot'sImp1191¼MandatoryCount1141¾UnionSoldier114¾	Drew clear	9
28Feb75- 7Bow	fst	6f	:23	:47	1:12⅖	Clm 13500	1	3	2hd	21	2½	1hd	McCarron C J	b	114	2.90e	81-27	Dot's Imp 114hd Tsunami 1175 Ambermott 1171	Driving	12
10Feb75- 7Bow	fst	6f	:22⅖	:45⅕	1:09⅗	Clm 17500	3	3	24	26	614	718	McCarron C J5	b	109	1.90	77-19	Scam 1147 Love That Breeze 1144 Vasa Lopp 114nk	Tired	8
9Jan75- 7Bow	fst	6f	:22⅖	:46	1:11⅘	Clm 17500	3	3	2½	2hd	1½	2no	McCarron C J5	b	112	*1.20	84-24	Sea Rider 113no Dot's Imp 1124 Vesta's Dragon1142½	Just missed	8
30Nov74- 5Lrl	fst	6f	:23⅕	:46⅖	1:11⅕	3↑Clm 16000	5	2	2½	21½	2hd	1hd	McCarron C J5	b	111	*.90e	91-16	Dot's Imp 111hd You Can Do It 1163 Time OfPlenty112nk	Just up	8
9Nov74- 3Lrl	fst	6f	:23	:46⅘	1:10⅗	3↑Clm 12500	2	1	11½	1hd	1hd	1¾	McCarron C J5	b	115	*1.20	94-13	Dot's Imp 115¾ Vesta's Dragon 1205 High Road 1161	Driving	9
1Nov74- 4Lrl	fm	5f	Ⓣ:22⅕	:45⅗	:57⅗	3↑Clm 15000	7	2	1hd	21	33	44½	McCarron C J5		107	*2.10	95-08	Ducksummer 116½ Treetop 116hd Palace Jester 1163¾	Weakened	11
23Oct74- 6Lrl	fst	6f	:22⅘	:46	1:11	3↑Clm 15000	4	2	1hd	2½	22½	23¼	McCarron C J5	b	108	*1.30	89-18	National Resolve 1203¼ Dot'sImp1081½ImpressiveImp116¾	Gamely	8
27Sep74- 9Bow	fst	6f	:23⅕	:46⅘	1:11⅗	3↑Clm 10500	6	4	21	21½	11	11½	McCarron C J5	b	111	*.80	85-26	Dot's Imp 1111½ Little Seth 1161¾ Golden Moo Moo 1147	Driving	9
12Sep74- 7Bow	fst	6f	:23	:46⅘	1:11⅘	3↑Clm 8500	1	1	11½	1½	13½	15	McCarron C J5	b	111	2.50	84-23	Dot's Imp 1115 Better Bee Hip1161½JokersWild116nk	Mild urging	9

LATEST WORKOUTS Feb 7 Bow 3f my :39⅖ b

Copyright © 1979, by DAILY RACING FORM, INC. Reprinted with permission of copyright owner.

Rare Joel engaged in such brawls on April 13, April 20, May 31, June 23, and July 28. On May 31, he had a clear lead at the stretch call, but lost most of it by the wire.

Rare Joel Ch. g. 5, by Rare Pet—All's Wellesley, by Colonel Mike
Br.—Rare Pet Enterprises (NY)
Own.—Shapoff E L Tr.—Shapoff Stanley R **117**

	St.	1st	2nd	3rd	Amt.
1977	17	6	4	1	$51,080
1976	19	5	6	3	$39,840

28Jly77- 6Bel	fst	1⅟₁₆	:46⅗	1:11	1:41⅘	3↑Allowance	3	3	43	4¾	21	2¾	Day P	b	119	*2.30	92-15	Bold N Bizarre 119¾ Rare Joel 1193¾TripleTheScore113nk	Gamely	7
5Jly77- 2Bel	fst	1¼	:46⅗	1:37⅗	2:03⅗	3↑Clm 35000	5	3	414	22	1½	11¼	Day P	b	115	4.50	81-16	Rare Joel 1151¼ Bess's Boy 115hd Really Cooking 1172	Easily	7
23Jun77- 7Bel	fst	1⅟₁₆	:46	1:11	1:43⅘	3↑Clm 30000	5	5	57	52¾	2½	1¾	Day P	b	122	4.30	83-19	Rare Joel 122¾ Gentleman James II 1173 Jazziness 117½	Driving	7
8Jun77- 6Bel	fst	1⅛	:48	1:13⅗	1:51⅗	3↑Hcp 10000s	7	6	64½	4¾	1hd	11¼	Cordero A Jr	b	116	3.10	69-27	RareJoel1161¼PnutVendor1231CompnyCommnder120¾	Drew clear	8
31May77- 4Bel	fst	1⅟₁₆	:47⅕	1:12⅖	1:44⅖	Clm 18000	1	5	53	51¾	11½	1nk	Cordero A Jr	b	122	3.40	80-20	Rare Joel 122nk Don't Believe It 115½TropicMonkey1173½	Driving	10
23May77- 2Bel	fst	1⅟₁₆	:47	1:12⅘	1:44⅕	Clm 15000	10	4	31	1½	13	14½	Cordero A Jr	b	117	3.30	81-17	Rare Joel 1174½ Rumancoke 1102 Surf 1171½	Ridden out	14
2May77- 2Aqu	fst	7f	:22⅖	:45⅕	1:23⅕	Clm 16000	9	5	67½	59½	45	21½	Cordero A Jr	b	117	5.50	83-15	Trainer Mickey 1121½ Rare Joel 117hd Split Infinitive 1102	Wide	12
20Apr77- 2Aqu	fst	1⅛	⊡:49⅘	1:15⅖	1:54	Clm 15000	3	3	31	2½	1½	2nk	Cordero A Jr	b	115	4.90	82-14	Proud Romeo 112nk Rare Joel 115¾ Estornudo 1172	Gamely	8
13Apr77- 3Aqu	fst	1⅟₁₆	⊡:48⅖	1:14	1:47	Clm 14000	8	2	21	1hd	2hd	2¾	Cordero A Jr	b	117	7.40	82-13	Change of Venue 112¾RareJoel1172½TropicMonkey1172	Game try	8
2Apr77- 3Aqu	gd	6f	⊡:22	:45⅖	1:11	Clm 17500	1	3	48	411	64¾	55½	Martens G	b	115	17.60	88-09	Genuine Silver 1141¾ Elena's Boy 112½ Bold Jim 1172¾	Mild rally	7

LATEST WORKOUTS Sep 8 Bel 3f fst :37 b Sep 2 Bel 6f fst 1:14 b Aug 27 Bel 1 fst 1:41 h Aug 17 Bel tr.t 7f fst 1:28⅖ h

Copyright © 1979, by DAILY RACING FORM, INC. Reprinted with permission of copyright owner.

A study of 946 races found 617 such cases. Here is how those horses performed in their next starts, presumably after recapturing their breath.

NH	*NW*	*WPCT*	*MPCT*	*$NET*	*I.V.*
617	113*	18.3%	46.0%	$1.85	1.59

Hardly the figures one might expect from leg-weary horses. Perhaps a sustained drive from the stretch call to the wire (one furlong, or $\frac{1}{8}$ of a mile) is not all that taxing.

Suppose instead that we study horses involved in a prolonged drive from the quarter pole to the wire—within one length of the lead at each of the last three calls, or clear at the quarter pole, but in a photo at the wire. (For example, Dot's Imp on November 9, January 9, and February 28, or Rare Joel on April 13, April 20, and July 28.) Maybe this would be enough to tap a horse's energy reserve.

But, as the following figures prove, the answer is an emphatic "NO."

NH	*NW*	*WPCT*	*MPCT*	*$NET*	*I.V.*
388	78*	20.1%	47.9%	$2.11	1.75

And, surprisingly, horses that stood up to such a fight in a route did just as well as those that had done so in a sprint.

Apparently, a horse that can survive prolonged pressure for the last quarter mile of a race is an admirable creature indeed, possessed of a strong will to win. Such a horse should be bet, rather than bet against.

○ THE STRETCH GAIN ○

Many handicappers believe that a horse able to come on strongly from the stretch call to the wire is on edge and ready to win. Once again, statistics fail to completely support an article of faith.

In the tabulation below, we study horses that, in their last starts, finished in the front half of their fields *and* within five lengths of the winners (if not themselves the winners) after improving their positions from stretch call to finish. By "improving" we mean that the horse passed at least two others *and* gained at least one length on the leader, *or* passed at least one rival *and* gained at least two lengths on the leader. Horses sprinting are required to have made their stretch gains in sprint races.

The recent performances of Rising Crest include two examples of stretch gains. On November 20, he passed one horse and gained a little more than two lengths from the stretch call to the wire. And on November 5, he passed two horses and gained more than one length. But on November 13, although he passed two horses in the last eighth, he did not gain a full length on the lead and so does not qualify for a stretch gain on that occasion.

Rising Crest — Own.—Testa Tuesdee — $18,000 — Ch. h. 5, by Rising Market—Pinecrest Miss, by Royal Serenade — Br.—Madden Preston (Cal) — Tr.—Testa Tuesdee — 119

	St.	1st	2nd	3rd	Amt.
1976	10	7	1	0	$19,732
1975	3	1	0	0	$5,100

20Nov76-	1Aqu	fst	6f	:22⅘	:46⅘	1:12	3↑Clm 15000	3	8	$7^{4\frac{1}{4}}$	4^{2}	$2^{1\frac{1}{2}}$	$1^{\frac{3}{4}}$	Hawley S	119	5.80	83-17	Rising Crest 119¾ KiltiePiper$117^{1\frac{1}{4}}$MonetaryPrinciple117^{2}	Driving	8
13Nov76-	3Aqu	fst	6f	:22⅘	:46⅕	1:11	3↑Clm 12500	9	5	4^{2}	3^{2}	$3^{\frac{1}{2}}$	1^{nk}	Martens G	117	4.80	88-19	Rising Crest 117^{nk} Satan's Question 113½ Stern 110^{nk}	Just up	9
5Nov76-	2Aqu	fst	6f	:22⅖	:45⅘	1:11⅗	3↑Clm c-8000	2	4	3^{2}	$4^{3\frac{1}{2}}$	$3^{1\frac{1}{2}}$	$1^{\frac{3}{4}}$	Venezia M	117	5.90	85-21	Rising Crest 117¾ Sky Treaty 112^{2} Joanne's Fling 117no	Driving	9
29Oct76-	1Aqu	fst	6f	:22⅗	:46⅗	1:12	3↑Clm 8500	3	4	3^{nk}	1^{hd}	$2^{\frac{1}{2}}$	$2^{3\frac{1}{2}}$	Venezia M	117	8.50	79-21	Monitoril$115^{3\frac{1}{2}}$RisngCrst117½On'sTooMny110^{nk}	Lasted for second	10
13Oct76-	4Bel	fst	7f	:22⅘	:46⅕	1:24⅗	3↑Clm 10000	10	4	$5^{2\frac{1}{2}}$	$3^{1\frac{1}{2}}$	3^{4}	6^{11}	Venezia M	117	5.10	68-16	Dorage $117^{1\frac{1}{2}}$ Good And Bold 122^{4} Lord Graustark $113^{2\frac{1}{2}}$	Tired	10
25Sep76-	2Bel	fst	6f	:22⅘	:45⅘	1:10⅘	3↑Clm 12500	3	2	$5^{2\frac{1}{4}}$	$5^{1\frac{1}{2}}$	$8^{3\frac{1}{4}}$	9^{4}	Rodriguez J A	117	*3.30	84-12	Roman Decade 117^{nk} Commercial Pilot 117^{hd}BiBidder117^{nk}	Tired	10
5Sep76-	4GM	fst	5f	:22⅘	:46⅖	:58⅗	3↑Handicap	6	4	$2^{\frac{1}{2}}$	1^{3}	1^{4}	1^{4}	Boudreau R	132	*.90	95-11	Rising Crest 132^{4} [D]Divine Dividend 114no Fringante106^{3}	Handily	6
25Jly76-	8GM	fst	5f	:22⅗	:46	:58⅖	3↑Handicap	5	4	1^{hd}	1^{hd}	1^{1}	$1^{1\frac{1}{4}}$	Boudreau R	124	*1.50	96-14	Rising Crest $124^{1\frac{1}{4}}$ SurpriseMike104^{7}IncenseKing124^{1}	Ridden out	7
11Jly76-	4GM	fst	5f	:22⅖	:46⅗	:59⅕	3↑Handicap	4	4	$2^{\frac{1}{2}}$	1^{hd}	1^{1}	$1^{1\frac{3}{4}}$	Boudreau R	112	*1.20	92-17	Rising Crest $112^{1\frac{3}{4}}$ Surprise Mike $105^{2\frac{3}{4}}$ Princess Lil 115^{2}	Driving	6
4Jly76-	4GM	fst	5f	:22	:46	:58⅗	3↑Allowance	6	4	2^{2}	$2^{\frac{1}{2}}$	$1^{1\frac{1}{2}}$	$1^{1\frac{1}{4}}$	Boudreau R	114	2.20	95-09	Rising Crest $114^{1\frac{1}{4}}$ Flowerball 109^{hd} Rocket Tread 115^{6}	Driving	8

LATEST WORKOUTS ●Nov 26 Bel 4f fst :46⅘ h Nov 10 Bel 4f fst :47⅘ h Nov 3 Bel tr.t 3f fst :38⅕ b

Plastic Surgeon's finish in the Rosemont Stakes qualified as a "stretch gain." But his rally on June 30 did not, because while passing two horses, he failed to gain at least one length on the leader. And his rally on April 13 failed to qualify because, while passing one horse, he failed to gain two lengths on the lead.

Plastic Surgeon * B. c. 3, by Dr Fager—Fashion Verdict, by Court Martial
Own.—Phipps O Br.—Phipps O (Ky) Tr.—Laurin R **117**

	St.	1st	2nd	3rd	Amt.
1973	12	4	5	3	$52,890
1972	5	1	2	1	$9,400

8Jly73- 8Del fst 1⅛ :46⅗ 1:10⅕ 1:42⅖ Rosemont 1 7 77½ 53½ 31½ 1¾ Cordero A Jr 114 1.90 97-10 PlasticSurgeon 114¾ DoubleEdgeSword 1142½ Annihilte'Em 1201½ Driving 9
30Jun73- 5Aqu fst 6f :21⅘ :44⅖ 1:08⅗ 3↑Allowance 6 1 43½ 43½ 41½ 21 Cordero A Jr 115 2.60 99-05 Timeless Moment 1121 Plastic Surgeon 1152 Black Balled 1151¾ Gamely 5
11Jun73- 8Bel fst 6½f :22⅘ :45⅗ 1:15⅖ 3↑Allowance 6 1 43½ 41¾ 1½ 1hd Cordero A Jr 115 3.30 102-05 Plastic Surgeon 115hd Sail Through 1154½ In Rhythm 1151½ Driving 6
2Jun73- 4Bel fst 7f :22⅘ :46 1:22⅕ 3↑Allowance 8 1 61¾ 41½ 1hd 1hd Cordero A Jr 114 *2.10 96-06 Plastic Surgeon 114hd Winds of Thought 1125 Balconaje 1183½ Driving 9
13Apr73- 7Aqu fst 1 :46 1:10⅖ 1:36 3↑Allowance 4 7 68½ 34½ 43½ 31¾ Cordero A Jr 114 3.00 85-20 New Hope 113nk Paternity 1141½ Plastic Surgeon 1145 No mishap 7
4Apr73- 6Aqu sly 7f :23⅖ :46⅗ 1:23⅖ 3↑Allowance 3 4 44½ 56 25 24 Cordero A Jr 112 3.90 80-21 Settecento 1124 Plastic Surgeon 1122½ I Summon 1112½ Second best 7
17Mar73- 6Aqu sly 6f :22 :44⅕ 1:09⅘ Allowance 8 7 53½ 43½ 34½ 35½ Ussery R 117 3.10 88-17 Timeless Moment 117hd Settecento 1145½ Plastic Surgeon 1172 Rallied 8
9Mar73- 6Aqu gd 6½f :22⅖ :45⅗ 1:16⅗ Allowance 7 5 33 32 22 2¾ Turcotte R b 119 *1.00 93-16 Raise And Rule 114¾ Plastic Surgeon 1193 Decimator 1142½ Gamely 7
1Mar73- 4Aqu fst 6f :22⅘ :45⅘ 1:11 Allowance 3 2 32½ 32 2½ 2nk Vasquez J b 116 *1.40 88-18 Old Charade 114nk Plastic Surgeon 1163 Raise And Rule 1143½ Sharp 6
7Feb73- 8Hia fst 7f :23⅕ :46 1:24 Allowance 8 5 43½ 32 1½ 1nk Vasquez J b 115 1.90 87-13 Plastic Surgeon 115nk Campus Cop 110hd Lord Gaylord 122hd Driving 9
LATEST WORKOUTS ●Jly 17 Bel 3f fst :34⅘ b Jun 26 Bel 3f fst :35 h ●Jun 19 Bel 3f fst :34⅘ h Jun 8 Bel 3f fst :36⅘ b

Kintla's Folly qualifies for a "stretch gain" in his last start, passing the one horse ahead of him at the stretch call and gaining more than two lengths in the run to the wire.

Kintla's Folly B. g. 4, by Run Like Mad—Kintla, by Mr Trouble
Own.—Newmeyer S M Br.—Davis S F (Fla) Tr.—Dutrow Richard E **113**

Turf Record	St.	1st	2nd	3rd		St.	1st	2nd	3rd	Amt.
	1	0	1	0	1976	10	7	1	1	$35,340
					1975	17	7	2	2	$33,976

30Jly76- 7Del fst 6f :21⅘ :44⅘ 1:10⅕ 3↑Clm 40000 5 3 32½ 21 2hd 12¾ Fann B b 120 3.40 94-18 Kintla's Folly 1202¾ Run Tell Run 107no Scam 1163½ Ridden out 5
16Jly76- 7Del fst 6f :21⅘ :45 1:10⅖ 3↑Allowance 5 4 1½ 11½ 11½ 11½ Fann B b 118 3.20 93-20 Kintla's Folly 1181½ Cut Corners 116nk Fly Past 1123 Driving 6
2Jly76- 2Aqu fst 6f :22⅕ :45⅕ 1:09⅗ 3↑Clm 45000 5 3 3½ 42 55 65½ Hernandez R b 117 4.70 89-14 Bright Discovery 1091 Checkerhall 1152½ Jaunty Jolly 114nk Tired 7
23Jun76- 8Pim fst 5f :22 :45 :57⅕ Clm 30000 5 5 21 2hd 13 11 Bracciale V Jr b 114 *.80 99-17 Kintla's Folly 1141 Jiva Coolit 114no Oxford Flight 1194½ Driving 6
11Jun76- 7Del fst 6f :22 :45⅕ 1:10⅖ Allowance 6 1 21 1½ 31½ 32¾ Woodhouse R b 112 1.40 90-22 Silver Hope 1212½ Bold Dave 121½ Kintla's Folly 1123 Tired 6
24Apr76- 4Pim fst 6f :23 :45⅘ 1:11⅕ Allowance 3 2 32½ 22½ 22 11¾ Bracciale V Jr b 119 *.50e 90-20 Kintla's Folly 1191¾ Gigli Saw 1151¾ Take ThePledge1121 Driving 7
12Apr76- 8Pim fst 6f :23⅕ :46⅕ 1:11⅗ Allowance 6 1 12 14 14 14 Poulin R R5 b 110 *.70 88-29 Kintla's Folly 1104 Ben S. 1123 Native Secret 112hd Ridden out 8
30Mar76- 5Pim fst 6f :23 :45⅘ 1:10⅗ Clm c-18500 7 1 1½ 14 12½ 14¼ McCarron C J b 119 *1.10 93-19 Kintla's Folly 1194¼ Rattle the Rye 1063Terriobu1142¾ Ridden out 8
19Mar76- 6Pim fst 6f :23 :45⅘ 1:12⅖ Clm 18500 2 1 11½ 14 13 12½ Kurtz J b 114 *1.40e 84-24 Kintla's Folly 1142½ Terriobu 114¾ Imapuncher 1142½ Driving 8
14Jan76- 3Bow fst 7f :22⅘ :45⅘ 1:25 Clm 18500 5 3 33 32 21½ 22 Kurtz J b 114 *.80e 78-31 Apres Vous 1092 Kintla's Folly 114nk King ofCornish1148 Gamely 8
LATEST WORKOUTS ●Sep 9 Bow 3f fst :34⅖ h ●Sep 3 Del 6f fst 1:12⅗ h Aug 29 Del 4f fst :49 b ●Aug 22 Del 6f fst 1:12⅕ h

Our study of 946 races located 802 horses that had made stretch gains in their latest starts. Here is how they performed in their next outings:

NH	*NW*	*WPCT*	*MPCT*	*$NET*	*I.V.*
802	108	13.5%	43.3%	$1.51	1.17

As the 1.17 impact value attests, many of these horses were able to retain their sharp form. But as a rule, this type of horse is overbet.

Most significantly, these horses failed to improve on the overall figures for horses that had most recently finished ahead of at least half their opponents (see page 74.)

The stretch gain proved significant for bettors only in sprint races, and only when the horse involved rallied to win, or lose by no more than a neck, in its most recent start, which must also have come in a sprint. Such horses had the following record:

NH	*NW*	*WPCT*	*MPCT*	*$NET*	*I.V.*
259	36	13.9%	38.2%	$2.29	1.31

○ BID, BUT HUNG—AN EARLIER MOVE ○

The major problem with the stretch gain is that many late-running horses fail to do much serious running at earlier stages, and consequently are seldom in position to catch the leaders at the end.

Perhaps an earlier move of similar vigor would be a better forecast of future success. Such a move would suggest not only good (or improving) form, but also the early speed needed to win.

In the tabulation below, we study horses that bid, but hung in their most recent races, which we require to be of distance similar to today's race (a sprint or a route). "Bid" means that the horse progressed between the first and second calls, or between the second and third calls. "Hung" means that the horse failed to improve its position in the final run to the wire.

More specifically, "bid" means that the horse moved (at either the second or third call) to a position in the front half of its field *and* within five lengths of the leader as a result of passing horses *and* gaining ground, for a total of at least three horses and/or lengths. That is, the horse either must have passed at least two rivals and gained one length on the lead, or passed one rival and gained at least two lengths on the lead. And "hung" means that the horse neither passed rivals nor gained ground from the stretch call to the wire. If the horse had moved into the lead at either the second or third call, it must have lost the race.

For example, Holding Pattern, in the Secretariat Stakes, moved into second place (well within the front half) at the stretch call by passing two horses and gaining five lengths, before weakening in the final eighth-mile.

Lady Love, on the other hand, bid at the second call in the Acorn Stakes—passing one rival and gaining two lengths—but (technically) did not hang at the end, gaining slightly from stretch call to wire. (At 15-1 odds in her next start, one could very easily overlook such hairsplitting.)

Middletown Billy, on the other hand, hung in his last race, his first in 5 weeks, but, according to the definition, did not bid. Although he did pass one horse between the second and third calls, he failed to gain a full two lengths on the lead.

Sproull D. bid when he took the lead at the second call—he passed two horses and gained a length and a half—and "hung," eventually losing the race.

Our study of 946 races located 534 horses that had bid but hung in their most recent race. Here is how they ran in their next starts:

NH	NW	WPCT	MPCT	$NET	I.V.
534	98	18.4%	46.8%	$1.94	1.63

Excellent results—better than those for horses that had run good races, or finished in the front half of their fields, in their latest starts.

And they can be improved. Add the additional requirement that the horse must have finished in the front half of its field after bidding but hanging, and the small dollar loss becomes a small profit.

NH	NW	WPCT	MPCT	$NET	I.V.
463	88	19.0%	48.2%	$2.10	1.69

○ TWO RUNS IN THE SAME RACE ○

The late Colonel E. R. Bradley, a famous owner and "improver of the breed" whose horses won several Kentucky Derbies, was particularly fond of horses that were able to come on a second time in a race. His "angle" is still effective today, but only in sprint races.

In the tabulation below, we study horses able to run within three lengths of the early lead in their last starts, only to lose ground (at least one length) and position (at least one horse passed them) between the first and second calls, before either gaining ground or position in the run from the stretch call to the wire, to finish in the front half of their fields or within 5 lengths of the winner.

Ring For Nurse, for example, employed this "up, back, up" running style when he won the Dragoon Stakes, and it was the portent of better things to come. Next out, he scored an eight-length victory in the Kindergarten Stakes, and then five days later took Monmouth's well-regarded Sapling Stakes, both at excellent prices.

Susan's Girl, on the other hand, provided a "marginal" example in the 1973 Beldame. Within two and a half lengths of the early lead, she had fallen back considerably before "coming on" again in the stretch—although finishing twelve lengths behind the victorious Desert Vixen, and losing ground to that rival in the final eighth, she did pass one rival from the stretch call to the wire.

A study of 646 sprint races turned up just 87 horses coming out of sprint races in which they had run in this "up, back, up" style. Here is how they ran in their next starts:

NH	NW	WPCT	MPCT	$NET	I.V.
87	20	23.0%	43.7%	$2.62	2.18

A study of 300 routes failed to produce similar, or even positive, results. Evidently, the inability to keep up with the pace in a route, once well situated, is a bad sign.

○ SURPRISE EARLY SPEED ○

Strangely, especially in light of the findings presented in Chapters 1 and 2, horses that flashed surprise early speed in their latest starts, once considered an excellent sign of imminent success, no longer do the job (if they ever did).

In the following tabulation, we study horses that had run among the first three *and* within two lengths (three lengths, if a route) of the lead at the first call in their most recent race, but which had failed to run among the first three *or* within two lengths (three lengths, if a route) of the lead at the first call in their two previous races. All three of these races must have been at distances similar (sprint or route) to that of today's race.

Automatic Harvey, when entered August 4, provided an excellent example, having surprised everybody when he sat right behind the early leader on July 27 after having been among the early trailers in his two previous starts.

Copyright © 1979, by DAILY RACING FORM, INC. Reprinted with permission of copyright owner.

A study of 946 races revealed little of interest:

NH	NW	WPCT	MPCT	$NET	I.V.
439	62	14.1%	35.5%	$1.61	1.23

Automatic Harvey's past performances also give an excellent example of why this "angle" is not producing the expected results. Harvey was able to win on July 27, the day he had the early foot. But on August 4, he reverted to his old style of running from far behind and, as usual, his stretch run was too late.

As suggested in Chapter 2, the idea is to catch a horse on the day it shows the early speed, not one race later. The "surprise speed last" angle apparently has its supporters "jumping on the bandwagon" one race too late.

FORM:
FAILURES

Thus far in our discussion of form, we have been looking mostly for positive characteristics in a horse's record. We now change the point of view and take a negative approach, asking whether a horse has failed to accomplish something that might have been expected of it.

○ GOOD RACES IN LAST THREE STARTS ○

It is a serious blot on a horse's record not to have run even one good race in its latest three starts. In the following study of 1,248 races, the "Yes" horses ran well in at least one of their last three starts. The "No" horses had not.

	NH	NW	WPCT	MPCT	$NET	%W	I.V.
Yes	7894	1068	13.5%	39.1%	$1.55	85.6%	1.16
No	2764	180**	6.5%	24.0%	$1.50	14.4%	0.56

The statistics for the negative characteristic "no good race last three starts" should be compared with those for "last race not good" (see page 75) and "no good races last 30 days" (see page 83). Although our latest potential elimination factor involves fewer starters than either of its predecessors, it does produce the lowest impact value of the three.

However, the other two approaches pack more clout, placing more than half the starters in the typical field in categories that produce only 65 to 75 percent of their share of the winners.

Still, it is safe to eliminate from serious consideration any horse that failed to run a good race in any of its last three starts. Which is not to suggest that any horse with a good race somewhere in its last three starts is a good bet for that reason alone. The $NET figure for the "Yes" category should dispel that notion.

○ BAD RACES SINCE LAST GOOD RACE ○

In the following tabulation, we present the results of a study of 946 races in which each horse was classified according to the number of bad races it had run since its last good race.

# Bad Races	NH	NW	WPCT	MPCT	$NET	%W	I.V.
None	3252	536	16.5%	43.9%	$1.66	56.7%	1.43
One	1734	188	10.8%	33.9%	$1.60	19.9%	0.94
Two or more	3223	222**	6.9%	25.6%	$1.36	23.5%	0.60

Horses entered after two or more bad (not good) races in succession are poor bets. But a horse that has turned in just one bad race since its last good race should not be dismissed on that account alone. The horse may very well have had a valid excuse for that poor performance—it may have come after a layoff, or at an unsuitable distance, or against horses of higher grade than the animal is capable of beating.

Consequently, it would seem wise to distinguish between recent poor races that indicate a failure to live up to reasonable expectations, and recent poor races that probably should not be held against a horse's record.

○ FAILURES—A DEFINITION ○

We propose the following definition of failure:

"A bad (not good) race since a horse's most recent good race is considered a *failure* if, in that race, the horse failed to live up to what it had accomplished in the good race, or failed to accomplish what it will be asked to accomplish in today's race."

This definition has implications with respect to both class and distance.

In terms of class, it means that the horse must not have run poorly against animals of the same class or cheaper than it had opposed in that good race. Nor must it have run poorly against animals of the same class or cheaper than it will face today.

In terms of distance, two possibilities arise. If today's race is at the same distance as the most recent good race (simply, both sprints, or both routes), the horse must not have run poorly at that distance against the appropriate class horse. If today's race and the good race involve different distances (one a sprint, the other a route), the horse is expected to have run well at both kinds of distances when entered against the appropriate class horse.

Differences between classes in the claiming ranks should be determined according to the table on page 11. Par times (to be discussed in Chapter 16) should be used to determine the class, in terms of claiming price, of the various kinds of allowance races at different tracks. We will assume that an allowance classification is one class better than the claiming class with the same par times.

The two examples that follow should help clarify the various implications of the definition of failure.

Suppose first that a horse's four most recent races look like this:

6 furlongs	$13,000	4^4
$1\frac{1}{16}$ miles	$13,000	8^{12}
$6\frac{1}{2}$ furlongs	$16,000	5^7
6 furlongs	$10,000	2^1

The horse's last good race came four starts ago, against $10,000 claiming sprinters. Consequently, the horse is expected to have raced well in subsequent starts against $10,000 (or cheaper) sprinters.

None of the horse's last three performances is good. Nor are they failures to run back to the horse's last good race. Whether these races were, in fact, failures depends on the conditions of today's race.

If entered today in a sprint, the horse's recent route performance can be ignored. If entered today against $10,000 (or cheaper) sprinters, its last two sprint efforts can be forgiven. The horse did not indicate in its last good race that it could handle $13,000 or $16,000 horses, nor will it have to beat such horses today.

But if entered against $13,000 sprinters today, the horse has one failure on its record. In its last start, it failed to accomplish exactly what is being asked of it today. If entered against $16,000 sprinters, its latest two sprints both must be regarded as failures to run well in the same company (or cheaper) it runs today.

Should the same horse be entered today in a route, class alone determines which of its recent efforts were failures. The horse has demonstrated that it can run well in a sprint, and is now being asked to run well in a route. Consequently, a poor race at either distance may possibly be regarded as a failure.

If this horse is entered today against $10,000 routers, it has no failures on its record—there is no reason to expect the horse to run well against $13,000 or $16,000 horses, at any distance, nor to penalize it for not having done so.

If the horse is entered today against $13,000 routers, its two most recent starts resulted in failures. If entered against $16,000 (or better) routers, all three of its recent poor efforts must be considered failures.

Suppose that a second horse's recent form looks like this:

$1\frac{1}{8}$ miles	$13,000	8^{12}
6 furlongs	$16,000	5^8
$1\frac{1}{16}$ miles	$20,000	9^{20}
$1\frac{1}{16}$ miles	$35,000	8^{15}
$1\frac{1}{16}$ miles	$25,000	1^2

Since this horse's last good race came against $25,000 routers, its first and third most recent starts must be considered failures (to run back to that good race), regardless of the conditions of today's race. Unless the horse is entered today in a sprint, its recent sprint race can be ignored—otherwise, it must be regarded as a failure, regardless of classification today. And unless the horse is entered today against $35,000 (or better) stock, its performance four races back can be ignored.

There are certain extenuating circumstances under which a race that would ordinarily be termed a failure can be forgiven. They are:

1. Any race immediately after a layoff of 31 days or more. Most horses are not ready for a top effort in their first race after being rested.

2. Any race immediately before a layoff of 31 days or more. A horse may throw in an uncharacteristically poor race prior to a layoff, indicating to its trainer that it needs a rest.

3. Any race in which the horse had a valid excuse for a poor effort. "Blocked," "bumped," "checked," "forced wide," and "poor start" are all valid excuses. In a route, a far outside post position may be considered a valid excuse. For a come-from-behind horse, a sloppy track may excuse a poor performance. Physical problems such as "bore out," "lugged in," or "bled," are not valid excuses.

4. For a filly or mare, any race against males.

5. For a three-year-old claimer, any race against older claiming horses.

6. For a horse whose last good race came on dirt, and whose record indicates no good races on grass, any race on grass.

7. For a horse whose last good race came on grass, and whose record indicates no good races on dirt, any race on dirt.

Tree Of Knowledge, when entered October 8, had no failures on his record. Those two poor performances came one before and the other after a layoff of approximately seven weeks.

Copyright © 1979, by DAILY RACING FORM, INC. Reprinted with permission of copyright owner.

Al Hattab's poor performance in the Leonard Richards is not considered a failure, coming in the Jersey Derby winner's career debut on grass. However, had he been entered in a grass race, rather than the Lamplighter Handicap, which he won on the main track, his last race would have been a failure.

Copyright © 1979, by DAILY RACING FORM, INC. Reprinted with permission of copyright owner.

Likewise, Bailar's poor showing on dirt August 25 was not counted as a failure on September 14 because his recent record (last ten starts) gave no indication of dirt-running ability. As far as can be seen, Bailar was a turf specialist.

Copyright © 1979, by DAILY RACING FORM, INC. Reprinted with permission of copyright owner.

These excuses, and all distance considerations, are suspended when a horse takes a considerable drop in class. By "considerable" we mean a drop of at least two classes to a level at least two classes below that of the horse's most recent good race.

For example, when the gallant old gelding Wicked Man returned to the races on November 5, 1977, after an absence of more than a year and a half, he "came off" a race in which he had taken a two-class drop (the claiming prices on March 22 ranged from $11,500 to $9,500). Although his performance in that race was almost "good"—he missed a good race by half a length—it must be termed poor especially in light of the drop in class and the comment "returned sore." Consequently, although that race preceded a layoff, it must be counted as a failure the day he returned.

Wicked Man * Ch. g. 10, by Rattle Dancer—Dillifilly, by With Regards
Own.—Rinaldi N E $8,500 Br.—Hillview Farms (Mich) Tr.—Dutrow Richard E 116

	St.	1st	2nd	3rd	Amt.
1976	5	0	3	0	$4,740
1975	9	5	3	0	$23,050

22Mar76- 5Pim fst 6f :23 :46⅘ 1:12⅗ Clm 11500 4 1 2hd 2½ 2hd 52½ Passmore W J 114 *.80e 80-24 Open Game 114¹ IThinkNoEvil106hd TheCrease109¾ Returned sore 8
29Feb76- 6Pen fst 6f :22 :45⅕ 1:10⅕ Clm 15000 2 2 22½ 21 22½ 24½ Fitzgerald R 115 *.40 90-18 Winning Point 1074½ Wicked Man 115³ Sir Virge116nk Weakened 6
10Feb76- 8Bow fst 7f :24 :47⅗ 1:25⅗ Allowance 2 1 2hd 1hd 21 48½ Passmore W J 115 *1.10 68-26 Famous Jim 1124¾ Gillingham 112¾ Doctor Po 112³ Speed, tired 6
28Jan76- 8Key my 6f :23 :47⅗ 1:13⅕ Allowance 3 2 21 11 2hd 21 Black A S 115 *.80 75-33 Bold Who 119¹ Wicked Man 115¹⁰ Roman Scythe 113⁴ Gamely 5
10Jan76- 7Bow fst 6f :22⅗ :45⅗ 1:11⅖ Allowance 2 3 2½ 22 22 2nk Passmore W J 117 *1.70 86-23 Rico Nativo 107nk Wicked Man 117nk Gillingham 112½ Gamely 8
26Nov75- 6Lrl fst 7f :22⅘ :46⅕ 1:24⅖ 3↑Clm 19000 6 1 22½ 34½ 32½ 1½ McCarron C J 117 1.60e 89-17 Wicked Man 117½ King of Cornish 116³ Hunter F. 1121¼ Driving 9
18Nov75- 6Lrl fst 6f :22⅗ :46⅕ 1:11 3↑Clm c-15000 2 2 21½ 21½ 2hd 11 McHargue D G 119 *1.00 92-18 Wicked Man 119¹MontanaHour116²MandatoryCount109³ Driving 8
28Oct75- 7Lrl fst 6f :22⅗ :46⅖ 1:10⅘ 3↑Allowance 7 1 2hd 2hd 1hd 2¾ McCarron C J b 113 *.30e 92-19 Shine It 110¾ Wicked Man 1132¾ Corny Luck 1131½ Gamely 8
15Oct75- 7Bow fst 6f :22⅘ :45⅗ 1:10⅖ 3↑Clm 18500 4 2 2hd 2hd 2hd 1hd McCarron C J 122 *.90 91-17 Wicked Man 122hd BoldEd114hdNoblePromise116⁶ HARD DRIVE 6
3Oct75- 4Bow fst 6f :22⅗ :45⅖ 1:11 3↑Clm 18500 6 1 3nk 11 11½ 1no Fann B 119 *1.10e 88-28 Wicked Man 119no Terriobu 1162¼ Raved 1133½ Driving 9
LATEST WORKOUTS ●Oct 29 Lrl 6f sl 1:17⅖ b Oct 22 Lrl 5f fst 1:05 b

Copyright © 1979, by DAILY RACING FORM, INC. Reprinted with permission of copyright owner.

Pres De Tu, on the other hand, dropped three classes upon his return to the races November 6. On that day, his poor race just prior to the layoff must be counted as a failure. In his second start, on November 13, he again is charged with one failure, this time for his poor performance the day he returned (and dropped in class).

Pres De Tu Gr. g. 4, by Tudor Grey—Snow Trick, by Snow Cat
Own.—Decap Stable $17,500 Br.—Switzer J (Fla) Tr.—Schwizer Albert 117

	St.	1st	2nd	3rd	Amt.
1976	11	3	1	1	$27,020
1975	5	0	2	0	$3,740

6Nov76- 2Aqu fst 6f :22⅗ :46⅕ 1:11⅗ 3↑Clm 18000 3 6 2½ 2hd 3nk 54½ Turcotte R b 117 4.60 80-19 Trainer Mickey 1101½ IrishFun1172¼ChaulkyLong113nk Weakened 8
28May76- 3Bel fst 7f :23 :46⅕ 1:24⅕ Clm 35000 8 1 4¾ 51½ 108½ 911 Turcotte R b 117 *2.50 70-21 Proud Romeo 113nk Checkerhall 1174¾ TrainerMickey108nk Tired 11
13May76- 6Bel fst 6f :22⅖ :45⅗ 1:10⅗ Clm 37500 4 4 53½ 41½ 2½ 21½ Turcotte R b 115 10.00 88-16 Jose Eduardo 1131½ Pres De Tu 115² Checkerhall 112nk Gamely 9
3May76- 6Bel fst 6f :22⅖ :45⅗ 1:10⅗ Clm 40000 4 3 22½ 33 41 44½ Turcotte R b 114 3.10 85-17 Trumpeter Swan1171½StillSailing1151½Judgmatic1171½ Weakened 9
17Mar76- 6Aqu my 6f :22⅗ :46⅕ 1:10⅘ Allowance 2 6 31 3nk 52½ 58¾ Turcotte R b 122 6.70 80-25 Yu Wipi 1151½ Desert Outlaw 115⁴ Naudi 115¾ Tired 7
17Mar76-Placed fourth through disqualification
12Mar76- 8Aqu fst 1⅛ :46⅕ 1:10⅗ 1:49⅗ Allowance 1 1 14 14 31½ 43½ Turcotte R b 115 4.70 84-18 DFramptonDelight110noCoHost115³HawainGulf110nk Drifted out 7
5Mar76- 6Aqu fst 1⅛ :49 1:13⅗ 1:51 3↑Allowance 3 1 13 11 32½ 54½ Turcotte R b 116 2.90 76-16 Knight of Honor 1201¾ Gallant Glory 116nk Co Host 116nk Tired 5
27Feb76- 6Aqu fst 6f :23 :46⅗ 1:11⅕ Allowance 1 3 1hd 11 1½ 1nk Turcotte R b 121 *1.60 87-21 Pres De Tu 121nk Naudi 116³ Enough 116¾ Driving 6
12Feb76- 7Aqu fst 6f :22 :45⅖ 1:10⅖ Allowance 1 4 21½ 21½ 12 11¾ Turcotte R b 114 *2.00 91-19 Pres De Tu 1141¾ Master Quico 114nk Danny Boy 1141½ Driving 7
22Jan76- 9Aqu fst 1 :46⅗ 1:12⅗ 1:40 Clm 25000 8 1 15 19 18 15 Turcotte R b 115 5.20 66-29 Pres DeTu115⁵FreedomCalling115²RoyalBook1162½ Never headed 8
LATEST WORKOUTS Nov 3 Bel tr.t 5f fst 1:05⅕ b Oct 14 Bel tr.t 4f fst :51⅗ b

Copyright© 1979, by DAILY RACING FORM, INC. Reprinted with permission of copyright owner.

Here, now, are the results of a study of 1,367 races, in which the contestants were classified according to the number of failures on their records.

Failures	*NH*	*NW*	*WPCT*	*MPCT*	*$NET*	*%W*	*I.V.*
None	6856	1027	15.0%	41.7%	$1.57	75.1%	1.22
One	2263	217	9.6%	32.4%	$1.40	15.9%	0.78
Two or more	2057	123**	6.0%	24.2%	$1.45	9.0%	0.49

Comparison with the figures for "Number of bad races since last good race" reveals that we have strengthened the negative categories "One" and "Two or more," although significantly reducing their numbers.

In other words, two (or more) failures is a worse sign than two (or more) bad races since a good race. And one failure is less forgiveable than one bad race following a good race.

The diminutive Dark Mirage scoring an easy victory in the 1968 Coaching Club American Oaks, to become the first filly to sweep New York's Triple Crown for Fillies series—the Acorn, Mother Goose, and Oaks.

Photo credit: Bob Coglianese

FORM:
USEFUL
ODDS
AND
ENDS

In this chapter, we will discuss four additional topics which, in some way, relate to a horse's present form or condition.

○ A RACE OVER THE TRACK ○

Whether or not a horse has had a race over the track is a problem that touches partly on form, and partly on class. A horse may be a champ at Charles Town, but its reputation in the hills of West Virginia will be of little help when it races against $20,000 claimers at Pimlico.

On the other hand, a $10,000 claimer shipping from Monmouth to Laurel faces no better or worse stock, but still has not had a race over the Laurel surface.

Some tracks are notoriously inhospitable to shippers. Calder has long had such a reputation. Aqueduct's new inner course, which is deeper than most surfaces, has such a reputation. Many horses successful over Aqueduct's main track still seem to need a race over the inner course before being able to cope with it.

But most tracks have no such reputation. The problem lies with the horse, and not the racing surface. Horses are creatures of habit. Until they become fully accustomed to their new surroundings, and until they recover from the stress of travel, they are likely to run below their best form.

A study of 946 races proves that horses without a race over the local track are at somewhat of a disadvantage. Here are the details.

	NH	NW	WPCT	MPCT	$NET	%W	I.V.
Race over track	6461	778	12.0%	36.4%	$1.56	82.2%	1.05
Others	1758	168	9.6%	28.0%	$1.39	17.8%	0.83

If we had asked instead "has the horse ever run in the money (1-2-3) over the local track?" we would have found a much stronger negative category:

	NH	NW	WPCT	MPCT	$NET	%W	I.V.
Yes	4392	624	14.2%	41.3%	$1.68	66.0%	1.23
No	3827	322	8.4%	26.9%	$1.36	34.0%	0.73

The starters are divided much more evenly here (actually 54-46 percent), yet almost two thirds of the winners fall in the YES category.

○ BEATEN FAVORITES ○

Many handicappers like to follow up on beaten favorites, particularly those that come back (soon) in a race of comparable class and distance to the one in which they were favored. They argue that there was a solid reason for the horse being favored in the first place, and that the horse stands a good chance of winning its subsequent start for that same reason. Perhaps the horse was a tardy favorite only because of poor racing luck, or because it needed a race, or a race over the track. Statistics support this line of reasoning. Beaten favorites do win far more than their share of races.

The tabulation below presents the results of a study of 556 races. The "NOT*" category refers to horses not favored in their most recent starts. The other three categories refer to horses that were favored last out, and separate them according to their finishes—first, second, third, or out of the money.

	NH	NW	WPCT	MPCT	$NET	%W	I.V.
Not*	4133	388	9.4%	30.9%	$1.45	69.8%	0.83
Won	312	72	23.1%	50.6%	$1.78	12.9%	2.04
2-3	253	59	23.3%	54.2%	$1.94	10.6%	2.06
Out	221	37	16.7%	44.8%	$1.44	6.7%	1.48

Beaten favorites clearly attract considerable support at the betting windows, even after running out of the money. But only those that managed to finish in the money are worthwhile betting propositions.

Punctual favorites do well in their next starts, winning more than twice their share. They repeat far more often than does the typical winner (see Chapter 6).

○ EXCUSE HORSES ○

Some bettors cannot seem to pass on horses that ran into traffic problems in their last race. They expect the horse to make amends, automatically. They fail to realize that no performance—not a win, nor a good race, much less an excuse—guarantees that a horse will run well enough to win its next start.

The fact that a horse ran into traffic last out does not imply that it will find clear sailing this time. Many excuse horses are come-from-behind types, and as such are especially prone to traffic problems. Many come-from-behind horses are chronic "excuse horses."

Statistics reveal that horses whose problems draw a comment such as "bumped," "blocked," "checked," or "forced wide" win no more and no less than their share of their next starts, but are heavily overbet. A study of 946 races found 273 such horses, with the following results:

NH	NW	WPCT	MPCT	$NET	I.V.
273	32	11.7%	30.0%	$1.30	1.04

Some horses are able to overcome difficulties and win, or lose by just a narrow margin. Oftentimes, however, the extra effort needed to overcome the problem drains the horse's energy reserves, and the animal will come up empty during the stretch run of its next race.

Numbered Account, for example, stumbled at the start of the Maskette Handicap, losing several lengths to her three rivals. She ran a powerful race to open three and a half lengths after seven furlongs, but had given her all. Although able to hold on and win the Maskette, the effort cost her dearly. She had little response in the stretch ten days later in the championship Beldame stakes.

Of a completely different color are horses whose problems were of a physical nature, and noticeable enough to draw comment. Our study of 946 races located 165 horses which either failed to run a straight course ("bore in," "bore out," or "lugged in"), presumably because of physical problems, or met with a more serious physical mishap ("sore," "lame," or "bled") in their last start. Here is how they ran, after escaping from the infirmary.

NH	NW	WPCT	MPCT	$NET	I.V.
165	20	12.1%	35.8%	$1.18	1.07

Obviously, the betting public should exercise more caution when backing the chances of a horse that displayed physical difficulties in its last start. That 1.07 impact value is probably misleading. Many of these horses ran decently last out—otherwise, their problem might never have been noticed. But they are bet as if they had run a solid race, and were likely to continue doing so.

○ BANDAGES ○

Almost everyone agrees that bandages on a horse's hind legs are *not* a sign that anything is seriously wrong with the horse. Many horses wear run-down bandages on their rear legs to prevent them from scraping their ankles or burning their heels.

Front bandages, on the other hand, can mean serious trouble. Long front bandages usually indicate tendon trouble, up front, where the horse can least tolerate it.

A study of 171 races produced the following statistics:

	NH	NW	WPCT	I.V.
Front bandages	239	18	7.5%	0.69
None	1330	153	11.5%	1.06

The vast majority of horses do not wear bandages on their front legs. Those that do apparently should be avoided, unless the handicapper knows for certain that the bandages are part of the horse's usual equipment, and that the horse has raced successfully in them in the past.

Some trainers, including some of the very best, such as Frank and David Whiteley, use front bandages rather freely—1976 champions Forego and Revidere wore them, Forego for the entire year. And 1974 Belmont winner Little Current wore front bandages in that smashing triumph, as do many of trainer Lou Rondinello's stakes runners.

CONSISTENCY

Thoroughbreds, like humans, possess varying degrees of intelligence and competitiveness. Some win their share of the races, some win more, and others don't win at all.

Some are driven by a fierce will to win, or at least give their best, every time they step on the racetrack. Others couldn't care less.

Some, including many of the better ones, seem to know what is expected of them. They enjoy getting out on the track and outrunning their opponents. Others have discovered that they will be fed regardless of how they perform on the track.

In this chapter, we study a few techniques for evaluating a horse's consistency. Our efforts in this direction will be frustrated somewhat by the fact that horses frequently race at unsuitable distances or against far superior opponents. Losing performances in unwinnable races frequently sully a horse's record, making the animal seem less consistent than it would be if properly placed.

○ WINNING PERCENTAGE ○

A horse's winning percentage can easily be calculated from the numbers in the earnings box in the upper right-hand corner of the *Daily Racing Form* past performances. The earnings box reveals the horse's number of starts, wins, seconds, and thirds (as well as earnings) during each of the last two years the horse competed.

The handicapper must decide whether to include *both* year's data in his calculations. Last year's figures may be misleading.

Because of injuries or advancing age, a consistent winner last year may no longer be capable of such form this year. Another horse, injured or inexperienced, may have had trouble last year, but this year may put it all together and become a consistent winner.

Logic suggests that old data be discarded, and that only the most recent information be used. The statistics support this conclusion, but not by a very large margin. So that the reader may compare, we present the results of both approaches.

In our first tabulation, horses in 938 races were grouped according to their winning percentage over the past two years.

PCT	NH	NW	WPCT	MPCT	$NET	%W	I.V.
0–10%	3501	335	9.6%	31.0%	$1.45	35.7%	0.83
11–20%	3015	337	11.2%	35.3%	$1.47	35.9%	0.97
21–30%	1139	171	15.0%	38.6%	$1.80	18.2%	1.31
31–40%	375	60	16.0%	44.5%	$1.54	6.4%	1.39
41% up	162	39	24.1%	45.7%	$2.43	4.2%	2.09

In the next tabulation, horses in 942 races[1] were grouped according to their winning percentage during the current year, provided they had started at least six times. Horses that had started five or fewer times during the current year had their winning percentage calculated on the basis of two years' racing.

PCT	NH	NW	WPCT	MPCT	$NET	%W	I.V.
0–10%	3463	324	9.4%	30.4%	$1.46	34.4%	0.82
11–20%	2922	324	11.1%	34.8%	$1.46	34.4%	0.97
21–30%	1160	164	14.1%	39.2%	$1.65	17.4%	1.23
31–40%	415	78	18.8%	46.7%	$1.84	8.3%	1.64
41% up	211	48	22.7%	46.9%	$2.12	5.1%	1.98

Although there is little to choose between these two approaches, the second does give a smoother progression, and is based on more up-to-date information, and so is (slightly) preferable.

· In neither case is the weakest category (0–10%) alarmingly weak, while the strongest category (41% up) presents but two plays per average day.

One additional point is worth mentioning: horses that have won frequently in the past will not win as often in the future. Perhaps this is the effect of the additional weight they will be forced to carry, or the rise in class they will be asked to take, or simply the fact that many of them will have passed the peak on their form cycle. After losing a few races,

[1] In 4 of these 942 races, the two-year winning percentages of all starters fell into the same category. This explains why the first study is based on only 938 races—the other four races offered no diversity, and so were eliminated.

they will get lighter weight assignments again, and can safely drop in class to a level that better suits their ability.

○ NUMBER OF WINS IN LAST TEN RACES ○

Many handicappers like to judge a horse's consistency on the basis of the ten (or fewer) past-performance lines in the *Daily Racing Form* on the day of the race. This consistency rating depends on how many times the horse won, or at least ran a good race, in its last ten starts. The ten races not only are the horse's most recent, but provide a large enough sample to be representative.

The following tabulation groups horses in 2,285 races according to "number of wins in last ten starts."

# Wins	NH	NW	WPCT	MPCT	$NET	%W	I.V.
0	5011	403	8.0%	28.2%	$1.30	17.6%	0.70
1	7191	748	10.4%	32.0%	$1.57	32.7%	0.91
2	4530	574	12.7%	37.7%	$1.52	25.1%	1.10
3	2011	324	16.1%	42.7%	$1.75	14.2%	1.39
4 up	1098	236	21.5%	52.2%	$1.83	10.3%	1.83

Obviously, any horse that has not been able to win in its last ten starts is a poor risk. The horse has probably grown accustomed to losing, and is not a good bet to break its slump. Even though it may look good in other respects, something will probably beat it to the wire.

Surprisingly, one of every four horses falls into this category of "winless wonders." In the next tabulation, we study winless ones that had run a good race in their last start.

NH	NW	WPCT	MPCT	$NET	I.V.
1053	130	12.3%	37.8%	$1.38	1.12

Promises, promises! Many of these horses had several good races in their records, but had not been able to win. Why should they change overnight?

A classic example of this type of "sucker bet" was New York's legendary bridesmaid, Jacques Who, whose past performances (for the day he finally won a race) appear below. Notice the incredible number of second place finishes—13 in 20 races as a three-year-old—and the enormous amount of money that went down the drain on this horse, race after race—tote-board odds of 3-1 or less in seven of the ten races showing. He paid a "generous" $6.60 when he finally won a race.

That's Jacques Who, caught in the act of winning a race at Aqueduct on March 29, 1975. This perennial bridesmaid never seemed to learn that first was better than second. On March 29, he charged from three and a half lengths behind at the stretch call to get up in the final strides. He was moving so fast, he lost his sense of timing, and accidentally won.
Photo credit: Bob Coglianese

Should one of these winless wonders actually break through and win a race, is it likely to win a second in succession? In the tabulation below, we study horses that had won their last race but showed no other wins in their past performance lines.

NH	NW	WPCT	MPCT	$NET	I.V.
545	70	12.8%	34.1%	$1.63	1.17

These figures, and those in the preceding tabulation, fall far short of those for all horses that had won, or run a good race, in their last start (see Chapter 6).

On the other hand, horses able to win three or more times in their latest ten starts will continue to win far more than their share of races, returning an average payoff of $1.78. Add a good race in the horse's last

Shelter Bay as a four-year-old defeating Loud (8) and Cougar II (3) in the 1970 Manhattan Handicap on Belmont's Widener turf course. This professional race horse rolled on like Old Man River, winning often in top company during the next four seasons, including a victory over turf champion Fort Marcy in the 1971 Bougainvillea at Hialeah.

Photo credit: Bob Coglianese

119

start, to guarantee that good form is not a thing of the past, and the figures improve:

NH	NW	WPCT	MPCT	$NET	I.V.
1038	217	20.9%	49.0%	$1.87	1.90

Once again, the figures for "good race last" improve significantly when there is some guarantee—this time, consistency—that the horse will reproduce its good form.

○ THE LIGHTLY RACED HORSE ○

Statistics show that a horse with two wins in five lifetime starts will win its next race as often as a horse with three wins in its last ten starts.

A study of lightly raced horses (fewer than ten career starts), entered in non-maiden races, produced winning frequencies for any combination of starts and wins. A comparison with known frequencies for "number of wins in last ten starts" suggested how to project "wins in fewer than ten starts" to "wins in ten starts." The results of that study are contained in the following table:

Wins

		0	1	2	3	4+
	1	0	4+	x	x	x
S	2	0	4+	4+	x	x
T	3	0	3	4+	4+	x
A	4	0	2	3	4+	4+
R	5	0	2	3	4+	4+
T	6	0	1	3	4+	4+
S	7	0	1	2	3	4+
	8	0	1	2	3	4+
	9	0	1	2	3	4+

To determine a lightly raced horse's likely number of wins in ten starts, look up the horse's number of career starts in the left-hand column of the table, and then find the number in the column corresponding to the horse's number of victories.

For example, if a horse has won once in four starts, look on line 4 in column 1 to find the number 2. This horse's win-consistency thus far in its career projects to two wins in ten starts.

It was in this manner that lightly raced horses were classified in the preceding study.

○ COUNTING OTHER DECENT FINISHES ○

Some handicappers prefer to measure a horse's consistency in terms more extensive than wins.

In the following tabulation, horses in 1,549 races are grouped according to the number of times they ran in the money (first, second, or third) in their last ten starts.

# In Money	NH	NW	WPCT	MPCT	$NET	%W	I.V.
0	637	24	3.8%	18.1%	$0.79	1.5%	0.34
1	1330	96	7.2%	22.5%	$1.59	6.2%	0.66
2	2398	221	9.2%	27.8%	$1.88	14.3%	0.84
3	2754	250	9.1%	29.3%	$1.41	16.1%	0.82
4	2583	282	10.9%	34.2%	$1.40	18.2%	0.99
5	2104	306	14.5%	40.2%	$1.80	19.8%	1.32
6	1294	194	15.0%	44.6%	$1.50	12.5%	1.36
7–10	977	176	18.0%	46.6%	$1.76	11.4%	1.64

Horses that have run in the money in at least half of their ten most recent starts can be counted on to continue winning considerably more than their share of races. But the betting public is well aware of this and ultra-consistent horses are usually overbet.

In our next tabulation, horses in 946 races are grouped according to the number of times they ran a good race (see page 9) in their last ten starts.

# Good Races	NH	NW	WPCT	MPCT	$NET	%W	I.V.
0	726	38	5.2%	22.5%	$0.91	4.0%	0.45
1	1073	86	8.0%	25.5%	$1.55	9.1%	0.70
2	1946	197	10.1%	31.1%	$1.51	20.8%	0.88
3	1686	179	10.6%	35.9%	$1.56	18.9%	0.92
4	1228	177	14.4%	41.4%	$1.69	18.7%	1.25
5	897	144	16.1%	41.0%	$1.62	15.2%	1.39
6	440	68	15.5%	45.9%	$1.47	7.2%	1.34
7–10	223	57	25.6%	52.0%	$2.07	6.0%	2.22

Those rare horses—there are two every nine races—that have run at least seven good races in their last ten tries seem to be potentially lucrative betting propositions.

Our statistics suggest that horses with fewer than ten past performance lines be projected into one of the categories 0,1,2,3,4,5,6, or 7–10 by multiplying their "in the money" or "good race" percentage by 10 (races), and then dropping the fractional part of the answer. For example, a horse that has run three good races in its last eight starts has a "good race" percentage of $\frac{3}{8}$, or 37.5%, or 3.75 good races per ten starts. Ignoring the .75, we project the horse into the three good races per ten starts category.

○ WINS, PLACES, AND SHOWS ○

Some "figure freaks" like to assign weights to the number of wins, places, and shows in a horse's record, and come up with a figure that rates the animal's consistency. They multiply the number of wins by one "magic number," the number of places by another such number, and the number of shows by still another, and then add. The horse with the highest total is the most consistent, according to their reasoning. The trick, of course, is to determine the exact ratios among the three different "magic numbers."

Armed with a statistical technique known as multiple regression (see Appendix B), the computer studied the number of wins, places, and shows for each of more than 5,000 horses' last ten starts, and came up with the ratio 6:3:1. In other words, wins should be multiplied by 6, places by 3, and shows by 1.

Using this formula, a horse's consistency rating can range from 0 (for the horse that ran out of the money in each of its last ten starts) to 60 (for the horse that won each of its last ten starts).

The following tabulation groups horses in 946 races according to their "multiple regression consistency" total (MRCT).

MRCT	NH	NW	WPCT	MPCT	$NET	%W	I.V.
0–6	2965	224	7.6%	25.4%	$1.42	23.7%	0.66
7–15	3192	373	11.7%	36.5%	$1.49	39.4%	1.02
16–21	1197	174	14.5%	41.9%	$1.64	18.4%	1.26
22–up	865	175	20.2%	48.5%	$1.84	18.5%	1.76

So it appears that horses in the 0–6 range are poor betting risks. Horses whose total is 22 or higher win far more than their share of races and, although not producing a profit, average a return far above the parimutuel average of $1.64.

Actually, this approach has little advantage. The 0–6 category includes mostly horses that have failed to win in their last ten starts. And most horses with at least three recent wins fall in the 22–up category. So the multiple regression approach does not seem to have any advantage over the "number of wins in last ten starts" approach, which has the advantage of being easier to calculate.

○ CONSISTENCY AND DISTANCE ○

Consistency seems completely independent of the distance factor. All the studies produced essentially the same findings for both sprints and routes.

CLASS:
EARNINGS

Class is probably *the* most important factor in the outcome of a race. How often have you seen a horse win impressively, wire to wire, then move up in class for its next race, only to quit readily when a classier animal looks it in the eye? It happens every day. Some horses happen to be better than others, and they know it. The lesser ones know it, too.

Ray Taulbot, in his renowned *Thoroughbred Racing—Playing For Profit* (Amerpub, 1951), defined class as reserve racing energy:

> A high-class horse is simply an animal that owns a high degree of reserve racing power, which it can call upon to either set or force a pace so fast that it burns out the cheaper horse's store of reserve racing energy, leaving the high-class animal with sufficient power to go on and win the race, sometimes in slower time than the lower-grade horse has previously run the distance.

As Taulbot implied, final time should not be mistaken for class. Just because a horse shows the fastest time at the distance does not mean that it is the class of its field. A horse that beats $5,000 claimers in 1:11 for six furlongs may very well run up the track in a $10,000 race run in 1:11.4.

How, then, is class to be measured? One obvious possibility is by means of the horse's earnings record. The better (classier) horses run for the higher purses, and win their fair share (if not more) of those purses.

There are basically three different ways the handicapper may use the earnings information that appears in the upper right-hand corner of

124

the *Daily Racing Form* past performances. Each has its advantages and disadvantages.

○ TOTAL EARNINGS ○

First, and most simply, the horses in a race may be ranked according to their total earnings over the past two years. A study of 1,700 races (sprints and routes, claiming and allowance races) produced the following statistics:

Rank	NH	NW	WPCT	MPCT	$NET	%W	I.V.
First	1715	266	15.5%	42.9%	$1.40	15.6%	1.41
Second	1704	247	14.5%	39.1%	$1.51	14.5%	1.32
Third	1720	215	12.5%	39.9%	$1.55	12.6%	1.14
Front Half	2857	305	10.7%	33.2%	$1.72	17.9%	0.97
Rear Half	7205	667	9.3%	28.6%	$1.55	39.2%	0.84

Not very promising. Although horses ranked in the top three win considerably more than their share of races, the betting public is aware of this, and bets accordingly. The underachievers—horses with earnings in the lower half of their fields—win almost 40 percent of all races. Their impact value of 0.83 is low, but not alarmingly so.

Total earnings figures can be misleading, because they often tend to reflect past form, rather than current form. The lightly raced horse with good present form would most likely be downgraded in such figures. And horses that earn the top rankings may very well have burned themselves out in the process and need a rest, some time to spend their hard-earned cash.

○ AVERAGE EARNINGS PER START ○

Total earnings figures tend to overrate horses that race often, although perhaps not very well too often, vis-à-vis lightly raced but consistent horses. Yet there is something to be said for the durable horse that gets to the races two, three, or four times a month. Such an animal is not as likely to go bad during a race as are less active, more fragile horses.

For rating purposes, an alternative to total earnings might be average earnings. In the tabulation below, the horses in each of our 1,700 races have been ranked according to average earnings per start—

dividing the total earnings of each by its number of starts. Earnings and starts for the current year only have been used whenever possible. However, when a horse had started fewer than six times during the current year, the previous year's totals were added to obtain a truer average. Here are the results:

Rank	NH	NW	WPCT	MPCT	$NET	%W	I.V.
First	1803	362	20.1%	48.4%	$1.84	21.3%	1.82
Second	1822	274	15.0%	42.8%	$1.43	16.1%	1.36
Third	1811	243	13.4%	40.9%	$1.59	14.3%	1.22
Front Half	2961	308	10.4%	31.0%	$1.70	18.1%	0.95
Rear Half	6804	513	7.5%	26.3%	$1.45	30.2%	0.69

Note: *All earnings figures have been rounded to the nearest $100. This caused ties in rank which otherwise would not have existed, particularly when averages were taken.*

This is somewhat better than the total earnings tabulation. Horses ranked first in average earnings are a much stronger group than those ranked first in total earnings. And those in the bottom halves of their fields with respect to average earnings are weaker than their counterparts in total earnings. Nevertheless, even though horses ranked first in average earnings won 80 percent more than their share of races and finished in the money almost half the time, they still cost their backers eight cents on the dollar.

Average earnings figures tend to make a consistent cheaper horse look better than a classier but less consistent rival. Yet the statistics indicate that the number one horse in average earnings is a better bet than the number one horse in total earnings—it is more likely to win, and it is a more favorable betting proposition.

Average-earnings-per-start combines both class (earning power) and consistency. Add a good race last start to the fact that a horse ranks first in its field in average earnings, as assurance that the horse's form is not a thing of the past, and the figures approach the break-even point:

NH	NW	WPCT	MPCT	$NET	I.V.
828	206	24.9%	54.8%	$1.90	2.26

○ AVERAGE PURSE ○

It is possible to use a horse's earnings record to compute the size of the average purse for which it has successfully competed in the past. Unfortunately, the calculations required must reflect the purse distribution at the track or tracks where the horse has raced. And there is no one formula that is used in every state, or at every track in a given state, or for every race at a given track.

Most tracks award 60 percent of the purse to the winner. Some still give 65 percent, others as low as 55 percent. Some tracks award purse money to the fifth, and even sixth, finishers. Others go back no further than fourth. Some tracks pay a certain amount to all starters, and divide the rest among the first four finishers. And some tracks divide stakes purses differently from overnight purses.

Perhaps the best approach would be to use the most widely used purse distribution formula: 60-22-12-6. In many states, 60 percent of the purse is awarded to the winner, 22 percent to the second finisher, 12 percent for third, and the remaining 6 percent for fourth.

The average purse for which a horse has competed successfully is then determined by multiplying its win total by .60, its place total by .22, its show total by .12, and its fourths total by .06, adding, and then dividing the sum into the total earnings.

DeLite Jr., for example, had 10 wins, 6 seconds, and 3 thirds in 1976. Looking over his past-performance lines, we find no fourths (or fifths or sixths, if necessary) showing. So we calculate

$$10 \times .60 + 6 \times .22 + 3 \times .12 + 0 \times .06 = 7.68$$

and then divide into his earnings for the year, $46,425, to get

$$\$46,425/7.68 = \$6044.92 .$$

This means that the average purse for which DeLite Jr. competed successfully in 1976 was approximately $6,045.

Copyright © 1979, by DAILY RACING FORM, INC. Reprinted with permission of copyright owner.

The horse that gets the highest figure from all these calculations is supposedly the "class" of its field, having successfully competed for the highest purses during the past year or two. Of course, the figures give no indication of how frequently the horse was successful when competing for such a purse. Neither do they indicate whether the horse is presently in condition to compete for such a purse, or any other.

In the tabulation below, we have ranked the horses in our 1,700 races according to the size of the average purse for which they had successfully competed. Once again, we have used only the current year's earnings figures, provided the horse had started at least six times during the year.

Rank	NH	NW	WPCT	MPCT	$NET	%W	I.V.
First	1756	210	12.0%	33.7%	$1.47	12.4%	1.09
Second	1741	237	13.6%	38.7%	$1.69	13.9%	1.23
Third	1708	235	13.8%	39.7%	$1.68	13.8%	1.25
Front Half	2889	335	11.6%	34.9%	$1.55	19.7%	1.05
Rear Half	7107	683	9.6%	30.2%	$1.53	40.2%	0.87

This is by far the weakest of the three approaches—the swing in impact values is very slight, the top-ranked category weaker, and the rear-half category stronger, than for the other two approaches.

"Average successful purse" figures can be compared with the purse for which the horse is competing today to determine whether the horse is entered above or below its proper class. Simply divide the "average successful purse" by today's purse. The answer you get will be a percentage.

DeLite Jr., for example, was entered in a race worth $4,800. So his percentage figure would be

$$\$6044.92/\$4800 = 1.26,$$

or 126 percent of today's purse. Had he been entered instead in a race with a purse of $7,000, his figure would have been

$$\$6044.92/\$7000 = 0.86,$$

or just 86 percent of the purse.

For the sake of classification, we shall regard a horse as moving up in company over the average class of its successful (first, second, third, fourth) races during the most recent year or two, if the percentage is less than 90. We shall say the horse is dropping if the percentage is 110 or higher. Otherwise, we rule that the horse is running in approximately the same company against which it has successfully competed in the past year or two.

DeLite Jr. has a rating of 126 percent, and so is considered to be dropping from the level of his average successful race of 1976, even though his last four races had come against the same kind of beast he will be facing today. His past performances feature six good races against $6,500–$8,500 stock, and he had beaten better than that earlier in the year.

The following tabulation indicates how the horses in our 1,700 race sample performed when classified in this manner:

	NH	NW	WPCT	MPCT	$NET	%W	I.V.
Going Up	6751	668	9.9%	30.2%	$1.56	39.3%	0.90
Same Class	3725	458	12.3%	37.6%	$1.64	26.9%	1.12
Dropping	4725	574	12.1%	35.7%	$1.47	33.8%	1.10

Once again, we find little significant information. Horses racing for approximately the same kinds of purses as have rewarded them in the past appear to do best. Those moving up face the obvious

Majestic Prince (middle) defeats Arts & Letters (inside) and Dike (outside) in the 1969 Kentucky Derby.

Photo credit: Lexington Herald-Leader

obstacle—tougher competition. And many of those competing at a lower level than previously may no longer be the horses they used to be.

Perhaps the problem with this, and the other two earnings approaches, is that class cannot be completely separated from current form. A horse may outclass its opponents, but unless it is in shape will not be able to beat them today.

Consistency being related to form as well as to class, you can better understand why the average earnings approach, which combines earning power with consistency, appears strongest of our three evaluation methods.

○ EARNINGS AND DISTANCE ○

Our studies reveal that none of our three approaches to earnings figures is more (or less) powerful as predictors in sprint races than it is in routes—nor in allowance races, rather than claiming races.

CLASS:
CHANGES
IN
CLAIMING
PRICE

Earnings power is not the only way to measure a horse's class. One could also consider the quality of the animals the horse has been competing (successfully) against. Unless the handicapper is familiar with the ability of most of the horses on the grounds, this means simply looking at the claiming prices for which the horse has been entered, or determining the type of allowance races in which the horse has been competing.

In the allowance ranks, this measure of class is usually fairly stable and easy to determine. If a horse is entered in an NW3 race, it is usually fair to assume that its most recent allowance races, back to its last win, were also in NW3 company. That win was probably in an NW2 race, as were all prior allowance races, back to a second win. That win (if it shows in the past performances) was probably in an NW1 race, and the win before that in a maiden race. This is generally the way things work in the restricted allowance ranks.

If a horse is entered in a classified allowance race, some knowledge of its past opponents is necessary to determine how long the animal has been competing in the classified division, and when it graduated from the restricted allowance ranks.

In the claiming ranks, on the other hand, horses constantly move up or down in class, seeking the proper level for present ability. The tabulations that follow all pertain to claiming races only, and are an attempt to determine where (if anywhere) the advantage lies in such races.

Does the horse dropping in class have an advantage? Or perhaps the sharp horse moving up enjoys greater success than expected. Or should one play the horse going neither up nor down? The studies that follow will help answer these questions.

To help in determining whether a claiming runner is moving up or down in class, we will use the "claiming ladder," as described on page 12.

○ CLAIMING PRICE LAST START ○

In our first tabulation, each horse in 945 claiming races has been classified according to the change in class from its last start. Horses coming out of allowance races have been classified separately.

Class Change	NH	NW	WPCT	MPCT	$NET	%W	I.V.
Down 2+	1007	147	14.6%	35.7%	$1.54	15.6%	1.27
Down 1	1431	171	11.9%	34.1%	$1.68	18.1%	1.04
Same	2897	317	10.9%	37.0%	$1.54	33.5%	0.95
Up 1	1483	192	12.9%	35.0%	$1.74	20.3%	1.13
Up 2+	833	81	9.7%	32.5%	$1.30	8.6%	0.85
Allowance	561	37**	6.6%	23.0%	$0.82	3.9%	0.57

These results are hardly conclusive. The vast majority of the starters in these races (71 percent) were racing within one class of their previous race. Those moving up one class did just as well (actually, slightly better) as those dropping one class, and both did slightly better than those not changing class at all. Horses dropping two or more classes were the most frequent winners, but also the most heavily bet.

To increase the likelihood that each race in the sample would include horses moving up and horses dropping down, our sample of 945 claiming races included none for the cheapest or the best claiming horses on the grounds. This probably explains the poor showing by horses dropping from allowance races. Allowance runners probably perform well in the highest-priced claiming events. Those that drop farther down are probably ill or injured, or may not have been authentic allowance stock to begin with.

In any event, our first class study suggests consideration of a horse's latest race in terms more elaborate than its class. How well the horse raced must also be pertinent. The table on the following page separates the horses in each of our six categories according to whether or not they had run a good race in their last start.

Aside from pointing out the obvious—that horses coming off a good race outperform those that are not as sharp, regardless of class—these figures reveal a few other interesting points.

Horses dropping in class after a "not good" race do not win their share of races. The combined impact value for these two categories was 0.92.

Even worse off are horses that run a "not good" race and then do

DOWN TWO+ CLASSES

	NH	NW	WPCT	MPCT	$NET	I.V.
Good	273	65	23.8%	44.3%	$1.92	2.07
Others	1173	136	11.6%	35.1%	$1.42	1.01

DOWN ONE CLASS

	NH	NW	WPCT	MPCT	$NET	I.V.
Good	250	59	23.6%	49.6%	$1.97	2.05
Others	1181	112	9.5%	30.8%	$1.62	0.82

SAME CLASS

	NH	NW	WPCT	MPCT	$NET	I.V.
Good	1207	205	17.0%	49.0%	$1.60	1.48
Others	1697	113	6.7%	28.5%	$1.62	0.58

UP ONE CLASS

	NH	NW	WPCT	MPCT	$NET	I.V.
Good	941	150	15.9%	41.3%	$1.78	1.39
Others	542	42	7.7%	24.0%	$1.66	0.67

UP TWO+ CLASSES

	NH	NW	WPCT	MPCT	$NET	I.V.
Good	592	73	12.3%	38.0%	$1.49	1.07
Others	241	8	3.3%	19.1%	$0.84	0.29

ALLOWANCE LAST

	NH	NW	WPCT	MPCT	$NET	I.V.
Good	115	11	9.6%	23.5%	$1.27	0.83
Others	446	26**	5.8%	22.9%	$0.71	0.51

not drop in class, but rather remain in the same class or move up. Such animals are extremely poor betting risks, highly unlikely to be found in the winner's circle.

On the other hand, horses moving up or remaining in the same class after a good race win considerably more than their fair share. Their odds generally are not high enough to warrant a bet, however.

○ THOSE SUSPICIOUS DROPDOWNS ○

When a horse wins, it usually moves up in class for its next start. But what about the horse that drops down after running well in its most recent start? Is the horse dropping into an easy spot to steal a purse? Or is it dropping because something is physically wrong?

If the horse is running in allowance company, the former is probably true. But if the horse is a claimer, either could be true. A trainer who drops a horse in an effort to win a purse also risks losing the animal via a claim. In such situations, most trainers usually tip their hands by riding leading jockeys, taking no chances on losing both horse and purse.

But if a horse is ailing, the trainer may drop it in price, hoping that some other trainer will consider the animal a bargain, and take the problem off his hands.

Statistics indicate that sharp claiming horses dropping in class are excellent bets. They win almost twice their share of races, and cost their backers only three cents per wagered dollar. Add the requirement that the jockey must have ridden the horse in one of its good races, or be among the top five riders at the meeting, and this "angle" becomes slightly profitable:

NH	NW	WPCT	MPCT	$NET	I.V.
269	79	29.4%	54.3%	$2.13	2.55

Comparison of win and in-the-money percentages here reveals that more than 50 percent of these "sharp dropdowns" able to run in the money manage to win. These horses are probably not worth place and show bets. Either the horse is sound enough to assert its class and win, or it is ailing and may very well run out of the money.

Needless to say, the handicapper who can recognize a "hurting dropdown" will improve considerably his own chances of winning. Some of these signs, such as a suspicious layoff, the absence of workouts, or the inability to run a straight course, can be found in the *Daily Racing Form*. Others, such as front bandages, or excessive nervousness or kidney sweat, may be observed in the paddock and post parade before the race. And it never hurts to be familiar with an individual trainer's "modus operandi." With some trainers, a drop in price signals an attempt to win a purse. Other trainers drop a horse only when it is ailing or has been drained of every last ounce of run.

○ CLAIMING PRICE LAST GOOD RACE ○

In the next tabulation, horses in 946 claiming races are classified according to the change in class from their last good claiming race. In this tabulation, and the one immediately after it, horses whose past performances show no claiming races are placed in the ALLOWANCE category—such horses are racing in a claiming event for the first time in at least ten races, perhaps for the first time ever.

Horses whose past performances show claiming races, but no good claiming races, are classified as follows: first look for the most recent finish within three to five lengths of the winner, penalizing the horse one class; if no such race is found, look for the most recent finish within six to nine lengths, penalizing two classes; then a finish within ten to fourteen lengths, penalizing three classes; finally, the most recent finish, penalizing four classes.

So, for example, if a horse's best claiming showing is a 5^4 for $13,000, that performance is considered the same as a good race for $10,000, one class cheaper.

Here, then, are the statistics from our study of claiming horses classified according to class change from last good claiming race.

Class Change	NH	NW	WPCT	MPCT	$NET	%W	I.V.
Down 2+	1033	126	12.2%	34.1%	$1.28	13.3%	1.06
Down 1	1130	150	13.3%	36.7%	$1.73	15.9%	1.15
Same	2566	329	12.8%	39.6%	$1.67	34.8%	1.11
Up 1	1875	220	11.7%	33.9%	$1.58	23.3%	1.02
Up 2+	1474	114	7.7%	26.9%	$1.29	12.1%	0.67
Allowance	141	7**	5.0%	19.1%	$0.67	0.7%	0.43

Once again, there is little to choose from among those horses entered within one class of their most recent good race. Horses racing two or more classes below their recent good form are barely able to hold their own, and are heavily overbet. And horses attempting to move up two or more classes usually are not successful.

In our final tabulation along these lines, horses in 946 claiming races have been classified according to the class change from the best claiming effort (highest class good race) showing in their past performances.

Class Change	NH	NW	WPCT	MPCT	$NET	%W	I.V.
Down 2+	1719	244	14.2%	39.5%	$1.43	25.8%	1.23
Down 1	1393	181	13.0%	37.7%	$1.56	19.1%	1.13
Same	2081	260	12.5%	37.8%	$1.78	27.5%	1.09
Up 1	1581	166	10.5%	30.9%	$1.42	17.5%	0.91
Up 2+	1304	88	6.7%	25.8%	$1.43	9.3%	0.59
Allowance	141	7**	5.0%	19.1%	$0.67	0.7%	0.43

The value of "back class" is evident here. Most horses that are successful when moving up in class were able to run well because they previously had been competitive in that class or higher. Horses moving up to a class where they had never been successful before, or had even attempted before, are not worthwhile bets.

Yeyo, for example, could have been expected to handle his class rise on March 20—he had competed successfully against far better horses during his 1975 campaign.

Copyright © 1979, by DAILY RACING FORM, INC. Reprinted with permission of copyright owner.

○ THE RECENT CLAIM ○

A horse that has just been claimed must move up in class. That, or be forced to the sidelines for a month. In most states, the rules require that a newly claimed animal race at a minimum 25 percent increase in claiming price for one month, or not race in claimers at all.

Consequently, horses recently claimed would appear to be at a disadvantage in their first few starts under new ownership. Either they must remain inactive for a month, which is unremunerative, or they must compete against animals that supposedly outclass them.

Were the picture really this depressing, far fewer claims would be made. But many trainers have the knack for claiming horses just as they are coming to hand and ready to move up. Others see the hole card, and can transform a horse practically overnight.

Banderlog is an excellent example of what an astute trainer can do with a willing, though ailing, animal. Two weeks after being claimed from a fair performance against $7,500 platers, he defeated $10,000 stock, avenging two earlier losses at the same level. Trainer Pancho Martin must have seen something in this old warhorse other than heart. Otherwise, why claim an eight-year-old, with a history of unsoundness, that had failed in its only two recent attempts against better horses?

Copyright © 1979, by DAILY RACING FORM, INC. Reprinted with permission of copyright owner.

But we are interested in the facts, not speculation, and the facts indicate that a recently claimed horse is a good bet only if it has won since being claimed. The following tabulation studies 809 claiming races in which at least one of the starters had been claimed from one of its latest three races.

	NH	NW	WPCT	MPCT	$NET	I.V.
No Claim	5252	589	11.2%	33.8%	$1.57	0.98
c-Last Race	685	79	11.5%	33.9%	$1.53	1.01
c-Won Since	176	40	22.7%	51.7%	$1.70	1.99
c-Good Since	344	49	14.2%	43.6%	$1.26	1.25
c-Poor Since	633	52	8.2%	28.6%	$1.27	0.72

Horses in the NO CLAIM category went unclaimed in each of their three most recent starts. All other categories refer to horses that had recently been claimed. Those claimed from their latest start are included in the c-LAST RACE category. Those that won or ran a good race since being claimed are included in the similarly named categories. And those yet to run a good race since being claimed are found in the c-POOR SINCE category.

Obviously, horses that have run poorly since being claimed are not likely to improve. And a horse claimed in its last start is not automatically a good bet.

Horses that have run a good race since being claimed do well, but not as well the typical horse coming off a good race. It should be pointed out, though, that some of the horses in the c-GOOD SINCE category did not run a good race last out, but in their first start after being claimed.

Of particular interest is the c-WON SINCE (not won last, necessarily) category. These horses do better than the typical winner trying to repeat. Apparently, if a trainer is able to get a claimed horse to win one of its first two starts in its new colors, the horse is likely to win again, often moving even farther up in class.

Horses claimed from races in which they ran well (a good race) frequently run well in their first starts for their new owners, but not as often as horses coming out of good races in which they went unclaimed.

NH	NW	WPCT	MPCT	$NET	I.V.
384	59	15.4%	39.6%	$1.66	1.35

The 1.35 impact value for this group is slightly lower than the 1.41 I.V. for all horses coming off good races.

And what of claimed horses whose first starts for their new stables take place a month or more after the claim? They do badly:

NH	NW	WPCT	MPCT	$NET	I.V.
111	10	9.0%	25.2%	$1.19	0.79

A layoff helps nobody's horse.

WEIGHT

They say that weight can slow down a freight train. It certainly has stopped many a great race horse. The giant gelding Forego is the latest to succumb to a racing secretary's "admiration"—138 pounds didn't help him in the 1977 Suburban, nor did 137 in the Brooklyn.

Ordinary horses seldom are required to carry extreme weights. The conditions for allowance and claiming races usually stipulate a maximum weight of about 122 pounds. And when does a horse get to carry top weight? Precisely when it is in top shape, having recently won a race or two of similar class.

What effect does weight have on thoroughbred performance? That is the central question to be answered in this chapter.

○ THE EFFECT OF WEIGHT ON SPEED ○

A study of approximately 30,000 past performance lines revealed the not so surprising fact that horses carrying higher weights tend to run faster than less-burdened rivals. Horses carrying 120 pounds ran, on the average, $\frac{1}{5}$ of a second (one length) faster than did horses carrying 110 pounds. The statistical technique known as linear regression (see Appendix B) produced the formula that one pound is worth .09 lengths, in favor of the horse carrying the *higher* weight.

Obviously, it is not the added weight that makes horses run faster. Rather, horses carrying the higher weights are better horses in better condition than their rivals.

This same study revealed that horses dropping three pounds or more from their previous start tended to run $\frac{1}{5}$ of a second slower than they had in that start. Horses adding three pounds or more tended to run slightly more than $\frac{1}{5}$ of a second faster than they had in their previous start. And horses that carried within two pounds of what they carried in their previous race tended to run as fast as they had in that race.

Contrary to popular belief, then, picking up weight is a good sign, and dropping a few pounds is not.

(Note: this study used for speed figures sums of *Daily Racing Form* speed ratings and track variants, adjusted for distance, as will be explained in Chapter 17.)

○ TODAY'S WEIGHT ○

A study of 942 races proves that horses carrying the higher weights are more successful, and more lucrative betting propositions, at sprint distances. First, we have a study of 643 sprints:

Weight	NH	NW	WPCT	MPCT	$NET	%W	I.V.
100–109	545	50	9.2%	30.8%	$1.30	7.8%	0.85
110–112	811	98	12.1%	33.8%	$1.96	15.2%	1.11
113–115	2163	186	8.6%	29.7%	$1.36	28.9%	0.78
116–117	1495	171	11.4%	34.1%	$1.57	26.6%	1.03
118–119	418	67	16.0%	40.4%	$1.60	10.4%	1.42
120 up	345	71	20.6%	48.7%	$2.04	11.0%	1.86

And then, a study of 299 routes:

Weight	NH	NW	WPCT	MPCT	$NET	%W	I.V.
100–109	212	27	12.7%	33.5%	$1.61	9.0%	1.03
110–112	406	54	13.3%	39.7%	$1.90	18.1%	1.08
113–115	762	87	11.4%	35.6%	$1.40	29.1%	0.92
116–117	653	75	11.5%	36.1%	$1.17	25.1%	0.93
118–119	213	33	15.5%	44.6%	$1.66	11.0%	1.29
120 up	167	23	13.8%	38.3%	$1.42	7.7%	1.11

Horses carrying 118 pounds or more win far more than their share of sprints, but this is not quite true in routes. It seems to be much more difficult to carry in excess of 120 pounds over a route distance.

As we have said, high weight today usually follows a recent win in comparable class. If a horse's most recent race was sharp, if it is assigned 120 pounds or more today, and if it is entered in a sprint, you have an excellent bet, as the following figures show:

Last Race	NH	NW	WPCT	MPCT	$NET	I.V.
Good	205	54	26.3%	57.6%	$2.18	2.34
Won	125	32	25.6%	58.4%	$2.40	2.23

But not so in routes:

Last Race	NH	NW	WPCT	MPCT	$NET	I.V.
Good	95	17	17.9%	46.3%	$1.86	1.49
Won	65	14	21.5%	50.8%	$1.70	1.80

A horse does not qualify for the top weight assignment in a race solely on the basis of one recent win. Read the conditions for a six-furlong claiming race run at Monmouth Park in November of 1976:

For three year olds and upwards,
three-year-olds	121 pounds
older	122 pounds

Non-winners of three races
since July 8 allowed	3 pounds
—two races since July 8 allowed	5 pounds
—a race since July 8 allowed	7 pounds

In order to qualify for top weight of 121–122 pounds, a horse must have won at least three times since July 8. Precisely the highly consistent horses discussed in Chapter 12—three or more wins in last ten starts. We already know that these horses do well, and are worthwhile bets—especially when their last start indicates they are in form.

○ **WEIGHT CONCESSIONS** ○

The following study indicates that the top-weighted horse (or horses) are the most likely to win, a fact well known to the betting public. In the tabulations below, horses are classified according to the number of pounds of difference between their imposts and those of the top-weighted horses in their fields. First, a study of 644 sprints:

Pounds	NH	NW	WPCT	MPCT	$NET	%W	I.V.
Top	1179	187	15.9%	40.8%	$1.52	29.0%	1.42
1–4	2444	266	10.9%	32.9%	$1.76	41.3%	0.98
5–8	1646	142	8.6%	29.8%	$1.30	22.0%	0.77
9 up	515	49	9.5%	31.1%	$1.39	7.6%	0.85

And then 300 routes:

Pounds	NH	NW	WPCT	MPCT	$NET	%W	I.V.
Top	561	83	14.8%	42.3%	$1.45	27.7%	1.19
1–4	869	105	12.1%	37.5%	$1.35	35.0%	0.97
5–8	724	76	10.5%	33.7%	$1.43	25.3%	0.85
9 up	265	36	13.6%	35.5%	$1.94	12.0%	1.10

The top-weighted horses were slightly more successful in sprints. And horses carrying nine pounds or more below top weight did much better in routes, accounting for the highest $NET in this particular study.

○ WEIGHT ON, WEIGHT OFF ○

Is a shift in weight from one race to the next of any significance? A study of 943 races produced mixed and inconclusive results:

Weight Shift	NH	NW	WPCT	MPCT	$NET	%W	I.V.
Down 4+ Lbs.	1151	145	12.6%	33.6%	$1.70	15.4%	1.10
Down 2–3 Lbs.	1145	121	10.6%	33.4%	$1.41	12.8%	0.92
Within 1 Lb.	3671	393	10.7%	34.8%	$1.59	41.7%	0.93
Up 2–3 Lbs.	1087	139	12.8%	36.9%	$1.53	14.7%	1.11
Up 4+ Lbs.	1143	145	12.7%	33.8%	$1.27	15.4%	1.10

Some horses picking up weight do well, while others shedding poundage do equally as well. Apparently, weight shifts are of little importance, in either sprints or routes.

○ PREVIOUS WEIGHT-CARRYING EXPERIENCE ○

Another question that might be asked is the following: "If a horse is carrying high weight, how well has it done in the past when carrying at least as many pounds at today's distance or longer?"

According to the computer, the ideal breakoff point between "high" and "low" weight is 118 pounds. Any horse carrying 118 pounds or more is either toting top-weight or receiving the smallest weight concession prescribed in the conditions of the race.

In the tabulations below, horses were placed into one of four possible categories. Any horse carrying 117 pounds or less went into the

LOWER category. Horses carrying 118 pounds or more fell into one of the following three categories:

YES: The horse's past performances indicate that it has run a good race at today's distance or longer under today's weight or higher.

NO: All races showing in the horse's past performances at today's distance or longer under today's weight or higher were "not good."

???: The horse's past performances include no race at today's distance or longer under today's weight or higher.

Here are the results, first for a study of 382 sprints:

	NH	NW	WPCT	MPCT	$NET	%W	I.V.
Lower	2643	244	9.2%	30.7%	$1.44	63.9%	0.82
Yes	299	64	21.4%	50.8%	$1.90	16.8%	1.90
No	208	29	13.9%	33.2%	$1.68	7.6%	1.27
???	256	45	17.6%	45.3%	$1.78	11.8%	1.58

And then, for 196 routes:

	NH	NW	WPCT	MPCT	$NET	%W	I.V.
Lower	1232	140	11.4%	34.9%	$1.46	71.4%	0.93
Yes	109	22	20.2%	47.7%	$1.72	11.2%	1.78
No	103	16	15.5%	44.7%	$1.81	8.2%	1.29
???	166	18	10.8%	36.8%	$1.29	9.2%	0.89

The advantage clearly lies with horses carrying 118 pounds or more, regardless of whether or not they had ever been successful under such weight before. But horses inexperienced carrying 118 pounds or more did much better in sprints.

○ **RUNNING STYLE** ○

A study of 422 horses carrying 123–124 pounds (high weight in New York at the time of the study) revealed that horses carrying high weights do best when racing in front.

FCP	NH	NW	WPCT	MPCT	$NET	I.V.
1	41	15*	36.6%	58.5%	$3.75	3.30
2–3	111	27	24.3%	57.7%	$1.65	2.21
4–7	185	30	16.2%	42.7%	$1.27	1.46
8–12	85	6**	7.1%	16.5%	$1.74	0.64

Perhaps this is a bit redundant. The horses carrying top weight have been running well (winning), and horses that win often usually have early speed.

The key point to be made is that it is difficult for a horse carrying a heavy package to put that burden in motion more than once during a race. These heavyweights cannot afford to be blocked or knocked off stride during the running. When they are racing up front, there is less chance of this.

○ CONCLUSION ○

The weight factor is not what mathematicians would call an independent variable. Rather, it is a function of recent form and class. The better horses that appear to be in shape carry the top weights, and outperform their less-burdened rivals.

	SR	DV	SF
Vosburgh Handicap	100	15	119
United Nations Handicap		Grass	
Washington Park Handicap	100	13	118
Whitney	91	22	121
Brooklyn Handicap	97	17	128
Suburban Handicap	98	11	123
Californian	91	12	120
Roseben Handicap	94	17	115
Vosburgh Handicap	93	17	114
Hawthorne Gold Cup	88	13	114
Woodward	82	20	116
New Hampshire Sweeps	100	18	113
Rockingham Special	100	15	112
Arlington Classic	81	29	115
Jersey Derby	97	20	123
Withers	97	18	120
Gotham	90	16	111
Champagne	90	17	112
Cowdin	78	24	105
World's Playground	86	24	108
Allowance	88	17	105
Maiden	88	20	103

SR: Speed ratings, based on track records in effect September 30, 1978.
DV: Accurate daily variants (see Chapter 17).
SF: Adjusted speed figures (see Chapter 17).

DR. FAGER

Three of the greatest weight-carrying feats in racing history were turned in by the immortal Dr. Fager in the last three starts of his career. First, he carried 134 pounds to a world's record (which still stands) for the mile, winning the Washington Park Handicap at Arlington Park by ten lengths. Then, he traveled to Atlantic City, where he was assigned 134 pounds for the United Nations Handicap. In his turf debut, despite racing wide on a wet course he disliked, he beat Advocator by a neck while spotting Fort Marcy, the previous year's grass champion, 16 pounds. And then, back home in New York, he shattered Aqueduct's seven-furlong record under 139 pounds, while running away from the likes of Kissin' George and Jim J. in the Vosburgh Handicap.

Dr. Fager ⊗						B. c (1964–Fla), by Rough'n Tumble—Aspidistra, by Better Self		1968	8	7	1	0 $406,110
						Tartan Stable J. A. Nerud (Tartan Farms)		1967	9	7	0	1 $484,194
								1966	5	4	1	0 $112,338

Copyright © 1979 by DAILY RACING FORM, INC. Reprinted with permission of copyright owner.

Photo credit: Bob Coglianese

Vosburgh Handicap—139 lbs.

Washington Park Handicap—134 lbs.

United Nations Handicap—134 lbs.

SPEED
HANDICAPPING:
PAR
TIMES

The better the horse, the faster it runs. When in form and entered at the proper distance, it covers that distance more rapidly than its inferior opponent can—barring the occasional effects of racing luck.

Yet inferior horses sometimes win their races in faster official times than are recorded by better horses. This causes confusion. When the better winner finally meets the lesser one and defeats him (sometimes in slower time than expected), numerous horsemen and handicappers take the phenomenon as evidence that time is an undependable measure of thoroughbred quality. "Class is the thing," they say, "not time."

Speed handicappers know better. They know that time and class are inseparable. To understand the relationship between time and class, it is necessary to recognize that the official time of a race may be misleading, having been affected by weather and the texture of the racing strip. This is why speed handicappers calculate daily variants—numbers that compensate for the effects of weather and track maintenance on official running times.

After an accurate daily variant has modified an official running time (or a *Daily Racing Form* speed rating) earned by the winner of a $25,000 claiming race and the time (or speed rating) earned on another day by the winner of a $10,000 claiming race, it will be discovered in

Table 1

	6F	1¹⁄₁₆ M.	CLF	MSW	2-MSW
Ak-Sar-Ben (Aks)	1:11.1(B)	1:45.1(A)	1:10.3	1:12	1:06.2(B)
Albuquerque (Alb)	1:11 (C)	1:46.1(C)	1:11.1	1:12.3	
Aqueduct(Inner)(Aqu)	1:12	1:47 (A)	1:10.4	1:12	1:12 (D)
Aqueduct(Main)(Aqu)	1:11.2(B)	*1:51.4(A)	1:10	1:11.1	1:11.2(D)
Arlington (AP)	1:11 (A)	*1:51.2(A)	1:10	1:11.2	1:11.4(B)
Atlantic City (Atl)	1:10.4(A)	1:44.4(C)	1:09.4	1:11	1:11.2(B)
Bay Meadows (BM)	1:10.3(B)	1:44.1(A)	1:09.4	1:11	1:11.2(D)
Belmont (Bel)	1:11.3(B)	1:44.2(A)	1:10.1	1:11.2	1:11.3(C)
Beulah (Beu)	1:11.4(C)	1:45.2(A)	1:11.4	1:13	1:13 (D)
Bowie (Bow)	1:11.1(D)	1:45.4(D)	1:10.1	1:11.3	1:11.4(C)
Calder (Crc)	1:12(D)	1:46.2(C)	1:11.1	1:12.2	1:12.3(D)
Caliente (AC)	1:09.2(D)	1:42.4(E)	1:09.3	1:10.4	
Centennial (Cen)	1:09.4(B)	1:44.2(A)	1:09.4	1:11.1	1:11.3(B)
Churchill Downs (CD)	1:11.3(E)	1:46.3(C)	1:10.3	1:11.4	1:11.4(D)
Delaware (Del)	1:11.2(C)	1:45.4(A)	1:10.2	1:11.4	1:12.2(B)
Del Mar (Dmr)	1:09.3(B)	1:42.3(A)	1:08.1	1:09.2	1:10(B)
Detroit (Det)	1:12.1(B)	1:47.3(B)	1:11.3	1:13	
Ellis Park (ElP)	1:12 (E)	*1:53.2(C)	1:11.4	1:13	1:13.4(B)
Fair Grounds (FG)	1:11.2(B)	1:45.3(A)	1:10.3	1:11.4	1:12 (D)
Fairmount (FP)	1:11.2(A)	1:45.3(A)	1:11.3	1:13	
Finger Lakes (FL)	1:11.3(D)	1:46.1(D)	1:11.4	1:13.1	
Florida Downs (FD)	1:12.1(C)	1:48.1(C)	1:11.3	1:13	
Fort Erie (FE)	1:11.3(C)	1:44.4(C)	1:10.4	1:12	1:12.2(B)
Fresno (Fno)	1:08.4(B)	1:42 (A)	1:08.4	1:10.1	1:10.2(A)
Garden State (GS)	1:13 (C)	1:48 (C)	1:12.1	1:13.2	
Golden Gate (GG)	1:10.2(B)	1:44.3(A)	1:09.2	1:10.3	1:05.2(A)
Gulfstream (GP)	1:10.4(C)	1:44.3(B)	1:09.3	1:10.4	0:59 (A)
Hawthorne (Haw)	1:10.4(B)	1:44.2(A)	1:09.4	1:11.1	1:11.4(C)
Hialeah (Hia)	1:10.3(C)	*1:50.1(A)	1:09.2	1:10.3	0:58.4(A)
Hollywood (Hol)	1:10.1(B)	1:43.3(A)	1:08.4	1:10	1:10.3(B)

SPECIAL DISTANCES

Aqueduct : 1 Mile = 1:37.3

Belmont : 1½ Miles = 2:31.3

Laurel : 1 Mile = 1:38.2

Laurel : Laurel Futurity = 1:43.2

Keeneland : @7½ F = 1:28.2

Keeneland : 2 YOS MSW at 4½ F = 0:52.4

Churchill Downs : 1 Mile = 1:38.2

Churchill Downs : 2 YOS MSW at 5F = 0:59.3

Ellis Park : 1 Mile = 1:39.1

Arlington : 1 Mile = 1:36.4

Arlington : 1¹⁄₁₆ Miles = 1:45.4

Waterford : @1 Mile = 1:36.3

most cases that the horse of higher quality has earned the higher figure. Which is to say that it has run faster—regardless of whether its official running time (or speed rating) was faster or not.

The basis for daily variants and speed figures is a table of par

Track					
Juarez (Jua)	1:10.4(D)	1:45.1(C)	1:11.2	1:12.3	1:11.1(C)
Keeneland (Kee)	1:11(E)	1:44.4(D)	1:10	1:11.1	1:12(C)
Keystone (Key)	1:10.4(C)	1:44.2(C)	1:10	1:11.2	1:15.1(C)
Latonia (Lat)	1:14(H)	1:48.3(E)	1:13.4	1:15	1:12.1(D)
Laurel (Lrl)	1:11.4(C)	*1:52.2(C)	1:10.4	1:12.1	1:11.1(B)
Longacres (Lga)	1:09.3(A)	1:43.2(A)	1:09.2	1:10.3	1:14.2(C)
Louisiana Downs (LaD)	1:13(C)	1:48.2(A)	1:12.4	1:14.1	1:12.3(C)
Meadowlands (Med)	1:12.1(A)	1:46.2(A)	1:11	1:12.2	1:11.1(B)
Monmouth (Mth)	1:10.4(B)	1:45(A)	1:09.4	1:11	—
Narragansett (Nar)	1:11.2(C)	1:45.2(A)	1:11.2	1:12.3	—
Oaklawn (OP)	1:12.2(B)	1:46.3(A)	1:11.2	1:12.3	—
Penn National (Pen)	1:10.4(B)	1:45.1(A)	1:10.1	1:11.3	1:13(B)
Pimlico (Pim)	1:12(C)	1:45(A)	1:11	1:12.2	—
Pleasanton(Pln)	1:10 (B)	1:43.1(A)	1:10	1:11.2	1:05.1(A)
Portland Meadows(PM)	1:12 (B)	1:45.4(B)	1:12.1	1:13.3	1:07.2(A)
River Downs (RD)	1:11.3(C)	1:46 (C)	1:11.3	1:12.4	1:13.1(B)
Rockingham (Rkm)	1:11.1(B)	1:45 (A)	1:10.3	1:11.4	1:12.1(B)
Sacramento (Sac)	1:09.1(B)	1:42.2(A)	1:09.1	1:10.3	1:10.4(A)
Santa Anita (SA)	1:10.2(B)	1:43.4(A)	1:09	1:10.1	1:10.3(C)
Santa Fe (SFe)	1:11.1(B)	1:45.3(A)	1:11.2	1:12.4	1:12.4(B)
Santa Rosa (SR)	1:10.3(B)	1:43.4(A)	1:10.3	1:12	1:12.1(A)
Saratoga (Sar)	1:10.3(C)	*1:51.1(A)	1:09.1	1:10.2	1:10.4(B)
Stockton (Stk)	1:10.2(B)	1:44(A)	1:10.2	1:11.4	1:12 (A)
Suffolk Downs (Suf)	1:11 (B)	1:44.3(A)	1:10.2	1:11.4	1:11.4(C)
Sunland (Sun)	1:11 (C)	1:44.3(C)	1:11	1:12.2	1:12.2(D)
Thistledown (Tdn)	1:12.3(C)	1:47.1(A)	1:12.3	1:14	1:14.2(C)
Turf Paradise (TuP)	1:09.2(B)	1:42.4(C)	1:09.1	1:10.3	1:10.3(D)
Waterford (Wat)	1:10.2(B)	1:43.3(A)	1:10.4	1:12.1	—
Woodbine (Wo)	1:11.1(C)	1:45.2(C)	1:10.2	1:11.3	1:11.4(C)
Yakima Meadows (YM)	1:10.3(A)	1:44 (A)	1:10.4	1:12.1	—

* indicates 1¼ miles, rather than 1 1/16 miles.

times—the times normal for each class of race at each distance on an average day at any race track in North America. Comparison of official running times with these par figures indicates whether a track was faster or slower than par on a given day, and by how much.

○ THE PAR TIMES TABLES ○

A computer study of hundreds of thousands of races at all distances on all North American tracks not only has established these par times for each class and distance, but has shown that the differences among various norms are standard and predictable. After par times have been established for one class of race—we use older (3up or 4up) male $10,000 claimers as our base—certain patterns can be used to es-

Table 2

	1 Turn	2 Turns	3 Turns	CLF	MSW	2-MSW
Assiniboia Downs (AsD)	6F=1:10.4(A)	1M=1:38(C)		1:11.2	1:12.4	1:12.4(B)
Atokad (Ato)	4F=0:45.2	6F=1:12.4(A)	1 1/16M=1:46.1(A)	1:13	1:14.2	1:15.4(C)
Balmoral (Bml)		6F=1:17.2(B)	1 1/16M=1:53.2(C)	1:10.4	1:12.2	
Berkshire Downs(BD)	5F=1:04	@6 1/2F=1:30.4	@1 1/8M=2:05	1:31.3		
Cahokia Downs(Cka)	5F=0:58.3(D)	6 1/2F=1:19.1(D)	1M=1:39.3	1:19.2	1:20.4	
Charles Town(CT)	4 1/2F=0:52.4	6 1/2F=1:20.2(A)	1 1/16M=1:47(B)	1:20.1	1:21.2	
Columbus (Neb) (Cls)		6F=1:12.3(B)	1 1/16M=1:46(B)	1:12.4	1:14.1	1:15.3(C)
Commodore Downs (Com)	5F=0:59.4(D)	6 1/2F=1:20.4(C)	1M=1:40.3(C)	1:21.2	1:22.3	
Delta Downs (DeD)	5F=1:00(B)	6 1/2F= 1:21.1(B)	1 1/16M=1:47(A)	1:21.2	1:22.3	1:01.2(A)
Evangeline Downs (EvD)	5F=0:58.4(B)	6 1/2F=1:20.2(B)	1M=1:40(A)	1:20.3	1:21.4	1:00.3(A)
Exhibition Park (EP)		6 1/2F=1:18.1(C)	1 1/16M=1:45.3(C)	1:18	1:19.1	
Fonner (Fon)	4F=0:45.3	6F=1:12.1(C)	1M=1:38.3(A)	1:12.2	1:13.4	0:47.1(A)
Great Barrington (GBF)	5F=1:01.4	@6 1/2F=1:28.1	@1 1/16M=1:51.4	1:29		
Green Mountain (GM)	5F=0:59	7 1/2F=1:33(A)	1M=1:39.2(A)	1:33.2	1:34.4	
Greenwood (Grd)	4 1/2F=0:53.1	7F=1:26.1(A)	1 3/4M=2:00(A)	1:25.3	1:26.4	1:27.1(D)
Hazel Park (HP)	4F=0:46.2	6 1/2F=1:20(B)	1M=1:41.2(C)	1:19.3	1:21	
Jefferson Downs (JnD)	5F=0:59(B)	6 1/2F=1:20.2(B)	1 70M=1:44.2(A)	1:20.2	1:21.4	1:22.1(B)
La Mesa (LaM)	6F=1:10.4(G)	1 1/16M=1:45.3(E)		1:11	1:12.2	1:12.2(B)
Lethbridge (Lbg)		@5F=0:58.3	@7F :1:27.4	0:59.1	1:00.3	
Lincoln (Neb) (LnN)	4F=0:46	6F=1:12.4	1 1/16M=1:47.2(E)	1:13	1:14.2	1:15.3(B)
Lincoln Downs (LD)	5F=0:59.3	7F=1:27.3(A)	1M=1:40.4(C)	1:27.3	1:28.4	
Los Alamitos (LA)		6F=1:11.1(A)	1 1/16M=1:44(A)	1:10.2	1:11.4	1:12.1(D)
Marquis Downs (MD)		6F=1:11.4(B)	1M=1:38.3(B)	1:12.2	1:13.4	
Marshfield (MF)	@5F=1:03.3	@6 1/2F=1:27.1	@1 1/16M=1:52.2	1:28		
Northhampton (Nmp)	@5F=0:57.3	@6 1/2F=1:23	@1 1/16M=1:52.2	1:23.4		
Northlands (NP)	3 1/2F=0:40	6F=1:11.3(B)	1M=1:38.2(A)	1:12	1:13.2	1:14(B)
Park Jefferson (PJ)		6F=1:12.3	7F=1:27.2	1:13.1	1:14.3	
Playfair (Pla)		6F=1:12(E)	1 1/16M=1:45(C)	1:12.1	1:13.3	1:14.3(A)
Pocono Downs (Poc)	3 1/2F=0:38	6F=1:12.3(C)	1M=1:40(B)	1:13	1:14.2	

150

Track						
Pomona (Pom)		6F=1:10.1(B)	$1\frac{1}{16}$M=1:44.3(A)	1:10.1	1:11.2	1:11.2(C)
Prescott Downs (Pre)		$5\frac{1}{2}$F=1:06.1(G)	7F=1:27.3	1:06.4	1:08.1	1:08.2(B)
Rillito (Ril)	4F=0:46	6F=1:12(C)	1M=1:39.2(E)	1:12.3	1:14	1:14
Ruidoso Downs (Rui)		6F=1:13.1(C)	1M=1:41.1(C)	1:13.2	1:14.4	1:14.4(B)
Salem (Sal)		6F=1:13.2(D)	1M=1:40.1(C)	1:13.4	1:15.1	1:15.2(C)
Sandown Park (San)	$3\frac{1}{2}$F=0:39.4	$6\frac{1}{2}$F=1:22.1	1M=1:43.3(E)	1:22.1	1:23.3	—
Shenandoah Downs (ShD)	6F=1:09.4(B)	6F=1:13(A)	1M=1:40.4(C)	1:12.4	1:14	1:14
Solano (Sol)	4F=0:46.4	$1\frac{1}{16}$M=1:43.2(A)		1:09.4	1:11.1	1:05(A)
Sportmans (Spt)	4F=0:45.3	$6\frac{1}{2}$F=1:18	$1\frac{1}{16}$M=1:46.3(B)	1:17.2	1:18.4	1:18.4(D)
Stampede (Stp)		6F=1:11.1(C)	$1\frac{1}{16}$M=1:44.4(C)	1:11.3	1:13	—
Thistledown (Inner) (Tdn)	5F=1:00.2	1M=1:43.2(A)		1:00.2	1:01.4	—
Timonium (Tim)	4F=0:46.1	$6\frac{1}{2}$F=1:18.1	$1\frac{1}{16}$M=1:46.4(A)	1:17.3	1:19	1:19(B)

SPECIAL DISTANCES

Pocono Downs: @$6\frac{1}{2}$F=1:17.1	Park Jefferson : $5\frac{1}{2}$F=1:07.1
Great Barrington : @$5\frac{1}{4}$F=1:06.2	Park Jefferson : $1\frac{1}{16}$M=1:48(C)
Jefferson Downs : @6F=1:13.3	Prescott Downs : $1\frac{1}{16}$M=1:49
Sportsmans : 6F=1:13	Greenwood : $1\frac{1}{16}$M=1:46
Cahokia Downs : 1^{70}M=1:43.2	Lethbridge : 5F=0:59.3
Cahokia Downs : @ $1\frac{1}{16}$M=1:45.4	Lethbridge : 7F=1:29.1
Hazel Park : 6F=1:13.3	Lethbridge : $1\frac{1}{16}$M=1:50.2
Thistledown Inner : $7\frac{1}{2}$F=1:37.1	Stampede : 7F=1:24.2
Rillito : $7\frac{1}{2}$F=1:32.3	Assiniboia Downs : 7F=1:24.4

tablish par times for all other classes, and for races restricted to fillies and mares, to three-year-olds, or to two-year-olds.

The first step in creating a par-times table for a given track is to locate that track on either Table 1 or Table 2. If the track is one mile or longer in circumference, it can be found on Table 1, which includes (among other things) par times for older male $10,000 claimers at six furlongs and $1\frac{1}{16}$ miles (in some cases, $1\frac{1}{8}$ miles). All the smaller tracks (the "bullrings") can be found on Table 2, which lists pars for older male $10,000 claimers at the most frequently used one-, two-, and three-turn distances. Par times for special distances (one-turn routes, special chutes, etc.) are included at the bottom of both tables.

Listed with each[1] par time is a letter referring to one of the sprint or route patterns found in Table 3. These patterns determine the differences between the $10,000 par times at the different sprint or route distances.

Table 3

SPRINT PATTERNS

	4F →	$4\frac{1}{2}$F →	5F →	$5\frac{1}{2}$F →	6F →	$6\frac{1}{2}$F →	7F →	$7\frac{1}{2}$F
A:	:06	:06	:06.1	:06.1	:06.2	:06.2	:06.3	
B:	:06	:06.1	:06.1	:06.2	:06.2	:06.3	:06.3	
C:	:06.1	:06.1	:06.2	:06.2	:06.3	:06.3	:06.4	
D	:06.1	:06.2	:06.2	:06.3	:06.3	:06.4	:06.4	
E:	:06.2	:06.2	:06.3	:06.3	:06.4	:06.4	:07	
F:	:06.2	:06.3	:06.3	:06.4	:06.4	:07	:07	
G:	:06.3	:06.3	:06.4	:06.4	:07	:07	:07.1	
H:	:06.3	:06.4	:06.4	:07	:07	:07.1	:07.1	

ROUTE PATTERNS

	1M →	$1\frac{1}{16}$ M →	$1\frac{1}{8}$M →	$1\frac{3}{16}$M →	$1\frac{1}{4}$M
A:	:06.3	:06.3	:06.4	:06.4	
B:	:06.3	:06.4	:06.4	:07	
C:	:06.4	:06.4	:07	:07	
D:	:06.4	:07	:07	:07.1	
E:	:07	:07	:07.1	:07.1	

	1M →	1^{40}M →	1^{70}M →	$1\frac{1}{16}$M
:06.3:	:02.2	:01.4	:02.2	
:06.4:	:02.2	:01.4	:02.3	
:07 :	:02.2	:02	:02.3	
:07.1:	:02.3	:02	:02.3	

Belmont, for example, has pars of 1:11.3 for six furlongs and 1:44.2 for $1\frac{1}{16}$ miles (see Table 1), and calls for sprint pattern B and route pattern A. Consequently, the par for six and a half furlongs is :06.2 seconds slower than the par for six furlongs, and the par for seven furlongs is :06.3 slower than the par for six and a half furlongs. Likewise, the

[1] If a par time appears without such a letter, that track cards races at no other distance around the same number of turns.

one-mile par is :06.3 faster than the $1\frac{1}{16}$ mile par, while the $1\frac{1}{8}$ mile par is :06.3 slower than the $1\frac{1}{16}$ mile par. This gives the following list of $10,000 par times for Belmont's six basic distances:

$$
\begin{aligned}
6 \text{ furlongs} &= 1{:}11.3 \\
6\tfrac{1}{2} \text{ furlongs} &= 1{:}18 \\
7 \text{ furlongs} &= 1{:}24.3 \\
1 \text{ mile} &= 1{:}37.4 \\
1\tfrac{1}{16} \text{ miles} &= 1{:}44.2 \\
1\tfrac{1}{8} \text{ miles} &= 1{:}51
\end{aligned}
$$

(We choose to omit pars for the infrequently used $1\frac{3}{16}$, $1\frac{1}{4}$, and $1\frac{1}{2}$ mile distances. Pars for two-year-olds at the $5\frac{1}{2}$-furlong distance will be discussed later.)

Monmouth (see Table 1) has a six-furlong par of 1:10.4 and a $1\frac{1}{16}$ mile par of 1:45, and also calls for sprint pattern B and route pattern A. Consequently, Monmouth's 1 mile par is :06.3 faster than its $1\frac{1}{16}$ mile par, and its $1\frac{1}{8}$ mile par :06.3 slower. Monmouth also cards races at the one mile, 70 yards distance. Table 3 also contains a "pattern" indicating how to determine one mile, 40 yards, and one mile, 70 yards pars, relative to the difference between the pars for one mile and $1\frac{1}{16}$ miles. If that difference is :06.3, as it is at Monmouth, par for one mile, 70 yards is :02.2 faster than par for $1\frac{1}{16}$ miles. Here, then, are the $10,000 pars for Monmouth's five basic distances:

$$
\begin{aligned}
6 \text{ furlongs} &= 1{:}10.4 \\
1 \text{ mile} &= 1{:}38.2 \\
1 \text{ mile, 70 yds.} &= 1{:}42.3 \\
1\tfrac{1}{16} \text{ miles} &= 1{:}45 \\
1\tfrac{1}{8} \text{ miles} &= 1{:}51.3
\end{aligned}
$$

This is the second step of the process: Using Table 1 or Table 2 and the patterns in Table 3, determine the par times for older male $10,000 claimers at all frequently used distances. The reader is assured that large enough samples were used in determining these times, so that the par times for the various distance at each track are accurately correlated.

Note that $10,000 claiming horses run six furlongs in 1:10.2 at both Santa Anita and Golden Gate. However, this same class of horse runs $1\frac{1}{16}$ miles in 1:43.4 at Santa Anita, but covers the same distance in only 1:44.3 at Golden Gate. Every track has its own unique characteristics, attributable to its shape, the texture of its racing surface, or the prevailing direction of the wind. These combine to affect racing times at each track. Above all, these differences among tracks defeat any attempt to use a single set of par times at all tracks. The handicapper must use the par times that apply to his particular track—or his figures will be useless.

Some tracks just happen to be faster than others. The par times tables make these differences precise. A $10,000 claiming horse at Longacres normally runs six furlongs in a quick 1:09.3. Its counterpart at Belmont covers the same distance in a more pedestrian 1:11.3. This does not mean that a $10,000 horse at Longacres is a better (faster) animal than its counterpart in New York, but rather that the Longacres racing surface is more conducive to fast times.

New York fans can learn from the par times tables that Aqueduct's new Inner Track is $\frac{3}{5}$ slower than the older main track at six furlongs, and that Saratoga is at least $\frac{4}{5}$ faster than any of the down-state tracks at that distance. New Jerseyites will discover that the Meadowlands is a full seven lengths slower than Monmouth. Fans throughout the country will be able to make precise comparisons of times at different tracks in their locale.

○ PAR TIMES FOR CLAIMING RACES ○

The third step in the process of creating par times tables is to adjust the par times for $10,000 claiming races to obtain par times for all other claiming classes at all distances. Table 4 indicates, in fifths of a second, what these adjustments are.

Table 4

	$3\frac{1}{2}$F	4F	$4\frac{1}{2}$F	5F	$5\frac{1}{2}$F 6F $6\frac{1}{2}$F	7F $7\frac{1}{2}$F	1M 1^{40}M	1^{70}M $1\frac{1}{16}$M	$1\frac{1}{8}$M
$50,000	−3	−4	−5	−5	−6	−7	−9	−9	−10
$40,000	−3	−4	−5	−5	−6	−6	−8	−8	−9
$35,000	−3	−4	−5	−5	−5	−5	−7	−7	−8
$30,000	−3	−4	−5	−5	−5	−5	−6	−6	−7
$25,000	−2	−3	−4	−4	−4	−4	−5	−5	−6
$20,000	−2	−2	−3	−3	−3	−3	−4	−4	−4
$18,000	−2	−2	−2	−2	−2	−2	−3	−3	−3
$15,000	−1	−1	−2	−2	−2	−2	−2	−2	−2
$13,000	−1	−1	−1	−1	−1	−1	−1	−1	−1
$10,000	0	0	0	0	0	0	0	0	0
$8,500	+1	+1	+1	+1	+1	+1	+1	+1	+1
$7,500	+1	+1	+1	+2	+2	+2	+2	+2	+2
$6,500	+1	+1	+1	+2	+3	+3	+3	+3	+3

	3½F	4F	4½F	5F	5½F 6F 6½F	7F 7½F	1M 1^{40}M	1^{70}M 1$\frac{1}{16}$M	1⅛M
$5,000	+2	+2	+2	+3	+4	+4	+4	+4	+4
$4,000	+3	+3	+3	+4	+5	+5	+5	+5	+5
$3,500	+3	+3	+3	+4	+5	+5	+5	+6	+6
$3,200	+4	+4	+4	+5	+6	+6	+6	+7	+7
$3,000	+4	+4	+4	+5	+6	+6	+7	+8	+8
$2,500	+5	+5	+5	+6	+7	+7	+8	+9	+9
$2,000	+5	+5	+6	+7	+8	+8	+9	+10	+11
$1,750	+6	+6	+7	+8	+9	+9	+10	+11	+12
$1,500	+6	+6	+7	+8	+9	+10	+11	+12	+13
$1,250	+6	+7	+8	+9	+10	+11	+12	+13	+14
$1,000	+6	+7	+8	+9	+10	+11	+13	+14	+15

So $5,000 claimers normally run six furlongs $\frac{4}{5}$ of a second slower than $10,000 claimers do, at any track. And $20,000 claimers normally cover 1⅛ miles $\frac{4}{5}$ of a second faster than $10,000 claimers do. Anywhere.

As an example of how to use Table 4, we use the par times for older male $10,000 claimers at Belmont as the base from which to construct the complete par times table for older male claiming horses at Belmont (see Table 5).

Table 5

BELMONT CLAIMING PAR TIMES

	6F	6½F	7F	1M	1$\frac{1}{16}$M	1⅛M
$50,000	1:10.2	1:16.4	1:23.1	1:36	1:42.3	1:49
$35,000	1:10.3	1:17	1:23.3	1:36.2	1:43	1:49.2
$25,000	1:10.4	1:17.1	1:23.4	1:36.4	1:43.2	1:49.4
$20,000	1:11	1:17.2	1:24	1:37	1:43.3	1:50.1
$15,000	1:11.1	1:17.3	1:24.1	1:37.2	1:44	1:50.3
$13,000	1:11.2	1:17.4	1:24.2	1:37.3	1:44.1	1:50.4
$10,000	1:11.3	1:18	1:24.3	1:37.4	1:44.2	1:51
$8,500	1:11.4	1:18.1	1:24.4	1:38	1:44.3	1:51.1
$7,500	1:12	1:18.2	1:25	1:38.1	1:44.4	1:51.2
$6,500	1:12.1	1:18.3	1:25.1	1:38.2	1:45	1:51.3
$5,000	1:12.2	1:18.4	1:25.2	1:38.3	1:45.1	1:51.4
$3,500	1:12.3	1:19	1:25.3	1:38.4	1:45.3	1:52.1

Note: *This table omits several "in-between" classes listed on Table 4— namely, $40,000, $30,000, $18,000, and $4,000. Their sprint pars are identical to those for similarly priced classes, as set forth in Table 4. Their route pars fill in the gaps on this table.*

○ PAR TIMES FOR ALLOWANCE RACES ○

The fourth step in the process of constructing par times tables deals with allowance races.

Par times at six furlongs (or the most frequently used sprint distance) for older male classified (CLF) allowance and maiden special weight (MSW) races at any given track can be found in columns 3 and 4 of Table 1, or in columns 4 and 5 of Table 2. These six-furlong pars point to the claiming classification that shares its pars at all distances with the CLF or MSW races.

At Belmont, for example, the six-furlong par for MSW races is 1:11.2, same as the six-furlong par for $13,000 claiming horses. Consequently, all MSW pars will equal the par at the distance for $13,000 claimers.

Similarly, Belmont's six-furlong par for CLF allowances is 1:10.1, which is $\frac{1}{5}$ faster than par for $50,000 claimers. So all of Belmont's CLF pars will be $\frac{1}{5}$ faster than the par at the distance for $50,000 claimers.

Once the MSW pars have been determined, pars for the restricted allowance races (NW1, NW2, and NW3) follow according to the following pattern:

	Sprints	Routes
MSW	0	0
NW1	−2	−3
NW2	−4	−5
NW3	−5	−7

This means, for example, that the average NW1 sprint is run $\frac{2}{5}$ of a second faster than the average MSW sprint. And the average NW3 route is run $\frac{7}{5}$ faster than the average MSW route.

Our statistics indicate that par times for stakes races should be set $\frac{2}{5}$ of a second faster than pars for CLF allowance races, regardless of distance.

Using Belmont as an example once again, here is a table of par times for allowance races for older males:

	6F	6½F	7F	1M	1 1/16 M	1⅛M
Stakes	1:09.4	1:16.1	1:22.3	1:35.2	1:42	1:48.2
CLF	1:10.1	1:16.3	1:23	1:35.4	1:42.2	1:48.4
NW3	1:10.2	1:16.4	1:23.2	1:36.1	1:42.4	1:49.2
NW2	1:10.3	1:17	1:23.3	1:36.3	1:43.1	1:49.4
NW1	1:11	1:17.2	1:24	1:37	1:43.3	1:50.1
MSW	1:11.2	1:17.4	1:24.2	1:37.3	1:44.1	1:50.4

Our study has also shown that average times for the MSW and restricted (not classified) allowance races vary according to the time of the year. Such races are faster early in the year, simply because more talented horses are still eligible to run in them. Our statistics show the following seasonal variations:

January-February	$-\frac{2}{5}$
March-April-May	$-\frac{1}{5}$
June-July-August	0
September-October	$+\frac{1}{5}$
November-December	$+\frac{2}{5}$

For tracks that run split or exceptionally long meetings, the MSW par listed in the table reflects a year-long average. The reader should be aware that running times may be slightly faster early in the year (meet), then slower towards the end of the year (meet).

The par times for the CLF and MSW races allow the reader, at a glance, to compare the caliber of racing at different tracks. Oaklawn Park, for example, presents slightly better racing than does the Fair Grounds, because classified allowance horses at Oaklawn tend to run as fast as $35,000 claimers there, while their counterparts at Fair Grounds match times with $25,000 claimers. Both are far superior to Louisiana Downs, where classified horses run as fast as $13,000 claimers.

There still remains the problem of where allowance horses of different grades fit into the claiming ranks, and vice versa, at a given track. Just because an NW2 race in New York averages as fast as a $35,000 claiming race does not necessarily imply that a $35,000 horse can move into an NW2 race and be successful, or even competitive. Nor does it imply that an NW2 horse will meet with instant success against $35,000 claiming company.

A small matter called "class" must be considered. An NW2 race might be filled with inexperienced horses that will eventually become stakes runners. Even at this early stage of their development, they probably possess that "touch of class" that allows them to trounce claiming animals that appear, at least on paper, capable of running just as fast.

On the other hand, many claiming horses running for a $35,000 tag have probably, at some time in their careers, won allowance races. They climbed the allowance ladder as far as they could, perhaps all the way to the top, and then entered the claiming ranks when age or infirmities began to affect them. In other words, many of the entrants in a $35,000 claiming race were once good enough to win an NW2 race. The question that must be answered, of course, is whether they are good enough *now* to win such a race, or to beat horses of that caliber.

The answer to this question varies with the locality. The serious reader would be wise to investigate for himself what price claiming horse is competitive in the different types of allowance races run at his local track(s).

○ PAR TIMES FOR MAIDEN CLAIMING RACES ○

Most horses running in maiden claiming races have neither the talent to compete successfully in MSW races nor the experience to do well in straight (non-maiden) claiming races of the same price. Our study reveals that the typical maiden claiming sprint is run one full second slower than the average straight claimer of the same price. Maiden claimers at a mile or longer normally are $\frac{7}{5}$ slower than comparable straight claimers at the same distance.

For example, a maiden $20,000 claimer for older males at six furlongs will be run in 1:11 + :01 = 1:12 (on the average) at Belmont. The same kind of horse will cover $1\frac{1}{16}$ miles in 1:43.3 + $\frac{7}{5}$ = 1:45.

○ PAR TIMES FOR RESTRICTED CLAIMING RACES ○

Apparently, the winner of a typical maiden claiming race must improve several lengths to be competitive in a straight claiming race of comparable price. But not all claiming races are open to all horses on the grounds. Some, especially at smaller tracks, are restricted to horses that have yet to win one, two, or three races since leaving the maiden ranks (two, three, or four races lifetime). The following table, which uses straight claiming races as the base, shows how to determine par times for claiming races restricted to limited winners:

	Sprints	Routes
Straight Claiming	0	0
NW3	$+\frac{1}{5}$	$+\frac{2}{5}$
NW2	$+\frac{2}{5}$	$+\frac{3}{5}$
NW1	$+\frac{3}{5}$	$+\frac{5}{5}$
Maiden Claiming	$+\frac{5}{5}$	$+\frac{7}{5}$

At River Downs, for example, a $10,000 claiming race restricted to horses aged three years and up that have yet to win two races other than a maiden race (NW2) has par time of 1:11.3 + $\frac{2}{5}$ = 1:12 at six furlongs, or 1:46 + $\frac{3}{5}$ = 1:46.3 at $1\frac{1}{16}$ miles.

158

○ PAR TIMES FOR FILLIES AND MARES ○

Races restricted to fillies and mares are slower than male races of equivalent class or claiming price. How much slower? Our studies show that the average sprint for females is $\frac{2}{5}$ of a second slower than a sprint for males of the same class. In races at a mile or longer, the times for females are $\frac{3}{5}$ slower.

So, for example, par time for older $15,000 fillies and mares running six furlongs at Belmont equals $1:11.1 + \frac{2}{5} = 1:11.3$. And par time for older $7,500 fillies and mares going $1\frac{1}{16}$ miles at Belmont is $1:44.4 + \frac{3}{5} = 1:45.2$.

○ PAR TIMES FOR THREE-YEAR-OLDS ○

When three-year-olds race against older horses they receive a weight allowance, the size of which decreases as the year moves along. This allowance is supposed to compensate for the fact that the three-year-old thoroughbred has yet to reach physical maturity.

Consequently, one would expect par times for races restricted to three-year-olds to be somewhat slower than those for races among older horses of comparable class. This is so, and the differences decrease as the year passes.

The table below shows those differences in fifths of a second, and the dates on which the differences change. The differences appear in the left and right margins, the dates in the body of the table.

	6F	6½F	7F	$1M–1^{40}M$	$1^{70}M–1\frac{1}{16}M$	$1\frac{1}{8}M$	
+9						Jan. 1	+9
+8						Feb. 1	+8
+7					Jan. 1	Mar. 15	+7
+6					Feb. 15	May 1	+6
+5				Jan. 1	Apr. 15	June 1	+5
+4		Jan. 1	Jan. 1	Apr. 15	June 1	July 1	+4
+3	Jan. 1	Feb. 1	Mar. 15	June 1	July 1	Aug. 1	+3
+2	Apr. 15	June 1	June 15	July 15	Aug. 15	Sept. 15	+2
+1	July 1	Aug. 1	Aug. 15	Sept. 15	Oct. 15	Dec. 1	+1
0	Nov. 1	Dec. 1	Dec. 15	——	——	——	0

For example, reading down the six furlongs column of the table, we find that par time for three-year-olds at six furlongs should be set $\frac{3}{5}$ of a second slower than par for older horses of comparable class early in the year. The difference should be reduced to $\frac{2}{5}$ on April 15, and then to $\frac{1}{5}$ on July 1. After November 1, there is no difference.

The other five columns read in the same manner, from top to bottom. Here, for example, are the par times for races restricted to three-year-old $10,000 claimers at Belmont on or about June 10:

$$6 \text{ furlongs} = 1:11.3 + \tfrac{2}{5} = 1:12$$
$$6\tfrac{1}{2} \text{ furlongs} = 1:18 \quad + \tfrac{2}{5} = 1:18.2$$
$$7 \text{ furlongs} = 1:24.3 + \tfrac{3}{5} = 1:25.1$$
$$1 \text{ mile} = 1:37.4 + \tfrac{3}{5} = 1:38.2$$
$$1\tfrac{1}{16} \text{ miles} = 1:44.2 + \tfrac{4}{5} = 1:45.1$$
$$1\tfrac{1}{8} \text{ miles} = 1:51 \quad + \tfrac{5}{5} = 1:52$$

In one exceptional case, the times for three-year-olds appear out of phase with the times for older horses. High-priced ($25,000–$50,000) three-year-old claiming races early in the year tend to average a few points slower than par. Many of the horses in these races run with highly inflated price tags, and are destined to run much cheaper later in the year, after competition has revealed their true worth. On the other hand, high-priced claiming races for older horses attract horses of established value, many of whom had been competitive in allowance races in their younger days. A little older and slower now, they are still far superior to the average three-year-old running for a similar claiming price early in the year. It would be unreasonable to expect these youngsters to run within "scale" time of their older counterparts.

○ PAR TIMES FOR TWO-YEAR-OLDS ○

Our study of two-year-old times was complicated by the fact that the vast majority of two-year-old races are run at sprint distances, a high percentage at six furlongs or shorter. Consequently, it is impossible to make a valid statement concerning how fast a two-year-old can be expected to run a given route distance, and we will not attempt to do so.

The computer has, however, been able to make an accurate assessment of two-year-old sprint times. The last column of both Table 1 and Table 2 contains par times for two-year-old MSW races at six furlongs,[1] together with a letter indicating the season to which the time applies.

[1]Some tracks scheduled so few races for two-year-olds that it was impossible to calculate accurate par times, and so none is listed. For those tracks which do not race during the latter half of the year, the table includes a par for a distance shorter than 6 furlongs. At tracks where 6 furlongs is not "the" sprint distance, the par for the appropriate distance is listed.

Our study revealed that there were basically four different "seasons" for two-year-old par times:

(A)   January through June,
(B)   July and August,
(C)   September and October,
(D)   November and December.

The study also indicated a ⅕ of a second difference between any two consecutive time periods.

At Belmont, for example, the two-year-old MSW par is 1:11.3, during time period C—the Fall Championship meet. Belmont also cards six-furlong races for juveniles during July, one time period earlier. Par that month would be 1:11.4, one tick slower than during September and October.

Once a two-year-old time at six furlongs is known, times for the other sprint distances follow from the appropriate sprint pattern, with one major exception: the differences between six and six and a half, and six and a half and seven furlongs tend to be ⅕ more than the pattern indicates.

At Belmont, which requires sprint pattern B, the difference (for two-year-olds) between six and six and a half furlongs is :06.3 (rather than :06.2), and the difference between six and a half and seven furlongs :06.4 (rather than :06.3). So, during September and October, Belmont's two-year-old MSW par at six and a half furlongs is 1:11.3 + :06.3 = 1:18.1; at seven furlongs, the par is 1:18.1 + :06.4 = 1:25.

Pars at distances shorter than six furlongs are determined according to the appropriate sprint pattern. So Belmont's two-year-old MSW par at five and a half furlongs during July is 1:11.4 − :06.2 = 1:05.2. During May and June, this par is 1:12 − :06.2 = 1:05.3 (notice that 1:12 is used here for 6 furlongs—⅕ slower than during July—to account for moving back one more time period).

Once the MSW pars are known, allowance pars follow from the allowance pattern (as used for older horses). Juvenile stakes pars tend to average ⅗ faster than MSW pars during time period (A), with the difference an additional ⅕ more for each succeeding time period.

Par times for two-year-old maiden claiming races at six furlongs differ from the par for the same class straight claimer for older horses according to the following table:

Time Period	Difference
A	$+\frac{12}{5}$
B	$+\frac{11}{5}$
C	$+\frac{10}{5}$
D	$+\frac{9}{5}$

One full second of these differences is the usual difference between maiden and straight claiming. The rest has to do with the age difference, and decreases as the year progresses. Recall that three-year-old maiden claimers at six furlongs during January tend to average $\frac{8}{5}$ slower than do straight claimers of comparable price. So the two-year-old pars seem to "fit" with the pars for older horses.

At Belmont, a $25,000 maiden claimer for two-year-olds at six furlongs during September would have an expected time of $1:10.4 + \frac{10}{5} = 1:12.4$. During July, the par would be $1:13$—$\frac{1}{5}$ slower.

As the season progresses, the fields for two-year-old non-maiden claiming races grow stronger and stronger. Toward the end of the year, they actually begin to resemble straight claiming races, rather than claimers restricted to horses that have yet to win two, three, or four races lifetime.

Consequently, the differences between the pars for two-year-old maiden and straight claiming grow larger as the year passes. Our study suggests the following differences:

Time Period	Difference
A	$+\frac{2}{5}$
B	$+\frac{2}{5}$
C	$+\frac{3}{5}$
D	$+\frac{4}{5}$

So a $25,000 claiming race for two-year-olds at six furlongs during September at Belmont would have a par of $1:12.4 - \frac{3}{5} = 1:12.1$, which is $\frac{3}{5}$ faster than the par for a $25,000 maiden claiming race. The same type of race run at Belmont during July would have a par of $1:13 - \frac{2}{5} = 1:12.3$.

Since the majority of juvenile races are for maidens, a table of two-year-old par times should highlight the maiden pars, leaving the differences between maiden and non-maiden races to be committed to memory. The table below, for Belmont, demonstrates how this can be done:

	$5\frac{1}{2}$F	$5\frac{1}{2}$F	6F	6F	$6\frac{1}{2}$F	7F
Stakes	1:05	1:04.3	1:11	1:10.3	1:17.1	1:24
NWl	1:05.1	1:05	1:11.2	1:11.1	1:17.4	1:24.3
MSW	1:05.3	1:05.2	1:11.4	1:11.3	1:18.1	1:25
MDN $50,000	1:06.2	1:06.1	1:12.3	1:12.2	1:19	1:25.4
MDN $35,000	1:06.3	1:06.2	1:12.4	1:12.3	1:19.1	1:26
MDN $25,000	1:06.4	1:06.3	1:13	1:12.4	1:19.2	1:26.1
MDN $20,000	1:07	1:06.4	1:13.1	1:13	1:19.3	1:26.2
MDN $15,000	1:07.1	1:07	1:13.2	1:13.1	1:19.4	1:26.3
MDN $13,000	1:07.2	1:07.1	1:13.3	1:13.2	1:20	1:26.4
MDN $10,000	1:07.3	1:07.2	1:13.4	1:13.3	1:20.1	1:27
	May/June	July		September/October		

○ CONCLUSION ○

At this point, the reader is advised to form par times tables for each of his local tracks, plus any others he may wish to follow on a daily basis. These tables can be written on the two sides of a sheet of paper. On one side, include the pars for older male claiming and allowance races at all frequently used distances; on the other side, pars for two-year-old maiden races, and perhaps some note on seasonal time allowances for three-year-olds. Adjustments for maiden races, and for races restricted to fillies and mares, can easily be committed to memory.

Note that our par times apply only to races on dirt tracks. Turf racing is a separate problem best approached in terms of established or potential grass-running ability as indicated in past performances or bloodlines (see Chapter 22).

We have omitted par times for two-year-old route races, marathon routes (races at $1\frac{3}{16}$ miles or longer, although par times for $1\frac{3}{16}$ or $1\frac{1}{4}$ miles can be determined using one of the route patterns), state-bred races, starter allowances, and starter handicaps. However, the running times or speed ratings for any such race no longer than $1\frac{1}{4}$ miles can still be converted into accurate rating figures with the daily variants calculated according to the instructions in the next chapter.

The reader is also assured that these daily variants will compensate should a particular track become noticeably faster or slower during future seasons.

SPEED HANDICAPPING: DAILY VARIANTS

If you know the normal running time for each class, sex, and age group at each distance at your track, it takes only a few minutes to determine whether the track was fast or slow—and to what extent—during a particular afternoon or evening. When you modify speed ratings or official running times with daily variants calculated in accordance with the instructions that follow, you can tell whether one contender has been outperforming others. You often find that a horse with relatively slow running times or low speed ratings has actually been the fastest runner.

○ THE PROCEDURE ○

The daily variant shows whether the track was faster or slower than normal—and by how much—during the course of a single program. The handicapper calculates the variant by comparing the official running time of each race (on dirt) with its par time (if known), noting the deviation from par in fifths of a second, and then averaging the day's (or evening's) deviations.

Deviations from par should be listed in terms of (a) whether each individual race time was faster or slower than par, and (b) the number of fifths of a second of each deviation. For example, a race that was $\frac{2}{5}$ faster than par would be listed as FAST 2. If slower by $\frac{3}{5}$, it would be SLOW 3.

On days when a track is slow, races at a mile or longer usually produce running times with larger deviations. Research shows that if sprints are SLOW 2, routes will be roughly SLOW 3. This "time lag" is evident in Table 4 of the preceding chapter. At six furlongs, $1,000 horses run 3.1 seconds slower than $50,000 horses. At 1 $\frac{1}{16}$ miles, the difference is 4.3 seconds, a ratio of approximately 3:2.

For the most accurate variant on slow days, therefore, the handicapper should reduce route deviations by one third, bringing them into phase with sprint deviations. The resultant average of the day's deviations becomes the sprint variant for that day. To apply that variant to the speed rating or final time of a horse that ran in a route on that day, the handicapper increases the sprint variant by 50 percent. This process usually does not apply on days when a track is fast—route deviations then do not necessarily become larger than sprint deviations.

To illustrate this process, here are the calculations for an imaginary day of racing at Belmont Park. We assume the date to be June 20. Make sure you understand how each par time has been determined.

Race	Conditions	Par	Time	Deviation	Revised Deviation
1.	3up MSW at 1$\frac{1}{16}$ miles	1:44.1	1:44.4	Slow3	Slow2
2.	3F Mdn $15,000 at 6F	1:13	1:12.3	Fast2	Fast2
3.	2 YOS Mdn $35,000 at 5$\frac{1}{2}$F	1:06.3	1:07.1	Slow3	Slow3
4.	3 YOS $10,000 at 6$\frac{1}{2}$F	1:18.2	1:18.2	Par	Par
5.	3 YOS CLF at 1 mile	1:36.2	1:37.4	Slow7	Slow5
6.	3upF NW2 at 7F	1:24	1:24.4	Slow4	Slow4
7.	3F NWl at 6F	1:11.4	1:12.3	Slow4	Slow4
8.	4up CLF at 6F	1:10.1	1:10.2	Slow1	Slow1
9.	4up $15,000 at 1$\frac{1}{8}$ miles	1:50.3	1:50.2	Fast1	Fast1

Note: *Since the day's races appeared a little slower than par, the deviations for the three routes were reduced by one third.*

When all the day's deviations cluster around some SLOW or FAST number, it is perfectly safe to add them, divide by the number of races used in the calculation, and accept the average as the day's variant. For the example above, the variant works out to SLOW 2: The six SLOW races total SLOW 19 while the other three races total FAST 3, for a net of SLOW 16 over 9 races—an average of (approximately) SLOW 2.

On some days, the first five races may be slower than par and the last four may be faster. Or sprints may be faster than par and routes slower. Situations of this type arise for a variety of reasons:

1.   Rainfall may affect track speed during a program.

2.   A track may become slower between the first and last races if drying after a rain. Or if it becomes thoroughly dry during the program, it may be faster at the end of the day than at the beginning.

3.   At a one-mile or longer track, the clubhouse turn is used only for route races and may be slower than the rest of the strip.

4.   Between-race activity of the maintenance crew may increase or reduce track speed.

5.   Shifting winds may help early speed horses to fast final times in some races and slow them to a walk in others, producing slower final times.

Some handicappers overlook these facts, simply lumping all the day's fast and/or slow deviations from par, striking an arithmetical average and using the resultant number as a variant. They do surprisingly well, considering the number of errors they commit. They would achieve more accurate variants and better selections if they applied the following principles:

1.   If the day's sprints were fast (or slow) and the routes were the opposite, and if there were at least two routes on the program, the handicapper should make two separate variants, one for sprints and one for routes. (In this case, it is unnecessary to scale down slow route deviations.)

2.   If the track was fast during one part of the program and slow during the remainder (or vice versa), and if the difference was not attributable to sprints being fast and routes being slow (or vice versa), the handicapper should compute two separate variants—one for races 1, 2, and 3 (for example), and the other for races 4 through 9.

On other days, one or two races may seem totally out of phase with the rest. A deviation of FAST 3 on a day when the other eight races were all run considerably slower than par should be regarded with suspicion.

If distance was not the cause of an abnormally SLOW or FAST deviation, the handicapper should check the *Daily Racing Form* result chart in search of an explanation such as an artificially slow pace, or a speedball breaking free and winning by fifteen lengths, or a severe traffic jam, or a fallen horse. If some such reason turns up, the handicapper can assume that the footing was about as fast (or slow) during that race as during the ones that immediately preceded or followed it. The race's odd deviation from par should be excluded from the calculation of the variant. And the variant should be supplemented with a reminder that the time of the race, and the speed ratings of its horses, should not be taken seriously. Subsequent performances by horses that ran in the race will usually cast ample light on their current speed and class. Until then, their performances previous to the race should suffice for handicapping purposes. But insofar as speed ratings and variants are concerned, the race should be ignored pending further information.

Other unusual deviations from par arise when contenders are off form or a winner proves to be much better than the class of its race might suggest—as when a talented young horse moves up through the allowance ranks. Deviations of the first kind mentioned should be excluded from the calculations of the variant. Those of the second kind may be excluded as well, although in the case of a horse winning by a large margin in exceptionally fast time, it is possible to determine a reasonable deviation for the race. Simply reduce the winning margin to two lengths (the average margin of victory), and then make a similar adjustment in the official running time of the race. For example, a winning margin of eight lengths must be reduced by six lengths, and so $\frac{6}{5}$ must be added to the race's final time. This provides a good guess as to how fast a "typical" winner of such a race would have run.

In either case, when handicapping (at a later date) the performances of horses that ran in either of these kinds of races, the day's variant can be used to modify their speed ratings or final times.

○ USING VARIANTS WITH FINAL TIMES ○

A simple way to rate horses for handicapping purposes is to modify their official running times with the variants for the days on which the races were run.

We assume that the individual horse's final time was the winner's time plus one fifth of a second for each beaten length. Beaten margins of less than half a length are not counted. Half a length is regarded as a full length. Thus, if a horse was beaten by $3\frac{3}{4}$ lengths in a race officially timed in 1:09, we regard its own final time as 1:09.4.

To compare final times at the *same distance over a given track*, modify each running time with the applicable daily variant. Remember to increase slow variants by 50 percent for use with route performances. A variant of SLOW 4 means that the track was four ticks slow, delaying the average winner by that many fifths of a second. In more normal racing conditions, therefore, each horse that ran well would have finished about $\frac{4}{5}$ sooner. This means that $\frac{4}{5}$ must be subtracted from each running time. A handicapper who preferred this method to the ones discussed below could list a SLOW 4 as −4, and a FAST 5 as +5. Why does FAST become plus? When the track is abnormally fast, the horses are credited with faster official running times than they could otherwise achieve. To find out how fast they actually ran on a FAST day, it is necessary to *add* fifths to their running times.

To compare times run at *different distances over the same track* (or at the same distance, for that matter), adjust each time with the correct variant, as above, then find the adjusted time in its proper distance column on the track's par times table, and note the class of race to which that adjusted time corresponds. Example: A horse's final time, plus or minus the variant, for a race at $1\frac{1}{16}$ miles at Oaklawn turns out to be 1:46, which falls midway between par for $20,000 and $15,000 horses. Classify that performance at $17,500. In the same field, another contender's latest final time, plus or minus the variant, was 1:43.2 at a mile and 70 yards at Oaklawn. That is par for a $20,000 winner.

When rating a performance that took place at *another track* for which you also compile variants, follow exactly the same procedure. Find the class of race that corresponds to the adjusted time, and rate the horse accordingly.

Needless to say, it pays to compile variants for all tracks whose names crop up frequently in the past-performance records of the horses that run at your track. That, or be forced to take out-of-town final times at face value, unmodified by accurate variants, usually not good handicapping practice. Of course, if a horse ships from a track of lower quality than your own, you can safely ignore it until it establishes its form in local competition.

○ YOUR OWN SPEED RATINGS ○

Many handicappers prefer speed ratings to final times. One easy plan is to assign a rating of 100 to all the $10,000 par times at each track. At each distance, times faster than the $10,000 pars are assigned ratings above 100, one point for each fifth of a second difference. Times slower than these pars are rated below 100.

A SLOW 3 variant is now a +3, because a slow track produces artificially low speed ratings (slow times) which need to be *increased* by the variant. And a FAST 4 variant is now −4, the extra-speedy track having enabled horses to run faster than they could in normal circumstances. Their speed ratings must be *lowered*.

In the previous example, the horse with the modified final time of 1:46 for a $1\frac{1}{16}$ mile race at Oaklawn has gone $\frac{3}{5}$ faster than the $10,000 par, earning 103. And the other horse has run $\frac{4}{5}$ faster than its $10,000 par, earning 104.

○ DAILY RACING FORM SPEED RATINGS ○

The speed ratings published in the *Daily Racing Form* are calculated by subtracting one point from 100 for each fifth of a second difference between a race's official running time and the track record for the distance. For example, if a six-furlong race at Hollywood Park (track record: 1:07.2) is run in 1:10, its speed rating would be 87, because the difference between 1:07.2 and 1:10 is $\frac{13}{5}$, and $100 - 13 = 87$.

Form speed ratings can be modified by an accurate daily variant as above: *add* for a SLOW track, or *subtract* for a FAST track. If our six-furlong race at Hollywood Park took place on a SLOW 3 day, its adjusted speed rating would be $87 + 3 = 90$. On a FAST 2 day, it would become $87 - 2 = 85$.

Even when modified by a variant, however, *Form* speed ratings present difficulties. Because they are based on local track records, some of which are abnormally fast and others abnormally slow, *Form* speed ratings at different distances or different tracks do not lend themselves to direct comparison with each other.

For example, here are the speed ratings associated with a par race for older male $10,000 claimers at the different distances run at Belmont:

6 furlongs	=	84	(1:11.3 − 1:08.2 = 16)
6½ furlongs	=	86	(1:18 − 1:15.1 = 14)
7 furlongs	=	79	(1:24.3 − 1:20.2 = 21)
1 mile	=	79	(1:37.4 − 1:33.3 = 21)
1$\frac{1}{16}$ miles	=	80	(1:44.2 − 1:40.2 = 20)
1$\frac{1}{8}$ miles	=	72	(1:51 − 1:45.2 = 28)

At Calder, $10,000 horses get the following figures:

6 furlongs	=	94	(1:11.3 − 1:10.2 = 6)
6½ furlongs	=	96	(1:18.1 − 1:17.2 = 4)
7 furlongs	=	91	(1:25 − 1:23.1 = 9)
1 mile, 70 yds.	=	95	(1:43.1 − 1:42.1 = 5)
1$\frac{1}{16}$ miles	=	90	(1:45.4 − 1:43.4 = 10)
1$\frac{1}{8}$ miles	=	92	(1:52.3 − 1:51 = 8)

This is clearly an unacceptable state of affairs. If a $10,000 claimer at Calder "runs its race" at six furlongs, it gets a speed rating of 94. If its counterpart at Belmont runs a par race, it rates only 84, but is not a slower horse because of it. Or a mile race for $10,000 claimers at Belmont might feature one contender coming out of a par race at $1\frac{1}{16}$ miles and another from a recent par race at $1\frac{1}{8}$ miles. Comparison of their speed ratings can only be misleading.

Unless adjustments for distance and track can be made, *Form* speed ratings cannot be a reliable means for separating contenders. But adjustments can be made, and the Speed Rating Adjustment Table on pages 172 and 173 indicates how. After adjusting a speed rating with an accurate daily variant, simply *add* the SR adjustment number for the particular track and distance.

For example, a six-furlong race run in 1:10 at Hollywood Park on a SLOW 3 day earns a speed rating of 87, adjusted to 90 because of the variant. Looking up the table, we find an SR adjustment figure of +14 for six furlongs at Hollywood. Adding this, we get a final figure of $90 + 14 = 104$.

Our SR adjustment figures simply reflect the difference between the $10,000 par and the existing track record at the distance. For example, if the $10,000 par equals an 85 speed rating, the SR adjustment for the distance will be +15.

Consequently, after the daily variant and the appropriate SR adjustment figure have modified the *Form* speed rating, a par (average) race for older male $10,000 claimers will earn a net figure of 100, regardless of distance, or track, or track conditions.

For those who do not care to calculate variants, or for those confronted with shippers from tracks for which variants may not be available, the SR adjustment irons out artificial differences among ratings, producing better results than can be obtained with raw *Form* speed ratings alone.

Remember, the SR adjustment is just the difference between a local $10,000 par and the track record at the distance. To keep the SR figures up to date, be careful to check the table of track records that appears above the *Form* past performances. If you find that any new record was set at your track during the previous meeting, compare the new record with the old.[1] For every fifth of a second difference between the two, *add* one point to the corresponding SR adjustment figure, and use the new SR for races at the current meeting.

[1]The entire Speed Rating Adjustment Table is based on track records in effect on September 30, 1978. These track records can be calculated by *subtracting* the adjustment figure from the $10,000 par time. For example, at Aqueduct, the seven-furlong track record is $\frac{1}{5}$ faster than the $10,000 par of 1:24.2—that is, 1:20.1.

○ THE EASTERN FORM VARIANT ○

In Eastern editions of the *Form*, each speed rating is accompanied by a track variant. The *Form* variant states the average number of fifths of a second between the day's running times and the track records for the various distances that were run. A variant calculated in that way tells as much about the quality of the horses that ran on the given day as it does about the speed of the track.

If you have ever come to New York for the Belmont Stakes, you have witnessed a perfect example of this flaw. Even if the weather and track conditions were identical for the two days, the *Form* variant for Friday will be much higher than the *Form* variant for Saturday, Belmont day. The reason is that the Saturday card will consist almost exclusively of allowance races, while the Friday card will contain several claiming and maiden claiming races. The better animals running on Saturday will run much closer to the track records than did Friday's winners. Of course, this produces a much lower *Form* variant for Saturday.

If a minor track presented a card of eight $1,500 claiming races topped by a feature for $10,000 sprinters, the *Form*'s track variant would be determined for the most part by the times for the eight $1,500 races. By comparison, the time for the $10,000 horses would be outstanding. Adding the *Form* variant to the $10,000 winner's *Form* speed rating will produce a figure in the 108–110 range. Top-class sprinters in New York seldom run to such high figures. But, had a $10,000 race been run on the Belmont day program, its speed figure would have come out well below 100.

○ IMPROVING THE FORM VARIANT ○

Easterners can now obtain an extremely accurate version of the track variant published in their copies of the *Form*, one that reflects only the speed of the racing surface on the particular day. Simply calculate a daily variant by the par-time method explained above, and then use it to modify the track's Par Variant, the number that appears in the last column of the Speed Rating Adjustment Table.

For example, if a day's racing at Bowie turned out to be FAST 3, subtract 3 from Bowie's Par Variant of 25, making the daily variant 22. And if a night's racing at the Meadowlands produced a figure of SLOW 2, add 2 points to Meadowlands Par Variant of 19, making that night's variant 21. Remember, a SLOW 2 variant becomes SLOW 3 for routes.

TRACKS	4F	4.5F	5F	5.5F	6F	6.5F	7F	7.5F	1M	1.40-1.70	8.5F	9F	9.5F	10F	PV
AK-SAR-BEN	0	0	6	14	19	0	16	0	17	0	20	22	0	0	20
ALBUQUERQUE	0	0	10	10	12	0	0	0	0	0	20	17	19	16	20
AQUEDUCT(INNER)	0	0	6	12	16	0	16	0	22	21	0	17	19	31	17
AQUEDUCT(MAIN)	0	0	7	13	14	0	21	0	23	0	22	24	0	28	17
ARLINGTON	2	0	4	7	13	0	12	0	11	0	9	20	22	19	16
ASSINIBOIA DOWNS	3	0	5	12	6	0	16	0	0	0	19	20	0	0	18
ATLANTIC CITY	0	0	7	14	0	0	0	0	8	22	13	12	0	0	18
ATOKAD PARK	0	0	21	25	7	0	0	0	19	0	27	28	10	20	19
BALMORAL	0	0	0	13	14	0	0	0	0	0	20	22	14	24	22
BAY MEADOWS	0	0	11	16	14	0	21	0	21	0	17	0	0	0	30
BELMONT	0	0	24	0	33	0	0	0	0	12	15	48	0	0	25
BERKSHIRE DOWNS	0	-3	5	7	13	0	18	0	13	17	23	15	12	15	16
BEULAH PARK	6	0	1	2	8	0	13	0	10	18	13	0	0	0	15
BOWIE	0	-3	8	6	10	0	14	0	0	4	11	10	4	11	15
CAHOKIA DOWNS	0	-8	-1	0	5	0	12	0	0	11	15	18	7	11	19
CALDER	7	0	4	0	17	0	14	0	23	0	25	25	0	0	20
CALIENTE	1	0	3	12	12	0	8	0	0	4	16	0	0	0	15
CENTENNIAL	4	0	11	7	15	0	15	0	12	0	16	21	12	28	14
CHARLES TOWN	0	0	7	7	12	0	16	0	0	20	20	25	12	24	14
CHURCHILL DOWNS	0	7	6	10	0	0	0	0	12	0	13	15	0	0	20
COLUMBUS(NEB)	0	11	11	13	16	0	0	0	26	0	19	19	11	16	15
COMMODORE DOWNS	0	6	3	0	9	0	10	0	14	-5	0	35	33	0	22
DELAWARE	6	6	0	0	16	0	11	0	16	8	17	20	13	0	17
DEL MAR	5	2	8	6	14	0	2	0	2	12	17	17	17	13	19
DELTA DOWNS	0	0	7	9	0	0	0	0	0	8	6	3	-3	0	15
DETROIT	8	12	11	8	12	0	16	0	16	19	13	10	10	0	21
ELLIS PARK	0	6	3	0	0	0	0	0	0	8	9	8	13	13	16
EVANGELINE DOWNS	6	6	0	10	11	0	0	0	0	33	11	35	37	23	15
EXHIBITION PARK	6	6	0	6	13	0	0	0	0	0	19	23	27	33	31
FAIR GROUNDS	2	5	4	7	12	0	0	0	0	14	-3	20	0	0	24
FAIRMOUNT	6	6	2	4	14	0	0	0	22	12	16	0	0	15	17
FINGER LAKES	0	5	8	0	0	0	0	0	0	2	17	3	-3	0	15
FLORIDA DOWNS	0	0	4	4	3	0	0	0	0	19	17	10	0	21	21
FONNER PARK	0	0	7	11	4	0	0	0	0	9	6	11	13	13	16
FORT ERIE	0	-3	-3	7	11	0	12	0	0	8	13	13	13	11	15
FRESNO	16	0	7	0	22	0	0	0	22	0	11	0	0	0	31
GARDEN STATE	0	0	4	9	13	0	0	0	22	33	19	37	23	44	24
GOLDEN GATE	0	0	0	2	0	0	0	0	0	0	23	27	33	0	19
GREAT BARRINGTON	11	0	3	7	37	0	10	0	0	-3	-3	0	0	0	19
GREEN MOUNTAIN	0	0	4	0	0	0	10	0	0	20	20	0	15	19	17
GREENWOOD	0	0	6	0	13	0	16	0	24	0	22	23	0	0	24
GULFSTREAM	0	0	2	10	12	0	13	0	0	0	24	25	0	29	17
HAWTHORNE	7	0	0	0	0	0	0	0	0	0	15	19	19	0	18
HAZEL PARK	0	0	10	13	17	0	17	0	19	0	23	19	20	21	15
HIALEAH	0	0	8	13	13	0	15	0	0	14	0	0	0	0	20
HOLLYWOOD	5	0	0	0	7	0	0	0	0	0	0	0	0	21	15
JEFFERSON DOWNS	0	5	2	0	17	0	16	0	0	15	18	19	0	21	15
JUAREZ	0	0	0	13	12	0	17	19	0	-1	0	22	21	13	15
KEENELAND															

KEYSTONE	0	0	2	2	12	14	13	0	0	0	9	18	21	0	16	18
LA MESA	-6	-3	5	6	5	0	6	3	11	0	0	9	14	0	0	13
LATONIA	0	0	0	17	22	24	0	0	29	0	0	33	33	0	0	29
LAUREL	0	0	9	0	13	0	14	0	19	0	0	13	16	12	17	19
LETHBRIDGE*	0	5	-1	0	0	18	9	0	0	0	0	5	0	0	0	16
LINCOLN DOWNS	0	0	11	0	0	0	23	18	20	0	20	21	0	0	0	22
LINCOLN(NEB)	4	0	0	0	9	0	0	0	17	0	13	15	15	0	0	18
LONGACRES	0	0	6	5	12	11	0	0	14	0	0	12	17	0	15	19
LOS ALAMITOS	0	0	0	0	6	4	3	0	0	0	0	8	9	0	0	10
LOUISIANA DOWNS	0	0	0	0	13	13	10	0	0	0	13	20	12	0	0	20
MARQUIS DOWNS	0	0	0	2	4	0	0	0	4	0	0	9	0	0	0	15
MARSHFIELD FAIR	0	0	4	0	0	9	0	0	0	0	0	-2	0	0	0	14
MEADOWLANDS	0	0	0	0	16	0	0	0	0	0	19	21	32	0	20	19
MONMOUTH	0	0	5	5	14	0	0	0	19	0	17	20	23	0	24	18
NARRAGANSETT	0	0	6	4	11	0	0	0	0	0	14	16	14	21	-5	19
NORTHHAMPTON FAIR	0	0	14	0	0	6	0	0	0	0	0	16	0	0	0	21
NORTHLANDS	1	0	0	4	8	0	0	0	9	0	0	25	0	0	0	16
OAKLAWN	0	0	0	12	17	0	0	0	0	0	25	25	23	13	14	21
PARK JEFFERSON	0	0	0	5	7	0	10	0	0	0	7	8	0	0	0	20
PENN NATIONAL	0	0	5	6	10	0	0	0	12	0	14	20	7	16	9	15
PIMLICO	0	0	11	7	14	0	0	0	0	0	0	20	16	22	4	20
PLAYFAIR	0	0	0	2	9	15	0	0	9	0	15	6	14	0	0	22
PLEASANTON	0	0	0	6	4	0	0	0	0	0	4	10	13	5	10	12
POCONO DOWNS*	4	0	0	7	8	13	0	0	6	0	18	0	0	0	0	16
PORTLAND MEADOWS	0	4	7	14	13	0	0	0	15	0	11	13	12	5	6	22
POMONA	0	0	0	-1	5	0	0	0	0	0	0	11	12	0	6	12
PRESCOTT DOWNS	0	0	-2	7	0	0	6	0	0	0	0	9	0	0	0	15
RILLITO	3	0	0	3	4	4	4	9	2	0	0	3	-7	0	0	11
RIVER DOWNS	0	0	4	11	15	0	0	0	0	0	17	21	19	11	24	22
ROCKINGHAM *	0	0	9	3	12	0	0	0	0	12	17	15	17	13	27	18
RUIDOSO DOWNS *	5	0	0	8	8	9	9	10	11	0	0	13	17	0	0	14
SACRAMENTO	0	0	0	1	1	0	0	0	0	0	0	7	11	0	2	10
SALEM	0	0	0	8	10	0	0	0	12	0	0	11	0	0	0	20
SANDOWN	0	0	0	0	0	18	0	0	29	0	34	25	0	0	0	31
SANTA ANITA	0	1	0	6	13	14	14	0	17	0	0	18	21	0	24	15
SANTA FE	0	3	8	9	11	8	11	0	12	0	0	16	-1	0	4	18
SANTA ROSA	0	0	0	7	9	0	0	0	10	0	0	12	3	0	0	16
SARATOGA	0	0	0	4	13	11	17	0	0	0	0	0	21	13	23	13
SHENENDOAH DOWNS*	4	0	0	8	11	0	0	0	12	0	9	15	0	0	0	18
SOLANO	0	0	-1	4	5	0	0	0	7	0	0	8	6	0	1	12
SPORTSMANS	10	0	0	0	14	13	0	0	20	0	0	19	21	0	0	20
STAMPEDE PARK	1	0	0	2	4	-8	2	0	7	0	0	5	10	0	0	16
STOCKTON	0	0	0	2	2	0	0	0	9	0	0	11	4	0	10	13
SUFFOLK DOWNS	0	2	5	0	14	0	0	0	13	0	11	14	15	13	19	20
SUNLAND	5	8	8	10	13	13	0	0	10	0	0	13	16	1	6	18
THISTLEDOWN(INNER)	0	0	9	0	0	0	0	18	24	0	20	0	0	0	0	20
THISTLEDOWN(MAIN)	8	10	12	12	19	0	0	0	24	20	17	26	30	25	20	26
TIMONIUM	5	0	0	0	0	9	0	0	9	0	8	13	10	0	0	15
TURF PARADISE	0	1	7	7	10	8	0	0	11	0	0	16	7	5	8	17
WATERFORD	0	-6	2	3	6	0	0	0	3	0	-3	8	14	0	-3	14
WOODBINE	0	0	5	7	13	16	13	0	0	0	11	18	19	17	25	18
YAKIMA MEADOWS	0	5	9	12	8	0	0	0	11	0	0	3	3	0	5	18

Thus, 3 points would be added to Meadowlands 19 to obtain the variant (22) to be used with route speed ratings earned on that evening.

A track's Par Variant is the average *Form* variant for that track. It is highly coordinated with the $10,000 par times presented in the preceding chapter. Both were determined from the same sample of races.

The Par Variant, modified by an accurate daily variant, is used in exactly the same way as the Eastern *Form*'s own variant—both were designed to be added to the *Form* speed rating.

But whether it is the *Form* variant or this more accurate substitute that is added to a *Form* speed rating, the resultant SR+TV figures can be misleading. The following two examples will explain the problem.

Take a look first at what happens when the Par Variant for Belmont is added to that track's $10,000 par speed ratings:

$$
\begin{array}{lll}
\text{6 furlongs} & : 84 + 18 = 102 \\
6\frac{1}{2}\ \text{furlongs} & : 86 + 18 = 104 \\
\text{7 furlongs} & : 79 + 18 = 97 \\
\text{1 mile} & : 79 + 18 = 97 \\
1\frac{1}{16}\ \text{miles} & : 80 + 18 = 98 \\
1\frac{1}{8}\ \text{miles} & : 72 + 18 = 90 \\
\end{array}
$$

Obviously, adjustments will have to be made to iron out differences among figures obtained at different distances.

Then, consider what happens when Suffolk Downs's Par Variant is added to its $10,000 par speed ratings:

$$
\begin{array}{lll}
\text{6 furlongs} & : 86 + 20 = 106 \\
\text{1 mile} & : 87 + 20 = 107 \\
\text{1 mile, 70 yds.} & : 89 + 20 = 109 \\
1\frac{1}{16}\ \text{miles} & : 86 + 20 = 106 \\
1\frac{1}{8}\ \text{miles} & : 85 + 20 = 105 \\
\end{array}
$$

So an average $10,000 claiming race for older male horses will produce a speed figure well above 100, regardless of distance, on a par day at Suffolk Downs. The reason is that a $10,000 horse is a topnotcher at Suffolk, where the average horse is probably worth about $3,500. Now it is the times of average horses that are mainly responsible for a track's Par Variant (or daily *Form* variant). Consequently, when a $3,500 variant is added to a $10,000 speed rating, the resultant speed figure for the $10,000 horse comes out well above 100. Too high, clearly, if these figures are to be used for comparing a $10,000 horse at Suffolk with a $10,000 horse running elsewhere.

Consequently, SR+TV figures must be adjusted not only to equalize figures obtained at different distances, but also to equalize figures obtained by the same class of animal running at different tracks, particularly if the "quality of racing" presented at the tracks is noticeably different.

One adjustment irons out all inequities caused by distance and class of racing.

The adjustment for a particular distance at a specific track can be found in the SR+TV Adjustment Table on pages 176 and 177.

These adjustments simply reflect the difference between the SR adjustment figure for the distance and the track's Par Variant. For example, the SR+TV adjustment figure for six furlongs at Belmont is $16 - 18 = -2$. For $1\frac{1}{8}$ miles at the same track, the adjustment is $28 - 18 = +10$.

SR+TV adjustment figures are simple to use. First, add the *Form* speed rating and a variant—either the *Form* variant, or the appropriate Par Variant modified by an accurate daily variant. Then make the one adjustment called for by the distance and track.

For example, a six-furlong race run in 1:10 at Hollywood Park on a SLOW 3 day earns an SR+TV figure of $87 + 19 = 106$ (the 19 variant is 3 above Hollywood's 16 Par Variant). At the six-furlong distance, Hollywood calls for an adjustment of -2, so the adjusted SR + TV for the race is $106 - 2 = 104$.

This one adjustment insures that an average race for older male $10,000 claimers will receive a speed figure of 100, regardless of distance or track, *provided that an accurate variant has been added* to the race's *Form* speed rating. The adjustment compensates for the exact amount by which the sum of the $10,000 par speed rating and the track's Par Variant misses 100.[2]

For users of the Eastern *Form*, this is the ideal approach. It results in highly accurate figures for local races, figures that are compatible with the slightly less accurate ones obtainable for shippers (by adding their *Form* speed ratings and *Form* variants, and making the proper SR + TV adjustment). To obtain compatible figures for local horses and shippers, users of other editions of the *Form* are advised to use the modified *Form* speed rating, as described above.

Although the *Form* variant is much less satisfactory than one based on par times, computer studies show that it is a helpful supple-

[2]The adjustment involves the following arithmetic: Speed Rating+Par Variant+(SR adjustment—Par Variant), which reduces to Speed Rating + SR adjustment. If the speed rating is for a $10,000 par time, this sum will equal 100, because of the way the SR adjustment was defined.

TRACKS	4F	4.5F	5F	5.5F	6F	6.5F	7F	7.5F	1M	1-40	1-70	8.5F	9F	9.5F	10F	PV
AKSAR-BEN	0	0	-12	-6	-8	-10	0	-3	0	0	0	-3	2	0	0	20
ALBUQUERQUE	0	-14	-10	-4	-8	0	0	-5	0	-4	-12	0	-4	0	-4	19
AQUEDUCT(INNER)	0	-8	-5	-3	-4	0	0	-5	-7	2	-2	-2	-14	14		17
AQUEDUCT(MAIN)	0	-12	-10	-7	-6	-4	0	-1	-5	-7	-2	-10	9			19
ARLINGTON	-14	-7	-9	-10	-2	-8	0	-4	-8	-3	-3	-1	0	0	0	18
ASSINIBOIA DOWNS	0	0	-13	-14	0	-2	0	-6	0	-10	0	-3	2	4	0	29
ATLANTIC CITY	-15	0	-7	-11	-4	0	0	-5	-1	-7	-5	-6	-6	-9	1	16
ATOKAD PARK	0	0	-8	-8	-11	0	0	0	-2	0	0	3	-9	19	19	18
BALMORAL	0	0	0	-6	-4	-7	0	-4	0	0	0	0	10	-4	-1	29
BAY MEADOWS	0	0	-7	-4	-11	0	0	-4	0	-7	0	0	-4	0	6	16
BELMONT	0	0	0	-7	-2	0	0	-5	2	3	0	3	1	-9	-8	38
BERKSHIRE DOWNS	0	-14	-14	-7	0	-7	0	0	-3	-7	0	-6	-6	-2	-9	19
BEULAH PARK	0	-14	-12	0	-9	0	0	-3	-5	0	0	-4	-6	-13	-10	25
BOWIE	-10	0	24	21	0	0	7	0	-3	-7	0	2	-6	-14	-14	15
CAHOKIA DOWNS	-19	0	-13	-13	0	-7	0	-3	-5	-4	-7	-3	-13	-5	-5	15
CALDER	-23	0	-16	-11	-11	0	-2	0	-5	-2	-7	-2	-19	-15	-5	15
CALIENTE	-12	0	-16	-10	0	0	-5	-5	-4	-1	0	-4	-1	-2	-6	19
CENTENNIAL	-18	0	-16	0	0	-2	0	-7	-6	6	0	0	0	-8	21	19
CHARLES TOWN	0	-17	-10	0	0	-7	0	-6	0	-7	0	-5	-7	-10	0	21
CHURCHILL DOWNS	-15	0	0	0	0	-6	0	-4	0	-5	-6	0	0	0	0	16
COLUMBUS(NEB)	0	0	0	-9	-4	0	0	-4	-9	0	-5	0	-7	-7	-12	14
COMMODORE DOWNS	0	-9	-8	-4	-8	0	0	-4	-2	-2	0	9	2	-2	-10	14
DELAWARE	-18	-14	-15	0	-7	-5	0	-2	-3	3	0	0	7	2	4	26
DEL MAR	0	-15	-14	0	-7	-11	0	-27	-14	0	0	-1	0	-1	-1	17
DELTA DOWNS	-16	0	-10	-15	0	0	0	-3	0	0	0	0	-4	0	0	21
DETROIT	0	0	-10	-5	0	-6	0	-3	-7	0	-6	-2	-7	0	-5	19
ELLIS PARK	-13	-14	-11	-13	0	-5	0	-3	-7	-2	-2	0	0	3	-13	21
EVANGELINE DOWNS	0	0	-13	-12	-4	0	0	-5	-9	-22	-6	-11	-13	-5	-5	16
EXHIBITION PARK	0	-12	-4	-13	-5	0	0	-8	-12	0	-1	-6	-22	0	-1	15
FAIR GROUNDS	0	0	-10	-18	-5	0	4	-4	-12	-8	0	-3	-5	-5	-11	16
FAIRMOUNT	0	0	-11	-24	-9	0	0	-5	-5	0	2	2	26	-1	-11	31
FINGER LAKES	0	-15	-20	-24	13	0	0	-9	-8	0	-27	1	5	11	-11	22
FLORIDA DOWNS	0	-20	-20	0	0	-6	0	0	-8	0	-1	0	5	7	-11	24
FONNER PARK	-8	0	0	0	0	-3	0	-2	0	0	1	-2	7	4	8	17
FORT ERIE	0	-14	0	-7	-2	0	0	0	0	-4	0	0	3	5	12	18
FRESNO	0	0	0	-5	-5	0	0	-3	0	0	6	-3	6	6	6	17
GARDEN STATE	-14	0	-12	-8	-1	0	0	-3	3	0	7	3	0	-15	-3	21
GOLDEN GATE	0	0	-8	-8	-1	0	0	-1	2	-22	0	0	-7	3	20	20
GREAT BARRINGTON	-15	0	0	0	0	0	0	-3	0	0	-5	0	-12	-4	-2	11
GREEN MOUNTAIN	0	-10	0	0	-2	2	0	2	0	0	-6	2	-7	-7	6	15
GREENWOOD																
GULFSTREAM																
HAWTHORNE																
HAZEL PARK																
HIALEAH																
HOLLYWOOD																
JEFFERSON DOWNS																
JUAREZ																
KEENELAND																

KEYSTONE	0	0	-16	-16	-6	-4	-5	0	0	0	-9	0	3	0	-2	18
LA MESA	-19	-16	-8	-7	-8	0	-7	-10	-2	0	0	-4	1	0	0	13
LATONIA	0	0	0	-12	-7	-5	0	0	0	0	0	4	4	0	0	29
LAUREL	0	0	-10	0	-6	0	-5	0	0	0	0	-6	-3	-7	-2	19
LETHBRIDGE*	0	-11	-17	0	0	2	-7	0	0	0	0	-11	0	0	0	16
LINCOLN DOWNS	0	0	-11	0	0	0	1	-4	-2	0	-2	-1	0	0	0	22
LINCOLN(NEB)	-14	0	0	0	-9	0	0	0	-1	0	-5	-3	-3	0	0	18
LONGACRES	0	0	-13	-14	-7	-8	0	0	-5	0	0	-7	-2	0	-4	19
LOS ALAMITOS	0	0	0	0	-4	-6	-7	0	0	0	0	-2	-1	0	0	10
LOUISIANA DOWNS	0	0	0	0	-7	-7	-10	0	0	0	-7	0	-8	0	0	20
MARQUIS DOWNS	0	0	0	-13	-11	0	0	0	-11	0	0	-6	0	0	0	15
MARSHFIELD FAIR	0	0	-10	0	0	-5	0	0	0	0	0	-16	0	0	0	14
MEADOWLANDS	0	0	0	0	-3	0	0	0	0	0	0	2	13	0	1	19
MONMOUTH	0	0	-13	-13	-4	0	0	0	1	0	-1	2	5	0	6	18
NARRAGANSETT	0	0	-13	-15	-8	0	0	0	0	0	-5	-3	-5	2	-24	19
NORTHHAMPTON FAIR	0	0	-7	0	0	-15	0	0	0	0	0	-5	0	0	0	21
NORTHLANDS	-15	0	0	-12	-8	0	0	0	-7	0	0	9	0	0	0	16
OAKLAWN	0	0	0	-9	-4	0	0	0	0	0	4	4	2	-8	-7	21
PARK JEFFERSON	0	0	0	-15	-13	0	-10	0	0	0	-13	-12	0	0	0	20
PENN NATIONAL	0	0	-10	-9	-5	0	0	0	-3	0	-1	5	-8	1	-6	15
PIMLICO	0	0	-9	-13	-6	0	0	0	0	0	0	0	-4	2	-16	20
PLAYFAIR	0	0	0	-20	-13	-7	0	0	-13	0	-7	-16	-8	0	0	22
PLEASANTON	0	0	0	-6	-8	0	0	0	0	0	-8	-2	1	-7	-2	12
POCONO DOWNS*	-12	0	0	-9	-8	-3	0	0	-10	0	2	0	0	0	0	16
PORTLAND MEADOWS	0	-18	-15	-8	-9	0	0	0	-7	0	-11	-9	-10	-17	-16	22
POMONA	0	0	0	-13	-7	0	0	0	0	0	0	-1	0	0	-6	12
PRESCOTT DOWNS	0	0	-17	-8	0	0	-9	0	0	0	0	-6	0	0	0	15
RILLITO	-8	0	0	-8	-7	-7	-7	-2	-9	0	0	-8	-18	0	0	11
RIVER DOWNS	0	0	-18	-11	-7	0	0	0	0	0	-5	-1	-3	-11	2	22
ROCKINGHAM	0	0	-9	-15	-6	0	0	0	0	-6	-1	-3	-1	-5	9	18
RUIDOSO DOWNS	-9	0	0	-6	-6	-5	-5	-4	-3	0	0	-1	3	0	0	14
SACRAMENTO	0	0	0	-9	-9	0	0	0	0	0	0	-3	1	0	-8	10
SALEM	0	0	0	-12	-10	0	0	0	-8	0	0	-9	0	0	0	20
SANDOWN	0	0	0	0	0	-13	0	0	-2	0	3	-6	0	0	0	31
SANTA ANITA	0	-14	0	-9	-2	-1	-1	0	2	0	0	3	6	0	9	15
SANTA FE	0	-15	-10	-9	-7	-10	-7	0	-6	0	0	-2	-19	0	-14	18
SANTA ROSA	0	0	0	-9	-7	0	0	0	-6	0	0	-4	-13	0	0	16
SARATOGA	0	0	0	-9	0	-2	4	0	0	0	0	0	8	0	10	13
SHENENDOAH DOWNS*	-14	0	0	-10	-7	0	0	0	-6	0	-9	-3	0	0	0	18
SOLANO	0	0	-13	-8	-7	0	0	0	-5	0	0	-4	-6	0	-11	12
SPORTSMANS	-10	0	0	0	-6	-7	0	0	0	0	0	-1	1	0	0	20
STAMPEDE PARK	-15	0	0	-14	-12	-24	-14	0	-9	0	0	-11	-6	0	0	16
STOCKTON	0	0	0	-11	-11	0	0	0	-4	0	0	-2	-9	0	-3	13
SUFFOLK DOWNS	0	-18	-15	0	-6	0	0	0	-7	0	-9	-6	-5	-7	-1	20
SUNLAND	-13	-10	-10	-8	-5	-5	0	0	-8	0	0	-5	-2	-17	-12	18
THISTLEDOWN(INNER)	0	0	-11	0	0	0	0	-2	4	0	0	0	0	0	0	20
THISTLEDOWN(MAIN)	-18	-16	-14	-14	-7	0	0	0	-2	-6	-9	0	4	-1	-6	26
TIMONIUM	-10	0	0	0	0	-6	0	0	-6	0	-7	-2	-5	0	0	15
TURF PARADISE	0	-16	-10	-10	-7	-9	0	0	-6	0	0	-1	-10	-12	-9	17
WATERFORD	0	-20	-12	-11	-8	0	0	0	-11	0	-17	-6	0	0	-17	14
WOODBINE	0	0	-13	-11	-5	-2	-5	0	0	0	-7	0	1	-1	7	18
YAKIMA MEADOWS	0	-13	-9	-6	-10	0	0	0	-7	0	0	-15	-15	0	-13	18

ment to the raw speed ratings (see Chapter 18). The average *Form* variant differs from one based on par times by two points. In particular, *Form* variants on weekends and holidays tend to be two points lower than variants based on par times.

It is necessary to keep the Par Variants (and therefore, SR + TV adjustment figures) up to date. The Par Variant should be *increased* by one point as soon as the local six furlong[3] track record becomes $\frac{2}{5}$ faster than the record as of September 30, 1978. No change is necessary for a difference of $\frac{1}{5}$ at that distance. The handicapper also should remain aware of changes in the track record at the route distance most frequently run at the individual track. When it becomes $\frac{4}{5}$ faster than the record as of September 30, 1978, one point must be *added* to the Par Variant for that track.

For a final check, bear in mind that the SR + TV adjustment figure should be exactly equal to the number obtained by subtracting the (possibly revised) Par Variant from the SR adjustment for the distance.

○ TWO WORDS OF WARNING ○

First, if it becomes necessary to compare sprint and route rating figures, do not overlook the "time lag." All route figures should be adjusted by one third *towards 100*. For example, a route figure of 103 must be reduced to 102, its equivalent at the sprint distances. And a route figure of 94 must be *increased* to 96.

But remember, it is not good handicapping practice to rate a horse for sprint purposes based on how fast it has run at route distances. To be considered a contender in a sprint race, a horse must have demonstrated ability at sprint distances, and it is best to rate the horse off such races.

On the other hand, our study of the distance factor (see Chapter 5) revealed that lack of recent activity at route distances was not a serious shortcoming for a horse entered in a route. Consequently, it would seem reasonable to rate a contender in a route off its recent sprint figures. Of course, a horse whose past performances suggested lack of ability at route distances would not likely be considered a contender in a route race. Nor would a sprint type in a route field featuring other sprint types also likely to battle for the early lead.

And second, avoid the temptation to mistake final time for class.

---

[3]Actually, the most frequently used sprint distance, which at most tracks is six furlongs.

A horse that wins in fast time against cheaper may not be able to stand the rise in class its speed figures suggest.

Suppose, for example, that a horse earns a speed figure of 104 while beating $10,000 claiming stock at six furlongs. The horse has run $\frac{4}{5}$ faster than par for its classification, and in time equal to par for $25,000 animals. But can the horse now move up four classes into $25,000 company and be competitive?

Most winners, no matter how fast they won against cheaper, would not be able to stand such a sharp rise in price, and the reason is class. Unless the horse had previously, and preferably recently, shown that it could compete with $25,000 claimers, it should not be expected to race well against them just because it ran very fast against $10,000 claimers.

So how is a horse like this to be treated? Although we have no statistics to back this up, experience working with speed figures suggests that 50 percent of the difference gives an accurate barometer of the horse's present ability. So our $10,000 horse probably could stand a two- (half of four) class rise into $15,000 company.

The 50 percent principle works well in the opposite direction, too. A horse that earned a speed figure of 96 winning a $10,000 claiming sprint is probably not a solid $10,000 horse, unless it won the race very easily, or the low figure ($\frac{4}{5}$ below expectations) was due to unusually slow early fractions. If the figure is a true indication of the horse's best effort, it probably would be more successful racing two classes below $10,000, against $7,500 claimers. It was probably just lucky to have caught a weak field when it beat "$10,000" horses.

In terms of time (speed figures), the 50 percent principle translates as follows: Rather than use a speed figure at face value, average it with the speed figure corresponding to the par time for the race. For example, if an older male $10,000 claimer earned a speed figure of 104, its "class-speed" figure would be 102, the average of 104 and 100, the speed figure for a par race for older male $10,000 claimers.

Who was faster, Secretariat or Ruffian? The speed figures suggest that Ruffian was the faster sprinter, but that Secretariat was stronger over a distance of ground. Judge for yourself.

Ruffian

Ruffian Dk. b. or br. m. 5, by Reviewer—Shenanigans, by Native Dancer
Br.—Janney Mr–Mrs S S Jr (Ky)
Own.—Locust Hill Farm Tr.—WHITELEY F Y JR

	St.	1st	2nd	3rd	Amt.
1975	6	5	0	0	$179,356
1974	5	5	0	0	$134,073

6Jly75-	8Bel	fst	1¼	:44⅗	1:35⅖	2:02⅘	Match Race	1	1	—	—	—	—	Vasquez J	121	*.40	— —	Foolish Pleasure 126 Ruffian 121	Broke down	2
21Jun75-	8Bel	fst	1½	:49	2:03⅕	2:27⅘	ⒻC C A Oaks	5	1	14	11½	13	12¾	Vasquez J	121	*.05	81–12	Ruffin1212¾EqulChnge1219LetMeLinger1212¼	Confidently ridden	7
31May75-	8Aqu	fst	1⅛	:47⅗	1:11⅗	1:47⅘	ⒻMotherGoose	6	1	11½	12	18	114	Vasquez J	121	*.10	96–07	Ruffian 12113½ Sweet Old Girl 1212 SunandSnow1212½	Easy score	7
10May75-	8Aqu	fst	1	:45⅗	1:09⅗	1:34⅖	ⒻAcorn	3	1	11	13	17	18¼	Vasquez J	121	*.10	94–08	Ruffian 1218¼ Somethingregal 121no Gallant Trial 1211	In hand	7
30Apr75-	8Aqu	fst	7f	:22⅘	:45	1:21⅕	ⒻComely	3	5	11	11½	16	17¾	Vasquez J	113	*.05	95–16	Ruffian 1137¾ Aunt Jin 1132½ PointInTime1132	Slow start,handily	5
14Apr75-	8Aqu	fst	6f	:23	:45⅘	1:09⅖	ⒻAllowance	2	3	11	1½	12	14¾	Vasquez J	122	*.10	96–17	Ruffian 1224¾ Sir Ivor's Sorrow 113hd Channelette 1132	Easily	5
23Aug74-	8Sar	fst	6f	:22⅕	:44⅘	1:08⅗	ⒻSpinaway	2	1	12	13	17	113	Bracciale V Jr	120	*.20	97–10	Ruffian 12013 Laughing Bridge 1201½ Scottish Melody1205	Easily	4
27Jly74-	8Mth	fst	6f	:21⅗	:44⅕	1:09	ⒻSorority	3	3	1½	1hd	1½	12¼	Vasquez J	119	*.30	95–15	Ruffian 1192¼ Hot N Nasty 11922 Stream Across 1194	Driving	4
10Jly74-	8Aqu	fst	5½f	:21⅘	:44⅖	1:02⅘	ⒻAstoria	2	2	11	13	16	19	Bracciale V Jr	118	*.10	99–15	Ruffin1189LughingBridg11512OurDncingGirl1153¼	Speed to spare	4
12Jun74-	8Bel	fst	5½f	:22⅖	:45⅕	1:03	ⒻFashion	3	4	11½	11½	14	16¾	Vasquez J	117	*.40	100–12	Ruffian 1176¾ Copernica 11713 Jan Verzal 117nk	Ridden out	6
22May74-	3Bel	fst	5½f	:22⅕	:45	1:03	ⒻMd Sp Wt	9	8	13	15	18	115	Vasquez J	116	4.20	100–15	Ruffian 11615 Suzest 1135 Garden Quad 116½	Ridden out	10

LATEST WORKOUTS May 29 Bel 4f fst :46⅖ b May 24 Bel 4f fst :47⅗ b May 18 Bel 4f fst :47 b ●May 9 Bel 3f fst :34⅗ b

Photo credit: Bob Coglianese

Probably the greatest filly ever produced in this country, Ruffian storms to victory in the 1974 Spinaway at Saratoga in an incredible—for a two-year-old filly—1:08.3.

	SR	DV	SF
C.C.A. Oaks	81	16	117
Mother Goose	96	14	117
Acorn	94	14	113
Comely	95	17	116
Allowance	96	17	110
Spinaway	97	12	109
Sorority	95	14	105
Astoria	99	18	112
Fashion	100	18	111
Maiden	100	17	110

SR: *Speed rating, based on track records in effect September 30, 1978.*
DV: *Accurate daily variants.*
SF: *Adjusted speed figures.*

Photo credit: Bob Coglianese

The beauty and power of Ruffian—captured as she wins the 1975 Coaching Club American Oaks.

181

Secretariat

Secretariat X — Ch. h. 5, by Bold Ruler—Somethingroyal, by Princequillo

Own.—Meadow Stable — Br.—Meadow Stud Inc (Va) — Tr.—Laurin L

Turf Record St.	1st	2nd	3rd	Year	St.	1st	2nd	3rd	Amt.
2	2	0	0	1973	12	9	2	1	$860,404
				1972	9	7	1	0	$456,404

28Oct73- 8WO	fm	1⅝ Ⓣ	:47⅖	1:11⅗	2:41⅘	3↑ Can Intern'l	12	2	$2^{1\frac{1}{2}}$	1^{5}	1^{12}	$1^{6\frac{1}{2}}$	Maple E	b 117	*.20	96-04	Secretariat $117^{6\frac{1}{2}}$ Big Spruce $126^{1\frac{1}{2}}$ Golden Don $117^{\frac{3}{4}}$	Ridden out	12
8Oct73- 7Bel	fm	1½ Ⓣ	:47	1:11⅗	2:24⅘	3↑ Man o' War	3	1	1^{3}	$1^{1\frac{1}{2}}$	1^{3}	1^{5}	Turcotte R	b 121	*.50	103-01	Secretariat 121^{5} Tentam $126^{7\frac{1}{2}}$ Big Spruce $126^{\frac{1}{2}}$	Ridden out	7
29Sep73- 7Bel	sly	1½	:50	1:13⅖	2:25⅘	3↑ Woodward	5	2	$2^{\frac{1}{2}}$	1^{hd}	$2^{1\frac{1}{2}}$	$2^{4\frac{1}{2}}$	Turcotte R	b 119	*.30	86-15	Prove Out $126^{4\frac{1}{2}}$ Secretariat 119^{11} Cougar II $126^{\frac{1}{2}}$	Best of rest	5
15Sep73- 7Bel	fst	1⅛	:45⅗	1:09⅕	1:45⅖	3↑ Marl Inv. H	7	5	$5^{1\frac{1}{4}}$	$3^{\frac{1}{2}}$	1^{2}	$1^{3\frac{1}{2}}$	Turcotte R	b 124	*.40e	104-07	Secretariat $124^{3\frac{1}{2}}$ Riva Ridge 127^{2} Cougar II $126^{6\frac{1}{2}}$	Ridden out	7
4Aug73- 7Sar	fst	1⅛	:47⅘	1:11	1:49⅕	3↑ Whitney	3	4	3^{1}	$2^{\frac{1}{2}}$	2^{hd}	2^{1}	Turcotte R	b 119	*.10	94-15	Onion 119^{1} Secretariat $119^{\frac{1}{2}}$ Rule by Reason 119^{2}	Weakened	5
30Jun73- 8AP	fst	1⅛	:48	1:11⅕	1:47	Invitational	4	1	1^{3}	$1^{2\frac{1}{2}}$	1^{6}	1^{9}	Turcotte R	b 126	*.05	99-17	Secretariat 126^{9} My Gallant 120^{nk} Our Native 120^{17}	Easily	4
9Jun73- 8Bel	fst	1½	:46⅕	1:09⅘	2:24	Belmont	1	1	1^{hd}	1^{20}	1^{28}	1^{31}	Turcotte R	b 126	*.10	113-05	Secretariat 126^{31} Twice A Prince$126^{\frac{1}{2}}$MyGallant126^{13}	Ridden out	5
19May73- 8Pim	fst	$1\frac{3}{16}$	:48⅕	1:11⅖	1:54⅖	Preakness	3	4	$1^{\frac{1}{2}}$	$1^{2\frac{1}{2}}$	$1^{2\frac{1}{2}}$	$1^{2\frac{1}{2}}$	Turcotte R	b 126	*.30	98-13	Secretariat $126^{2\frac{1}{2}}$ Sham 126^{8} Our Native 126^{1}	Handily	6
19May73-Daily Racing Form Time1:53 2/5.																			
5May73- 9CD	fst	1¼	:47⅖	1:11⅘	1:59⅖	Ky Derby	10	11	$6^{9\frac{1}{2}}$	$2^{\frac{1}{2}}$	$1^{\frac{1}{2}}$	$1^{2\frac{1}{2}}$	Turcotte R	b 126	*1.50e	103-10	Secretariat $126^{2\frac{1}{2}}$ Sham 126^{8} Our Native $126^{\frac{1}{2}}$	Handily	13
21Apr73- 7Aqu	fst	1⅛	:48⅕	1:12⅕	1:49⅘	Wood Mem	6	7	6^{6}	$5^{5\frac{1}{2}}$	$4^{5\frac{1}{2}}$	3^{4}	Turcotte R	b 126	*.30e	83-17	Angle Light 126^{hd} Sham 126^{4} Secretariat $126^{\frac{1}{2}}$	Wide, hung	8
7Apr73- 7Aqu	fst	1	:45⅕	1:08⅗	1:33⅖	Gotham	3	3	1^{hd}	1^{2}	$1^{\frac{1}{2}}$	1^{3}	Turcotte R	b 126	*.10	100-08	Secretariat 126^{3} Champagne Charlie 117^{10}Flush$117^{2\frac{1}{2}}$	Ridden out	6
17Mar73- 7Aqu	sly	7f	:22⅕	:44⅘	1:23⅕	Bay Shore	4	5	5^{6}	5^{3}	1^{hd}	$1^{4\frac{1}{2}}$	Turcotte R	b 126	*.20	85-17	Secretarit$126^{4\frac{1}{2}}$ChmpgneChrlie$118^{2\frac{1}{2}}$Impecunious126^{no}	Mild drive	6
18Nov72- 8GS	fst	$1\frac{1}{16}$	:47⅖	1:12	1:44⅖	Garden State	6	6	$4^{6\frac{1}{4}}$	3^{3}	$1^{1\frac{1}{2}}$	$1^{3\frac{1}{2}}$	Turcotte R	b 122	*.10e	83-23	Secretariat $122^{3\frac{1}{2}}$ Angle Light $122^{\frac{1}{2}}$ Step Nicely $122^{\frac{3}{4}}$	Handily	6
28Oct72- 7Lrl	sly	$1\frac{1}{16}$	:45⅘	1:11⅖	1:42⅘	Laurel Fut	5	6	5^{10}	5^{3}	1^{5}	1^{8}	Turcotte R	b 122	*.10e	99-14	Secretariat 122^{8} Stop The Music 122^{8} Angle Light 122^{1}	Easily	6
14Oct72- 7Bel	fst	1	:45⅕	1:09⅘	1:35	Champagne	4	11	$9^{8\frac{1}{2}}$	$5^{3\frac{1}{2}}$	$1^{\frac{1}{2}}$	1^{2}	Turcotte R	b 122	*.70e [D]	97-12	[D]Secretariat 122^{2} Stop The Music 122^{2} Step Niiely$122^{1\frac{1}{2}}$	Bore in	12
14Oct72-Disqualified and placed second																			
16Sep72- 7Bel	fst	6½f	:22⅗	:45⅗	1:16⅖	Futurity	4	5	$6^{5\frac{1}{2}}$	$5^{3\frac{1}{2}}$	1^{2}	$1^{1\frac{3}{4}}$	Turcotte R	b 122	*.20	98-09	Secretariat $122^{1\frac{3}{4}}$ Stop The Music 122^{5}SwiftCourier$122^{2\frac{1}{2}}$	Handily	7
26Aug72- 7Sar	fst	6½f	:22⅘	:46⅗	1:16⅕	Hopeful	8	8	$9^{6\frac{1}{2}}$	1^{hd}	1^{4}	1^{5}	Turcotte R	b 121	*.30	97-12	Secretariat 121^{5} Flight To Glory 121^{nk} TopTheMusic121^{2}	Handily	9
16Aug72- 7Sar	fst	6f	:22⅘	:46⅕	1:10	Sanford	2	5	5^{4}	4^{1}	$1^{\frac{1}{2}}$	1^{3}	Turcotte R	b 121	1.50	96-14	Secretariat121^{3}Linda'sChief121^{6}NorthstarDncer$121^{3\frac{1}{2}}$	Ridden out	5
31Jly72- 4Sar	fst	6f	:23⅕	:46⅖	1:10⅘	Allowance	4	7	$7^{3\frac{3}{4}}$	$3^{\frac{1}{2}}$	1^{hd}	$1^{1\frac{1}{2}}$	Turcotte R	b 118	*.40	92-13	Secretariat $118^{1\frac{1}{2}}$ Russ Miron 118^{7} Joe Iz $118^{2\frac{1}{2}}$	Ridden out	7
15Jly72- 4Aqu	fst	6f	:22⅕	:45⅖	1:10⅗	Md Sp Wt	8	11	$6^{6\frac{1}{2}}$	4^{3}	$1^{\frac{1}{2}}$	1^{6}	Feliciano P^{5}	b 113	*1.30	90-14	Secretariat 113^{6} Master Achiever $118^{\frac{3}{4}}$ Be On It 118^{4}	Handily	11
4Jly72- 2Aqu	fst	5½f	:22⅖	:46⅕	1:05	Md Sp Wt	2	11	10^{7}	$10^{8\frac{3}{4}}$	$7^{5\frac{1}{2}}$	$4^{1\frac{1}{4}}$	Feliciano P^{5}	b 113	*3.10	87-11	Herbull118^{nk}MsterAchiever118^{1}Flet'NRoyl118^{no}	Impeded, rallied	12

Photo credit: Bob Coglianese

In perhaps the most powerful performance in racing history, Secretariat wins the 1973 Belmont (and the Triple Crown) by an incredible 31 lengths, shattering the track record by 13 lengths.

	SR	DV	SF
Canadian International		Grass	
Man O'War		Grass	
Woodward	86	17	123
Marlboro	100	10	120
Whitney	88	20	116
Arlington Invitational	99	19	123
Belmont	100	15	135
Preakness	"103"	18	123
Kentucky Derby	100	13	134
Wood Memorial	83	18	108
Gotham	99	10	114
Bay Shore	85	17	106
Garden State	83	24	111
Laurel Futurity	99	19	112
Champagne	93	18	114
Futurity	94	18	108
Hopeful	94	16	108
Sanford	90	20	110
Allowance	86	20	106
Maiden	90	14	101
Maiden	87	15	97

Photo Credit: Bob Coglianese

Secretariat first asserted himself as a championship contender with this victory over Linda's Chief (outside) in the 1972 Sanford at Saratoga.

SPEED
HANDICAPPING:
SPEED
FIGURES
AS
PREDICTORS

Thus far, we have said little, if anything, about how well speed figures predict the outcomes of races. Before this problem can be approached, one important decision must be made: On *how many* races should a horse's final speed figure be based? And *which* races?

The obvious point of the first question is that a speed figure based on just one race can be misleading. Exceptionally fast or slow early fractions in that race may have paved the way for a final time that does not represent the contestant's true abilities. Clearly a speed figure based on a larger sample of races would be more representative, tending to "average out" one uncharacteristically fast or slow performance.

On the other hand, accurate speed figures require a lot of work. The more races used, the more calculations there are to perform, and the longer the whole process takes. Obviously, the fewer races needed for accurate figures the better.

Our computer studies have shown that reasonable results can be obtained using just two races. Our studies also revealed in no uncertain terms that speed figures hold up much more frequently in sprints than in routes. Several different approaches to speed figures were tried. Each led to the same conclusion. Final times are more important in sprints. Final times mislead more often in routes, possibly because early pace in distance races has a more telling effect on the race's final time.

Since there is a marked difference between sprints and routes, we will study sprints first, and then make some remarks about routes.

○ SPRINTS ○

There are basically two different ways to use speed figures.

In the first approach that we will study, speed figures are used as indicators of a horse's speed when it runs well. The rest of the handicapping process discloses whether or not the horse is likely to run well today.

In the table below, the horses in 400 sprints were ranked with respect to their average speed figures in their last two good performances. For the sake of comparison, speed figures were calculated in four different ways, using:

1. *The Form speed rating.*
2. *The Form speed rating modified by the appropriate SR adjustment figure.*
3. *The sum of the Form speed rating and the Form track variant.*
4. *The sum of the Form speed rating and the Form track variant modified by the appropriate SR+TV adjustment figure.*

The table below gives the impact values of each method for the three horses of highest rank in each field, other horses ranked in the front halves of their fields, and those in the rear halves.

Rank	SR	Modified SR	SR+TV	Modified SR+TV
First	1.09	1.60	1.46	1.65
Second	1.63	1.45	1.50	1.54
Third	1.27	1.10	1.34	1.25
Front Half	0.95	1.00	0.86	0.84
Rear Half	0.75	0.64	0.68	0.61

These findings emphasize the value of the Speed Rating Adjustment Tables. Notice how the modified figures "straighten out" the unmodified ones, producing impact values that decrease steadily from top rank to bottom. The modified SR+TV approach appears best of all, producing a stronger first three categories and a weaker REAR HALF category than any of the other three methods.

Here, in more detail, are the statistics using the modified SR+TV method for this particular approach to speed figures:

Rank	NH	NW	WPCT	MPCT	$NET	%W	I.V.
First	504	98	19.4%	44.6%	$1.74	24.5%	1.65
Second	464	84	18.1%	45.7%	$1.84	21.0%	1.54
Third	398	59	14.8%	43.5%	$1.62	14.8%	1.25
Front Half	618	58	9.4%	33.7%	$1.19	14.5%	0.84
Rear Half	1417	101	7.1%	27.0%	$1.39	25.3%	0.61

Note: there were many ties in rank.

Apparently, horses ranking in the bottom halves of their fields with respect to this type of speed figure have but a slim chance of winning or producing profits for their backers.

A good race last out is always a good sign, and usually strengthens another good sign. Here is how horses performed when (a) they were ranked first by this modified SR+TV method and (b) their last race was good.

	NH	NW	WPCT	MPCT	$NET	I.V.
Good Race	204	59	28.9%	58.8%	$1.90	2.40
Won	106	27	25.5%	55.7%	$1.75	2.13
Lost	98	32	32.7%	62.2%	$2.06	2.71

Apparently, those that ran well last out, but did not win, and therefore did not have to move up in class or carry more weight, are the best bets here.

A second approach to speed figures is to make them reflect the horse's present form. In other words, the horse will be penalized for a recent poor race by having its figure for that race count toward its overall rating.

Once again, we shall average two races to obtain a horse's final figure. We will be guided in our selection of these races by the concept of "failure" discussed in Chapter 10. Here is how it works.

Locate the horse's most recent good race, going back no farther than five races in the published record. Then determine how many failures have occurred since that good race.

If the horse has two or more recent failures on its record, we average the horse's speed figures for the two most recent failure races. Yudy Eye, for example, has failed twice (on September 12 and 27) since his last good race, and therefore must be rated on the September 12 and 27 races.

Yudy Eye

Own.—Hawk Crest Farm

B. g. 3, by Good Behaving—Manta H, by Manteau
$8,500
Br.—Rosoff A (Fla)
Tr.—Schwizer Albert

117

	St.	1st	2nd	3rd	Amt.
1977	16	2	3	1	$21,440
1976	15	5	0	1	$25,350

27Sep77- 2Bel my 7f	:23%	:47½ 1:25	Clm 11500	3 5	86½ 55 58	59½ Turcotte R	b 115	6.70	68–21 Nurse Chaser 117nk Last Family 117½ Mike Palm 117½	Outrun 8
12Sep77- 9Bel fst 6f	:23%	:47½ 1:13%	Clm c–8500	5 7	98½ 96½ 99½	916 Hernandez R	117	4.60	58–21 Theatrical Beau 117hd Bold Fly 1191½ Big Apple 1175	Dull try 11
29Aug77- 1Bel fst 1⅛	:47	1:11½ 1:45	Clm 11500	6 5	56½ 35 24	49½ Cauthen S	115	3.60	67–19 VeryDistinguished117hdDiWithStrngth117½Frmrco117hd	Weakened 8
19Aug77- 1Sar fst 7f	:22%	:45½ 1:24	Clm 13000	1 7	64½ 56½ 61½	21½ Trosclair A J	113	*3.60	84–14 Deal With Strength117½YudyEye113½JudgeRoot115no	Wide rally 10
10Aug77- 2Sar fst 7f	:23%	:46½ 1:25	Clm 14000	6 2	85 84½ 63½	43½ Hernandez R	117	*2.60	77–15 Butchcee 117½ Malachi 113½ Nurse Chaser 117hd	Wide 9
4Aug77- 9Sar fst 1⅛	:47½	1:12 1:51%	Clm 15000	9 3	33 42½ 24	37½ Hernandez R	117	*3.00	70–13 Taxi Cab Driver 117½ Mood Thirteen 1086 Yudy Eye 117½	Tired 9
20Jly77- 5Bel fst 1	:46%	1:11½ 1:37%	Clm 20500	2 8	88½ 67 461	48½ Hernandez R	115	3.90	71–19 VeryDistinguished117½Marlago1154½SeneyBer115½	Pinched back 8
6Jly77- 8Bel fst 7f	:23%	:46½ 1:24%	Clm 15000	7 1	62½ 52½ 1½	11½ Hernandez R	113	3.70	79–16 Yudy Eye 113½ Seaney Bear 1194½TaxiCabDriver117½	Ridden out 8
25Jun77- 9Bel fst 7f	:23%	:47¾ 1:25%	Clm 12500	7 2	51½ 42 1hd	11½ Hernandez R	117	3.90	73–18 Yudy Eye 117½ Make Our Move 1191 Judge Root 117no	Driving 11
17Jun77- 7Bel fst 6f	:23	:47 1:12%	Clm 11500	8 4	32 22 2½	24½ Hernandez R	115	14.50	71–22 Early Leader 1154½ Yudy Eye 115½ L'Aig Promise 117nk	Gamely 10

Predetermine *

Own.—Sommer S

Ro. g. 5, by Determined Man—Sara Will, by John William
Br.—Nolan N C (Va)
Tr.—Martin F

115⁵

	St.	1st	2nd	3rd	Amt.
1976	5	1	1	0	$11,700
1975	27	9	8	0	$57,875

27Feb76- 6Aqu fst 6f	:23	:46¾ 1:11½	Allowance	6 1	2hd 31	55 66¾ Santiago A	b 119	2.50	80–21 Pres De Tu 121nk Naudi 116¾ Enough 116¾	Tired 6
10Feb76- 4Aqu fst 6f	:22%	:45½ 1:10½	Allowance	2 3	2hd 2hd 1½	1½ Cordero A Jr	b 122	*1.00e	90–18 Never Retreat 1151½ Fiveontheside 116nk Naudi 114no	Weakened 6
20Jan76- 4Aqu fst 6f	:22%	:45½ 1:10	Allowance	1 2	1hd 1½ 11¼	11¼ Cordero A Jr	b 117	*.70	93–16 Predetermine 1171¼TrainerMickey116½MasterQuico116½	Driving 6
17Jan76- 4Aqu fst 6f	:23%	:47 1:11	Allowance	6 2	1hd 31¼ 41½	11¼ Santiago A	b 115	*1.30	83–22 Umin 121nk Proud Romeo 114¾ Fiveontheside 111¾	Weakened 7
3Jan76- 4Aqu sly 6f	:22%	:45½ 1:11	Allowance	3 2	11 1hd 2¼	2¾ Cordero A Jr	b 115–	*.80	87–18 Umin 114¾ Predetermine 115¾ Proud Romeo 109¼	Gamely 6
22Dec75- 7Aqu fst 6f	:22%	:46 1:09%	3 ↑ Allowance	6 3	31½ 2½ 2¾	22½ Maple E	b 120	1.70	94–16 Amerrico 118¾ Predetermine 1201½ Umin 115¾	Gamely 6
11Dec75- 4Aqu fst 7f	:22%	:46 1:22%	3 ↑ Clm 25000	2 3	2hd 1hd 16	16½ Maple E	b 120	*.90	87–15 Predetermine 1183 Bostons Boy 114½ Whickery 114½	Driving 12
26Nov75- 4Aqu fst 6f	:22%	:45½ 1:23%	3 ↑ Clm c–18000	3 1	31½ 31 2½	11½ Tejeira J	b 118	4.00	88–15 Predetermine 1183 Bostons Boy 114² Whickery 114½	Driving 12
15Nov75- 4Aqu fst 6f	:22%	:45½ 1:10½	3 ↑ Clm c–14000	2 1	11 21 1hd	11 Pincay L Jr	b 118	2.90	90–15 Predetermine 1201 Our Town 113² Bostons Boy 116¾	Hard drive 10
8Nov75- 1Bel sly 6f	:22%	:46 1:11%	3 ↑ Clm 12500	1 1	11½ 11 1nk	11 Pincay L Jr	b 118	*1.70	86–12 Predetermine 118² Six No Trump 109nkDirtyDan1181½	Ridden out 9

LATEST WORKOUTS Feb 21 Bel tr.t 4f fst :48 h   ●Feb 19 Bel tr.t 3f gd :35½ h   Feb 8 Bel tr.t 4f fst :47½ h   Jan 30 Bel tr.t 4f sl :49% h

Gustavus Adolphus *

Own.—Tanenbaum S

Dk. b. or br. g. 4, by Gustav—Painted Lady, by Cormac
$40,000
Br.—Ohstrom R R (Va)
Tr.—Martin J

1·22

Turf Record				St.	1st	2nd	3rd	Amt.
St.	1st	2nd	3rd	1973 17	8	1	1	$58,205
1	0	0	0	1972 21	4	2	2	$24,750

13Jly73- 8Aqu fst 1¼	:46% 1:10% 1:49	3 ↑ Clm 40000	2 3	34½ 34 1hd	13½ Cordero A Jr	b 115	*1.10	91–14 Gustavus Adolphus 115²½ Cheriepe 102² Trupan 113¹	Driving 7
29Jun73- 9Bel fst 1⅛	:48 1:12 1:48%	3 ↑ Clm 40000	3 1	1hd 2hd 1½	1¾ Cordero A Jr	b 116	*1.40	93–13 Gustavus Adolphus 116¾ Cristobal 115nk High Center 114¼	Driving 7
5Jun73- 9Bel fst 1⅛	:46½ 1:10½ 1:47%	3 ↑ Clm 40000	1 1	1½ 14 1nk	1nk Cordero A Jr	b 114	1.70	94–08 Trupan 112no Gustavus Adolphus 114¹½ Camoweal 112¾	Missed 6
29May73- 3Bel gd 1⅛	:45% 1:11% 1:44%	3 ↑ Clm 35000	6 1	41 3½ 1nk	1nk Cordero A Jr	116	1.70	86–22 Gustavus Adolphus 116nk Paraje 116¾ In Camera 116¼	Driving 7
22May73- 7Bel fst 1	:45% 1:10% 1:09%	3 ↑ Allowance	1 1	1½ 1hd 1½	1hd Arellano J	b 116	*1.40	90–08 Loud 113¹ Whitey II 113hd Rule by Reason 119⁵¼	Stumbled break 6
5May73- 7Aqu fst 1⅛	:46½ 1:10% 2:01¾	3 ↑ Grey Lag H	1 2	2½ 3½ 41½	8¹² Castaneda M	b 111	6.90	76–17 Summer Guest 116⁹½ Loud 111hd Traffic Cop 114¹M	Tired 12
23Apr73- 7Aqu fst 1	:45% 1:10% 1:35%	3 ↑ Allowance	2 1	2½ 21 1hd	1¾ Cordero A Jr	b 114	3.40	82–22 Gustavus Adolphus 114¾ Onion 115² Rule by Reason 117¹	Driving 7
11Apr73- 9Aqu fst 1	:45% 1:10% 1:36%	3 ↑ Allowance	1 1	11 1½ 1hd	1½ Cordero A Jr	b 114	*2.40	91–17 Gustavus Adolphus 114² Date the Note 116¾½ Pierce Luck 109¾½	Driving 7
27Mar73- 4Aqu fst 1⅛	:46 1:10% 1:51%	3 ↑ Allowance	4 1	18 1¼ 1hd	1⁵ Cordero A Jr	b 120	*2.40	90–12 Gustavus Adolphus 120¹² Christobal 120³ Sentimentalist 112¾½	Handily 6
21Mar73- 3Aqu fst 1	:45% 1:11% 1:36%	Allowance	3 6	6⁹ 5¹⁸ 5¹⁴	Venezia M	b 114	4.80	71–18 Head of the River 114² Flying Crimson 109⁴ Quinnox 115½	Outrun 9

LATEST WORKOUTS Jly 9 Bel tr.t 5f fst 1:00% h   Jun 23 Bel tr.t 6f my 1:17 b   Jun 15 Bel tr.t 5f fst 1:03% b

Jim J. ×

H. H. Polk   E. Yowell

Ch. c (1964–Md), by First Landing—Sunelia, by More Sun
(H. H. Polk)

125

	St.	1st	2nd	3rd	Amt.
1968	14	6	3	1	$121,231
1967	15	3	5	2	$77,555

23Oct68- 7Bel fst 6f	:22% :45% 1:09½	SportPageH 4	5	87½ 75 33½	23½ JVelasquez	126	4.60	95–15 Dewan 126nk Jim J. 126² Royal Exchange 115¹	Rallied 7
28Sep68- 8Atl	fst 1½	:45½ 2:41:21¾	Atl.CityH	4 2	52½ 37 38	4⁹ WBlum	126	*1.00	82–19 JimJ.126h d–AirKing1113h OurMichael114nk	Forced wide, just up 7
24Jly68- 7Aqu sly 6f	:22 :45 1:10½	GravesendH	2 4	42 3¼ 1hd	1½ ACorderoJr	124	3.90	92–19 JimJ.124h d–AirKing1113h OurMichael114nk	Forced wide, just up 7
10Jly68- 8Mth fst 6f	:21% :44½1:09½	RumsonH	2 4	43 32½ 1h	1½ CBaltazar	122	*2.50	94–15 Jim J. 122½ R. Thomas 123nk Air King II 113no	Was drawing clear 9
20Jun68- 8Mth gd 6f	:23 :46%1:11½	Allowance	3 3	31 1½ 12	1½ JVasquez	124	*0.70	86–26 Jim J. 124⁵ Future Bold 121¹² Crowned King 118³	Handy score 7
25May68- 8GS	fst 1⅛	:47¼1:11½1:48%	CamdenH	1 3	38 35 24	25 JVelasquez	114	*1.10	89–19 King'sPalace1125 Jim J.114¹ Swoonaway111½nk	Best of others 8
13May68- 8Pim	fst 1½	:48¼1:12¾1:44½	JenningsH	4 2	33 1hd 1h	2hd JVasquez	120	*0.80	88–17 Rock Talk 115h Jim J. 120³ Exceedingly 120²½	Couldn't hold winner 6
23Apr68- 8GS	fst 6f	:22% :44½1:08%	Ch'ryHillH	1 1	54 53½ 33	34½ JVelasquez	121	*1.30	90–12 Tumiga 119²½ Jim J. 121⁵ Pappa Steve 114²½	No match for winner 6
10Apr68- 7Aqu fst 7f	:22% :45%1:09%	TobogganH	4 2	54 7³½ 3½	2hd ACorderoJr	113	11.90	94–18 Jim J. 119¹½ Air King II 1152 Mr. Washington 124²	Won going away 7
2Mar68- 5Hia	fst 7f	:22% :45%1:22	Allowance	4 4	5³ 4½ 2hd	2½ ACorderoJr	124	*0.90	99–11 Jim J. 119½ Bold Tactics 115⁵ Straight Deal 112²	Driving 7
17Feb68- 7Hia	fst 7f	:23 :45½1:22	Allowance	2 5	32 35½	4⁴ ACorderoJr	124	4.30	94–17 Great Power 115nk Jeronia 121⁵ Jim J. 124³	Well placed, hung 7

LATEST WORKOUTS Oct 30 GS 4f fst :47 h   Oct 21 GS 4f gd :47% h   Oct 16 GS 3f fst :37 b   Oct 12 Atl 5f fst 1.09 b

Our Hero

Own.—Phipps Ogden

Dk. b. or br. c. 4, by Bold Ruler—Dorine, by Aristophanes
Br.—Phipps O (Ky)
Tr.—Russell John W

120

Turf Record				St.	1st	2nd	3rd	Amt.
St.	1st	2nd	3rd	1976	13	4	2	1	$88,140
1	0	0	0	1975	14	4	2	1	$55,882

4Sep76- 8Key fst 6f	:22 :44% 1:09½	3 ↑ Garrison H	2 6	55½ 46½ 711	616 Shoemaker W	b 126	9.40	77–18 Relent 120⁵ Kirby Lane 1241½ Soy Numero Uno 137no	Tired 7
30Aug76- 8Sar fst 6f	:23½ :46 1:09½	3 ↑ Fall Hi Wt H	2 7	65 55½ 8	2 7 Phelps B	b 117	5.50	95–20 Our Hero 1172 North Call 119¼ Crafty Drone 118nk	Drew clear 9

30Aug76–Run in two divisions, 6th & 8th races.

25Jly76- 8Aqu fst 7f	:23% :44% 1:21	3 ↑ Tom Fool H	4 2	32 32½ 53½	610 Montoya D	b 115	5.10	69–24 El Pitirre 114½ Nalees Knight 110¾ Honorable Miss 1181½	Tired 6
3Jly76- 6Aqu fst 6f	:22% :45% 1:09%	3 ↑ Allowance	5 1	11½ 1½ 1½	1hd Cordero A Jr	b 119	1.30	96–13 Our Hero 119¹ Promised City 117½ Sailors Watch 122½	Driving 5
12Jun76- 4Atl fst 6f	:22% :44% 1:09	3 ↑ Premier H	8 4	42 32½ 21	21½ Cordero A Jr	b 119	1.40	95–16 North Call 1172 Our Hero 117½ Old Mystery 122½	Gamely 10
5Jun76- 4Bel fst 6f	:22% :45% 1:10	3 ↑ Allowance	4 3	23 2hd 1½	2hd Cordero A Jr	b 119	1.40	92–15 Our Hero 118½ Sailors Watch 116no Sunny Clime 109no	Driving 10
24Apr76- 8Hol fst 7f	:22 :44½ 1:20%	3 ↑ L. Angeles H	7 3	41 41½ 63½	54½ Pierce D	114	16.70	90–14 Century's Envoy 123²HomeJerome117½SportingGoods120½	Wide 8
16Apr76- 8Aqu fst 6f	:22 :45 1:09%	3 ↑ Gravesend H	8 2	63½ 75½ 73½	733 Velez R I	b 112	10.20	93–19 Our Hero 112½ Valid Appeal 117½ NaleesKnight117hd	Ridden out 8
3Apr76- 7Aqu fst 6f	:22 :45% 1:10	3 ↑ Allowance	7 2	41½ 31½ 2½	1½ Velez R I⁵	b 113	15.50	81–19 Due Diligence 1172 Pompini 113² Gallant Bob 129½	Wide 11
13Mar76- 8Aqu sly 6f	:21% :45% 1:10%	3 ↑ Toboggan H	9 6	76½ 78 75½	711 Cordero A Jr	b 113	15.50		

13Mar76–Placed sixth through disqualification.

LATEST WORKOUTS Sep 19 Bel 6f fst 1:13 h   Sep 13 Bel 5f fst 1:01 b   Aug 22 Sar tr.t 5f fst 1:02 h   Aug 12 Sar 6f fst 1:19 b

Forage

Own.—Perry W H

Ch. g. 3, by Herbager—Respected, by Round Table
Br.—Claiborne Farm (Ky)
Tr.—Maloney J W

110

	St.	1st	2nd	3rd	Amt.
1972	13	4	3	0	$40,709
1971	5	1	M	0	$1,540

14Oct72- 6Bel fst 7f	:23 :46½ 1:22%	3 ↑ Allowance	5 2	25 24 22	11½ Pincay L Jr	114	5.50	89–12 Forage 1141½ Sir Dagonet 113¼ Peace Corps 121¹	Driving 6
9Aug72- 7Sar fst 1⅛	:47½ 1:11½ 1:49%	Jim Dandy	6 5	59½ 66 78	68½ Pincay L Jr	114	3.10	84–14 Tentam 114²½ True Knight 115hd Halo 114¹	Tired 10
22Jly72- 7Aqu fst 1⅛	:47% 1:10% 2.00	3 ↑ Suburban H	6 4	75½ 64 74½	64½ Baeza B	113	3.90e	92–09 Hitchcock 113² West Coast Scout 120nk Naskra 116½	Fell back 8
8Jly72- 6Aqu fst 1⅛	:23 :45½ 1:10%	Allowance	3 4	2½ 21½ 1½	1½ Vasquez J	113	3.50	92–09 Forage 1133 Icecapade 122½ Tidy Beau 113½	Driving 8
27Jun72- 6Aqu fst 6f	:22% :45 1:15%	3 ↑ Allowance	1 7	75½ 53½ 24	21 Vasquez J	112	4.40	90–15 Tentam 1152 Forage 112³½ Gay Gallant 112¾½	Held on 8
10Jun72- 6Bel fst 1⅛	:48 1:10% 1:41%	3 ↑ Allowance	4 5	53½ 22 2½	2½ Marquez C H	115	*1.30	90–14 Tentam 1115 Forage 115¾ Straight and Level 113¾	Best of others 7
31May72- 7Bel fst 1¼	:47% 1:10 1.34%	Withers	5 5	54½ 45 45	44½ Marquez C H	126	36.40	91–16 Key To The Mint 126½ Icecapade 126½½ Zulu Tom 126½	Raced Wide 10
24May72- 5Bel fst 1⅛	:46% 1:11% 1:51	Allowance	5 5	54 45 45	45 Marquez C H	113	4.60	91–12 Icecapade 116² Chevron Flight 122no Windjammer 122¹	Raced wide 5
22Apr72- 7Aqu sly 1⅛	:47% 1:11% 1:49%	Wood Mem	5 5	55 54 5⁸	5¹² Marquez C H	126	11.40	84–12 UpperCase 126½ TrueKnight 126⁴ HeadofTheRiver 126¾½	Lacked rally 12
8Apr72- 7Aqu fst 1⅛	:47% 1:11% 1.36%	Gotham	11 6	63½ 63½ 31½	64½ Adams L	115	9.60	81–19 Freetex 126¹ Eager Exchange 122⅓ Upper Case 126hd	Lacked room 13

LATEST WORKOUTS Oct 27 Bel 4f fst :37 b   Oct 21 Bel 4f gd :49 b   Oct 13 Bel 3f fst :36½ b   Oct 10 Bel 5f fst 1.00 b

If the horse has failed exactly once since its last good race, we use that good race and the failure race to compute its figure. Predetermine is such a horse, having failed on February 27 to run back to his good effort of February 10. His rating, therefore, is based on his last two starts.

If the horse has not failed since its last good race, we then look for its second most recent good race. If two failures occurred between that race and the most recent good race, we ignore it and rate the horse on just the recent good race. Otherwise, we compute the horse's figure as the average of the two good races.

The last two races of Gustavus Adolphus were good, and so his rating is simply the average of his figures for those two races.

Jim J., on the other hand, has one bad race sandwiched between two good performances, not enough to cancel out the second good race. He is rated off his performances in the Gravesend and Sport Page Handicaps.

Our Hero shows two bad performances between his latest two good races, but neither rates as a failure, coming immediately before and after a five-week layoff. Our Hero, therefore, is rated off his allowance win at Aqueduct on July 3 and the Garrison Handicap on September 4.

Forage also shows two bad races between recent good efforts that are not considered failures. Entered October 28 in an allowance race, his last two good efforts were also in allowance company, and so his poor performances in stakes competition are not failures. He is rated off his latest two good races.

Handsome Tod is another story—he has several poor races between his latest two good efforts. All are failures because he is entered July 25 at six furlongs. Consequently, Handsome Tod's rating is based on one race, his latest.

Should a horse show no recent good race we use its last two races at today's distance (sprint or route) to calculate its figure, provided these races occurred within the animal's last five starts. Otherwise, we simply use the horse's last two races, regardless of distance.

Here is how the impact value statistics worked out for this type of speed figure, over the same sample of 400 sprints as above. Once again, for the sake of comparison, we have used the four different methods.

Rank	SR	Modified SR	SR+TV	Modified SR+TV
First	1.40	1.84	1.78	2.02
Second	1.46	1.48	1.58	1.48
Third	1.38	1.26	1.12	1.08
Front Half	1.18	0.95	0.81	0.88
Rear Half	0.59	0.56	0.64	0.55

This table shows that improved results can be expected from this particular approach to speed figures. Each calculation method yields nice, steadily decreasing impact values, with the modified SR+TV method again proving best. Notice the especially strong FIRST category in column 4 and the anemic REAR HALF category (in all four columns).

Here, in more detail, are the statistics for the modified SR+TV method:

Rank	NH	NW	WPCT	MPCT	$NET	%W	I.V.
First	488	116	23.8%	50.4%	$1.94	29.0%	2.02
Second	455	79	17.4%	46.6%	$1.77	19.8%	1.48
Third	399	51	12.8%	40.6%	$1.21	12.8%	1.08
Front Half	600	59	9.8%	33.5%	$1.32	14.8%	0.88
Rear Half	1459	95	6.5%	26.0%	$1.41	23.8%	0.55

Had the top-ranked horse run well in its last start, we would find only slight improvement in the dollar figures, but considerable improvement in the percentage of winners:

	NH	NW	WPCT	MPCT	$NET	I.V.
Good	296	87*	29.4%	58.8%	$1.97	2.44
Won	146	42	28.8%	58.9%	$2.01	2.40

That this second approach should prove the better of the two comes as no surprise. It adds a second dimension—form—to the naked speed figures of the first approach.

Some might argue, however, that rating horses off poor performances produces artificially low figures—horses are not perservered with when hopelessly beaten, adding excess lengths to their final margins of defeat. While this is a valid point, remember that it only affects performances termed failures. And horses with recent failures on their records can be considered "non-contenders," according to the study discussed in Chapter 10. It is of little concern, then, that the ratings of such horses are downgraded a few points because they were not pressured in the late stages of a recent inexcusably poor performance.

○ ROUTES ○

These two approaches to speed figures, and all others studied, were not nearly as effective in handicapping routes (1 mile–1⅛ miles).

Here first is a study of 300 routes in which the horses have been ranked according to the average of their modified SR+TV's for their last two good races:

Rank	NH.	NW	WPCT	MPCT	$NET	%W	I.V.
First	378	59	15.6%	47.9%	$1.69	19.7%	1.26
Second	304	56	18.4%	45.7%	$1.69	18.7%	1.47
Third	310	39	12.6%	40.7%	$1.40	13.0%	1.00
Front Half	386	54	14.0%	36.0%	$1.81	18.0%	1.19
Rear Half	1041	92	8.8%	30.4%	$1.21	30.7%	0.71

And if the horses in the same 300 races had been ranked using the "failures" method described above:

Rank	NH	NW	WPCT	MPCT	$NET	%W	I.V.
First	415	54	13.0%	38.1%	$1.39	18.0%	1.05
Second	281	43	15.3%	44.8%	$1.56	14.3%	1.21
Third	287	48	16.7%	42.9%	$1.74	16.0%	1.32
Front Half	398	54	13.6%	41.2%	$1.58	18.0%	1.15
Rear Half	1038	101	9.7%	31.8%	$1.35	33.7%	0.78

In neither case does the top-ranked horse prove the most frequent winner. Any horse ranked in the top half of its field appears dangerous, and as likely to win as the horse ranked first.

○ CONCLUSION ○

Most handicappers use the factors of current form, distance, class, and early speed to identify the probable contenders in a race, and then speed figures, to separate the contenders.

In this chapter, we have asked speed figures to stand alone. We have found that a handicapper using only speed figures to make his selections can survive betting sprint races. Had the figures been applied exclusively to logical contenders, better results might be expected.

But route races are a different story. Speed figures apparently cannot stand alone in routes. Other factors must first point out logical contenders. We will see in Chapter 24 that this can be done effectively, that speed figures are a valid concern when handicapping a route race.

Regrettably, the past performance data upon which the studies presented in this chapter were based could not be supplemented with accurate daily variants. The reader is assured, however, that any adjustments or modifications designed to produce speed figures more accurate than those published in the *Daily Racing Form* are worth the effort. They can only serve to increase his own percentage of winning selections *without affecting the odds board*.

Our studies in this chapter have proven the effectiveness of both the SR and the SR+TV adjustments. The addition of an accurate daily variant could only improve the results even more.

SPEED
HANDICAPPING:
TWO
EXAMPLES

In this chapter we discuss two races in which speed figures were the determining factor in making a selection. Other handicapping factors eliminated few horses as possible contenders in either race.

○ **RACE #1** ○

Aqueduct's new inner dirt track was labeled FAST as eight horses entered the starting gate for the seventh race on Saturday, December 11, 1976. The race was at six furlongs, for horses in the Classified Division that had not won $6,100 twice in almost a full year—essentially, horses that had not won two allowance races in New York since December 15, 1975.

Fiveontheside

Own.—Brant P

B. g. 4, by Lt Stevens—Out Guess, by Alhambra
Br.—Lehrman L E (Md)
Tr.—Glynn Sanford

	Turf Record	St.	1st	2nd	3rd	Amt.
119	2 0 0 0	1976	16	1	2	4	$29,420
		1975	9	2	2	1	$18,230

30Dec76–	8Aqu fst 7f	:22⅖ :45	1:23½	3 ↑ Allowance	2 8	66¼ 67	66¼ 75	Santiago A	122	22.90	80–20 Chief Tamanaco 120nk Jacques Who117nk Banian1151¼	No mishap 8
22Dec76–	8Bel fst 7f	:23½ :47	1:23½	3 ↑ Allowance	5 4	21½ 2hd 2²	32½	Gustines H	122	22.90	82–21 Gitche Gumee 122½ Jeopardy 115½Fiveontheside122½	Weakened 7
10ct76–	8Bel sly 6f	:22½ :45½	1:10⅘	3 ↑ Allowance	6 7	45½ 42½	21	2no	Vasquez J	115	19.00	88–18 ⒹBonge 112no Fiveontheside 1153½ Scott M. 1151	Impeded 7

10ct76–Placed first through disqualification

9Aug76–	5Sar my 7f	:22½ :45½	1:24	3 ↑ Clm 35000	1 2	35	33½	42	32½	Cruguet J	117	5.90	83–20 DivineRoylty117½ChubbyCzech1151½Fiveonthesid117½	Wide, hung 8
27July76–	5Aqu fst 6f	:22½ :45½	1:10⅘	3 ↑ Allowance	9 7	75¾ 75	64½	45½	Velasquez J	117	6.40	84–22 Checkerhall 119³ Divine Royalty 122²½ Russ Miron 1131½	Rallied 10
26July76–	6Bel fm 7f	ⓣ:23	1:23½	3 ↑ Allowance	3 5	65	54½	43	45½	Velasquez J	119	22.60	86–11 Story Rights 113hd Debtor's Haven 112½ Austin 1131½	No mishap 9
20Jun76–	3Bel fst 6f	:22½ :45½	1:09⅘	3 ↑ Allowance	3 5	53	64½	67½	57½	Cruguet J	117	9.30	86–05 Line Officer 1123 Clean Bill 113¹ Story Rights 1113	Forced out 6
30May76–	6Bel fm 1	ⓣ:45⅘ 1:10	1:34⅗	3 ↑ Allowance	5 6	64½	66	67	712	Cruguet J	120	12.80	86–04 Fifth Marine 1152 Burundi 1151¼WiseRequest112nk	Broke outside 6
19May76–	6Bel sly 6f	:46⅖ 1:11⅗	1:43⅘	3 ↑ Allowance	4 3	22	21½	25	49	Cruguet J	120	14.50	77–17 Cinteelo 1067¾ BabyFaceBeau120nk GreenAsGrass1201½	Weakened 8
20May76–	6Aqu fst 1	:45⅘ 1:10	1:35⅘	3 ↑ Allowance	2 3	34	54	64	45½	Santiago A	120	18.10	84–17 Play The Red 112² Cabriolet II120½StoryRights114¾	No mishap 7

LATEST WORKOUTS ● Dec 9 Bel 4f fst :47 h ● Nov 26 Bel 6f fst 1:14 b

Mr. Barb

Own.—Hardin Sharen L

B. g. 4, by Barbizon—Above the Line, by Roman Line
Br.—Pin Oak Stud Inc (Ky)
Tr.—Hild Glen L

	Turf Record	St.	1st	2nd	3rd	Amt.
115	1 0 0 0	1976	24	2	5	7	$40,335
		1975	8	4	2		$45,862

30Dec76–	8Aqu fst 7f	:22½ :45	1:23½	3 ↑ Allowance	5 6	78½ 77½	34	42	Cruguet J	b 115	27.60	83–20 Chief Tamanaco 120nk JacquesWho117nk Banian1151¼	Raced wide 8
28Nov76–	8Key fst 6f	:22½ :45	1:11⅗	3 ↑ Allowance	6 6	64½ 94½	66	65	Wilson R	b 114	15.10e	78–27 North Call 119nk Kintla's Folly 1151½ Plain Pete 1141½	No excuse 9
12Nov76–	7Key fst 6f	:22½ :45½	1:11	3 ↑ Allowance	5 3	53½ 63½	44	47½	Hawley S	b 119	5.70	77–27 ⒹProud Kenn 112¹½ Plain Pete 114nk Bearer Bond 122⁶	Bumped 7

13Nov76–Placed third through disqualification

7Nov76–	7Pen fst 6f	:22½ :46½	1:11½	3 ↑ Allowance	1 6	52½ 41½ 21½	2no	Fitzgerald R	b 116	3.50	87–21 Old Mystery 113no Mr. Barb 1161½ Sid Said 1131	Missed 7
19Oct76–	8Mth fst 6f	:22	:44½ 1:09⅘	3 ↑ Allowance	4 4	54½ 44½ 34	31½	Edwards J W	b 119	6.30	88–20 Can You Beat That 117hd Old Mystery 1153 Mr.Barb119no	Rallied 4
2Oct76–	6Key gd 6f	:22½ :47½	1:10⅘	3 ↑ Allowance	2 4	44½ 66½ 59	49	Guadalupe J	b 122	15.10	81–22 Webelo 117⅓ Jaunty Jack 119²½ Orbit Round 117⁶	Sluggish 6
24Sep76–	8Mth fst 6f	:22½ :45½ 1:10	3 ↑ Allowance	3 3	1hd 2hd	1hd 1nk	Edwards J W	b 114	8.10	90–17 Mr. Barb 119nk Boy Emperor 119no Sweet Isaac 1192	Driving 9
15Sep76–	8Mth fm 5f	ⓣ:22⅘ :46	:58⅖	3 ↑ Allowance	6 3	73½ 76½ 74½ 43½	Edwards J W	b 115	18.10	87–19 Banian 1171¼ Sweet Isaac 1151¼ Run Tell Run 1221	Rallied 8
16Aug76–	8Atl fst 6f	:22½ :45	1:11⅖	3 ↑ Allowance	7 1	51½ 1hd 2hd 3½	Pettinger D	b 116	2.20	90–17 Jaunty Jack 119nk Packer Captain 1173 Mr. Barb 1142	Tired 7
28July76–	8Mth fst 6f	:22	:44½ 1:08⅘	3 ↑ Allowance	3 7	61½ 64½ 66½ 66½	Delahoussaye E	b 117	8.70	90–13 That Wing 115nd Mexican General113nk JoyfulHope113⁴	No factor 7

LATEST WORKOUTS Dec 10 Key 3f fr :36 b Dec 2 Key 3f fst :35 b Nov 19 Key 3f fst :37 h Oct 17 Key 3f fst :37 b

Jacques Who ✱

Own.—Wimpfheimer J D

Gr. h. 6, by Grey Dawn II—Lady Dulcinea, by Nantallah
Br.—Wimpfheimer J D (Ky)
Tr.—Sedlacek Woodrow

	Turf Record	St.	1st	2nd	3rd	Amt.
1175	23 4 2 2	1976	22	1	5	5	$57,900
		1975	19	1	2	1	$26,100

30Dec76–	8Aqu fst 7f	:22½ :45	1:23½	3 ↑ Allowance	8 1	8¹º 89½	54½	2hd	Cauthen S⁵	b 117	4.80	85–20 Chief Tamanaco 120nk JacquesWho117nkBanian1151¼	Just missed 8
27Nov76–	6Aqu fst 7f	:22½ :46	1:11	3 ↑ Allowance	2 8	88½ 73½	31	31½	Cordero A Jr	b 122	7.60	87–21 Naudi 1151½ Wing South 115½ Jacques Who 122²¾	Hung 8
12Nov76–	8Aqu fst 7f	:23	:46½ 1:24⅗	3 ↑ Allowance	3 4	45½ 41½	1½	1¹	Cordero A Jr	b 115	7.50	84–24 Jacques Who 115¹ Cliff Chesney 1132½ Wing South 115½	Driving 6
22Oct76–	8Bel fst 7f	:23½ :47	1:23½	3 ↑ Allowance	3 7	75½ 75¾	64	64½	Maple E	b 115	6.10	80–21 Gitche Gumee 122½ Jeopardy 115½ Fiveontheside 122½	Outrun 7
7Oct76–	7Bel fst 6f	:22½ :45½ 1:09⅘	3 ↑ Allowance	7 6	63½ 53	21	1hd	Maple E	b 115	6.50	91–13 Gitche Gumee 117⁵ SkyCommander1153¼JacquesWho115½	Rallied 7
10Sep76–	8Bel sly 7f	:23½ :45½ 1:23⅘	3 ↑ Allowance	6 6	64½ 66	41½	2hd	Maple E	b 115	5.50	86–16 Run Tell Run 115hd JacquesWho1152GayPrelude109²	Just missed 7
20Aug76–	6Sar fst 6f	:22½ :45½ 1:09⅘	3 ↑ Allowance	5 9	69	68½	68	611	Vasquez J	b 119	11.70	82–07 Nalees Rialto 1192½ Gitche Gumee 119hd Kirby Lane1141½	Trailed 6
4Aug76–	7Sar fm 1	ⓣ:46⅘ 1:10½ 1:41½	3 ↑ Allowance	1 8	78½	58	416	Vasquez J	b 119	5.80	75–13 Duveen 1193 Best Laid Plans 114½ Face Mask 1192½	No threat 8
24July76–	7Aqu gd 1	ⓣ 1:13	1:36⅗	3 ↑ Allowance	6 3	63½ 63½ 52½ 45½	Day P	b 119⁴	8.20	— — Dorji 119½ Co Host 1194½ Brian Boru 119hd	Evenly 6

24July76–Dead heat

| 9July76– | 7Aqu fm 1 | ⓣ:47½ 1:11½ 1:36 | 3 ↑ Allowance | 4 4 | 42 | 53½ 62½ 63½ | Cordero A Jr | b 117 | 6.20 | — — Burundi 117hd Dorji 117½ Rough Punch 1141½ | Bid, weakened 8 |

LATEST WORKOUTS Nov 5 Aqu 3f fst :37 h

Silver Badge

Own.—Hobeau Farm

B. h. 5, by Poker—Silver True, by Hail To Reason
Br.—Whitney C V (Ky)
Tr.—Jerkens H Allen

	Turf Record	St.	1st	2nd	3rd	Amt.
122	13 1 3 2	1976	17	1	2	1	$30,148
		1975	25	3	6	3	$60,703

| 30Dec76– | 8Aqu fst 7f | :22½ :45 | 1:23½ | 3 ↑ Allowance | 6 2 | 33 | 32 | 88½ 88½ | Turcotte R | b 122 | 3.00 | 76–20 Chief Tamanaco 120nk JacquesWho117nkBanian1151¼ | Tired 8 |
| 23Oct76– | 6Kee fst 1¼ | :48 | 1:12½ 1:44⅘ | 3 ↑ Allowance | 2 2 | 31½ 61 | 2hd | 7¹² | Patterson G | b 111 | 15.50 | 83–19 Silver Badge 1111½ Easy Gallop 117² Topinabee 112½ | Driving 9 |

23Oct76–Run in two divisions, 6th & 7th races.

30Oct76–	7Kee fst 1	:47½ 1:12½ 1:44⅘	3 ↑ Allowance	1 1	2½	32½ 47½	6¹²	Espinoza A	b 112	3.00	81–14 Ilefetchit 113¹½ Country Boy Jim 122⁶ Yarao 1222½	Tired 6
21Sep76–	8Bel fst 6f	:22½ :46½ 1:16	3 ↑ Allowance	7 4	51½ 62½ 86½ 66½	Montoya D	b 115	28.80	86–17 Logical 117hd Piamem 117½ Gitche Gumee 1153	No factor 8
3Aug76–	8Sar fm 1	ⓣ:46⅘ 1:10½ 1:41⅘	3 ↑ Allowance	2 1	42½ 43½ 32	31	Vasquez J	b 115	8.10	87–16 Ribot Grande 117⁴ Camelford115nkSilverBadge115hd	Finished well 7
14Aug76–	7Sar fst 6f	:22	:44½ 1:09⅘	3 ↑ Allowance	1 8	88½ 78	76½ 76½	Montoya D	b 115	24.70	88–11 UnderTack117hdPortAuthority115hdJohnBryn1173	Stumbled start 8
3Jun76–	7Bel fm 7f	ⓣ:23	1:21½	3 ↑ Allowance	1 8	88½ 74	44	57½	Turcotte R	b 117	17.70	87–09 NoseForNose1181½UpperCurrent117nkDeterminedKing1151½	Tired 10
12Jun76–	7Mth fm 1⅙	ⓣ:46⅘ 1:10½ 1:41½	3 ↑ Allowance	3 7	64½ 31	87	811	Brumfield D	b 114	9.80	84–14 Hat Full 1143 Toujours Pret 1143 It's Freezing 116hd	Tired 10
31May76–	8CD sly 1⅙	:48½ 1:13	1:46	3 ↑ Mem. Day H.	1 3	11	11	1hd	2nk	Brown D	b 117	*1.10e	78–29 It's Freezing 116nk Silver Badge 1116 Skit Run 1194	6
19May76–	8CD fst 1⅙	:45½ 1:09½ 1:36⅘	Allowance	1 2	21½ 45½ 41½	Espinoza J C	b 116	*1.00e	79–19 ⒹSatan's Hills 113no Jim Dan Bob 1131½ Yamanin 1164½	6

LATEST WORKOUTS Nov 27 Aqu tr.t 4f fst :48⅘ h

Great Above

Own.—Somer S

Dk. b. or br. c. 4, by Minnesota Mac—Ta Wee, by Intentionally
Br.—Tartan Farms Corp (Fla)
Tr.—Martin Frank

	Turf Record	St.	1st	2nd	3rd	Amt.
115	5 2 2 0	1976	12	6	1	0	$3,420
		1975	6	0	1	0	$56,364

24Nov76–	8Aqu fst 6f	:21½ :44½ 1:09⅘	3 ↑ Clm c–40000	2 8	53½ 54½ 78½ 78½	Woodhouse R	b 117	*3.20	83–14 Checkerhall 1151½ Banian 1173 Bonge 1158½	No threat 8
6Nov76–	4Aqu fst 6f	:22½ :46	1:11⅘	3 ↑ Clm 45000	2 7	43½ 41½ 3nk 41½	Woodhouse R	b 113	4.20	86–27 Christoforo 117nk Jaunty Jolly 113hd Townsand 1171	Evenly 7
30Oct76–	7Aqu fst 6f	:22½ :46	1:11⅖	3 ↑ Clm 45000	7 6	52½ 54	32	53½	Woodhouse R	b 115	9.50	87–16 Kintla's Folly 1151 Chief Tamanaco 1153 Jaunty Jack 1152	Tired 9
24Oct76–	2Bel fst 7f	:23½ :46½ 1:23	3 ↑ Clm 45000	1 1	11	11	11	11	Woodhouse R	b 117	5.50	88–18 Chief's Holiday 117⅛ Great Above 117⅘ Bold Play 1173½	Gamely 9
7Oct76–	7Bel fst 7f	:23½ :45½ 1:22⅖	3 ↑ Clm 50000	4 3	21	31	55	58½	Woodhouse R	b 117	11.90	80–13 Gitche Gumee 117⁵ Sky Commander 1153 Laertes 1173	Tired 7
23Sep76–	8Bel fst 6f	:22½ :45	1:09⅘	3 ↑ Clm 50000	2 6	65	67½ 714 710	Velez R I	b 117	8.20	75–12 Sunny Clime 117½ Jackson Square 117½GabeBenzur114no	Outrun 7
17Nov75–	8Aqu fst 6f	:45½ 1:09½ 1:35	Lucky Draw	3 5	43½ 41½ 52½ 63½	Cruguet J	117	3.80e	87–12 Pitirre 119no Rushing Man 119½ NalesRialto 1171½	Off slowly 8
2Nov75–	8Bel sly 1	:46½ 1:10	1:34½	Allowance	6 5	31½ 31	33½	Cruguet J	114	2.60e	93–12 Guards Up 1143½ ValidAppeal119nkGreatAbove114no	Broke slowly 7
17Oct75–	8Aqu fst 1⅙	:47½ 1:11½ 1:42½	3 ↑ Allowance	1 8	64½ 74	31	1nk	Vasquez J	113	*2.20	90–11 Great Above 113nk I'm On Top 1172½ New Alibhai 1152½	Driving 8
4Oct75–	8Bel fm 1	ⓣ:45½ 1:10½ 1:35½	3 ↑ Allowance	5 12	12	12	2nk	Velez R I⁵	108	*2.60	92–11 PmperedJbneh116nk GretAbove1081¾WhiskyPoppl112½	Weakened 8

LATEST WORKOUTS ● Dec 5 Bel tr.t 4f fst :47½ h ● Nov 22 Bel 4f fst :47⅘ h Nov 16 Bel 4f fst :48⅘ b Nov 6 Bel 4f fst :48½ b

Banian

Own.—Marsh J D

Ch. g. 6, by Nashua—Vapors, by Swoon's Son
Br.—Pin Oak Stud Inc (Ky)
Tr.—Cantey Joseph B

	Turf Record	St.	1st	2nd	3rd	Amt.
115	10 4 0 1	1976	18	5	2	3	$37,510
		1975	13	3	3	1	$29,935

30Dec76–	8Aqu fst 7f	:22½ :45	1:23½	3 ↑ Allowance	3 4	21½ 2hd 2nd 3½	Maple E	b 115	8.20	84–20 Chief Tamanaco 120nk Jacques Who 117nkBanian1151¼	Weakened 8
24Nov76–	8Aqu fst 6f	:21½ :44½ 1:09⅘	3 ↑ Clm c–40000	3 1	1½	11	11	1¹	Maple E	b 115	*3.20	91–14 Checkerhall 1151½ Banian 1173 Bonge 1158½	Gamely 8
22Nov76–	8Aqu fst 6f	:22½ :46	1:11⅖	3 ↑ Clm 50000	3 1	1½	11	4nk	59	Maple E	b 114	10.90	84–27 Christoforo 117nk Jaunty Jolly 113hd Townsand 1171	Tired 9
15Sep76–	8Mth fm 5f	ⓣ:22½ :45	:57⅘	3 ↑ Allowance	8 1	11	1hd 1¹	1nk	Stephen K	b 117	*1.10	91–19 Banian 1171¼ Sweet Isaac 1151¼ Run Tell Run 1221	Driving 8
7Sep76–	8Mth fm 6f	ⓣ:22½ :45	1:09⅘	3 ↑ Allowance	5 2	1½	1¹	14	14½	MacBeth D	b 117	*2.60	98–12 Banian 1174½ Don't Be Late Jim 114no In The Swing 114½	Driving 6
17Aug76–	8Mth fm 6f	ⓣ:21½ :45	1:09⅘	3 ↑ Allowance	6 1	1hd 2hd 2nd 3½	Thomas D	b 115	13.10	84–15 Lord Arlen 1192 Sweet Isaac 1113 Our Hermis 115½	Gave way 8
5Aug76–	7Mth fst 6f	:21½ :45	1:09⅘	3 ↑ Allowance	8 2	1hd 2hd 2½	3½	Marble W M	b 117	6.20	83–14 Mexican General 113⁴ Banian 1151¼ Sweet Isaac 117⁵	Hung 7
31July76–	6Mth fst 6f	:21½ :45½ 1:10½	3 ↑ Allowance	1 8	1hd 1½	1½	1hd	Thomas D	b 117	*2.50	87–15 Come On Jay 119² Midnight Joker 1163 Banian 117⁶	Weakened 5
14July76–	6Pim fm 5f	ⓣ:22½ :45½ :58⅘	3 ↑ Allowance	1 3	1¹	1½	16	1nk	McCarron C J	b 122	*1.70	99–01 Banian 122nk Smokey Topaz 1192½ Rowley 113½	Easily 6
22Jun76–	8Mth fm 6f	ⓣ:22½ :45½ 1:09⅘	3 ↑ Allowance	8 1	1¹	11	16	1nk	MacBeth D	b 117	8.30	96–07 Jaunty Jolly 109² Silent Song 1141½ Banian 117nk	Good try 9

LATEST WORKOUTS Dec 10 Bel 3f fst :36 bg Dec 2 Bel 3f fst :35½ bg Nov 23 Bel 4f fst :35⅘ bg Nov 20 Bel 5f fst 1:00¾ hg

Port Authority							Dk. b. or br. c. 4, by Delta Judge—Hidden Reef, by Cohoes Br.—Green Mr-Mrs R L (Ky) Tr.—Schmitt William F								**115**		Turf Record St. 1st 2nd 3rd 1 0 0 0		St. 1st 2nd 3rd Amt. 1976 17 1 3 5 $39,920 1975 14 3 0 3 $21,960
Own.—Miron Julie																			
23Nov76- 8Aqu	fst	6f	:22⅕	:46	1:11	3↑Allowance	8 2	31½	41½	74	75½	Venezia M	b 115	3.50	83-21	Naudi 115¾ Wing South 115½ Jacques Who 1222¾		Gave way	9
15Oct76- 8Bel	fst	6f	:22⅕	:45⅘	1:10⅘	3↑Allowance	6 2	23	24	21	33¼	Maple E	b 115	5.10	86-19	Piamem 115¾ Ramahorn 1152¾ Port Authority 115hd		Hung	9
7Oct76- 7Bel	fst	6f	:22⅖	:45⅕	1:09⅖	3↑Allowance	1 4	32	42	44	44¾	Maple E	b 115	2.20	90-13	Gitche Gumee 117½ Sky Commander 1153¾JacquesWho115½		Tired	7
13Sep76- 8Bel	fst	6f	:22⅖	:45⅕	1:09⅖	3↑Allowance	7 6	33½	21½	21	3¾	Maple E	b 115	5.70	94-11	Nebr. Harvest108½PromisedCity119nkPortAuthority115½		Good try	7
2Sep76- 8Bel	sly	7f	:22⅗	:45⅕	1:21⅗	3↑Allowance	3 5	55½	55½	48½	513	Cruguet J	b 115	5.60	82-09	Forage 1193 Packer Captain 1178 Lefty 1152		No factor	6
24Aug76- 7Sar	fst	6½f	:22⅗	:45⅖	1:16⅕	3↑Allowance	1 5	43½	43	22	34¼	Cruguet J	b 115	*.90	90-16	Relent 1151¼ Piamem 1153 Port Authority 1151¼		No excuse	6
14Aug76- 7Sar	fst	6f	:22	:44⅘	1:09⅖	3↑Allowance	4 5	43	42½	2hd	2hd	Cruguet J	b 115	13.70	93-11	Under Tack 117hd Port Authority115hdJohnBryn1173		Just missed	8
8May76- 7Bel	fst	6f	:22⅗	:45⅗	1:09⅘	Allowance	4 2	1½	12	12	21¼	Cruguet J	b 115	13.50	92-14	Pompini 1191¼ Port Authority 115½ Wishing Stone 115nk		Gamely	7
26Apr76- 6Aqu	fst	6f	:22⅖	:45⅘	1:10⅖	Clm 45000	5 5	72¾	42	1½	1¾	Maple E	b 113	6.20	91-14	Port Authority 113¾ Kratos 1081 Judgmatic 117¾		Driving	9
19Apr76- 6Aqu	fst	7f	:22⅘	:45⅖	1:23	Clm 42500	6 4	41½	42½	41½	32	Maple E	b 115	*1.90	84-18	Malign 1171¾ Umin 113nk Port Authority 1152½		Steadied, hung	7
LATEST WORKOUTS		Nov 20 Bel tr.t 4f fst :50⅗ b					Nov 9 Bel tr.t 3f fst :38 b												

Let's take a look at how the eight horses compared on speed figures:[1]

Since Banian (at 7-5) and Checkerhall (at 9-5) were the two favorites (the other six attracted little attention at the pari-mutuel windows), we will look at them first.

BANIAN has had three good races at Aqueduct since his recent layoff, and his figures appear to be getting better:

Dec. 3	Aqueduct	7f	$84+20=104+4=108$
Nov. 24	Aqueduct	6f	$91+17=108-3=105$
Nov. 8	Aqueduct	6f	$85+24=109-3=106$

The animal is in shape, is relatively fresh, and its last race at seven furlongs was outstanding, considering its tendency to tire at six furlongs. Add to this the fact that he figures to be alone on the early lead, and you can see why Banian was made the favorite over Checkerhall, who had just beaten him.

CHECKERHALL returned to peak form in his last, running by Banian in the last sixteenth. Several races in his past performances indicate that he will probably be able to duplicate this effort:

Nov. 24	Aqueduct	6f	$92+17=109-3=106$
July 22	Aqueduct	6f	$90+19=109-3=106$
July 2	Aqueduct	6f	$94+15=109-3=106$
June 17	Belmont	6f	$90+17=107-2=105$
June 7	Belmont	6f	$89+19=108-2=106$

It is fair to say that, when in shape, Checkerhall is a consistent 106.

FIVEONTHESIDE comes out of the same seven-furlong race as Banian, in which he was never a factor although racing for the first time in 6 weeks. He also showed little against Checkerhall at six furlongs on July 22. His only 1976 win in 16 tries came on a disqualification. His best races indicate that he is not fast enough to beat the two favorites at six furlongs:

[1]Accurate daily variants were available for all 1976 races run at Aqueduct, Belmont, Saratoga, and Monmouth, and were used in the calculations in place of the *Form* variant. For races run at other tracks, the *Form* variant was used.

Oct. 22	Belmont	7f	$82 + 19 = 101 + 3 = 104$
Oct. 1	Belmont	6f	$88 + 15 = 103 - 2 = 101$
Aug. 9	Saratoga	7f	$83 + 17 = 100 + 1 = 101$

MR. BARB was gaining ground in the stretch against Banian last out, but his previous races suggest that he is not fast enough to catch that rival at six furlongs:

Dec. 3	Aqueduct	7f	$83 + 20 = 103 + 4 = 107$
Nov. 7	Penn Nat.	6f	$87 + 21 = 108 - 7^* = 101$
Oct. 19	Monmouth	6f	$88 + 20 = 108 - 4 = 104$
Sept. 24	Monmouth	6f	$90 + 18 = 108 - 4 = 104$

JACQUES WHO has already won his race for the year, and passed Banian in the last strides last out. His recent efforts credit him with no speed points, a serious flaw at six furlongs. Unless the speed figures deceive, he improved sharply last out:

Dec. 3	Aqueduct	7f	$85 + 20 = 105 + 4 = 109$
Nov. 23	Aqueduct	6f	$87 + 19 = 106 - 3 = 103$
Nov. 12	Aqueduct	7f	$78 + 21 = 99 + 4 = 103$
Sept. 10	Belmont	7f	$83 + 14 = 97 + 3 = 100$

SILVER BADGE, a recent stakes winner, and the highweight at 122 pounds, appears entered at an unsuitable distance. He tired badly chasing Banian in his last, and is probably just out for the exercise. None of the sprint races in his past performances are even decent.

GREAT ABOVE was just claimed by Pancho Martin, and the excellent workout on December 5 raises the possibility that New York's leading trainer may have ironed out a few problems. Recent speed figures suggest that this once classier colt would be a solid contender on his best effort:

| Nov. 8 | Aqueduct | 6f | $86 + 24 = 110 - 3 = 107$ |
| Oct. 21 | Belmont | 7f | $86 + 18 = 104 + 3 = 107$ |

Although soundly beaten by both Checkerhall and Banian in his last start, Great Above did finish ahead of Banian on November 8.

PORT AUTHORITY returned from a six-week freshening with a dull effort on November 23. His recent figures indicate that he will have to improve sharply to contend in this field:

| Oct. 15 | Belmont | 6f | $86 + 18 = 104 - 2 = 102$ |
| Sept. 13 | Belmont | 6f | $94 + 13 = 107 - 2 = 105$ |

*1976 adjustment

Before making a selection among these horses, one problem must be resolved. Perhaps you have noticed it. That seven-furlong race involving Banian, Jacques Who, Mr. Barb, Fiveontheside, and Silver Badge appears to have received a suspiciously high figure. Banian figured to get worse, not better, at seven furlongs. Jacques Who inexplicably improved six points off his recent good efforts. Mr. Barb got a figure three points above his previous high. And Fiveontheside ran a poor race, yet received a figure equal to his previous high.

It would seem wise, then, to distrust the figure for this race, and rate the horses involved on the basis of their other races.

On this premise, four more horses can be eliminated as serious contenders: Fiveontheside, Mr. Barb, Jacques Who, and Port Authority. None figures capable of running within two to three lengths of Banian, Checkerhall, or Great Above at six furlongs. Three of these horses, we should note, could have been eliminated for other reasons. Jacques Who, for having no speed points, and both Fiveontheside and Port Authority for returning to the races with a poor effort (see Chapter 8).

This leaves us with three contenders. Both Banian and Checkerhall are sharp and fresh, each making his fourth start after a layoff. Banian is coming back eight days after his latest effort, and figures to set an uncontested pace. Checkerhall is a very consistent animal at six furlongs, and comes off a victory over Banian. Great Above was just claimed by the circuit's leading trainer, and has the best figures in the field. Anyone willing to forgive his recent failure against his major rivals here would have found the 15-1 odds very attractive.

As it turned out, Martin had worked his magic on Great Above, who won the race, but was disqualified (for the third time in his career) for bearing in during the stretch run. The chart tells the full story.

SEVENTH RACE Aqueduct DECEMBER 11, 1976	6 FURLONGS (INNER DIRT). (1.11⅕) ALLOWANCE. Purse $25,000. 3-year-olds and upward which have not won two races of $6,100 since December 15. Weight, 3-year-olds, 120 lbs. Older, 122 lbs. Non-winners of a race of $6,100 since October 1 allowed 3 lbs. Of such a race since September 1, 5 lbs. Of such a race since July 15, 7 lbs. (Maiden, claiming and starter races not considered.)

Value of race $25,000, value to winner $15,000, second $5,500, third $3,000, fourth $1,500. Mutuel pool $251,698, OTB pool $116,323. Exacta Pool $263,925. OTB Exacta Pool $225,782.

Last Raced	Horse	Eqt.A.Wt	PP	St	¼	½	Str	Fin	Jockey	Odds $1
24Nov76 6Aqu7	ⒹGreat Above	b 4 115	6	6	2²	2³	1hd	1no	Vasquez J	15.60
24Nov76 6Aqu1	Checkerhall	b 5 115	1	4	4½	3²	3⁵	2¹¾	Cordero A Jr	1.80
3Dec76 8Aqu3	Banian	b 6 115	7	1	1¹½	1¹	2¹	3¹	Maple E	1.40
3Dec76 8Aqu4	Mr. Barb	b 4 115	3	5	7⁵	6²	4¹½	4¾	Cruguet J	14.40
3Dec76 8Aqu7	Fiveontheside	4 119	2	7	5²	5½	6¹	5²	Santiago A	26.70
3Dec76 8Aqu2	Jacques Who	b 6 117	4	8	8	8	7¹½	6³¾	Cauthen S5	7.00
3Dec76 8Aqu8	Silver Badge	b 5 122	5	2	6hd	7³	8	7½	Velasquez J	10.10
23Nov76 8Aqu7	Port Authority	b 4 115	8	3	3hd	4¹½	5hd	8	Hernandez R	11.20

Ⓓ-Great Above Disqualified and placed third.

OFF AT 3:19, EST. Start good, Won driving. Time, :22⅘, :46⅕, 1:11 Track fast.

(NEW TRACK RECORD)

$2 Mutuel Prices:			
1-(A)-CHECKERHALL	5.60	3.00	2.80
7-(G)-BANIAN		2.80	2.60
6-(F)-GREAT ABOVE			5.40

$2 EXACTA 1-7 PAID $15.20.

Checkerhall—dk b or br. rig, by Times Roman—Oh Missie, by Oh Johnny. Trainer Barrera Oscar S. Bred by Ortlieb C (Ky).

GREAT ABOVE started to move after BANIAN following the first furlong, engaged that one on the outside settling for the stretch run, drifted in and tended to drift induring the last eighth, just got up. After a claim of foul was lodged by the jockey of CHECKERHALL, GREAT ABOVE was disqualified and placed third, for appearing to bother BANIAN the most. CHECKERHALL raced to the inside throughout, might have been intimidated through the last eighth, but never appeared to lose momentum before barely missing. BANIAN went to the front on his own courage, went along easily past the midway point, then failed to keep up in the drive while in tight between horses. MR. BARB raced inside while finishing his race with good energy. FIVEONTHESIDE dropped from a striking position on the turn, then gained late. JACQUES WHO made a belated bid. SILVER BADGE was outrun. PORT AUTHORITY had no visible excuse.

Owners— 1, Somer S; 2, Chankin T; 3, Marsh J D; 4, Hardin Sharon L; 5, Brant P; 6, Wimpfheimer J D; 7, Hobeau Farm; 8, Miron Julie.

Trainers— 1, Martin Frank; 2, Barrera Oscar S; 3, Cantey Joseph B; 4, Hild Glen L; 5, Glynn Sanford; 6, Sedlacek Woodrow; 7, Jerkens H Allen Schmitt William F.

Copyright © 1979, by DAILY RACING FORM, INC. Reprinted with permission of copyright owner.

Interestingly, the race was run in 106. If only the figures were always that accurate!

Note: The reader will find it a useful exercise to rank the horses in this field using the two approaches to speed figures discussed in the preceding chapter. With the exception of Great Above (and the unrated Silver Badge), the "failures" approach picks out the horse's last two good races. The recent poor efforts of Fiveontheside and Port Authority came after layoffs, while both Checkerhall and Mr. Barb have just one failure between their latest two good races. The "average of last two good races" approach rates Great Above on top. The "failures" approach chooses either Banian or Checkerhall, depending on how Banian's race at seven furlongs is treated.

○ RACE #2 ○

The Select Handicap at Monmouth on July 17, 1974 presented a different situation. Eleven three-year-olds contested this six-furlong dash. Here is how they looked on paper:

8 MONMOUTH 6 FURLONGS

6 FURLONGS. (1.08) 27TH RUNNING SELECT HANDICAP. Purse $25,000 added. The owner of the winner to receive a trophy. 3–year–olds. By subscription of $25 each which should accompany the nomination, $100 to pass the entry box, $150 to start with $25,000 added of which 65% of all monies to the winner; 20% to secnd; 10% to third and 5% to fourth. Weights, 5 p.m., Friday, July 12, 1974. Starters to be named through the entry box by the usual time of closing. Closed Monday, July 1, 1974 with 31 nominations.

Margaret's Beau *
Own.—Bright View Farm
Dk. b. or br. c. 3, by Bold Lad—Twice Cited, by Double Jay
Br.—Taylors Purchase Inc (Ky)
Tr.—Bardaro A J
114

	St.	1st	2nd	3rd	Amt.
1974	6	4	0	0	$17,300
1973	0	M	0	0	

5Jly74- 8Mth	gd	6f	:22	:44⅘	1:10⅗	Allowance	6	1	1¹	12½	1²	1¾	Miceli M	b 115	*1.80	87-21	Margaret's Beau115¾ CastInBronze117⁴ OddsAndEvens115¹	Driving 6
25Jun74- 7Mth	sly	6f	:22	:45⅕	1:11⅗	3↑ Allowance	8	1	1hd	12½	1⁷	16½	Miceli M	b 115	7.50	82-28	Margaret'sBeau1156½ FlashAct113⁴ AntiqueBrandy120no	Easy score 9
11Jun74- 6Bel	fst	6f	:22⅖	:46⅕	1:10	3↑ Allowance	6	6	1³	1½	3⁷	5¹⁵	Velasquez J	b 108	7.50	78-14	Princely Native 1159½ Jomar 1123½ Turn To Bo 1131½	Slow start 6
29May74- 8Lib	fst	6f	:22⅖	:46	1:11⅕	Sentinel	8	4	1hd	2½	42½	67½	Miceli M	112	5.10	81-20	Wing South 121½ Silver Hope 121⁴ Groton Guy 112²	Tired 9
20May74- 7GS	fst	6f	:22⅘	:46⅗	1:13⅖	3↑ Allowance	6	3	11½	1²	1⁵	1½	Miceli M	113	*1.00e	77-24	Margaret's Beau113½ PrivateCircle115² DecidedlyEm's1221¼	Driving 10
23Apr74- 6Hia	fst	6f	:22⅖	:45⅗	1:11⅕	3↑ Md Sp Wt	8	4	1¹	11½	1²	1⁴	Miceli M	114	2.10	87-21	Margaret's Beau 114⁴ Wally B. 1144½ Poker Hound 114⁴	Driving 9

LATEST WORKOUTS Jly 15 Mth 4f fst :50⅖ b Jly 11 Mth 5f fst 1:01⅖ h Jly 1 Mth 4f gd :51 b Jun 21 Mth 5f fst 1:01 h

Copyright © 1979, by DAILY RACING FORM, INC. Reprinted with permission of copyright owner.

Realman ✱
Own.—Blum Maribel G

Gr. c. 3, by Gray Phantom—Iwantwhatiwant, by Primate
Br.—Thornton T C (Ky)
Tr.—Handy G R

					St.	1st	2nd	3rd	Amt.
				110	1974	11	3	1	$18,101
					1973	8	4	1	$11,448

5Jly74- 8Mth gd 6f	:22	:44½ 1:10½	Allowance	3 5 57½ 511 610 612	Blum W	b 113	4.90	75-21 Margaret's Beau 115¾ Cast In Bronze117⁴ OddsAndEvens115¹ Tired 6
21Jun74- 8Crc fst 6f	:22½	:46 1:12¾ 3↑Allowance	4 2 13 12 1½ 65¼	Salinas J	b 113	1.90	86-19 ⑤Somewhat Striking108ⁿᵒ Mike A.1082¼ FireyNoon113¹ Speed, tired 8
8Jun74- 9Crc fst 6f	:22½	1:12	Citrus H	4 3 11 11½ 1¼ 43	Marquez C	b 119	*1.20	90-14 Star Lance 119¼ Trusted 116½ Do It My Way 122¹ Speed, tired 7
29May74- 9Crc fst 6f	:23	:46½ 1:12¼	Allowance	6 2 11 11½ 2½ 31	Salinas J	b 119	1.70	89-19 Do It My Way 122¹ Star Lance 122ⁿᵈ Realman 119⁴ Speed, tired 7
19Mar74- 9Hia fst 6f	:22½	:45½ 1:10½	Allowance	2 4 1hd 2hd 3hd 97	Rivera M A	b 113	*.60	85-13 Friendly Bee 115³ Semi Royal 114ⁿᵏ Mark The Prince 117¹ Used up 9
5Mar74- 9Hia fst 7f	:23	1:23	Bahamas	2 8 11 12 14 2¾	Rivera M A	b 113	8.60	90-08 Hasty Flyer 112¾ Realman 115²½ Gold and Myrrh 112¹ Gamely 14
24Feb74- 4PR fst 5½f	:22½	:47 1:07	Allowance	1 4 11½ 12 14 15½	Machado V5	b 113	*.40	— — Realman 113⁵½ Miraflores 106ⁿᵒ Guanajibena 110²½ Easily 7
17Feb74- 7PR fst 1½	:47½	1:13½ 1:48½	Washington	2 1 17 21½ 26 711	Mendoza C	b 120	1.50	— — My Eye 120² Sunglasses 120² Noel George 120²½ Used early 8
3Feb74- 1PR fst 1	:47½	1:13¾ 1:39¾	Allowance	2 2 15 14½ 14 14	Mendoza C	b 120	*.10	— — Realman 120⁴ Darold's Dream 112³¼ Maremoto 112¹ Easily 7
18Jan74- 4PR sly 6f	:22½	:46½ 1:12¾	Allowance	7 2 15 14½ 13 13½	Mendoza C	b 114	*.40	— — Realman 113⁶³½ Sunglasses 120⁷½ Danubio 115²¼ Easily 7
LATEST WORKOUTS	Jly 12 Mth ① 5f fm 1:03 b			Jly 2 Mth 4f gd :47 h			● Jun 20 Crc 3f fst :35¾ h	Jun 15 Crc 4f fst :49 b

---

The Grok ✱
Own.—Miami Lakes Stable

B. c. 3, by All Hands—Oh Susan, by Shannon II
Br.—Casse N E (Fla)
Tr.—Arcodia A

						Turf Record			St.	1st	2nd	3rd	Amt.
				114		St. 1st 2nd 3rd			1974	12	2	3	$17,774
						7 1 2 1			1973	11	2	2	$13,200

29Jun74- 8Mth gd 6f	:22½	:45½ 1:10½ 3↑Allowance	1 3 11½ 12½ 1½ 31	Iannelli F	b 109	12.40	85-20 Key To The Gun 111ⁿᵏ Twin Time 122¾ The Grok 109²¼ Weakened 7
8Jun74- 6Mth fm 1 ① :48½	1:12½ 1:36¾	Allowance	2 6 75½ 65½ 9¹¹10¹⁵	Broussard R	b 114	5.20	77-12 Silver Florin 124½ I'm On Top 116¹ R. Tom Can 114³ Outrun 10
8Jun74-Run in Two Divisions, 6th and 8th Races.							
29May74- 7Mth fm 1	:49	1:13¼ 1:38¼	Allowance	3 5 56¼ 62¾ 51¾ 54	Iannelli F	b 116	*1.50	78-18 Sokokis 120¼ Hat Full 114² David's Pinecone 109¼ Checked 6
11May74- 9Crc fm 1	:47½	1:12¼ 1:36¾	Boca Raton H	3 4 33 11 2hd 33	Iannelli F	b 118	*1.80	92-05 Commanding Lead108¹½ Dorrin'sWay1191½ TheGrok1182½ Gave way 13
11May74-Run in two divisions, 8th and 9th races.							
22Apr74- 9Hia fst 6f	:22	:45½ 1:10½	Allowance	5 2 45 33 11 13	Iannelli F	b 111	2.40	88-20 The Grok 111³ Swoon's Lass 120¾ Rule Fair 113²¼ Handily 7
10Apr74- 9Hia fst 7f	:22	:45½ 1:23¾	Allowance	2 3 2107¼ 64½ 3ⁿᵏ 32⅓	Iannelli F	b 111	28.00f	87-15 Mark The Prince116ⁿᵒ Eric'sChamp120²½ TheGrok111²½ Wide, hung 15
4Mar74- 9GP fst 1½	:46½	1:11½ 1:49	Florida Dby	4 2 23 52¾12¹⁸11¹¹⁷	Torres J E	b 122	16.80f	72-11 Judger 118¼ Cannonade 122⁵ Buck's Bid 118ⁿᵏ Early speed 16
22Feb74- 9GP fm 1½ ①	1:45½	Allowance	5 3 2hd 14 16 1hd	Torres J E	b 113	4.60	85-21 The Grok 112hd Butterbump 114¹½ Sir Jason 112¾ Just lasted 9
9Feb74- 6GP fst 1	:47½	1:11½ 1:37½	Allowance	1 1 1½ 12 12 2hd	Torres J E	b 114	14.70	92-10 Shady Character 114hd The Grok 112¾ R.TomCan113ⁿᵏ Just missed 8
30Jan74- 5GP fst 6f	:22½	:45½ 1:11½	Allowance	7 8 11½10¹º10¹1¹¹ 95	Rivera M A	b 114	49.00	78-22 DustyLnePrince113¹ CoolSpringPrk113ⁿᵏ LordForestar122¾ Outrun 11
LATEST WORKOUTS	Jly 14 Mth 5f fst 1:04⅖ b			Jly 9 Mth 4f fst :50 b			Jun 25 Mth 4f hy :48 b	Jun 6 Mth 4f fst :49 b

---

Az Igazi
Own.—Straus J R

Dk. b. or br. c. 3, by Time Tested—Fashionably, by Bald Eagle
Br.—Walden B P (Ky)
Tr.—Pardue H C

						St.	1st	2nd	3rd	Amt.
				117		1974	4	1	1	$20,500
						1973	8	4	2	$52,165

28Jun74- 8Aqu fst 6f	:22½	:45½ 1:09 3↑Allowance	6 2 11 11 24 2hd	Mayorga W	113	4.00	93-15 Lonetree 116⁵ Az Igazi 113hd Tap The Tree 119⁵ Gamely 6
10Jun74- 8Bel fst 6f	:22½	1:10 3↑Allowance	6 2 22 22 12 1hd	Mayorga W	110	*2.10	93-16 Az Igazi 110hd Halo 115ⁿᵏ Special Affair 112ⁿᵏ Driving 6
27May74- 6Bel fst 6f	:22½	:44½ 1:09½ 3↑Allowance	1 1 1hd 2hd 3hd 2hd	Moon L5	102	5.30	94-11 Dirty Dan 112ⁿᵏ El Espanoleto 111ⁿᵒ Az Igazi 102½ Held on 7
29Apr74- 8Aqu fst 6f	:22½	:45½ 1:10¾	Allowance	6 2 3ⁿᵏ 52¾ 65 7¹²	Mayorga W	117	5.30	79-16 Be A Native 116²½ El Espanoleto117ⁿᵏ ⑤TrentonJoe113¹¼ Bothered 9
29Apr74-Placed sixth through disqualification							
25Aug73- 7Sar fst 6f	:22½	:45½ 1:16¾	Hopeful	5 4 33¼ 41½ 65¼ 7¹⁶	Gustines H	121	*1.00	80-08 Gusty O'Shy121½ TkByStorm121²½ PrincofRson121²¼ Stumbled start 7
15Aug73- 7Sar fst 6f	:23	:46½ 1:10¾	Sanford	5 1 11 12 13 12	Venezia M	121	*.60	87-14 Az Igazi 121² Prince of Reason 121⁶ Totheend 121hd Ridden out 6
6Aug73- 7Sar fst 6f	:21½	1:11	Sar. Special	5 2 24 23 21½ 1½	Venezia M	117	*1.30	85-18 Az Igazi 117½ Gusty O'Shay 117ⁿᵏ Lakeville 117½ Driving 5
27Jly73- 7Aqu fst 6f	:22½	:45 1:11	Tremont	3 2 1½ 11 1hd 2½	Venezia M	117	2.90	94-14 Raise A Cup 120½ Az Igazi 117¾ Big Latch 120½ Gamely 6
30Jun73- 4Aqu fst 5½f	:22½	:45 1:04	Allowance	1 1 11½ 1½ 11½ 11½	Venezia M	117	3.50	93-05 Az Igazi 117¹½ PleaseSucceed117½ CorporateHeadache117¹½ Driving 9
18Jun73- 3Aqu fst 5f	:22½	:46½ 1:00	Md 35000	1 1 1½ 11½ 1½ 11½	Venezia M	117	3.70	92-12 Az Igazi 117¹ Mike A. 117¹¼ Lakeville 117¼ Driving 10
LATEST WORKOUTS	Jly 16 Bel tr.t 3f fst :35½ h			● Jly 11 Bel 5f fst :59 h			Jly 5 Bel 1 fst 1:39⅖ h	● Jun 22 Bel 7f sly 1:26 h

---

Silver Hope
Own.—Udouj Mrs H J

B. c. 3, by Ingrained—Jane Jay, by Double Jay
Br.—Udouj Mr-Mrs H J (Ark)
Tr.—Battles O

							Turf Record			St.	1st	2nd	3rd	Amt.
				119			St. 1st 2nd 3rd			1974	8	3	2	$28,510
							1 0 0 0			1973	5	3	0	$18,877

19Jun74- 8Lib fst 6f	:22½	:45½ 1:10¾	Allowance	3 2 12 12 13 15	Wilson R	b 123	*1.20	91-21 Silver Hope 123⁵ Groton Guy 113⁴ Second Pleasure 123¼ Driving 9
8Jun74- 3Mth fm 1 ①	:47½	1:11½ 1:38	Long Branch	5 2 43 74½ 75¼ 55¼	Wilson R	b 116	4.70e	80-12 Hat Full 114ⁿᵏ To The Rescue 116¹½ Never Explain 114² Bore out 9
8Jun74-Run in two Divisions, 6th and 8th Races.							
29May74- 8Lib fst 6f	:22½	:46 1:11½	Sentinel	5 3 52¼ 42 2hd 2½	Wilson R	b 121	5.90	89-20 Wing South 123½ Silver Hope 121⁴ Groton Guy 110² Gamely 9
11May74- 4CD fst 6f	:22	:46 1:12¾	Handicap	3 7 67½ 66 45 1ⁿᵏ	Wilson R	b 115	2.70	95-11 Silver Hope 115ⁿᵏ Brunate 118¹ Prayer Leader 114²½ Driving 7
27Apr74- 7CD fst 7f	:22½	:45½ 1:23½	Allowance	3 7 67½ 66 45 46½	Wilson R	b 115	19.50e	81-22 Cannonade 122½ J. R.'s Pet 122½ Destroyer 120ⁿᵏ No final rally 13
6Apr74- 8OP fst 170	:47	1:12½ 1:43½	Allowance	4 5 21 43½ 32 32½	Wilson R	b 114	8.70	77-24 Satan's Hills 113¹ Brunate 114ⁿᵏ Silver Hope 114ⁿᵏ Gamely 11
28Mar74- 6OP fst 6f	:22½	:46½ 1:12½	Allowance	1 5 1hd 2²½ 1½ 11½	Wilson R	b 122	*.40	89-21 Silver Hope 122¹½ Roman Knight 115¾ Ogan 122ⁿᵒ Drew out 8
12Mar74- 7OP fst 6f	:22½	:46½ 1:12½	Allowance	7 5 1hd 22½ 1½ 2¹½	Wilson R	b 122	*1.00	81-24 Count Fearless 122¹½ Silver Hope 122ⁿᵏ Chief Cherion 122¾ Tired 12
1Sep73- 6Lib fst 6f	:22	:45½ 1:12½	Allowance	1 5 1hd 22½ 11 11½	Moseley J W	115	*.80e	81-21 Silver Hope 115¹½ Neilson 115ⁿᵒ Moms Dads N' Mine 110⁹ Driving 7
11Aug73- 8Mth fst 6f	:21½	:44½ 1:10½	Sapling	1 9 53 56¼ 45 45	Moseley J W	122	3.80	86-15 Tisab 122¾ Wedge Shot 122ⁿᵒ Go For Love 122² Even effort 11
LATEST WORKOUTS	Jly 16 Mth 3f fst :36⅖ b			Jly 12 Mth 5f fst 1:02⅖ b			Jly 9 Mth 3f fst :37 b	Jly 3 Mth 5f fst 1:04⅗ b

---

Gala Double ✱
Own.—Leviton Gertrude

B. c. 3, by Spring Double—Right As Rain, by Rasper II
Br.—Glade Valley Farms Inc (Md)
Tr.—Bond B P

							Turf Record			St.	1st	2nd	3rd	Amt.
				113			St. 1st 2nd 3rd			1974	12	0	3	$7,250
							2 0 0 0			1973	13	3	1	$23,829

4Jly74- 7Mth fm 1½ ①	:47½	1:11½ 1:43½ 3↑Allowance	1 7 7¹¹ 76½ 74 88½	Solomone M	b 114	7.60	81-13 Twinkle Picker 113² Restless Jet 122² East Sea 111¹½ No factor 8
24Jun74- 8Mth fst 6f	:22½	:45½ 1:10½ 3↑Allowance	2 6 64¼ 64 52½ 32½	MacBeth D	b 116	*.80	84-21 Totheend 116¹½ Gala Double 116ⁿᵏ Crimson Twins 115¾ Slow early 6
13Jun74- 7Mth fst 6f	:22½	:46½ 1:09½ 3↑Allowance	3 4 75½ 43½ 32 2ⁿᵒ	MacBeth D	b 115	6.50	79-18 Best Of Il 114ⁿᵒ Gala Double 116⁴ Black Glove 115¾ Nosed 7
22May74- 8Pim fst 6f	:22½	:44½ 1:10½	Allowance	2 4 47¼ 37½ 25 31½	Kurtz J	b 115	2.90	93-15 Scam 120¹½ Be So Bold 117hd Gala Double 115²¼ Weakened 6
9May74- 6Pim sly 6f	:23	:46½ 1:11¾	Allowance	1 6 76½ 65¼ 55 59½	Cusimano G	b 115	10.60	87-15 Dvid'sPinecon120¾ GustyO'Shy112hd MrkThPrinc112¾ Finished well 10
25Apr74- 6Pim fst 6f	:23½	:47 1:11¾	Allowance	2 7 710 812 68½ 45½	Cusimano G	b 115	5.70	85-16 Half Shot 114⁷½ Pete Fox 109¾ Ima Duke 114ⁿᵏ Rallied 7
29Mar74- 7Pim gd 6f	:22½	:46½ 1:12½	Allowance	7 5 1hd 22½ 1½ 21½	Cusimano G	b 117	*1.00	56-23 GroundBreaker119⁴½ TheBrveChicken119²½ StrofMly119⁴ NO factor 7
7Mar74- 8Bow fst 1¼	:47½	1:13½ 1:46¾	Prince Geo	5 2 21 3¾ 512 5¹⁰	Cusimano G	b 119	13.00	66-17 Sherby 113¼ Jolly Johu 122¾ Hinky Dee 110¾ Early speed 7
18Feb74- 8Bow fst 1½	:48	1:12½ 1:46¾	Genl George	5 2 21 65¼ 610 62¹	Hawley S	b 119	9.10	60-31 Sharp Gary 122¹ Jolly Johu 119ⁿᵏ Ground Breaker 110ⁿᵒ Far back 16
LATEST WORKOUTS	Jly 16 Mth 3f fst :36⅘ b			Jly 12 Mth 3f fst :35¾ b			Jun 20 Mth 4f fst :47 b	Jun 10 Mth 3f fst :36 b

---

Hudson County ✱
Own.—Cohen R B

B. c. 3, by Black Mountain—Gem's Reward, by Armageddon
Br.—Silverman J C (Ky)
Tr.—Shapoff S R

						St.	1st	2nd	3rd	Amt.
				121		1974	9	2	1	$95,567
						1973	3	1	2	$7,341

28Jun74- 7Aqu fst 6f	:22½	:45½ 1:09½ 3↑Allowance	3 4 2hd 3ⁿᵏ 1hd 2½	Venezia M	b 112	*.90	92-15 Sports Editor 115ⁿᵏ No Bias 117½ Hudson County 112⁵ Weakened 7
8Jun74- 8Bel fst 1½	:49½	1:14 2:29½	Belmont	8 4 41 79½ 819 726	Venezia M	126	10.20	48-11 Little Current 126⁷ Jolly Johu 126ⁿᵒ Cannonade 126¾ Dropped back 9
18May74- 8Pim gd 1¼	:47	1:11¾ 1:54½	Preakness	10 2 51½ 73½ 11⁸ 811	Miceli M	126	5.20	74-11 Little Current 126⁷ Neapolitan Way 126¹ Cannonade 126½ Tired 13
4May74- 8CD fst 1½	:47½	1:11¾ 2:04	Ky. Derby	18 2 2½ 73¼ 54½ 32½	Miceli M	126	5.20f	75-15 Cannonade 126²½ Hudson County 126²¼ Agitate 126¾ Sharp try 23
20Apr74- 8Aqu fst 1½	:46½	1:11¾ 2:04	Wood Mem	8 2 21½ 54½ 52¾ 35¾	Miceli M	126	7.00	82-15 Rube The Great126hd FriendlyBee126¾ HudsonCounty126⁷ Rallied 11
20Apr74-Run in two divisions, 7th and 8th races.							
6Apr74- 7Aqu sly 1	:44½	1:10½ 1:36	Gotham	3 2 11 2½ 33 44½	Miceli M	121	*1.90	82-15 Stonewalk 121¾ L'Amour Rullah 116¾ Wing South 119¾ Tired 9
6Apr74-Run in two divisions, 7th and 8th races.							
16Mar74- 8Aqu sly 7f	:22	:44½ 1:22¾	Bay Shore	3 1 11½ 12 11½ 1hd½	Miceli M	114	8.70	88-11 HudsonCounty113¹½ FrankieAdms119⁵½ InstedOfRoses116¾ Driving 11
2Mar74- 8Aqu sly 7f	:22	:44½ 1:22¾	Swift	1 2 1½ 2hd 2½ 3ⁿᵏ	Miceli M	114	2.60	93-15 Noble Michael 114hd Accipiter114hd HudsonCounty114½ Driving 11
25Feb74- 6Aqu fst 6f	:22½	:46½ 1:12½	Allowance	4 3 54¾ 41½ 12 12½	Miceli M	122	*1.30	89-12 Hudson County 122¹½ Whoa Boy122⁴½ ThirdCavalry122² Ridden out 11
27Apr73- 6Kee sly 4½f	:22½	:46½ :52½	Lafayette	7 3 84 41½ 41½ 44	Miceli M	115	5.20	91-11 Mr. A. Z. 118¾ Hudson County 115⁵ Best Of It 116ⁿᵏ Gamely 10
LATEST WORKOUTS	● Jly 14 Mth 4f fst :46½ b			● Jly 10 Bel 4f fst :46 h			Jly 6 Bel 4f fst :48 b	Jun 24 Bel 7f sly :47 bg

Orders * — Dk. b. or br. c. 3, by Cornish Prince—Lady Lutza, by Roman Sandal
Own.—Rall Vivian E — Br.—Lovell Estate of & Wells (Ky) — Tr.—Smithwick D M — **113**

Turf Record	St.	1st	2nd	3rd		Year	St.	1st	2nd	3rd	Amt.
	1	0	0	1		1974	4	1	0	0	$5,880
						1973	11	3	1	3	$24,799

12Jly74- 8Mth	fst	6f	:22 :44⅘ 1:10	3↑Allowance	6 1 31½ 2½ 1½ 13	Passmore W J	112	2.30	90-18	Orders 1123 Country Tradition 115¾ You Can Do It 1143½	Driving	6
26Jun74- 8Del	fst	6f	:22⅕ :45⅖ 1:10⅕	3↑Allowance	5 2 24 33½ 34½ 57½	Pilar H	114	7.60	86-20	Scam 1224¾ Moving Cloud 114no Eric's Champ 1122½	In close	8
18Jun74- 8Del	fst	6f	:22⅕ :45 1:11⅗	Allowance	1 2 23½ 36½ 35 43¾	Pilar H	112	2.90	83-20	Moving Cloud 1121¼ Prince of Space 1152 You Bug Me 112½	Tired	6
3May74- 8Pim	sly	6f	:23 :46⅖ 1:11⅗	Allowance	7 1 22 21½ 22 74	Passmore W J	113	3.70	84-15	Dvid'sPinecone120¾ GustyO'Shy112hd MrkThPrinc112½	Speed, tired	10
29Dec73- 8Lib	gd	1	:46⅕ 1:12 1:40⅘	Allegheny	1 4 44½ 46 54 45½	Turcotte R L	114	6.50	64-29	Moms Dads N' Mine 1143 TrentonJoe117no WingSouth1142½	Evenly	8
21Dec73- 8Aqu	sly	1	:45⅘ 1:11⅗ 1:39	Allowance	3 3 35 3½ 22½ 34	Baltazar C	114	6.60	68-24	Beau Legend 1091 Cumulo Nimbus 1143 Orders 1141½	Tired	6
30Nov73- 7Lrl	fst	1	:46⅘ 1:12⅖ 1:38⅗	Allowance	2 2 1hd 1hd 2hd 32¾	Lee T	119	*.90	77-16	Mr. Sad 1191 Sahib Nearco 1191¾ Orders 119nk	Weakened	8
3Nov73- 8Lrl	fst	1 1/16	:46⅖ 1:12 1:43⅕	Lrl Fut'y	4 2 2hd 11 32½ 47¼	Lee T	122	7.70	90-12	Protgonist1223 HstyFlyer1223½ PrinceofReson122¾	Brushed at start	5
29Oct73- 6Lrl	sly	6f	:22⅖ :45⅗ 1:09⅘	Allowance	3 1 1hd 1hd 1½ 1¾	Lee T	115	9.10	100-15	Orders 115¾ Eastern Lord 1181½ Moving Cloud 1183½	Driving	7
23Oct73- 6Aqu	fm	1 Ⓣ	:46⅗ 1:11⅗ 1:36	Allowance	6 4 3nk 2hd 2½ 31½	Baltazar C	113	15.20	93-08	Talkative Turn 115nk Prod 1131¼ Orders 1136	Weakened	8

LATEST WORKOUTS ●Jly 10 Del 3f fst :34⅘ h ●Jly 6 Del 4f my :46⅖ h ●Jly 2 Del 1 fst 1:42⅗ b Jun 24 Del 4f my :50 b

Princely Native — Ch. c. 3, by Raise A Native—Charlo, by Francis S
Own.—Harbor View Farm — Br.—Harbor View Farm (Fla) — Tr.—Barrera L S — **119**

	St.	1st	2nd	3rd	Amt.
1974	5	4	0	0	$26,700
1973	0	M	0	0	

8Jly74- 6Aqu	fst	6f	:22⅘ :45⅗ 1:09⅗	3↑Allowance	1 1 1½ 1½ 13 12	Castaneda M	117	*.50	95-18	PrincelyNtive1172 SeeTheU.S.A.117hd JettoDmscus1171	Ridden out	6
24Jun74- 8Aqu	fst	1	:45 1:09⅘ 1:36⅖	Saranac	10 3 52½ 3½ 61¼ 62½	Castaneda M	117	2.00	82-12	Accipiter 123hd Best Of It 117¾ Hosiery 117nk	Tired	11
24Jun74-Placed fifth through disqualification												
11Jun74- 6Bel	fst	6f	:22⅖ :46⅕ 1:10	3↑Allowance	4 1 23 2½ 16 19½	Castaneda M	115	*.30	93-14	Princely Native 1159½ Jomar 1123½ Turn To Bo 1131½	Handily	6
27May74- 7Bel	fst	6f	:22⅖ :45 1:09⅘	Allowance	8 2 32 32½ 11½ 15½	Castaneda M	121	*1.50	94-11	Princely Native 1215½ Nile Delta 121¾ Take By Storm 1212½	Driving	10
22Apr74- 3Aqu	fst	6f	:22⅘ :45⅘ 1:10⅗	3↑Md Sp Wt	4 1 21½ 2hd 11½ 12½	Castaneda M	113	*1.30	90-14	PrincelyNative1132½ SeaSongster113nk DarkEncounter1082½	Driving	9

LATEST WORKOUTS ●Jly 4 Bel tr.t 5f fst 1:00 h Jly 1 Bel tr.t 3f fst :37⅕ b Jun 18 Bel tr.t 7f fst 1:28 b ●Jun 6 Bel tr.t 5f fst 1:00⅗ h

Muddy York — Ch. c. 3, by Viceregal—Its Ann, by Royal Gem II
Own.—Stollery Mrs A W — Br.—Angus Glen Farm Ltd (Can) — Tr.—Whitaker C — **110**

Turf Record	St.	1st	2nd	3rd		Year	St.	1st	2nd	3rd	Amt.
	1	0	1	0		1974	6	2	2	0	$9,205
						1973	4	1	2	0	$3,705

29Jun74- 7WO	sly	1¼	:47⅖ 1:14⅕ 2:09⅕	ⓈQueens Plate	14 1 14 68 922 814	Dittfach H	b 126	22.55	46-39	Amber Herod 1261½ Native Aid126hd Rushton'sCorsair1263	Used up	14
25May74- 7WO	fst	7f	:22 :45 1:21⅘	Marine	4 3 22½ 22½ 35 45½	Ryan M	b 112	3.80	95-12	InsteadOfRoses1192¼ RunninRoman1232½ Sam'sOwn119¾	Weakened	6
23Apr74- 6Kee	fst	7f	:22⅘ :45⅕ 1:24⅘	Allowance	1 1 2hd 1hd 2½ 1no	Ryan M	b 113	2.00Ⓓ	82-22	ⒹMuddy York113no NoAdvance1197 CrimsonSignal119½	Drifted out	7
23Apr74-Disqualified and placed second												
9Apr74- 6Kee	fst	6f	:21⅗ :45 1:10⅗	Allowance	8 6 2½ 1½ 13 13	Ryan M	b 114	6.70	89-17	Muddy York 1143 Creole Cross 1182 Bestead 1183½	Driving	9
14Mar74- 8FD	fst	6f	:21⅘ :45⅗ 1:12	3↑Allowance	7 1 16 15 11½ 2½	Ryan M	b 113	*.70	89-16	Gallant Smoke 111½ Muddy York 113no Top Lock 116hd	Gamely	9
21Feb74-10FD	fst	6f	:22⅖ :45 1:11	Allowance	7 2 12 13 15 13½	Ryan M	b 116	4.70	95-13	Muddy York 1163½ Joint Agreement 1163 Hy Value 120½	Ridden out	10
7Nov73- 7Grd	fst	1	:46⅗ 1:11 1:38	ⓈCarleton	3 1 2hd 56 57½ 68	Phipps J	b 112	9.50	82-17	Backstretch 1201¼ Noble Answer 1181¼ Cozy's Cousin 120no	Tired	10
13Oct73- 6WO	fm	*1 Ⓣ	:49⅗ 1:15⅘ 1:43⅘	ⓈAllowance	8 2 2½ 1hd 1½ 22½	Duffy L	b 122	2.50	76-25	Rushton'sCorsir1222½ MuddyYork1222¼ ScrtAssgnmnt122no	Gamely	8
30Sep73- 3WO	fst	7f	:23⅕ :46⅕ 1:25	ⓈMd Sp Wt	1 4 1½ 12 11½ 1nk	Gomez A	b 122	*1.50	85-13	Muddy York 122nk Do's Vigil 1176½ Pansancer 1223	Driving	9
19Sep73- 3WO	my	6½f	:22⅖ :45⅗ 1:19⅘	Md Sp Wt	6 6 11 12 13 2½	Gomez A	b 117	*1.90	73-24	Poor Native 122½ Muddy York 117¾ Pansancer 117hd	Gamely	12

LATEST WORKOUTS ●Jly 15 Mth 3f fst :34 h ●Jly 10 Mth 1 fst 1:40⅖ h

Best Of It — B. c. 3, by Creme dela Creme--Articana, by Arctic Prince
Own.—Bwamazon Farm — Br.—Bwamazon Farm (Ky) — Tr.—Basile A — **117**

	St.	1st	2nd	3rd	Amt.
1974	6	3	3	0	$42,639
1973	3	1	1	1	$6,520

24Jun74- 8Aqu	fst	1	:45 1:09⅘ 1:36⅖	Saranac	8 2 21½ 2hd 1hd 2hd	Brumfield D	b 117	5.40	85-12	Accipiter 123hd Best Of It 117¾ Hosiery 117nk	Gamely	11
13Jun74- 7Mth	fst	6f	:21⅘ :44⅖ 1:09⅘	3↑Allowance	1 3 22 21 1hd 1no	Brumfield D	b 114	*.40	91-18	Best Of It 114no Gala Double 1166 Black Glove 115¾	Driving	7
25May74- 8Bel	fst	1	:45⅘ 1:10⅗ 1:35⅗	Withers	8 5 41½ 2½ 1hd 21¾	Brumfield D	126	4.40	88-08	Accipiter 1261¾ Best Of It 126no Hosiery 1262½	Gamely	12
15May74- 7Bel	fst	6f	:22⅗ :46 1:10⅘	3↑Allowance	5 7 52½ 72¼ 41½ 21½	Brumfield D	114	2.70	87-16	Relent 1111½ Best Of It 114nk Cumulo Nimbus 113hd	Blocked	7
24Apr74- 5Kee	fst	6f	:21⅘ :44⅘ 1:10⅗	Allowance	1 5 1½ 1hd 12 18	Brumfield D	115	*.20	89-21	Best Of It 1158 My Native Land 1211½ Cammarrone 115hd	In hand	8
10Apr74- 5Kee	fst	6f	:22 :45 1:09⅘	Allowance	9 8 43 31½ 21 11	Brumfield D	115	*1.40	93-14	Best Of It 1151 T. V. Satan 1182 Nautilus 1151	Driving	11
17May73- 6CD	fst	5f	:22⅖ :46 :58⅗	Allowance	6 8 86 76 24 22½	Nichols J	118	*1.20e	93-18	Tisab 1222½ Best Of It 1185 No Advance 115no	Gamely	9
27Apr73- 6Kee	sly	4½f	:22⅕ :46⅖ :52⅗	Lafayette	4 7 54½ 53 35½	Nichols J	116	4.40e	86-11	Mr. A. Z. 118½ Hudson County 1155 Best Of It 116nk	Rallied	10
17Apr73- 4Kee	fst	4½f	:22⅘ :46⅖ :52	Md Sp Wt	2 5 21 11 15	Brumfield D	120	*1.30e	95-05	Best Of It 1205 High Crane 1201 Gwens Baby 120½	Driving	10

LATEST WORKOUTS Jly 16 Mth 4f fst :48⅗ b Jly 13 Mth 4f fst :48 b ●Jly 9 Mth 5f fst :59⅖ h Jly 5 Mth 6f fst 1:13 h

MARGARET'S BEAU won his last two in front-running style at Monmouth, but prior to that had been trounced by Select favorite Princely Native at Belmont and rival Silver Hope in Liberty Bell's Sentinel. He is the speed point leader (8) in the field, and his figures indicate improvement over earlier victories:

July 5	Monmouth	6f	87 + 21 = 108 − 4 = 104
June 25	Monmouth	6f	82 + 28 = 110 − 4 = 106
May 20	Garden State	6f	77 + 24 = 101 − 9 = 92
April 23	Hialeah	6f	87 + 21 = 108 − 5 = 103

But has he improved enough to compete with stakes horses?

REALMAN failed in his last two starts, and was without his usual early speed last out. Would be hard to take against allowance competition, to say nothing of stakes horses. Definitely not a contender.

THE GROK surprised with a good front-running effort against tough older horses last out, although the figures give him little chance in this field.

June 29	Monmouth	6f	$85 + 20 = 105 - 4 = 101$
April 22	Hialeah	6f	$89 + 20 = 109 - 5 = 104$
April 10	Hialeah	7f	$87 + 15 = 102 + 1 = 103$

AZ IGAZI has turned in three sharp efforts against good older horses in New York recently, and has been working well, although unraced for 19 days.

June 28	Aqueduct	6f	$93 + 15 = 108 - 3 = 105$
June 10	Belmont	6f	$93 + 16 = 109 - 2 = 107$
May 27	Belmont	6f	$94 + 11 = 105 - 2 = 103$

SILVER HOPE always gives a good account of himself at six furlongs, and his figure last time is an improvement over previous efforts:

June 19	Liberty Bell	6f	$91 + 21 = 112 - 7 = 105$
May 29	Liberty Bell	6f	$88 + 20 = 108 - 7 = 101$
May 11	Churchill Downs	6f	$95 + 11 = 106 - 7 = 99$

However, his last race came 28 days ago, and the absence of a recent sharp workout makes him look somewhat suspicious.

GALA DOUBLE has not won in twelve 1974 starts, is credited with no speed points, and comes from a route in which he trailed far behind. Even though his last two sprints are good, he must be eliminated from consideration as a possible winner.

HUDSON COUNTY went through the entire Triple Crown process, and then, 20 days later, started all over again with a sprint at Aqueduct. His figure in that race compares with those he earned in the Swift and Bay Shore:

June 28	Aqueduct	6f	$92 + 15 = 107 - 3 = 104$
March 16	Aqueduct	7f	$88 + 11 = 99 + 4 = 103$
March 2	Aqueduct	6f	$93 + 15 = 108 - 3 = 105$

In spite of sharp recent workouts, this horse is not likely to improve until given a chance to recuperate.

ORDERS finally found himself in his last start, just five days ago. Considering his low odds then, after three dull efforts in 1974, one has to wonder what he beat. His speed figure for the race is nothing special:

| July 12 | Monmouth | 6f | $90 + 18 = 108 - 4 = 104$ |

PRINCELY NATIVE has never lost a sprint, and his figures have gotten better with each succeeding race.

July 8	Aqueduct	6f	$95 + 18 = 113 - 3 = 110$
June 11	Belmont	6f	$93 + 14 = 107 - 2 = 105$
May 27	Belmont	6f	$94 + 11 = 105 - 2 = 103$
April 22	Aqueduct	6f	$90 + 14 = 104 - 3 = 101$

Photo credit: George Gugel

Princely Native winning the 1974 Select Handicap.

MUDDY YORK comes down from Woodbine where he failed in his quest for Canada's biggest race, the Queen's Plate. His figures at Keeneland make him look competitive with most of his opponents in the Select:

April 23	Keeneland	7f	$82 + 22 = 104 + 2 = 106$
April 9	Keeneland	6f	$89 + 17 = 106 - 2 = 104$

BEST OF IT has been running in good New York stakes company, but at the one-mile distance. His 1974 sprint efforts average to about 105:

June 13	Monmouth	6f	$91 + 18 = 109 - 4 = 105$
May 15	Belmont	6f	$87 + 16 = 103 - 2 = 101$
April 24	Keeneland	6f	$89 + 21 = 110 - 2 = 108$
April 10	Keeneland	6f	$93 + 14 = 107 - 2 = 105$

The figures literally shout "Princely Native." His latest victory earned a figure of 110, two points better than any of his opponents had ever run, and about five points higher than any of their recent averages. That victory had been achieved at the direct expense of the top-class older sprinter See The U.S.A., with whom he had fought for the early lead, and came just nine days ago. His previous sprint earned 105, and he probably could have gone faster if pressed.

Princely Native looked to be an improving young horse who had yet to reach his peak. If he ran his race, he figured to win by a clear margin.

He did run his race, beating Orders and Silver Hope by three lengths. He paid a decent $5.80, and earned a speed figure of 108 for his efforts. His nearest competitors ran right to their recent figures, but could not cope with a faster horse running to his figures.

MONMOUTH PARK

EIGHTH RACE
Monmouth
JULY 17, 1974

6 FURLONGS. (1.08) 27TH RUNNING SELECT HANDICAP. Purse $25,000 added. The owner of the winner to receive a trophy. 3-year-olds. By subscription of $25 each which should accompany the nomination, $100 to pass the entry box, $150 to start with $25,000 added of which 65% of all monies to the winner; 20% to second; 10% to third and 5% to fourth. Weights, 5 p.m., Friday, July 12, 1974. Starters to be named through the entry box by the usual time of closing. Closed Monday, July 1, 1974 with 31 nominations.

Value of race $28,825, value to winner $18,736, second $5,765, third $2,883, fourth $1,441. Mutuel pool $234,132.

Last Raced	Horse	Eqt.A.Wt PP St	¼	½	Str	Fin	Jockey	Odds $1
8Jly74 6Aqu1	Princely Native	3 119 5 4	22	11	12½	13	Castaneda M	1.90
12Jly74 8Mth1	Orders	3 113 9 1	42	21	22½	2¾	Passmore W J	13.10
19Jun74 8Lib1	Silver Hope	b 3 119 6 8	5hd	71	42½	32	Wilson R	12.20

Copyright © 1979 by Daily Racing Form, Inc. Reprinted with permission of copyright owner.

28Jun74 7Aqu3	Hudson County	b	3 121	8	7		6hd	8½	93	4no	Bracciale V Jr	4.00
28Jun74 8Aqu2	Az Igazi		3 117	4	6		3hd	41	3hd	51½	Mayorga W	6.00
4Jly74 7Mth8	Gala Double	b	3 113	7	9		11	92	6hd	6hd	MacBeth D	18.60
29Jun74 6Mth3	The Grok	b	3 116	3	11		10hd	11	108	71	Marquez C H	45.30
24Jun74 8Aqu2	Best Of It	b	3 118	11	2		96	6½	7hd	81	Broussard R	3.60
29Jun74 7WO8	Muddy York	b	3 112	10	3		72½	3½	5½	9nk	Blum W	21.00
5Jly74 8Mth6	Realman	b	3 110	2	10		8½	103	8hd	108	Gallitano G	90.00
5Jly74 8Mth1	Margaret's Beau	b	3 114	1	5		11	5½	11	11	Miceli M	25.60

OFF AT 5:41 1/2. Start good, Won driving. Time, :21⅗, :44⅕, 1:09⅕ Track fast.

$2 Mutuel Prices:				
	5–PRINCELY NATIVE	5.80	4.40	3.20
	9–ORDERS		11.20	7.80
	6–SILVER HOPE			6.20

Ch. c, by Raise A Native—Charlo, by Francis S. Trainer Barrera L S. Bred by Harbor View Farm (Fla).

PRINCELY NATIVE broke alertly, remained in close contention while reserved off the early pace, moved quickly to the lead when asked on the stretch turn, opened a clear lead but was kept under pressure through the final sixteenth. ORDERS, never far back racing outside horses early, moved nearest the pace on the stretch turn but could not gain in the final furlong. SILVER HOPE, within striking distance near the rail before a quarter, checked behind a wall of horses midway of the turn, responded between horses when clear but did not menace the winner. HUDSON COUNTY, forced to remain wide throughout, offered only a mild closing rally. AZ IGAZI, well placed early, lacked a strong finish. BEST OF IT was never in contention. MUDDY YORK was forced to stay wide. MARGARET'S BEAU weakened before a half and tired badly in the stretch.

Owners— 1, Harbor View Farm; 2, Rall Vivian E; 3, Udouj Mrs H J; 4, Cohen R B; 5, Straus J R; 6, Leviton Gertrude; 7, Miami Lakes Stable; 8, Bwamazon Farm; 9, Stollery Mrs A W; 10, Blum Maribel G; 11, Bright View Farm.

Overweight: The Grok 2 pounds; Best Of It 1; Muddy York 2.

Scratched—Totheend (3Jly74⁶Aqu⁴); Odds And Evens (5Jly74⁸Mth³); Second Pleasure (19Jun74⁸Lib³).

Note: Accurate daily variants were *not* substituted for *Form* variants in this example. Also, we have used the Liberty Bell six-furlong SR + TV adjustment for 1974: −7.

THE
WEAKER
SEX

Dr. Fager's half sister Ta Wee carries 140 pounds to victory over Distinctive (#8) and Towzie Tyke in the 1970 Fall Highweight, her second victory in that unusual fixture.

Is there a weaker sex in Thoroughbred racing? The recent exploits of fillies such as Dahlia, Allez France, Ivanjica, Shuvee, Dulcia, Drumtop, Ta Wee, Waya, My Juliet, and Honorable Miss seem to have disproved the myth that fillies and mares cannot compete successfully against males.

Obviously, a good female can compete against good males. But what about the average female of the allowance or claiming variety? Can she compete successfully against males of similar class?

Our study of final times (see Chapter 16) showed that races for females are slower, on the average, than races for males of comparable class. Par times for females tend to equal par times for males two classes cheaper. Invoking the 50 percent principle mentioned in Chapter 18, we are led to the conclusion that females can compete against males one class cheaper. This agrees with the traditional belief that a claiming female's price tag should be reduced by 20 percent to determine the caliber of males against whom she might compete successfully.

Photo credit: Bob Coglianese

Shuvee defeats Loud (outside) in the 1970 Jockey Club Gold Cup, her first of two consecutive victories in America's greatest endurance test.

○ AGAINST THE BOYS ○

When racing against males, female horses receive a weight allowance. According to the scale of weights, itself an admission of female inferiority, fillies and mares receive a five-pound break in the weights before September 1, and three pounds thereafter.

Using the generally accepted formulae that

4 pounds = 1 length ($\frac{1}{5}$ of a second) at 6 furlongs
3 pounds = 1 length ($\frac{1}{5}$ of a second) at 1 mile
2 pounds = 1 length ($\frac{1}{5}$ of a second) at 1$\frac{1}{8}$ miles,

we conclude that sprints for fillies and mares should average $\frac{1}{5}$ slower than sprints for males of comparable class, and routes $\frac{2}{5}$ slower.

But we know that the actual differences are $\frac{2}{5}$ in sprints and $\frac{3}{5}$ in routes. So the scale of weights shortchanges the gals. Since they are penalized in the weights, it would be logical to expect fillies and mares to fare poorly in competition against males.

Photo credit: Bob Coglianese

The "bionic filly" My Juliet runs away from Kentucky Derby-Belmont winner Bold Forbes (#4) in the 1976 Vosburgh.

206

Whether the weight assignments are to blame, or whether it is simply because the female Thoroughbred usually cannot match the speed and endurance of the male Thoroughbred of equivalent class, fillies seldom defeat males. Here are the results of a study of 722 fillies and mares that raced against males:

NH	NW	WPCT	MPCT	$NET	I.V.
722	53**	7.3%	27.6%	$1.07	0.66

These are negative results indeed, suggesting that fillies and mares should almost never be bet when running against males.

In sprints, where the premium is on speed rather than stamina, females stand a slightly "better" chance of beating males:

	NH	NW	WPCT	MPCT	$NET	I.V.
Sprints	403	33**	8.2%	26.1%	$1.21	0.74
Routes	319	20**	6.3%	29.5%	$0.89	0.50

○ THE FILLY WITH THE "FIGURE" ○

A filly coming off a good race is able to hold her own against males (I.V. = 0.96), but, surprisingly, is overbet:

Drumtop beats champion Fort Marcy (#5) in the 1971 Bowling Green Handicap at 1½ miles.

NH	NW	WPCT	MPCT	$NET	I.V.
257	29	11.3%	32.3%	$1.42	0.96

Even when the filly ranks first in average earnings per start in a field of males:

NH	NW	WPCT	MPCT	$NET	I.V.
87	6**	6.9%	31.0%	$0.35	0.59

or when the filly ranks first in speed figures (the "failures" approach discussed in Chapter 18):

NH	NW	WPCT	MPCT	$NET	I.V.
73	5**	6.8%	38.4%	$0.49	0.58

the results are dismal.

So it would seem fair to say that a filly running against the boys is far from a favorable betting proposition.

Photo credit: Bob Coglianese

Millionairess Dahlia romps to victory in the 1974 Man O' War, after spending much of the preceding week in quarantine in New Jersey after arriving in this country from France.

○ CONCLUSION ○

Computer studies suggest that fillies and mares are not as delicate as might be thought. When in competition against other females, they appear to be as rugged as males in competition with other males. In particular, the following appear to be true:

1. Female winners repeat as often as male winners.
2. Females carry high weights (120 pounds and up) against other females as well as males carry high weights against other males.
3. Females can withstand an all-out driving finish as well as males, and come back strongly in their next start, like males.

Then why do fillies and mares do so poorly in competition against males? And why do they run slower than males of comparable class? One possible answer lies in the simple fact that most females have value as potential broodmares after their racing days come to an end. Most males have no future at stud. Consequently, the female claimer runs for a higher price than does the male of comparable physical ability. Or she runs in allowance races, while the male runs for a price.

This line of reasoning would explain the differences between male and female par times, and the difficulty females have in defeating males of similar "face value." However, the statistics do not indicate that females meet with any greater success when dropped in claiming price to meet males of comparable ability:

	NH	NW	WPCT	MPCT	$NET	I.V.
Dropping	496	37**	7.5%	26.6%	$1.13	0.63
Others	226	16**	7.1%	29.6%	$0.95	0.60

TWO-YEAR-OLD
RACING

The two-year-old Thoroughbred can be a most unpredictable animal, especially early in its career. In April and May, when most of the entrants in juvenile maiden races are making their debuts, the parade to the post often turns out to be as exciting as the race itself!

Many two-year-old races can be handicapped very quickly— there is not that much information available for the player to ponder. This does not mean, however, that these races are easy to handicap. Several characteristic factors often cloud the crystal ball.

First, there is inexperience. Not only must the player decide whether to give serious consideration to a horse making its debut, but he must also be aware that some other inexperienced horse, racing greenly, might interfere with the horse he has played.

Second, there is consistency. It is often difficult to determine whether a young inexperienced horse can be relied on to duplicate a previous good performance.

Third, there is the learning process. Some horses learn their lessons very quickly, others take more time. It is not uncommon to see a juvenile "put it all together" overnight and win at a big price, even though its past performance lines gave little indication that improvement was imminent.

Finally, there is the common juvenile malady, bucked shins. Every youngster must buck its shins. Some do so before getting to the races, others after. Bucked shins might explain today's poor performance. Or they may explain why a horse ran poorly in its last start and has since been out of action for a couple of months.

○ FAVORITES ○

In spite of these possible causes of upsets, two-year-old favorites fare slightly better than favorites in general. A study of 831 juvenile favorites found them slightly superior in all major categories.

NH	NW	WPCT	MPCT	$NET	I.V.
831	296*	35.6%	68.8%	$1.87	3.03

Two-year-old form holds up very well. One possible reason is that the typical two-year-old has not yet soured on racing—the nagging injuries that are a part of racing are still to come.

Another reason, one we will explore in this chapter, is the fact that accurate speed figures are especially effective in juvenile races.

The following breakdown indicates that two-year-old favorites are most reliable in non-maiden and non-claiming races.

	NH	NW	WPCT	MPCT	$NET	I.V.
Maiden	517	169	32.7%	66.0%	$1.82	2.94
Non-maiden	314	127	40.4%	73.6%	$1.95	3.43
Claiming	376	126	33.5%	65.2%	$1.89	2.85
Non-claiming	455	170	37.4%	71.9%	$1.86	3.18

○ EARLY SPEED ○

Early speed, so important at six furlongs, is even more so in short two-year-old dashes of five and five and a half furlongs. Here are the results of a study of 240 of these races:

FCP	NH	NW	WPCT	MPCT	$NET	%W	I.V.
1	240	77*	32.1%	61.3%	$4.31	32.1%	3.17
1–3	720	172*	23.9%	56.4%	$3.15	71.7%	2.36
Front Half	505	42**	8.3%	30.5%	$1.46	17.5%	0.82
Rear Half	1150	26**	2.3%	13.9%	$0.56	10.8%	0.22

More than 70 percent of these races, which were run at major East and West Coast tracks, were won by horses among the first three at the first call.

Forecasting which juveniles will have early speed and which will not can be quite frustrating, however. Many youngsters come away from the starting gate very slowly in their first or second starts, looking over their surroundings, perhaps wondering what the other horses are doing. Such horses may not look like speed horses on paper. But as soon as they learn what their job is all about, they leave the gate much more quickly.

On the other hand, many trainers try to slow down promising juveniles that have shown excessive early speed in their initial races. Hoping to teach a horse to conserve its energy, they instruct the rider to restrain it slightly in the early going and come on in the stretch. But some horses do not take kindly to such treatment. They either set the pace in defiance of the jockey, or sulk (and quit) when they cannot get to the lead right away.

○ POST POSITION ○

Post position is especially important in five- and five-and-half-furlong dashes for juveniles, because they start much closer to the turn than do the more frequent six- to seven-furlong races. The effect of post position in sprints starting relatively near a turn was studied in Chapter 4.

○ MAIDEN RACES ○

With these preliminary remarks out of the way, we shall now, in effect, follow a two-year-old through its season. We begin by looking at maiden races, classifying the entrants according to how each finished in its latest start. Here are the results of a study of 1,114 maiden races:

Finish	NH	%H	NW	%W	WPCT	I.V.
Second	999	8.8%	218	19.6%	21.8%	2.22
Third	1021	9.0%	169	15.2%	16.6%	1.69
Out	6262	55.2%	469	42.1%	7.5%	0.76
Debut	3062	27.0%	258	23.2%	8.4%	0.86

Impact value statistics were approximately the same for both maiden special and maiden claiming races. However, maiden special races had a higher percentage of first-time starters, while maiden claiming races attracted more horses that had run out of the money in their most recent start.

But regardless of class, the advantage clearly lies with the horse that ran in the money in its last start. Unfortunately, these account for the winners of only 35 percent of all maiden races, leaving the other 65 percent to the unraced or the recently unsuccessful.

○ FIRST TIME STARTERS ○

Let's take a more detailed look at two-year-olds making their career debuts. Here are the results of a study of 1,073 of them (all of whom debuted in New York):

NH	NW	WPCT	MPCT	$NET	I.V.
1073	74	6.9%	23.3%	$1.10	0.70

Clearly, first-time starters are no bargains. And it makes no difference whether they debut in a maiden special or a maiden claiming race—the results are equally dismal.

Still, it remains a fact that horses making their debuts win 20 to 25 percent of all two-year-old maiden races. Is there any way to determine which first-starters are likely to run well?

Very little information is available on these horses—just the owner, the trainer, the breeding, and the recent workouts appear in the *Daily Racing Form*. Exceptional workouts often precede a good effort, but many win their first starts after mediocre workouts. Knowing a trainer's style with young horses is important, of course. Some do not rush their young horses, others are known for having a two-year-old ready to win at first asking.

Perhaps the most reliable indicator that a first-time starter will go well is the odds board. Juveniles bet below 6-1 in their debuts run much better than those that do not receive much betting support.

Betting	NH	NW	WPCT	MPCT	$NET	I.V.
Under 6-1	255	53	20.8%	47.1%	$1.64	2.12
Others	818	21**	2.6%	15.9%	$0.93	0.26

The wise bettor will not place any money on a first-time starter that the other bettors have ignored.

On the other hand, even though first-time starters bet below 6-1 must be regarded as serious threats to win, they do not help the player's cause versus the pari-mutuel takeout.

○ SECOND CAREER START ○

Here is the follow-up on our first-time starters,[1] showing how they raced in the second starts of their careers. Only slight improvement is evident.

NH	NW	WPCT	MPCT	$NET	%W	I.V.
887	79	8.9%	27.4%	$1.43	16.8%	0.91

Although the performance of these horses is on the negative side, they do account for almost 17 percent of all two-year-old maiden victories. So it would be wise to determine what (if anything) in the horse's debut performance is a solid indicator of imminent success.

Unfortunately, all the obvious factors, such as finish position, beaten lengths, and final time, can only be used to predict success for the horse, but not for the bettor. The information contained in the one past performance line cannot be hidden. If a first-time starter ran in the money, or close up, or in fast time, the promise is there for everyone to see. The horse is a strong candidate to run well again, but most likely will be overbet.

More specifically, a two-year-old able to run in the money, inside five lengths of a winner, or within three lengths of today's par time (after times are adjusted by a daily variant) in its debut stands better than a 50-50 chance to run in the money in its second start.

	NH	NW	WPCT	MPCT	$NET	I.V.
2–3 Finish	166	36	21.7%	51.2%	$1.36	2.22
W/in 5 Lengths	172	33	19.2%	52.3%	$1.34	1.96
W/in 3 of Par	129	35	27.1%	60.5%	$1.76	2.77

On the other hand, a horse that races dismally in its debut, finishing seventh or worse, is very unlikely to improve enough to win its second start. In our study, less than 4 percent did.

In summary, we have seen that although approximately 40 percent of all two-year-old maiden races are won by horses in the first or second starts of their careers, such horses are not profitable betting propositions. To whom, then, should the player turn in these races?

---

[1] Of the 1,073 horses studied, 74 won their debuts, leaving 999 others, of which only 887 raced again during the period surveyed.

We have already seen that maidens able to run in the money in their most recent start come back to win almost twice their share of the races. A study of 959 such animals discloses, however, that these horses are heavily overbet.

NH	NW	WPCT	MPCT	$NET	I.V.
959	191	19.9%	49.5%	$1.61	2.03

Those that had finished second performed slightly better than the ones that had finished third. But the racetrack audience placed great importance on that recent second-place finish, sending these horses to the post at average odds of $2.80 on the dollar, contrasted with odds of $4.10 for those that had finished third in their last starts.

Maidens that had finished within three lengths of the winner in their most recent efforts were more attractive betting propositions.

NH	NW	WPCT	MPCT	$NET	I.V.
465	114*	24.5%	54.6%	$1.82	2.50

But the best bets were maidens whose most recent performance resulted in a time no worse than one length slower than today's par (after times were adjusted by a daily variant).

NH	NW	WPCT	MPCT	$NET	I.V.
324	95*	29.3%	63.6%	$2.02	2.99

The value of having accurate speed figures, especially at the five- and five-and-a-half-furlong distances (where *Daily Racing Form* speed ratings usually are abnormally high—and misleading) is readily apparent.

Racing experience is important, but in a surprising way. Inexperienced horses able to finish in the money are usually better bets than experienced youngsters that have recently finished in the money.

Experience	NH	NW	WPCT	MPCT	$NET	I.V.
First Race	189	45	23.8%	51.9%	$1.48	2.42
Second Race	166	40	24.1%	53.6%	$2.03	2.45
Third Race	153	26	17.0%	41.2%	$1.45	1.73
Others	395	75	19.0%	51.9%	$1.66	1.93

So the youngster that runs in the money in the first or second start of its career is likeliest to win its next start. The one doing it in the second start of its career is much the preferable bet. Such a horse either has a poor first race on its record, which might help increase its odds, or it has two good races on its record, suggesting consistency. Contrast this with the horse that runs in the money in its debut. The latter has a clean record, and consequently will be overbet, but has yet to demonstrate whether it will be consistent or erratic.

○ A SPOT-PLAY SYSTEM FOR THE MAIDEN SPECIAL RACES ○

We have already seen that two-year-olds well bet in their debuts ran much better than those disregarded in the wagering. Many of those that lost at low odds are well worth following in their second, and possibly third, starts.

In the tabulation below, we study two-year-olds making their second career starts, in a maiden special race, that in their debuts (which also must have been in a maiden special race) either (1) were well bet—odds of 5-1 or lower, or (2) accumulated at least 15 points on the *Daily Racing Form* consensus the day of their debut, indicating selection by at least two *Form* handicappers—and then lived up to expectations by giving a reasonable account of themselves.

Acceptable debut performances can take several forms. For example, the horse may have fought it out every step of the race; or it may have weakened slightly after taking a clear lead; or tired somewhat after fighting for the lead; rallied slightly; raced evenly, though close up; rallied strongly after a slow start; or tired abruptly after dueling for the early lead following a slow break.

Sit in the Corner Dk. b. or br. c (1968–Ky), by Hail To Reason—Dunce Cap II, by Tom Fool 122 1970 2 1 0 1 $4,500
Greentree Stable J. M. Gaver (Greentree Stud, Inc.)
25Sep70-2Bel fst 6f .22⅘ .46⅖1.11 Md Sp Wt 9 3 2½ 1½ 13 17 LPincayJr 122 *2.20 90-13 Sit In The Corner 1227 Will Hays 1223½ Rum 122½ Mild drive 13
11Sep70-2Bel gd 6f .22⅘ .46⅕1.11 Md Sp Wt 9 3 32 31½ 33 33¼ LPincayJr 122 5.90 87-14 Hoist The Flag 1222½ Ogontz 122¾ Sit In The Corner 1226 Wide 11
LATEST WORKOUTS Oct 9 Bel 4f fst .50⅘ b Oct 5 Bel 7f fst 1.25⅕ h Oct 1 Bel 6f fst 1.13⅗ h Sep 29 Bel 4f fst .49⅕ b

His Majesty * B. c (1968–Ky), by Ribot--Flower Bowl, by Alibhai 122 1970 1 M 1 0 $1,210
Darby Dan Farm T. Rondinello (Mr.-Mrs. J. W. Galbreath)
13Nov70-6Aqu sly 6f .22⅘ .47⅕1.11⅕ Md Sp Wt 5 10 79 611 37 23½ BBaeza 122 5.00 83-22 Rough King 1223½ His Majesty 1221½ Warino 1224 Gamely 11
LATEST WORKOUTS Nov 26 Bel tr.t. 3f fst .38 b Nov 23 Bel 5f fst 1.01⅘ b Nov 19 Bel 4f sly .51⅗ b Nov 9 Bel 5f fst 1.00⅕ h

Joe Iz B. c. 2, by Disciplinarian—Betoken, by Dunce
Own.—Straus J R Br.—Jones W L Jr (Ky) Tr.—Pardue H C 122
St. 1st 2nd 3rd Amt. 1972 4 2 0 1 $11,280
8Aug72- 5Sar fst 6f .22⅘ .45⅘ 1.11⅗ Allowance 1 3 1½ 11½ 14 14½ Rotz J L b 118 5.00 88-13 Joe Iz 1184½ Biller's Brother 119hd Flight To Glory 1182½ Easily 6
31Jly72- 4Sar fst 6f .23⅕ .46⅖ 1.10⅘ Allowance 5 3 2hd 2hd 33 38½ Rotz J L b 118 11.70 83-13 Secretariat 1181½ Russ Miron 1187 Joe Iz 1182½ Weakened 7
17Jly72- 2Aqu fst 5½f .22⅕ .45⅘ 1.05⅕ Md Sp Wt 2 3 11½ 11½ 11½ 1½ Rotz J L b 118 *2.00 87-12 Joe Iz 118½ [D]Dirty Dan 1183 Dicks Boots 1184 Driving 10
8Jly72- 3Aqu fst 6f .22 .45⅗ 1.11⅖ Md Sp Wt 3 13 3nk 1hd 33 57½ Rotz J L b 118 5.70 78-09 Noble Descent 118no Plastic Surgeon 1186 Tropiquillo 118½ Gave Way 13
LATEST WORKOUTS Aug 14 Sar 4f fst .48⅕ b Jly 25 Bel 5f fst 1.00⅘ h Jly 16 Bel tr.t 3f fst .35⅘ h Jly 4 Bel 5f sly 1.01⅗ h

Copyright © 1979, by DAILY RACING FORM, INC. Reprinted with permission of copyright owner.

Not included in this study are second-time starters that had been well supported in their debuts only to trail far behind or quit badly after showing brief speed, unless (1) the horse had a valid excuse for its poor performance, such as a bad start; bad racing luck; or the inability to run a straight course (which could be corrected with experience, or a change in equipment); or (2) the horse has since been absent for at least one month, possibly an indication of bucked shins, as was the case with May I Rule, who won his second start July 24 at a nice $15.20 payoff; or (3) the horse switches today to a top five rider.

Big Bluffer B. c (1969–Ky), by Bold Ruler—Fool's Play, by Tom Fool 117 1971 3 1 1 0 $6,700
O. M. Phipps R. Laurin (O. M. Phipps)
9Jly 71-6Aqu fst 5½f.21⅘ .45⅕1.04⅕ Allowance 8 3 2h 2h 21½ 24 ACorderoJr b 122 5.10 88-17 Riva Ridge 1224 Big Bluffer 1221 Lucky Bidder 1222 Gamely 8
2Jun71-4Bel fst 5½f.23 .46⅘1.05⅘ Md Sp Wt 6 4 2h 1h 13 15 CBaltazar b 122 2.50 91-17 Big Bluffer 1225 Delineation 1222 Lucky Bidder 1221 Mild drive 9
10May71-3Aqu my 5f .22⅖ .46⅕ .59 Md Sp Wt 6 9 79½ 69 59½ 55¼ BBaeza 122 2.40 85-17 Futures Market 122½ No Le Hace 1224 Infant Prodigy 122½ Poor st. 10
LATEST WORKOUTS Jly 20 Bel 3f sly .36⅗ b Jly 15 Bel 4f fst .48 b Jly 1 Bel 5f fst 1.01⅕ h Jun 27 Bel 4f fst .49⅖ b

Riva Ridge B. c (1969–Ky), by First Landing—Iberia, by Heliopolis 117 1971 3 2 0 0 $10,500
Meadow Stable L. Laurin (Meadow Stud, Inc.)
9Jly 71-6Aqu fst 5½f.21⅘ .45⅕1.04⅕ Allowance 3 1 1h 1h 11½ 14 CBaltazar b 122 *2.20 92-17 Riva Ridge 1224 Big Bluffer 1221 Lucky Bidder 1222 Mild drive 8
23Jun71-2Bel fst 5½f.22⅗ .46⅕1.05 Md Sp Wt 2 2 1½ 2h 12 15½ CBaltazar b 122 2.00 95-15 Riva Ridge 1225½ Key To The Mint 1223½ Candyville 122h Mild drive 8
9Jun71-4Bel fst 5½f.23⅕ .46⅘1.05 Md Sp Wt 7 8 86½ 811 815 717 CBaltazar 122 2.30 79-12 SearchForGold1227TheGeneral 1223½CryingToRun1222 Bumped 10
LATEST WORKOUTS Jly 19 Bel 3f fst .34⅕ h Jly 15 Bel 4f fst .49 b Jly 6 Bel 4f fst .48⅕ h Jly 1 Bel 4f fst .47⅘ h

Singh Ch. c. 2, by Bold Ruler—Sari's Song, by Spy Song
Own.—Phipps Cynthia Br.—Headley H P Jr & Mrs H P (Ky) Tr.—Russell J W 119
St. 1st 2nd 3rd Amt. 1974 2 M 1 0 $1,980
17Aug74- 4Sar fst 6f :22 :45 1:10⅗ Md Sp Wt 5 3 32 31½ 22½ 2¾ Pincay L Jr 119 6.70 86-13 Ellora 119¾ Singh 119nk Real Terror 119hd Gamely 12
9Aug74- 3Sar fst 5½f :22⅕ :47⅘ 1:04⅗ Md Sp Wt 6 7 1213 1015 1013 816 Pincay L Jr 119 3.80 78-13 Laramie Trail 1194 Ellora 1191¼ [D]Jimbosanda 1195 Bore in 12
LATEST WORKOUTS Aug 1 Sar 5f fst :58⅘ hg Jly 26 Bel 4f fst :47⅖ hg Jly 20 Bel 5f fst 1:01 h

May I Rule Gr. g. 2, by Iron Ruler—Artismae, by Artismo
Own.—October House Farm Br.—October House Farm (Fla) Tr.—Wright Frank I 122
St. 1st 2nd 3rd Amt. 1976 1 M 0 0
19May76- 4Bel sly 5½f :22⅘ :46⅖ 1:04⅖ Md Sp Wt 8 8 62¼ 67¼ 67 59½ Vasquez J 122 5.10 83-17 [D]Something Rotten 1221½ Gulfo122nkDukeWayne1227 Off slowly 8
LATEST WORKOUTS Jly 18 Bel 5f fst 1:01⅖ b ●Jly 13 Bel 3f fst :34 h Jly 7 Bel 4f fst :46⅗ h Jly 3 Bel 3f fst :37⅖ b

Copyright © 1979, by DAILY RACING FORM, INC. Reprinted with permission of copyright owner.

The study also includes horses running in their third career starts that had been heavily supported in their debuts, providing one of the following conditions applies:

(1) The horse improved dramatically in its second start.

Take Off B. c (1969–Ky), by Sky High II—Special Style, by Roman 122 1971 2 M 1 0 $1,650
A. L. Rice F. I. Wright (Danada Farm)
7Jly 71-1Aqu fst 5½f.23⅖ .47 1.05 Md Sp Wt 10 11 51¼ 2½ 2h 2h JVasquez 122 15.60 88-16 On High 122h Take Off 1225 Determined Cosmic 1175 Gamely 11
30Jun71-4Aqu fst 5½f.23 .47 1.05⅘ Md Sp Wt 4 6 42 3½ 44½ 56 JVasquez 122 4.90 78-16 Stage Director 1221¼ The General 122½ Instinctive 1224 Weakened 6
LATEST WORKOUTS Jly 20 Aqu 3f sly .37 b Jly 13 Aqu 4f fst .47 hg Jun 26 Aqu 3f fst .35 hg Jun 23 Aqu 4f fst .47 h

Copyright © 1979, by DAILY RACING FORM, INC. Reprinted with permission of copyright owner.

(2) The horse had a valid excuse for losing its second race, such as traffic problems or a far-outside post.

Propellent — B. c. 2, by Damascus—Klondike Kate, by Mark-Ye-Well — Br.—Aitkin L F (Ky) — Tr.—Jacobs E — **119**
Own.—Allen H

St. 1st 2nd 3rd Amt.
1972 3 M 0 2 $2,400

17Aug72- 5Sar fst 6f .21⅗ .45⅗ 1.11⅕ Md Sp Wt 11 7 711 62¾ 41¼ 31¾ Velasquez J 119 5.10 89-08 Kup Runneth 119nk Infuriator 1191 Propellent 119nk Rallied 11
7Aug72- 4Sar fst 5½f .22⅗ .46⅖ 1.05⅗ Md Sp Wt 12 6 74¾ 73¾ 53¼ 33¼ Baeza B 118 6.80 85-11 Raise And Rule 1182 Spear Carrier 1181½ Propellent 1182½ Good try 12
26Jly72- 3Aqu fst 6f .22⅕ .46 1.11⅕ Md Sp Wt 2 6 14 13 24 48 Baeza B b 118 4.30 79-18 ChampagneCharlie 1183½ Whatbreeze 1183 MsterAchiever 1181½ Tired 11
LATEST WORKOUTS ●Aug 23 Sar 3f fst .34⅘ h Aug 13 Sar 5f fst 1.00 h Aug 2 Sar 5f fst 1.01 h ●Jly 21 Aqu 4f fst .46 hg

Copyright © 1979, by DAILY RACING FORM, INC. Reprinted with permission of copyright owner.

(3) The horse had a layoff of at least one month after its second start—suggesting bucked shins. Only horses that had run well, or with an excuse, in their debuts qualify under this condition. Gigli Saw, for example, showed good speed for half a mile in his debut, after breaking lengths behind his field. He paid $13.00 October 18 when he won his third career start, after recovering from bucked shins.

Gigli Saw — Ch. c. 2, by Dr Fager—Mile Barker, by Mossborough — Br.—Tartan Farm Corp (Fla) — Tr.—Schulhofer F S — **121**
Own.—Tartan Stable

St. 1st 2nd 3rd Amt.
1972 2 M 0 0

7Aug72- 4Sar fst 5½f .22⅗ .46⅖ 1.05⅗ Md Sp Wt 11 3 31½ 3½ 43 56¼ Woodhouse R b 118 14.90 83-11 Raise And Rule 1182 Spear Carrier 1181½ Propellent 1182½ Weakened 12
22Jly72 3Aqu fst 6f .22⅗ .46⅕ 1.10⅘ Md Sp Wt 7 9 21½ 31½ 611 719 Guadalupe J b 118 3.10 73-10 Blackthorn 1181 Gothic 1187 Tell It Like It Is 1086 Early Speed 9
LATEST WORKOUTS Oct 10 Bel tr.t 4f fst .49 h Oct 4 Bel tr.t 6f fst 1.18 b Sep 28 Bel tr.t 4f fst .49⅘ h Sep 16 Bel tr.t 4f fst .51 b

Copyright © 1979, by DAILY RACING FORM, INC. Reprinted with permission of copyright owner.

(4) The horse was sidelined for at least one month between its first and second starts, then requalified on the odds board prior to its second start. Mulready, for example, was held at 4-1 odds November 6, despite a poor showing in her debut.

Mulready — B. f. 3, by Dr Fager—Rare Stamp, by Prince John — Br.—Tartan Farms Corp (Fla) — Tr.—Nerud J A — **115**
Own.—Tartan Stable

St. 1st 2nd 3rd Amt.
1973 2 2 0 0 $7,800
1972 3 M 0 1 $1,440

15May73- 6Bel fst 6f :22⅕ :44⅘ 1:09⅗ ⒻAllowance 5 2 2hd 1½ 1½ 1¾ Woodhouse R 118 *2.20 96-04 Mulready 118¾ Desert Vixen 118hd Full Of Hope 1213 Driving 8
12Mar73- 3GP fst 6f :21⅘ :44⅖ 1:09⅘ ⒻMd Sp Wt 7 5 12 13 15 110 Iannelli F b 119 *1.50 93-14 Mulready 11910 Got Busy 119½ Art Deco 1192½ Easily 12
28Nov72- 3Aqu fst 6f :22⅕ :46 1:12⅘ ⒻMd Sp Wt 14 3 31 1½ 22½ 45¼ Woodhouse R b 120 *2.00 76-19 Yofit 1201¼ Play It Cool 1202½ Don't Get Caught 1201½ Wide 14
6Nov72- 2Aqu my 6f :22⅖ :45⅘ 1:11⅗ ⒻMd Sp Wt 10 6 1hd 12 1hd 32¾ Woodhouse R b 120 4.30 82-18 Lady Barbizon 1202 Timing 120¾ Mulready 120¾ Weakened 14
21Jly72- 4Aqu fst 6f :22 :45⅗ 1:11 ⒻMd Sp Wt 8 5 41½ 54¼ 57½ 68½ Woodhouse R 117 *2.80 79-10 Sparkalark 1175 ShimmeringBeauty 117¾ DivinePleasure 117½ No excuse 9
LATEST WORKOUTS ●Jun 1 Bel 4f fst :46 h May 28 Bel 4f sly :50 b May 12 Bel 4f fst :49⅕ b May 7 Bel tr.t 4f fst :49 b

Copyright © 1979, by DAILY RACING FORM, INC. Reprinted with permission of copyright owner.

Note: Only in (3) above is the horse required to have raced well, or with an excuse, in its career debut.

A four-year study in New York turned up 251 of these horses, with the following results:

	NH	NW	WPCT	MPCT	$NET	I.V.
Totals	251	79*	31.5%	61.8%	$2.73	3.21
Second Start	211	60	28.4%	58.8%	$2.48	2.90
Third Start	40	19*	47.5%	77.5%	$4.06	4.84

As a group, these horses performed almost as well as favorites, although obviously, many were not favored. Their success was to be expected. The confident manner in which they were bet, prior to ever having raced, indicates the word is out that they have some ability, and probably are not long for the maiden ranks.

Those that had been absent for at least one month after their debuts did slightly better than the group as a whole. There were 53 of them, including some that did not return until they were three-year-olds.

NH	NW	WPCT	MPCT	$NET	I.V.
53	20*	37.7%	71.7%	$3.63	3.84

Remember, we are talking about maiden races, in which the entrants are, for the most part, inexperienced and lightly raced. If these horses are talented, as their debut odds suggest, they will very often be able to overcome their lack of recent racing experience. And the fact that a horse is returning from a layoff certainly does not hurt its odds.

○ JUVENILE MAIDEN WINNERS ○

Most two-year-old maiden winners race next in an NW1 or an open claiming race. Early in the year, some proceed directly from the maiden ranks to stakes competition.

A follow-up study was made of all juvenile maiden winners in New York during the 1972-73 seasons, with the following results:

NH	NW	WPCT	MPCT	$NET	I.V.
500	66	13.2%	39.0%	$1.34	1.06

These horses are able to hold their own, but coming off a (maiden) win, are overbet.

The statistics reveal that maiden special winners are twice as likely to repeat:

	NH	NW	WPCT	MPCT	$NET	I.V.
MSW	262	44	16.8%	46.6%	$1.37	1.35
MDN CLMG	238	22	9.2%	30.7%	$1.32	0.74

In defense of the maiden claiming winners, it should be said that many race next in an NW1 race, often finding themselves overmatched. Others must overcome a rise in claiming price. Here is the breakdown.

	NH	NW	WPCT	MPCT	$NET	I.V.
NW1	89	6	6.7%	22.5%	$0.70	0.54
Up in Price	89	7	7.9%	32.6%	$1.36	0.63
Others	60	9	15.0%	40.0%	$2.91	1.20

Clearly, a two-year-old maiden claiming victor brought back at the same price (or lower) for which it won is at no disadvantage. Unfortunately, the owners of many two-year-olds become overly optimistic after their horse wins for the first time and enter the horse in a race where it is at a disadvantage.

Surprisingly, since maiden winners are overbet as a rule, the most impressive maiden winners are the overlays. If a two-year-old suggests exceptional ability, capturing its maiden victory by a large margin (five lengths or more), it is an excellent bet in its next start, as the following figures prove.

NH	NW	WPCT	MPCT	$NET	I.V.
72	21	29.2%	55.6%	$2.32	2.35

And if a youngster breaks its maiden in exceptionally fast time—at least two lengths faster than the par for the race in which it is now entered (after times have been adjusted by a daily variant)—it is also worth betting.

NH	NW	WPCT	MPCT	$NET	I.V.
62	20	32.3%	56.5%	$2.24	2.60

Approximately half of all two-year-old maiden races are won by horses making their first, second, or third career starts. Surprisingly, these are more likely to repeat in their first non-maiden starts.

Experience	NH	NW	WPCT	MPCT	$NET	I.V.
1, 2, 3 Races	255	39	15.3%	41.2%	$1.41	1.23
Others	245	27	11.0%	36.7%	$1.27	0.89

Of particular interest is the youngster that won its debut and now faces winners in the second start of its career. This undefeated potential "super star" is by far the most heavily bet former maiden. Although repeating at a somewhat higher rate than the typical maiden winner, it is hardly worth a bet.

Be particularly wary of the horse that wins wire-to-wire without challenge in its debut. It will probably be challenged for the early lead in its next start, and is likely to react badly. Only three of eighteen such horses in the study won their next starts, for a miserly average payoff of 84 cents per $2 bet.

The youngster that contests the early lead and is able to win in its racing debut is the most likely to repeat in its next start. Such horses have already demonstrated courage as well as ability. In 1972–73, these horses repeated at a 22.2 percent rate for an average payoff of $2.15.

○ OPEN WINNERS ○

Here is a study of how all two-year-old stakes, allowance, and open claiming winners in New York performed in their next starts during 1972–73:

NH	NW	WPCT	MPCT	$NET	I.V.
302	67	22.2%	50.3%	$1.40	1.79

Once again, the availability of accurate speed figures is crucial in separating the most likely repeaters from the rest. Those whose winning time was at least two lengths faster than par time for the race in which the animal is now entered had the following record:

NH	NW	WPCT	MPCT	$NET	I.V.
94	28	29.8%	52.1%	$2.10	2.40

○ RECENT ACTION ○

The recent action factor—a race within the past 30 days— usually so crucial in other races, appears to be of little significance among two-year-olds. All our studies (maiden and non-maiden races) have indicated that the absence of a race within the past 30 days in no way diminishes a two-year-old's chances of winning. As a matter of fact, winning percentages and average payoffs were slightly higher for those returning from layoffs.

Champagne Winners

New York's Champagne Stakes has long been a key factor determining the year's two-year-old champion. In fact, from 1964 to 1976, the first horse across the finish line in the Champagne was later named champion of his division. (Two Champagne winners, Hoist The Flag and Secretariat, were

221

disqualified.) The table below lists Champagne winners from 1964 to the present, and contains final times, speed ratings (based on track records in effect September 30, 1978), accurate daily variants (calculated as explained in Chapter 17), and final speed figures (that reflect an adjustment made for the distance—+3 at Belmont and +5 at Aqueduct, where the race was run from 1964 to 1967). The figures reveal that Spectacular Bid's Champagne was by far the fastest.

Champagne Winners 1964–1978

1978	Spectacular Bid	1:34.4	94 + 24	121
1977	Alydar	1:36.3	85 + 19	107
1976	Seattle Slew	1:34.2	96 + 15	114
1975	Honest Pleasure	1:36.2	86 + 19	108
1974	Foolish Pleasure	1:36	88 + 17	108
1973	Holding Pattern	1:36	88 + 14	105
1973	Protagonist	1:36	88 + 14	105
1972	Secretariat	1:35	93 + 18	114
1971	Riva Ridge	1:36.2	86 + 23	112
1970	Hoist The Flag	1:35.2	91 + 17	111
1969	Silent Screen	1:37.1	82 + 19	104
1968	Top Knight	1:35.1	92 + 18	113
1967	Vitriolic	1:34.3	93 + 15	113
1966	Successor	1:35	91 + 17	113
1965	Buckpasser	1:36.2	84 + 21	110
1964	Bold Lad	1:36.2	84 + 25	114

Note: the race was run in two divisions in 1973.

Photo credit: Bob Coglianese

Buckpasser, 1965

Photo credit: Bob Coglianese

Seattle Slew, 1976

Photo credit: Bob Coglianese

Alydar, 1977

223

Alydar Versus Affirmed

Alydar versus Affirmed—one of Thoroughbred racing's great rivalries, perhaps its greatest two-year-old rivalry ever. The greatness of these two young colts is reflected in their speed figures (the table below contains accurate daily variants and adjusted speed figures), highlighted by probable "record" performances in the Great American, Hopeful, Belmont Futurity, and Laurel Futurity. But the greatest testimony to their greatness lies in the fact that in spite of their furious, all-out battles, neither went off form or threw in a bad race. And the battle raged from June through October. Affirmed won the championship because he outgamed Alydar in their three head-to-head confrontations.

Alydar versus Affirmed
Speed Figures

Remsen	17	118
Laurel Futurity	32	118
Champagne	19	107
Futurity	16	113
Hopeful	15	111
Sanford	15	107
Sapling	21	104
Hollywood Juvenile	17	106
Tremont	16	106
Great American	18	108
Alydar's MSW	21	108
Youthful	19	102
Affirmed's MSW	23	101

Note: Speed figures are for the winner of each race, except the Remsen, in which Believe It finished two lengths ahead of Alydar.

Photo credit: Bob Coglianese

The Hopeful

The Great American

The Futurity

Alydar * Ch. c. 3, by Raise A Native—Sweet Tooth, by On-And-On
Br.—Calumet Farm (Ky)
Tr.—Veitch John M
Own.—Calumet Farm

125

	St.	1st	2nd	3rd	Amt.
1977	10	5	4	0	$285,026

26Nov77- 8Aqu	sly	1⅛	:47⅕	1:11⅘	1:47⅘	Remsen	5	4	4^{9}	$4^{5\frac{1}{2}}$	3^{5}	2^{2}	Velasquez J	b 122	*.60	94-13	Believe It 122^{2} Alydar $122^{1\frac{1}{2}}$ Quadratic 116^{6}	2nd best	5
29Oct77- 8Lrl	fst	1$\frac{1}{16}$	:48⅘	1:13⅗	1:44⅕	Lrl Fut'y	1	3	3^{1}	1^{hd}	2^{hd}	2^{nk}	Velasquez J	b 122	*.40	92-27	Affirmed 122^{nk} Alydar 122^{10} StarDeNaskra 122^{27}	Steadied,sharp try	4
15Oct77- 6Bel	my	1	:48⅕	1:12⅖	1:36⅗	Champagne	1	5	4^{2}	$5^{2\frac{3}{4}}$	$4^{1\frac{1}{2}}$	$1^{1\frac{1}{4}}$	Velasquez J	b 122	1.50	85-17	Alydar $122^{1\frac{1}{4}}$ Affirmed $122^{1\frac{1}{4}}$ Darby Creek Road $122^{1\frac{1}{2}}$	Ridden out	6
10Sep77- 8Bel	gd	7f	:23⅗	:46⅗	1:21⅗	Futurity	1	5	$3^{2\frac{1}{2}}$	2^{hd}	1^{hd}	2no	Maple E	b 122	1.50	94-10	Affirmed 122no Alydar 122^{11} NastyAndBold 122^{hd}	Short lead, missed	5
27Aug77- 8Sar	fst	6½f	:22⅘	:45⅕	1:15⅖	Hopeful	1	4	4^{4}	$4^{\frac{3}{4}}$	2^{hd}	$2^{\frac{1}{2}}$	Maple E	b 122	*1.00	97-11	Affirmed $122^{\frac{1}{2}}$ Alydar $122^{2\frac{1}{2}}$ Regal And Royal 122^{hd}	Steadied early	5
13Aug77- 8Mth	sly	6f	:22⅖	:45⅗	1:10⅗	Sapling	4	5	3^{4}	2^{3}	2^{hd}	$1^{2\frac{1}{2}}$	Maple E	b 122	*.60	87-17	Alydar $122^{2\frac{1}{2}}$ Noon TimeSpender $122^{4\frac{1}{2}}$ DominantRuler 122no	Easily	5
27Jly77- 8Bel	fst	6f	:23	:45⅘	1:10	Tremont	4	4	3^{3}	$3^{1\frac{1}{2}}$	1^{1}	$1^{1\frac{1}{2}}$	Maple E	124	*.40	92-16	Alydar $124^{1\frac{1}{2}}$ Believe It $117^{3\frac{3}{4}}$ Jet Diplomacy $124^{5\frac{1}{2}}$	Ridden out	5
6Jly77- 8Bel	fst	5½f	:22⅖	:45⅘	1:03⅗	Gr. American	7	7	$4^{2\frac{1}{2}}$	1^{hd}	$1^{1\frac{1}{2}}$	$1^{3\frac{1}{2}}$	Maple E	117	*.80	97-16	Alydar $117^{3\frac{1}{2}}$ Affirmed 122^{2} Going Investor 122^{4}	Ridden out	7
24Jun77- 4Bel	fst	5½f	:22⅘	:46⅕	1:04⅕	Md Sp Wt	9	8	$6^{3\frac{3}{4}}$	1^{hd}	1^{2}	$1^{6\frac{3}{4}}$	Maple E	122	*2.10	94-20	Alydar $122^{6\frac{3}{4}}$ Believe It 122^{1} Sauce Boat $117^{3\frac{1}{2}}$	Handily	10
15Jun77- 8Bel	fst	5½f	:22⅖	:45⅗	1:05	Youthful	7	9	9^{12}	9^{11}	5^{10}	5^{5}	Maple E	115	*1.80	85-17	Affirmed 119^{nk} WoodNative $119^{\frac{1}{2}}$ SensitiveNose $119^{2\frac{1}{2}}$	In close turn	11

Affirmed Ch. c. 2, by Exclusive Native—Won't Tell You, by Crafty Admiral
Br.—Harbor View Farm (Fla)
Tr.—Barrera Lazaro S
Own.—Harbor View Farm

	St.	1st	2nd	3rd	Amt.
1977	9	7	2	0	$343,477

29Oct77- 8Lrl	fst	1$\frac{1}{16}$	:48⅘	1:13⅗	1:44⅕	Lrl Fut'y	3	2	2^{1}	2^{hd}	1^{hd}	1^{nk}	Cauthen S	122	1.40	92-27	Affirmed 122^{nk} Alydar 122^{10} StarDeNaskra 122^{27}	Long, hard drive	4
15Oct77- 6Bel	my	1	:48⅕	1:12⅖	1:36⅗	Champagne	5	3	3^{2}	1^{hd}	$1^{\frac{1}{2}}$	$2^{1\frac{1}{4}}$	Cauthen S	122	*1.20	84-17	Alydar $122^{1\frac{1}{4}}$ Affirmed $122^{1\frac{1}{4}}$ Darby Creek Road $122^{1\frac{1}{2}}$	2nd best	6
10Sep77- 8Bel	gd	7f	:23⅗	:46⅗	1:21⅗	Futurity	2	2	$2^{\frac{1}{2}}$	1^{hd}	2^{hd}	1no	Cauthen S	122	*1.20	94-10	Affirmed 122no Alydar 122^{11} Nasty And Bold 122^{hd}	Strong drive	5
27Aug77- 8Sar	fst	6½f	:22⅘	:45⅕	1:15⅖	Hopeful	4	1	3^{2}	2^{hd}	1^{hd}	$1^{\frac{1}{2}}$	Cauthen S	122	2.30	98-11	Affirmed $122^{\frac{1}{2}}$ Alydar $122^{2\frac{1}{2}}$ Regal And Royal 122^{hd}	Good handling	5
17Aug77- 8Sar	fst	6f	:21⅘	:44⅗	1:09⅗	Sanford	3	2	$3^{5\frac{1}{2}}$	4^{3}	$2^{\frac{1}{2}}$	$1^{2\frac{3}{4}}$	Cauthen S	124	*1.30	92-15	Affirmed $124^{2\frac{3}{4}}$ TiltUp 122^{hd} JetDiplomacy 124^{nk}	Driving, very wide	6
23Jly77- 5Hol	fst	6f	:21⅗	:44⅖	1:09⅕	Juv. Champ	6	3	1^{hd}	$1^{\frac{1}{2}}$	1^{4}	1^{7}	Pincay L Jr	122	*.40	93-15	Affirmed 122^{7} He's Dewan 122^{6} Esops Foibles $122^{\frac{3}{4}}$	Easily	8
23Jly77-Run In Two Divisions, 5th & 8th Races.																			
6Jly77- 8Bel	fst	5½f	:22⅖	:45⅘	1:03⅗	Gr. American	1	1	1^{1}	2^{hd}	$2^{1\frac{1}{2}}$	$2^{3\frac{1}{2}}$	Cordero A Jr	122	4.60	93-16	Alydar $117^{3\frac{1}{2}}$ Affirmed 122^{2} Going Investor 122^{4}	No match	7
15Jun77- 8Bel	fst	5½f	:22⅖	:45⅗	1:05	Youthful	1	1	$2^{\frac{1}{2}}$	$2^{\frac{1}{2}}$	1^{hd}	1^{nk}	Cordero A Jr	119	3.40	90-17	Affirmed 119^{nk} Wood Native $119^{\frac{1}{2}}$ Sensitive Nose $119^{2\frac{1}{2}}$	Driving	11
24May77- 4Bel	fst	5½f	:23	:47⅖	1:06	Md Sp Wt	10	1	$1^{\frac{1}{2}}$	$1^{1\frac{1}{2}}$	1^{2}	$1^{4\frac{1}{2}}$	Gonzalez B^{5}	117	14.30	85-21	Affirmed $117^{4\frac{1}{2}}$ Innocuous $122^{3\frac{1}{2}}$ Gymnast 122^{2}	Ridden out	10

GRASS
RACING

Turf racing is an increasingly popular feature at Thoroughbred tracks in the United States and Canada. Each year, more races, including stakes, are run on our grass courses.

The reasons are substantial. Owners and trainers cherish the grass as a fountain of youth for many animals unable to earn their keep on dirt. Audiences enjoy the colorful spectacle and the handicapping challenge. And in an era of long seasons and short fields, turf racing is a boon to track management.

Although everyone appreciates the infield sport, it imposes more than ordinary frustration on horsemen and handicappers. Thoroughbreds with dismal main-track records sometimes surprise at large mutuels when tried (often in desperation) on the grass. Yet many good turf runners are helpless on dirt, and horses with keen dirt form flounder on the lawn. Form reversals—or upsets regarded as form reversals—seem more abundant on grass than in the dirt races with which we are all more familiar.

Why do certain horses prefer grass? Some experts feel that runners with long strides or high action are best suited to that surface. Others believe that a broad, low-heeled foot is a big help on turf. Still others speculate that some come-from-behind horses, discouraged by flying clods on most dirt tracks, are more likely to persevere on grass.

Alleged

A great triumph for American grass breeding—Alleged, a son of Hoist The Flag and the Prince John mare Princess Pout, wins the 1977 Prix de l'Arc de Triomphe, the world's richest Thoroughbred race. The sire, Hoist The Flag, shown winning the 1970 Champagne, appeared set to sweep the 1971 Triple Crown classics when a tragic injury ended his racing days and almost took his life. At stud, the son of Tom Rolfe has quickly assumed a position among this country's leading sires of grass runners. The dam, Princess Pout, shown winning the 1971 Sheepshead Bay Handicap, gained prominence as a four-year-old when tried on the grass, and became a multiple stakes winner on that surface.

Hoist The Flag

Princess Pout

○ BREEDING ○

All such ideas merit investigation. In this chapter, however, we will disclose the results of a study which demonstrates in unmistakable terms that breeding plays an essential role in a horse's affinity for the turf. Awareness of the breeding factor dispels much of the prevailing mystery and confusion. Appropriately bred animals that win their first starts on turf fully deserve to do so, even at huge mutuels. Many so-called form reversals are more apparent than real.

Outstanding turf runners often win their first races on grass and pay large mutuels. Here is a list of well-known stakes horses and the prices they paid in their turf debuts:

Elaine (by Round Table)	$110.40
Ethical Lady (dam by Intentionally)	$106.00
Princess Pout (by Prince John)	$90.00
Sir Jason (by Grey Dawn II)	$85.00
Glossary (by Prince John)	$80.60
Lightning Lucy (by Stage Door Johnny)	$60.60
Camelford (by Round Table)	$48.20
Erwin Boy (by Exclusive Native)	$39.20
Rich Soil (by Verbatim)	$36.20
Effervescing (by Le Fabuleux)	$34.60
Summertime Promise (by Nijinsky II)	$32.40
Caviar Kid (by One For All)	$31.80
Big Spruce (by Herbager)	$22.40
Glowing Tribute (by Graustark)	$21.80
Fifth Marine (by Hoist The Flag)	$16.20
Kittiwake (by Sea-Bird)	$14.80
Shredder (by Stage Door Johnny)	$14.60
London Company (by Tom Rolfe)	$13.40
Lie Low (by Dr. Fager)	$13.00

The male line of Prince Rose, especially through his son Princequillo, is prepotent. That is, its members tend to transmit grass racing talent to their offspring. Perhaps the most influential turf sires today are Princequillo's sons Round Table and Prince John. And the latter's son Stage Door Johnny is the best young turf sire in present-day American racing. Interestingly, neither Prince John (who raced only as a two-year-old), nor Stage Door Johnny (whose career ended after a three-year-old campaign of only four months) ever raced on grass.

Princequillo's granddaughter Pocahontas has produced the leading turf sires Tom Rolfe (by Ribot) and Chieftain (by Bold Ruler). His daughter Somethingroyal is the dam of turf sire Sir Gaylord, not to mention the great Secretariat, who won his only two grass races and whose offspring should go well on that footing. Another daughter, Quill, is the dam of turf stars Caucasus and One For All (already an outstanding turf sire), and is the granddam of turf champion Run The Gauntlet and the promising Music of Time. In addition to Run The Gauntlet, Tom Rolfe has also sired turf stars Droll Role and London Company, as well as the ill-fated super horse Hoist The Flag, who has quickly become one of the premier turf sires in the world, having sired an Arc de Triomphe winner (Alleged) in his second crop. Sir Gaylord is the sire of European champion Sir Ivor and the unfortunate, though talented, Drone.

Another strong influence in today's turf breeding is Prince Rose's son Prince Chevalier, from whom descend Czar Alexander, Pretendre,

Canonero II, Tobin Bronze, and Astray. A genealogical chart of the Prince Rose line appears on the next page.

Prince Rose descended from the immortal St. Simon, through his son Persimmon. Ribot also belongs to the St. Simon line, descending from his son Rabelais. But, as we shall soon see, the Ribots do not seem to move up on the turf (at least not on this continent).

Perhaps the most exciting new development in American turf breeding is the French import Le Fabuleux, the sire of Man O' War winner Effervescing and many other fine turf runners in his first crop to race in this country. Like Ribot, Le Fabuleux descends from St. Simon through his son Rabelais. But, unlike Ribot, his offspring really seem to improve when given the opportunity to race on grass.

The male line of Phalaris via his grandson Nearco dominates North American breeding, but is not noted for production of grass runners. Nevertheless, turf sires Sea-Bird, T.V. Lark, Mongo, Amerigo, and Nijinsky II are (or were) part of this line.

The Hyperion line is represented in grass breeding by Vaguely Noble (whose better runners seem to race in Europe) and Assagai. The Man O' War line remains prominent on grass through his great grandson Intentionally, whose sons In Reality and Tentam promise to sire good infield runners.

Other leading grass sires include Herbager and his son Grey Dawn II. Herbager has also sired the outstanding runners Big Spruce, Gleaming, Dike, and L'Heureux, all of whom liked the grass and will probably pass on this trait to their offspring. And the get of Vent du Nord, who is by Vandale, the sire of Herbager, should be kept in mind when they begin their grass careers.

Finally, there is the mysterious Exclusive Native, whose breeding suggests main track sprints (his racing career confirmed this), but whose offspring seem to excel at turf routes. Witness Erwin Boy, Teddy's Courage, Qui Native, Sisterhood, and Native Courier, to name the five most prominent to date.

○ BREEDING AND HANDICAPPING ○

An axiom of handicapping warns the forecaster against expecting a horse to do something the animal has not already demonstrated it can do. Sensible though the principle may be in most circumstances, it does not suffice on grass. The reason that so many good grass runners win at large mutuels in their turf debuts is that they are underbet by comparison with inferior opponents whose main recommendations are previous turf starts.

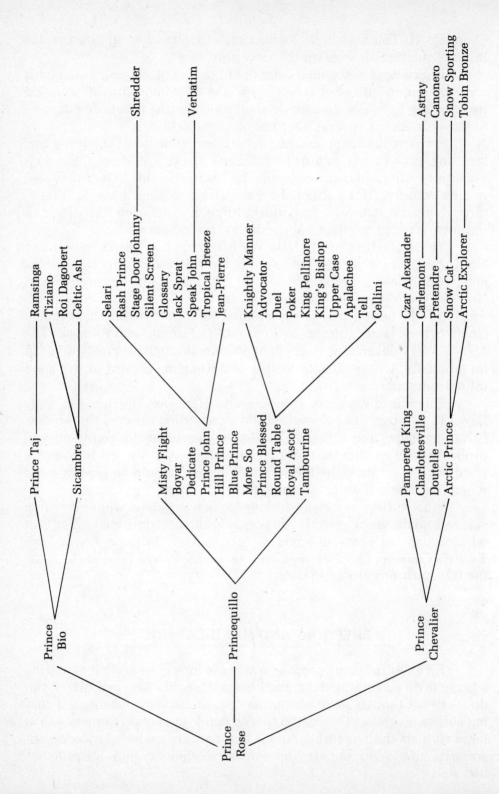

Ramsinga
Tiziano
Roi Dagobert
Celtic Ash

Shredder

Selari
Rash Prince
Stage Door Johnny
Silent Screen
Glossary
Jack Sprat
Speak John
Tropical Breeze
Jean-Pierre

Verbatim

Knightly Manner
Advocator
Duel
Poker
King Pellinore
King's Bishop
Upper Case
Apalachee
Tell
Cellini

Czar Alexander
Carlemont
Pretendre
Snow Cat
Arctic Explorer

Astray
Canonero
Snow Sporting
Tobin Bronze

Prince
Taj

Sicambre

Misty Flight
Boyar
Dedicate
Prince John
Hill Prince
Blue Prince
More So
Prince Blessed
Round Table
Royal Ascot
Tambourine

Pampered King
Charlottesville
Doutelle
Arctic Prince

Prince
Bio

Princequillo

Prince
Chevalier

Prince
Rose

232

How important is previous turf experience? A sample of 408 races turned up the following:

	NH	NW	WPCT	$NET	%W	I.V.
First Try	577	56	9.7%	$2.13	13.7%	0.83
Second Try	441	47	10.7%	$1.34	11.5%	0.91
Veteran	2483	305	12.2%	$1.46	74.8%	1.05

Turf veterans won 75 percent of these races, but the I.V. column shows that this was only 5 percent more than their fair share. Horses with little or no grass experience do fairly well. Those with no experience on the grass often pay shocking prices when they manage to win.

As these statistics suggest, grass experience does not necessarily signify grass ability. And the lack of grass experience does not necessarily mean inability. But what of horses that have already run on grass and have demonstrated a liking for it? The previous sample included 2,924 animals that had raced at least once on grass. They produced the following statistics:

	NH	NW	WPCT	$NET	%W	I.V.
Turf Winner	1831	248	13.5%	$1.59	60.8%	1.16
Turf Maiden	1093	104	9.5%	$1.21	25.5%	0.82

The figures show that previous grass winners have only a small advantage over grass maidens.

Evidently, some horses move up on grass sufficiently to win at the first or second asking on that surface, often at high odds. With that in mind, it seems appropriate to see whether horses well-bred for grass might be lucrative betting propositions even while inexperienced in turf competition.

We investigated the first and second grass races of 1,558 horses begotten by suspected turf sires. The results are stunning:

Sires Table

Sires	NH	NW	WPCT	MPCT	$NET	I.V.
Prince John	92	15*	16.3%	29.4%	$4.10	1.40
sons of P.J.	86	11	12.8%	29.1%	$1.89	1.10
Stage Door Johnny	52	21*	40.4%	55.8%	$4.64	3.47
Verbatim	12	6*	50.0%	75.0%	$9.68	4.29
Round Table	101	25	24.8%	56.4%	$4.00	2.12
sons of R.T.	112	10	8.9%	30.4%	$1.27	0.77
Sir Gaylord	59	11	18.6%	39.0%	$1.80	1.60
Sir Ivor	18	0	0.0%	22.2%	$0.00	0.00
Drone	18	2	11.1%	11.1%	$1.47	0.95
Ribot	56	7	12.5%	30.4%	$1.23	1.07
sons of Ribot	61	9	14.8%	44.3%	$2.05	1.27
Graustark	73	10	13.7%	35.6%	$1.16	1.18
Arts & Letters	19	0	0.0%	21.1%	$0.00	0.00
Tom Rolfe	82	11	13.4%	37.8%	$1.90	1.15
sons of T.R.	11	2	18.2%	63.6%	$1.33	1.56
Hoist The Flag	25	11*	44.0%	56.0%	$4.18	3.78
Chieftain	35	6	17.1%	42.9%	$3.42	1.47
T.V. Lark	87	17	19.5%	42.5%	$1.89	1.68
sons of T.V.L.	3	1	33.3%	33.3%	$2.93	2.86
T.V. Commercial	30	4	13.3%	43.3%	$2.63	1.14
Intentionally	35	6	17.1%	40.0%	$3.11	1.47
In Reality	35	2	5.7%	51.4%	$0.57	0.49
Dr. Fager	64	13	20.3%	37.5%	$2.63	1.74
Hawaii	10	1	10.0%	20.0%	$0.40	0.86
Mongo	54	9	16.7%	44.4%	$2.46	1.43
Assagai	57	5	8.8%	24.6%	$1.54	0.75
Sea-Bird	64	10	15.6%	28.1%	$2.44	1.34
sons of S.-B.	2	0	0.0%	0.0%	$0.00	0.00
Herbager	88	15	17.1%	39.8%	$2.20	1.46
sons of Herb.	5	1	20.0%	20.0%	$8.56	1.72
Grey Dawn II	48	8	16.7%	33.3%	$3.50	1.43
Vent du Nord	13	3	23.1%	46.2%	$3.34	1.98
Vaguely Noble	8	1	12.5%	37.5%	$0.35	1.07
Le Fabuleux	31	11	35.5%	58.1%	$3.81	3.05
Nijinsky II	29	9	31.0%	55.2%	$2.92	2.66
One For All	13	4	30.8%	69.2%	$5.80	2.64
Exclusive Native	23	5	21.7%	60.9%	$3.30	1.87
Bolero	6	3	50.0%	83.3%	$5.07	4.29
John's Joy	10	1	10.0%	40.0%	$0.48	0.86
Princequillo Line**	102	19*	18.6%	38.2%	$3.25	1.60
Prince Rose Line**	139	19	13.7%	36.7%	$2.20	1.17

**Descendants of these sires not individually listed in the table

A similar situation occurs with horses whose dams were sired by one of these suspected turf sires:

Broodmare Sires Table

Broodmare Sires	NH	NW	WPCT	MPCT	$NET	I.V.
Princequillo	159	22	13.8%	34.0%	$1.34	1.19
Princequillo Line	175	37*	21.1%	40.0%	$3.61	1.81
Prince Rose Line	76	15*	19.7%	42.1%	$3.49	1.69
Prince John	111	23	20.7%	45.1%	$3.01	1.78
Round Table	81	19	23.5%	46.9%	$4.74	2.01
Sir Gaylord	55	7	12.7%	38.2%	$2.28	1.09
Ribot	42	11	26.2%	42.9%	$3.65	2.25
sons of Ribot	5	1	20.0%	60.0%	$1.56	1.72
Amerigo	56	10	17.9%	33.9%	$2.49	1.53
Intentionally	43	8	18.6%	39.5%	$4.32	1.60
Bolero	35	8	22.9%	40.0%	$1.89	1.96
John's Joy	42	8	19.1%	35.7%	$3.97	1.63
T.V. Lark	27	6	22.2%	63.0%	$1.25	1.91
Herbager	21	2	9.5%	47.6%	$0.87	0.82
Grey Dawn II	1	0	0.0%	100.0%	$0.00	0.00
Mongo	13	2	15.4%	76.9%	$2.09	1.32
Sea-Bird	5	0	0.0%	40.0%	$0.00	0.00
Tom Rolfe	3	0	0.0%	0.0%	$0.00	0.00
Chieftain	10	1	10.0%	40.0%	$0.84	0.86

The small samples, of course, do injustice to the younger broodmare sires Tom Rolfe, Sea-Bird, Chieftain, and Grey Dawn II.

For full appreciation of these two tabulations, let us now combine them, and present additional detail. In the following presentation, the top line covers all 2,591 first- or second-time starters included in our study because of influential sires or maternal grandsires. The second line isolates those who went to the post at odds of less than 10-1.

	NH	NW	WPCT	MPCT	$NET	I.V.
All	2591	460*	17.8%	40.0%	$2.56	1.52
Low Odds	1543	387*	25.1%	51.4%	$2.32	2.15

Extraordinary results indeed. These horses win and run in the money much more consistently than their odds might suggest they should. And they return their backers an average profit of better than 25 cents on the wagered dollar. Those at less than 10-1 do even better than the group as a whole, except in the average payoff department. The study found 73 winners at odds of 10-1 or higher, illuminating a rich source of longshots.

The following tabulation also deals with appropriately bred horses in their first and second turf starts. It shows that the sire and maternal grandsire are almost equally influential. However, if both sire and maternal grandsire are turf influences, results are all the better.

	NH	NW	WPCT	MPCT	$NET	I.V.
Sire	1868	324*	17.3%	39.2%	$2.49	1.49
Broodmare Sire	960	180*	18.8%	41.2%	$2.88	1.61
Both	237	44*	18.6%	39.2%	$3.26	1.59

○ HAIL PRINCE ROSE! ○

The study reconfirms the prepotency of the Prince Rose line. Grouping every surveyed horse with Prince Rose blood on either side, we found 1,627 starters, with the following figures:

NH	NW	WPCT	MPCT	$NET	I.V.
1627	297*	18.3%	39.6%	$2.86	1.57

Although not listed in the Sires Table, both Blue Prince and Misty Flight, two sons of Princequillo, have proven to be successful grass sires, as have Prince Taj and Pretendre, both of whom descend from Prince Rose.

Surprisingly, only Advocator among the sons of Round Table has sired horses that seem to move up on the grass. And among the offspring of Prince John, only Stage Door Johnny, Tropical Breeze, Speak John, and the latter's son Verbatim appear to be carrying on the family tradition.

Consequently, young stallions such as King Pellinore, Tell, King's Bishop, Upper Case, Bicker, Apalachee, Cellini (all sons of Round Table), Shredder (by Stage Door Johnny), Glossary, and Jack Sprat (the last two by Prince John, the latter being a ¾-brother to Stage Door Johnny) should be closely scrutinized when their first crops begin to race on the grass.

On the other hand, it becomes clear that the Ribot line has shown no preference for the grass (with the exception of the Tom Rolfe's, who were included in the Prince Rose group). Of the Ribots, we found 256 starters, with the following record:

NH	NW	WPCT	MPCT	$NET	I.V.
256	38	14.8%	37.1%	$1.72	1.27

Much of this "success" is due to Ribot himself as a broodmare sire, and not to Ribot or any of his sons (particularly Arts & Letters and Graustark) as turf sires. But obviously, many bettors expect the Ribots to move up on grass.

The influence of the late T.V. Lark as a turf sire has lessened as that great sire's last few crops have come to race on grass. The same can be said of Sir Gaylord, who, in addition, has failed to pass his

Princequillo blood on to his sons Sir Ivor and Drone, both of whom have been dismal failures thus far as sires of turf runners.

One reason for the continued success of this study is the fact that the list of turf stallions has been updated each year. With but one exception (Exclusive Native), new stallions have been selected from one of three categories:

1. Horses carrying the blood of stallions already on the list, particularly those that ran to their turf breeding. Look for the following young stallions to prove effective turf sires in the near future: Secretariat, Tentam, Big Spruce, Shredder, Majestic Light, King Pellinore, Fifth Marine, and Little Current.

2. American turf champions, even those whose breeding may not have forewarned of grass championships. One would expect the offspring of Cougar II, Snow Knight, and Youth to go well on the grass.

3. Foreign imports, especially ones that had already been successful at stud in Europe. Le Fabuleux spent a few years at stud in France before coming to this country. Watch the offspring of the recent French imports Caro and Lyphard, both of whom sired several outstanding horses in their first crops to race in Europe. And English Derby winner Roberto has already sired a number of real runners in his first crop, juveniles of 1977 who will be running on the grass as three-year-olds in 1978.

Not all of the additions to the turf stallion list have proven to be "live" turf sires. For that matter, several on the original list failed to live up to expectations. But it is a fairly safe bet that a few of the young stallions mentioned above will be among the leading turf sires of the next decade.

Grass Champions

1953	Iceberg II	1962	——	1971	Run The Gauntlet
1954	Stan	1963	Mongo	1972	Cougar II
1955	St. Vincent	1964	——	1973	Secretariat
1956	Career Boy	1965	Parka	1974	Dahlia
1957	Round Table	1966	Assagai	1975	Snow Knight
1958	Round Table	1967	Fort Marcy	1976	Youth
1959	Round Table	1968	Dr. Fager	1977	Johnny D.
1960	——	1969	Hawaii		
1961	T.V. Lark	1970	Fort Marcy		

Shredder

Ch. c. 4, by Stage Door Johnny—Cut It Up, by Tudor Minstrel
Br.—Greentree Stud Inc (Ky)
Tr.—Gaver John M
Own.—Greentree Stable

115

Turf Record	St.	1st	2nd	3rd			St.	1st	2nd	3rd	Amt.
	2	2	0	0		1975	3	2	0	0	$17,400
						1974	2	M	0	2	$2,160

6Sep75- 6Bel	fm	1 1/16 Ⓣ	:46⅖	1:11	1:41⅖	3↑ Allowance	2	2	2½	1^{hd}	1^{3}	1^{5}	Bracciale V Jr	112	1.40e	94-11	Shredder 112^{5} Candle Stand 116$^{3/4}$ Intrepid Hero 118$^{2\frac{1}{4}}$	Handily	9
23Aug75- 1Sar	fm	1⅛ Ⓣ	:47	1:10⅘	1:46⅗	3↑ Md Sp Wt	1	1	1$^{1\frac{1}{2}}$	1$^{1\frac{1}{2}}$	1^{4}	1^{9}	Bracciale V Jr	117	6.30	94-08	Shredder 117^{9} Copper Kingdom 117$^{1\frac{1}{2}}$ Spasoje 117no	Mild drive	12
16Aug75- 9Sar	fst	6f	:22⅗	:46	1:10⅘	3↑ Md Sp Wt	2	8	7^{5}	8^{6}	6^{8}	5^{13}	Bracciale V Jr	118	*1.90	73-14	Yu Wipi 118^{7} Something Gold 113^{3} The IrishLord118^{no}	No factor	11
9Sep74- 3Bel	fst	6f	:22	:46⅕	1:11⅕	Md Sp Wt	6	7	8$^{8\frac{1}{2}}$	6$^{4\frac{1}{2}}$	4$^{1\frac{1}{2}}$	3$^{2\frac{3}{4}}$	Turcotte R	121	*1.00	84-13	Doug 121$^{1\frac{1}{2}}$ Lucky Limey 121$^{1\frac{1}{2}}$ Shredder 121$^{1\frac{1}{2}}$	Rallied	11
2Sep74- 3Bel	sly	6f	:22⅗	:45⅘	1:10⅘	Md Sp Wt	7	3	1^{hd}	1^{hd}	2^{hd}	3^{4}	Turcotte R	121	*1.40	87-13	Lefty 121^{4} Co Host 121no Shredder 121^{7}	Weakened	7

LATEST WORKOUTS Aug 30 Bel 4f fst :49 b ●Aug 26 Sar 7f fst 1:26 h Aug 23 Sar 7f fst 1:28 b ●Aug 19 Sar 6f fst 1:11⅘ h

Shredder looked like a promising two-year-old, but his three-year-old debut raised serious questions regarding his long absence. These were quickly dispelled in what may well have been the most impressive grass maiden victory in the annals of racing, so impressive that he was heavily bet in his next start against stakes horses—and beat them easily.

Photo credit: Bob Coglianese

Shredder, shown here winning his grass debut at Saratoga, was possibly the most talented horse produced in this country never to compete in stakes races.

Majestic Light

B. c. 3, by Majestic Prince—Irradiate, by Ribot
Br.—Phipps O M (Ky)
Tr.—Russell John W
Own.—Phipps Ogden Mills

126

Turf Record	St.	1st	2nd	3rd			St.	1st	2nd	3rd	Amt.
	2	2	0	0		1976	8	3	0	3	$37,023
						1975	7	1	0	2	$8,400

15May76- 8GS	fm	1 1/16 Ⓣ			1:43⅕	Cavalcade H	9	8	9^{15}	7$^{9\frac{1}{2}}$	5$^{1\frac{3}{4}}$	1½	Barrera C		117	6.80	89-11	Majestic Light 117½ Chati 116^{2} Fabled Monarch 115^{3}	Driving	12
5May76- 8GS	fm	1 Ⓣ			1:39⅗	Allowance	7	7	7$^{5\frac{1}{2}}$	6^{4}	4$^{1\frac{1}{2}}$	1$^{3\frac{1}{2}}$	Barrera C		115	2.60	75-25	MjesticLight115$^{3\frac{1}{2}}$NoblAdmirl115$^{3/4}$GrtCombintion117$^{3/4}$	Ridden out	8
16Apr76- 5Aqu	fst	1	:46⅕	1:10⅖	1:36	Allowance	6	5	8^{9}	7^{10}	7^{10}	6^{9}	Baeza B	b	117	26.60	77-18	BestLidPlns119$^{1\frac{1}{2}}$Prctitioner117^{hd}FifthMrin122$^{1\frac{1}{2}}$	Ducked in start	8
11Mar76- 8Aqu	sly	1	:46⅘	1:12	1:37⅕	3↑ Allowance	2	2	2½	2$^{1\frac{1}{2}}$	3$^{3\frac{1}{2}}$	5$^{8\frac{1}{4}}$	Cordero A Jr	b	113	5.00	72-21	Be-A-Son 113$^{2\frac{1}{2}}$ Cabriolet II 116^{2} Top Cat 109$^{1\frac{3}{4}}$	Tired	6
28Feb76- 6Aqu	fst	1	:48⅖	1:13⅗	1:39⅕	Allowance	6	3	3^{1}	2^{hd}	1^{hd}	1$^{1\frac{1}{2}}$	Cordero A Jr		117	*1.40	70-22	MajesticLight117$^{1\frac{1}{2}}$Resilient115^{no}Mr.Internationl115$^{2\frac{3}{4}}$	Drew clear	6
20Feb76- 8Aqu	fst	1	:46⅗	1:11⅗	1:37⅖	Allowance	3	5	6^{8}	4^{6}	4^{4}	3$^{1\frac{1}{4}}$	Cordero A Jr		119	*1.30	78-22	Kupper 115^{hd} Distinctively 115$^{1\frac{1}{4}}$ Majestic Light 119$^{2\frac{3}{4}}$	Bumped	8
12Feb76- 8Aqu	fst	1	:47	1:11⅖	1:37⅕	Allowance	3	6	5^{2}	4^{2}	5$^{1\frac{3}{4}}$	3$^{1\frac{3}{4}}$	Cordero A Jr		115	*2.00	78-19	Rough Punch 115$^{1\frac{1}{2}}$ Resilient 115^{nk} Majestic Light115^{hd}	Steadied	8
7Jan76- 6Aqu	fst	1	:47⅕	1:11⅗	1:36⅖	Allowance	3	3	2½	2^{1}	3^{1}	3$^{4\frac{1}{4}}$	Cordero A Jr		122	2.60	80-13	NewCollection115^{4}BrillintBhvior115^{nk}MjsticLight122^{1}	Weakened	6
18Dec75- 4Aqu	fst	1	:47⅖	1:13	1:38⅕	Md Sp Wt	5	5	4^{6}	4$^{4\frac{1}{2}}$	2^{3}	1¾	Baeza B		122	2.40	75-25	Majestic Light 122¾ Distinctively122½NativeFloridian122^{8}	Driving	7
6Dec75- 1Aqu	fst	6f	:22⅕	:45⅕	1:10⅗	Md Sp Wt	4	5	9^{9}	7^{9}	6$^{7\frac{1}{4}}$	3$^{2\frac{1}{4}}$	Baeza B		122	20.60	88-13	NotblyDiffrnt122$^{1\frac{3}{4}}$PrsidntChrli117½MjsticLght122^{hd}	Finished fast	12
18Oct75- 3Bel	sly	6f	:23⅕	:46⅖	1:11⅖	Md Sp Wt	6	3	6$^{5\frac{1}{4}}$	6$^{4\frac{1}{2}}$	5$^{9\frac{1}{2}}$	6$^{8\frac{1}{2}}$	Martens G		122	24.80	76-17	PrivteThoughts112$^{1\frac{1}{2}}$LordHenribe122$^{2\frac{3}{4}}$JudgndJury122^{3}	No factor	8
21Sep75- 4Bel	my	1	:47⅘	1:12⅘	1:37⅘	Md Sp Wt	9	5	5$^{2\frac{1}{4}}$	4^{5}	8^{18}	8^{25}	Cordero A Jr		122	6.10	54-19	Art Above All 122^{10} Royal Mission 115^{nk} Si Si You 122$^{8\frac{1}{2}}$	Tired	10
11Sep75- 4Bel	fst	7f	:23⅖	:46⅗	1:24⅗	Md Sp Wt	4	3	4$^{2\frac{1}{2}}$	5$^{3\frac{1}{2}}$	3^{5}	3$^{6\frac{1}{2}}$	Hole M		120	10.30	72-18	Bonge 120^{3} Full Catch 120$^{3\frac{1}{2}}$ Majestic Light 120¾	Even try	10
29Aug75- 3Bel	fst	7f	:23⅕	:47	1:25⅗	Md Sp Wt	7	3	5^{1}	5$^{2\frac{3}{4}}$	4$^{4\frac{1}{2}}$	4$^{7\frac{1}{4}}$	Hole M		120	8.90	67-22	Half Magic 120¾ Full Catch 120$^{6\frac{1}{2}}$ Finger Paints 120no	Tired	7
16Aug75- 2Sar	fst	6f	:22⅘	:46⅖	1:11⅘	Md Sp Wt	7	9	7$^{5\frac{1}{4}}$	5$^{6\frac{1}{2}}$	6$^{8\frac{1}{2}}$	6^{10}	Hole M		120	8.40	71-14	Bakor 120$^{4\frac{1}{2}}$ Bold Sunrise 120$^{1\frac{3}{4}}$ National Flag 120¾	No factor	10

LATEST WORKOUTS ●Jun 1 Bel 1 fst 1:40⅖ h May 27 Bel 6f fst 1:13 h May 22 Bel 5f fst 1:02⅘ b May 12 Bel 5f fst 1:02⅕ b

John Russell felt all along that Majestic Light had considerable talent, but it was not until he tried the colt on grass that he could be sure. The confidence gained in these grass races quickly propelled Majestic Light into a major stakes winner on both grass and dirt, a colt with one of the most devastating moves around a turn in racing history. In Majestic Light, we see the Ribot grass influence manifested in its most common form—through one of his daughters.

Music of Time — Ch. c. 3, by Northern Dancer—First Feather, by First Landing
Own.—Rokeby Stable — Br.—Mellon P (Va) — Tr.—Miller Mack — 115
Turf Record: St. 1st 2nd 3rd: 1 1 0 0 — St. 1st 2nd 3rd Amt.: 1977 3 1 1 0 $9,480; 1976 0 M 0 0
28Jun77- 5Bel fm 1 1/16 (T):46⅗ 1:10⅗ 1:41⅗ 3↑Md Sp Wt 8 2 21½ 1hd 11½ 14 Velasquez J b 114 3.20 93-07 MusicofTime1144ForwardView1143Soldier'sLark1142¼ Ridden out 12
30May77- 1Bel fst 7f :23 :46 1:24 3↑Md Sp Wt 2 4 31½ 3nk 2½ 21½ Vasquez J 113 4.70 80-14 Forecast 1121½ Music of Time 1131½ Caribert 1128½ Weakened 9
23May77- 3Bel fst 6f :22⅘ :46⅗ 1:11 3↑Md Sp Wt 1 3 1hd 21 32 44¾ Velasquez J 112 4.10 82-17 Stab 112hd True Colors 1074½ Decision Revoked 112hd Weakened 11
LATEST WORKOUTS Jly 4 Bel 4f fst :51⅗ b — Jun 26 Bel 4f sly :48 h — Jun 22 Bel 5f fst 1:00⅕ h — Jun 19 Bel 5f fst 1:01 h

Copyright © 1979, by DAILY RACING FORM, INC. Reprinted with permission of copyright owner.

Mack Miller and John Russell are more than just two of America's leading trainers. They are perhaps the two best when it comes to preparing a young three-year-old for a career as a grass runner. Interestingly, neither requires grass bloodlines to be successful. Music Of Time is a typical example of Miller's work—lightly raced, but well prepared when the grass racing season begins. Although his breeding does not immediately suggest grass, his dam did produce a turf champion, Run The Gauntlet, by turf sire Tom Rolfe.

Drumtop — B. f (1966–Ky), by Round Table—Zonah, by Nasrullah
J. B. Moseley — R. Laurin — (Mrs. G. G. Proskauer) — 111
1969 5 1 1 1 $7,750
1968 3 1 0 1 $4,125
24Jun69–6Bel fm 7f (T) 1.22⅘ f– Allow 7 4 43 31½ 12 15 ACorderoJr b 109 3.60 94– 7 Drumtop 1095 What Goes On 113½ Take A Stand 1142½ Mild dr. 10
10Jun69–6Bel fst 6f .22⅘ .46⅖1.12⅗ f– Allow 8 11 98¾ 88 75 31½ ACorderoJr b 109 7.60 80–18 Mlle. Roulette 110h Modest Martha 1091½ Drumtop 109¾ Swerved 12
3Apr69–6Aqu fst 6f .21⅘ .44⅘1.11⅕ f– Allow 4 6 67 710 68 44½ BBaeza b 113 3.20 82–15 Battle Message 1111½ Grey Slacks 1224 Gay Divorcee 122h Rallied 8
27Mar69–7Aqu fst 7f .23 .46 1.23⅘ f– Allow 1 6 3nk 31½ 43½ 510 BBaeza b 112 *2.10 72–19 Haulover 1135 Winsome Lea 122no Mlle. Quille 1114 No excuse 9
18Mar69–6Aqu fst 6f .22⅘ .46 1.10⅗ f– Allow 2 5 41½ 31½ 1½ 22 RUssery b 116 29.20 88–18 Secret Verdict 1212 Drumtop 1161½ Mlle. Quille 1161 Gamely 10
27Aug68–5Aqu fst 6f .23⅗ .48⅗1.14⅕ f–MdSpWt 6 7 83¼ 41¼ 11 1¾ JLRotz b 119 2.10 72–25 Drumtop 119¾ Hit Song 1141½ Duchess Rae 109h In close, driving 10
15Aug68–4Sar fst 5½f.22⅖ .46⅗1.05⅖ f–MdSpWt 4 8 74¾ 66¾ 2½ 32¼ JLRotz b 119 7.60 88–12 Plane 1192 Elizabeth's Dancer 116nk Drumtop 119h Bid, tired 12
6Aug68–3Sar sly 5½f.22⅖ .46⅘1.06⅕ f–MdSpWt 1 12 1012 99 65½ 65¼ JLRotz b 119 27.80 81–15 Lily Of The Nile 1191½ Finest Jade 1191 Thera 1191½ No rally 12
LATEST WORKOUTS Jly 11 Bel 5f fst 1.02 b — Jly 5 Bel tr.t. 4f fst .50⅕ h — Jun 18 Bel 4f fst .49 b — Jun 4 Bel tc 5f fst 1.02⅗ b

Copyright © 1979, by DAILY RACING FORM, INC. Reprinted with permission of copyright owner.

One of the top grass mares of her era, Drumtop beat topnotch males, including champion Fort Marcy, in several major events, including the Hialeah Turf Cup, the Canadian International, and the Bowling Green. The daughter of Round Table appeared to be just an ordinary allowance runner until she tried the grass.

Lightning Lucy * — Ch. f. 3, by Stage Door Johnny—Lucy Letton, by Sir Gaylord
Own.—Vee-Nine Stable — Br.—Forest Retreat Farm Inc (Ky) — Tr.—Rigione J — 114
Turf Record: St. 1st 2nd 3rd: 3 2 0 0 — St. 1st 2nd 3rd Amt.: 1973 9 3 0 1 $19,380; 1972 2 M 0 0
23Jun73- 7Aqu sf 1 3/16 (T) 1:14⅘ 1:59⅘ 3↑(F)Shepsd Bay H 10 3 33 22½ 99¾ 1011 Pineda R b 110 8.60 60-29 Shearwater 112½ Inca Queen 1181¼ Aglimmer 1151¼ Tired 13
16Jun73- 6Bel fm 1 1/16 (T) 1:10 1:41⅕ 3↑(F)Allowance 6 6 64½ 22 1hd 13½ Wallis T5 b 107 2.20 96-06 Lightning Lucy 1073½ Eclat 1064½ Sassy Cyane 1112 Ridden out 10
7Jun73- 5Bel hd 1 1/16 (T) 1:10⅘ 1:41⅖ 3↑(F)Allowance 5 4 32 1½ 12 13 Pineda R b 111 29.30 95-04 Lightning Lucy 1113 Misty Devil 113½ Marismas 1144 Driving 10
28May73- 4Bel sly 1 1/16 :45⅘ 1:11 1:44⅕ 3↑(F)Allowance 5 1 11 22 58½ 618 Cardone E b 108 4.60 64-16 Rokeby Venus 1149 Last Cruise 1012½ Mixed Flight 1123 Used up 8
23May73- 1Bel sly 7f :22⅗ :45⅘ 1:24⅕ 3↑(F)Md 18000 3 2 1hd 13 14 15 Santiago A b 114 4.00 86-16 Lightning Lucy 1145 Arbee Eye 1124 Bright Magic 1123 Driving 8
17May73- 1Bel fst 6f :22⅘ :46⅗ 1:11⅗ 3↑(F)Md c-12500 7 5 2hd 2hd 32 53 Velasquez J b 114 *2.30 83-11 Sweet Fern 1141¼ Cockateel 112¾ Barbill 114½ Speed, tired 13
11May73- 4Aqu gd 6f :22⅗ :46⅗ 1:12⅗ 3↑(F)Md 20500 6 1 31½ 1hd 22 35½ Velasquez J b 114 9.20 74-19 Instant Start 1142 Island Flower 1143½ Lightning Lucy 114hd Weakened 6
24Apr73- 2Aqu fst 6f :22⅗ :45⅘ 1:12⅗ 3↑(F)Md 22500 9 6 88¼ 811 79 68¾ Velasquez J b 114 5.70e 71-22 Savage Market 1152½ Randy's Way 1142 Easter Bonnet 109¾ No excuse 12
16Apr73- 2Aqu fst 7f :23 :45⅘ 1:25 3↑(F)Md 25000 3 4 21 46½ 716 620 Arellano J b 114 16.50 56-17 Miss Rag Mop 1112½ Savage Market 1133 Happy Chile 114¾ Gave way 7
29Aug72- 4Bel fst 6f :22⅕ :46⅕ 1:11 (F)Md Sp Wt 8 8 79½ 1114 1121 1121 Velasquez J 119 6.70 68-09 I Encompass 1192½ Protesting Bid 11911 Admiral's Maid 1192 No speed 11
LATEST WORKOUTS Jly 2 Bel tr.t 4f fst :49⅘ b — Jun 14 Bel tr.t 4f gd :50⅕ b — Jun 5 Bel tr.t 4f fst :51⅗ b — May 6 Bel 5f fst 1:00⅘ h

Copyright © 1979, by DAILY RACING FORM, INC. Reprinted with permission of copyright owner.

Were it not for grass racing, Lightning Lucy probably would have amounted to nothing more than an erratic claiming filly. But she took an immediate liking to the grass, and went on to become a multiple stakes winner, including a victory over older rivals in the 1973 Diana at Saratoga.

Kittiwake — B. f (1968–Fla), by Sea-Bird—Ole Liz, by Double Jay
Mrs. Taylor Hardin — W. C. Stephens — (M. Andersen) — 113
1971 9 2 0 2 $19,345
1970 13 1 3 5 $14,530
18May71–8Aqu fm 1 1/8 (T) 1.44⅖ f– Allow 4 3 33½ 32½ 11 14 JVasquez 112 6.10 81–19 Kittiwake 1124 Hilo Hop 1091½ Brave Lady 1031½ Ridden out 7
5May71–6Aqu fm 1 1/8 (T) 1.45⅕ f– Allow 8 4 43½ 31½ 11½ 12 HGustines 109 6.40 77–23 Kittiwake 1092 Rousiana 113nk Scoring 109no Mild drive 12
12Apr71–6Aqu fst 7f .23⅕ .46⅖1.24⅖ f– Allow 3 6 2h 63½ 42 44½ CBaltazar 112 11.40 74–24 Tender Logic 1123½ Jillys Joy 112nk Aube Rouge 109¾ Tired 10
25Mar71–7Aqu fst 6f .23 .47⅖1.12⅘ f– Allow 6 5 2½ 2h 54¾ 58 JCruguet b 112 3.10 71–30 Punchs Penny 1091 Lullah Lullah 120h Camp Glow 1124 Tired 8
1Mar71–7Hia fst 6f .22⅕ .45⅖1.11⅗ f– Allow 8 9 106¾ 58 45½ 44¾ ACorderoJr b 118 14.70 81–19 Gain Or Loss 1213 Turiana 1161½ Our Dish 121nk Slow early 11
12Feb71–7Hia fst 6f .22 .45⅕1.11 f– Allow 2 6 33 22 2h 32 JCruguet b 115 3.20 85–14 OurPersonalTouch1211¾ RulersMistress121nk Kittiwake115nk Weak'd 12
5Feb71–6Hia fst 6f .22⅕ .45⅘1.12⅕ f– Allow 2 9 76¾ 46 45½ 46 JCruguet b 115 *2.80 77–21 Muriels Dream 1153½ Our Dish 1212 Im Adorable 121½ Poor start 10
29Jan71–6Hia fst 6f .22⅖ .45⅗1.11⅗ f– Allow 8 4 22 21½ 23 33½ JCruguet b 115 3.60 83–17 Aqua Belle 1152½ Swoons Symbol 115¾ Kittiwake 1153 Weakened 12
19Jan71–7Hia sly 6f .22⅗ .45⅗1.11⅘ Allowance 11 8 32½ 32½ 57½ 67½ JCruguet b 115 2.50 78–19 YouAreFlat1181½ SenseOfReason118½ MurielsDream1153 Tired 11
9Nov70–7Aqu fst 1 .45⅗1.10⅖1.36⅖ f–Demselle 13 5 63 52 98½ 99½ JCruguet 112 31.80 75–19 Inca Queen 1122½ Deceit 1221 Emperors Desire 114nk Tired 13
LATEST WORKOUTS Jun 3 Bel 3f fst .36⅗ b — May 29 Bel 4f fst .52 b — May 14 Bel 4f fst .50 b — May 1 Bel 3f sly .39 b

Copyright © 1979, by DAILY RACING FORM, INC. Reprinted with permission of copyright owner.

As a two-year-old, Kittiwake built up a reputation as a talented filly who didn't like to win. Close on several occasions in top company, she won just a maiden race. As a three-year-old, she seemed to lose interest completely—until introduced to grass racing. Like Majestic Light, the confidence she gained in grass racing rekindled her interest in dirt racing, and she went on to win stakes over both surfaces.

Fifth Marine — B. c. 3, by Hoist the Flag—Quillobelle, by Princequillo
Own.—Firman Pamela H — Br.—Firman Pamela H (Ky) — Tr.—Watters Sidney Jr — **126**
Turf Record: St. 2, 1st 2, 2nd 0, 3rd 0
1976: St. 7, 1st 4, 2nd 0, 3rd 2, Amt. $42,493
1975: St. 0, 1st M, 2nd 0, 3rd 0

5Jun76- 8Pim	yl	1 1/16 Ⓣ	:48⅕	1:12⅗	1:44	Annapolis H	5	4	31	2hd	12	14½	Agnello A	b 113	1.60	91-16 Fifth Marine 1134½ Ripon 1111½ Chati 116no Brisk hand ride 6
30May76- 6Bel	fm	1 Ⓣ	:45⅘	1:10	1:34⅗	3↑Allowance	7	5	42½	31	1hd	12	Turcotte R	b 115	7.10	98-04 Fifth Marine 1152 Burundi 1151¾ Wise Request 112nk Ridden out 10
17May76- 5Bel	fst	1	:45⅗	1:09⅘	1:35⅕	Allowance	4	5	511	512	512	610	Turcotte R	b 117	3.00	82-14 Quiet Little Table 1153RedAnchor115¾BidToFame115hd No factor 6
1May76- 6Aqu	sly	1	:45	1:09	1:34⅗	3↑Allowance	1	2	1hd	21	25	39	Turcotte R	b 115	1.80	84-13 Cinteelo 1048½ El Portugues 110½ Fifth Marine 1152 Weakened 7
16Apr76- 5Aqu	fst	1	:46⅕	1:10⅖	1:36	Allowance	5	3	34½	33½	32½	31½	Turcotte R	b 122	*1.90	84-18 BstLidPlns1191½Prctitionr117hdFifthMrin1221½ Bothered st., wide 8
3Apr76- 6Aqu	fst	1	:46⅖	1:11⅘	1:36⅘	Allowance	5	4	41	21½	21	1¾	Turcotte R	115	*.60	82-19 Fifth Marine 115¾ Areonative 1156 Genuine Silver 1153¾ Driving 7
20Mar76- 3Aqu	fst	6f	:22⅘	:45⅗	1:10⅘	3↑Md Sp Wt	1	9	52½	43½	41½	1½	Turcotte R	114	*.50	89-17 Fifth Marine 114½ Liberal 114nk Jeopardy 1131 Driving 9

LATEST WORKOUTS Jun 18 Bel 4f fst :48⅘ b — Jun 14 Bel Ⓣ 4f fm :48 b — ●May 27 Bel Ⓣ 5f fm 1:00⅖ h — May 16 Bel 3f fst :37 b

Copyright © 1979, by DAILY RACING FORM, INC. Reprinted with permission of copyright owner.

Fifth Marine came to the races with a big reputation, but appeared to be tailing off when given the opportunity to race on grass. With a victory over Majestic Light in the American Derby, he established himself as the best three-year-old grass runner in America. But a midsummer injury ended his season, and lesser horses captured the prestigious grass events of the fall.

Big Spruce — Dk. b. or br. c. 3, by Herbager—Silver Sari, by Prince John
Own.—Elmendorf — Br.—Elmendorf Farm (Ky) — Tr.—Nickerson V J — **114**
Turf Record: St. 3, 1st 1, 2nd 0, 3rd 0
1972: St. 11, 1st 4, 2nd 0, 3rd 2, Amt. $53,985
1971: St. 0, 1st M, 2nd 0, 3rd 0

11Aug72- 7Sar	hd	1⅛ Ⓣ		1.11	1.46⅖	3↑B Baruch	5	7	64¾	88¼	89¼	89¼	Cespedes R	b 116	*3.50	92-03 Scrimshaw 1091 Maraschino II 111¾ New Alibhai 1152 No factor 9
22Jly72- 8AP	fm	1⅛ Ⓣ		1.12⅕	1.50⅘	Amer Derby H	7	8	86½	98¾	87¼	75¼	Cespedes R	b 119	2.40	77-20 Dubassoff 1231¼ King's Bishop 1222½ Tri Jet 116½ Bumped 15
4Jly72- 7Aqu	gd	1 3/16 Ⓣ		1.12⅕	1.56⅘	Lexington H	8	4	54¼	32	11½	12	Cespedes R	b 115	10.20	86-14 Big Spruce 1152 Ruritania 1132 Tentam 1141½ Driving 11
24Jun72- 6Aqu	fst	1	.44⅘	1.09⅖	1.35⅗	3↑Allowance	5	5	78¾	46½	32	1nk	Cespedes R	b 112	3.00	89-10 Big Spruce 112nk John Rolfe 1104 Prime Prince 114nk Driving 7
10Jun72- 8Bel	fst	1½	.48	1.12	2.28	Belmont	5	9	913	915	715	514	Cespedes R	126	18.80	79-08 Riva Ridge 1267 Ruritania 126¾ Cloudy Dawn 1265 Passed tired ones 10
24May72- 8Bel	fst	1 1/16	.44⅖	1.09⅗	1.42⅖	Allowance	6	6	615	68	43½	1nk	Cespedes R	112	8.70	91-12 Big Spruce 112nk Avid 115¾ Head of The River 1154 Just up 7
6May72- 9CD	fst	1¼	.47⅗	1.11⅘	2.01⅘	Ky. Derby	15	12	1324	1328	718	714	Adams L	126	8.90f	77-11 Riva Ridge 1263¼ No Le Hace 1263½ Hold Your Peace 1263½ No factor 16
2May72- 8CD	gd	1	.45⅘	1.10⅖	1.36⅕	Derby Trial	2	12	1230	1228	817	614	Adams L	116	15.90	74-20 Key to the Mint 1222½ No Le Hace 1227 Dr. Neale 1162½ Late bid 12

LATEST WORKOUTS Aug 10 Sar Ⓣ 3f fm .37 h — ●Jly 16 Aqu 1 fst 1.46 b — Jly 11 Aqu 4f fst .52 b — Jun 19 Aqu 3f sly .37⅕ b

Copyright © 1979, by DAILY RACING FORM, INC. Reprinted with permission of copyright owner.

Big Spruce appeared outclassed in stakes company until he took on a tough field in the Lexington Handicap. In his grass debut, he convincingly defeated such top-class performers as Tentam, Dubassoff, and Ruritania. Strangely, he failed to reproduce this form until much later in his career.

Princess Pout — B. f (1966-Ky), by Prince John—Determined Lady, by Determine
Mrs. June H. McKnight — D. M. Smithwick — (Mrs. J. H. McKnight) — **108**
1970: 3, 1, 0, 1, $8,000
1969: 7, 1, 0, 1, $6,350

8Jly 70-7Aqu	fm	1 1/16 Ⓣ			1.43⅕	f- Allow	7	1	13	13	1h	3½	RUssery	120	*2.00	86-13 Top Round 118½ Watch Fob 120h Princess Pout 120½ No excuse 7
25Jun70-8Bel	fm	1 1/16 Ⓣ			1.43⅕	f- Allow	8	2	2½	11½	15	17½	RUssery	118	7.60	86-13 Princess Pout 1187½ Polly Piper 1181 Syzygy 118¾ Easily 8
12Jun70-6Bel	fst	7f	.22⅘	.46	1.24⅕	f- Allow	2	5	67¾	69	611	516	JLRotz	118	28.80	70-11 Royal Picnic 114¾ Bright Sun 111nk Lady Fortune 1142½ No factor 6
8Sep69-8Bel	my	1 1/16	.47	1.12⅗	1.45⅖	f- Allow	2	9	98¾	68	78½	412	DBThomas	118	8.10	65-22 Paisley Square 1158 Silver Braid 1131 Spin The Ball 1153 No mis'p 12
20Aug69-8Sar	hd	1 1/16 Ⓣ			1.42	f- Allow	2	8	711	54	21½	11	DBThomas	109	44.00	90-10 Princess Pout 1091 Pashamin 1103 Socializing 1111 Driving 11
12Aug69-5Sar	gd	1⅛	.48⅘	1.14⅖	1.54⅖	Md Sp Wt	5	4	68½	73½	53¾	57¾	DBThomas	111	11.00	61-23 Nasambro 116no Viaticus 1164 Millet 116¾ Had no mishaps 9
1Aug69-6Del	fst	170	.48	1.13⅘	1.45⅖	Md Sp Wt	3	12	1223	915	79½	33¼	ENelson	110	36.30	70-21 Someday Or Now 110¾ Gay Talk 1122½ Princess Pout 110¾ Rallied 12
21Jly 69-9Del	my	170	.48⅘	1.14⅕	1.45⅕	f-MdSpWt	8	7	817	822	824	821	ENelson	114	7.20	53-22 Honey Bumps 1142½ Lovely Judge 1091½ Cyfling *144 Showed noth'g 8
3Jly 69-1Aqu	fst	6f	.22⅘	.46⅖	1.11	f-MdSpWt	3	9	910	1015	1016	1016	JCruguet	b 116	42.00	72-15 Kushka 1162½ Eiberta E. 116¾ Deliberately 1161½ Never close 11
26Jun69-1Bel	fst	6f	.23⅗	.47	1.11⅗	f-MdSpWt	1	8	73¾	78½	79	712	JCruguet	114	22.80	75-16 All A Jest 1141 Rolamile 1142½ Astolat 1142 Slow start 8

LATEST WORKOUTS Jly 1 Bel t.c. 4f fm .50 b — Jun 19 Bel tr.t. 5f sly 1.02 h — Jun 9 Bel 4f fst .50 b — Jun 4 Bel tr.t. 1m fst 1.47 b

Copyright © 1979, by DAILY RACING FORM, INC. Reprinted with permission of copyright owner.

Princess Pout couldn't get out of her own way on dirt, but once on grass, she even developed some early speed. She won four stakes on the grass, including two editions of the Sheepshead Bay, and the Benjamin F. Lindheimer against males. At stud, she has produced Alleged, winner of the 1977 and 1978 Arc de Triomphes.

○ SPRINT VERSUS ROUTE ○

Appropriately bred horses do not seem to care whether their first grass race is a sprint or a route. Some Thoroughbreds might be slightly hesitant during the early stages of a race on unfamiliar footing and therefore might be expected to fare somewhat better in a route than in a sprint. But our well-bred animals won more than their share in both sprints and routes, with the slightly lower sprint I.V. being compensated for by a slightly higher $NET.

Turf Debut	NH	NW	WPCT	MPCT	$NET	I.V.
Sprint	140	22	15.7%	39.3%	$2.97	1.35
Route	1418	235*	16.6%	38.9%	$2.87	1.42

We also found that a previous route attempt on the main track was no particular benefit. Turf-bred animals that have only sprinted before making their first starts on grass do not seem to be at a disadvantage—even though 90 percent of the horses in our sample made their turf debuts in races at a mile or longer.

Last Start	NH	NW	WPCT	MPCT	$NET	I.V.
Sprint	947	152*	16.1%	39.2%	$3.04	1.38
Route	611	105*	17.2%	38.5%	$2.63	1.48

○ PREVIOUS DIRT TRACK FORM ○

A horse bred for grass racing need not have shown good form on the main track prior to making its first start on the turf. The top line of the following table reviews those that had looked sharp on dirt in the race immediately previous to their grass bows. The second line studies runners that had quit badly or otherwise displayed nothing in the previous dirt start.

	NH	NW	WPCT	MPCT	$NET	I.V.
Good Form	596	123*	20.6%	45.6%	$2.60	1.77
Poor Form	962	134*	13.9%	34.7%	$3.05	1.20

Many an eventual turf stakes winner contributed to the totals on the second line, including Princess Pout, Ethical Lady, Effervescing, and Sir Jason. Of course, it takes courage to support the chances of a horse with terrible recent form. But if the horse is properly bred, is moving to the turf course for the first time, and faces no outstanding rival, the potential returns are large.

○ FIRST START VERSUS SECOND START ○

One would expect a turf-bred horse to improve in its second try on the grass. But statistics show that the experience of the first grass race has only a slight effect. Moreover, large mutuel overlays occur much more frequently in connection with a turf debut, before the horse has demonstrated its grass ability.

	NH	NW	WPCT	MPCT	$NET	I.V.
First Try	1558	257*	16.5%	39.0%	$2.88	1.42
Second Try	1033	203*	19.7%	41.4%	$2.09	1.69

The second start on the grass becomes more rewarding from a betting standpoint if the animal has not had a dirt race since its first turf start. Those that come right back on the grass do conspicuously better in their second grass attempts than those that have returned to the main track between their first and second grass starts.

	NH	NW	WPCT	MPCT	$NET	I.V.
Right Back	581	136*	23.4%	47.0%	$2.32	2.01
Others	452	67	14.8%	34.3%	$1.80	1.27

Horses that win their first grass starts do very well when they come right back on the grass, as the following statistics reveal.

	NH	NW	WPCT	MPCT	$NET	I.V.
Won Debut	147	50*	34.0%	59.2%	$2.47	2.92

And horses that lose their first turf start "with honor"—finishing within a length of the winner—do even better when they come right back on the grass.

	NH	NW	WPCT	MPCT	$NET	I.V.
Narrow Loss	85	31*	36.5%	64.7%	$2.62	3.13

It should be mentioned once again that an allowance winner is usually required to move up in class for its next start, whereas a loser, no matter how well it performed, is not. This, plus the benefit of the one race experience on grass, explains why those narrowly beaten in their turf bows do so well in their second attempts.

Here is a different way of examining those of our turf-bred horses whose second races on that footing came directly after their first, without interruption by one or more races on dirt. We divide the 581 horses into two categories. The first group includes those that won or finished within five lengths in their first try. The other includes all that finished farther back. How each group fared in second outings on turf is most revealing:

Second Starts	NH	NW	WPCT	MPCT	$NET	I.V.
Good Debuts	388	110*	28.4%	53.6%	$2.24	2.43
Not So Good	193	26	13.5%	33.7%	$2.48	1.16

Interesting. Although horses that won or finished within five lengths of a winner in their turf debuts came right back on grass and won more than twice as often as those who were beaten by more than five lengths in their turf bows, enough of the second group won at long odds to return an average profit of 48 cents for $2 bet—better than the group as a whole.

The statistics indicate that it would be sensible to give a turf-bred horse two races on that footing before deciding that the horse is unsuited to grass.

○ THE BAD APPLES ○

Most horses that do not come right back on the grass after their turf debuts should be regarded dubiously when they finally try grass again. The exceptions are those that display signs of sharp condition in the dirt race immediately preceding their second turf start.

The point becomes plain in the following statistics. The "Ready" group consists of horses that made good efforts or ran a bit short in such dirt races. The "Not Ready" group showed little and, as the figures shout, continued to show little on returning to grass.

Second Starts	NH	NW	WPCT	MPCT	$NET	I.V.
Ready	194	37	19.1%	37.6%	$2.14	1.64
Not Ready	258	30	11.6%	31.8%	$1.54	1.00

○ RESTRICTED ALLOWANCE RACES ○

Appropriately bred animals fare best when making their initial grass starts in restricted allowance races (MSW, NW1, NW2, and NW3 races). The fields for such races are usually cluttered with beasts that have become more or less permanent residents of the restricted allowance ranks, winning only when they catch a field of horses who, like themselves, are going nowhere.

When a horse bred for grass has the ability its breeding suggests, it can win its way through the restricted allowance ranks in short order. But not all well-bred horses run to their ancestry. Many of our turf-bred horses will quickly join the ranks of the "permanent residents," seldom, if ever, winning on the grass (or on dirt).

As our study has indicated, many of our suspected turf sires have failed to live up to their bloodlines or press releases. Prince John and Round Table stand alone in their generation, but they are getting old and may be losing their touch to some extent. Among the younger sires, Stage Door Johnny, Hoist The Flag, and Le Fabuleux appear the logical heirs to the crown. All of their offspring deserve backing when going greensward for the first time.

With other sires, it is best to look for some positive signs of

Photo credit: Bob Coglianese

Stage Door Johnny, shown beating Forward Pass in the 1968 Belmont, has become the premier turf sire in America, although he himself never raced on grass.

overall ability: sharp dirt form, the ability to close at the sprint distances, sharp workouts, strong support at the betting windows early in its career—anything that might suggest the animal has potential, the potential it might begin to realize when it starts running on the grass.

The record of Sisterhood, a daughter of Exclusive Native, was replete with positive signs, not the least of which was the identity of her sire. Her brief Santa Anita campaign revealed that she had some ability, and her sharp five-furlong workout at Belmont on June 2 attested to her physical well-being. Although her first race at Belmont was dismal, she showed sufficient signs of life—a sharp move around the turn—on June 22 to suggest the distinct possibility of a strong race in her grass debut on July 4. Heavy rains, however, forced that race off the grass, and Sisterhood finished "absolutely" over a racing surface heavily biased in favor of early speed types. That excusable performance only served to further darken her form, and add a few dollars to her odds on July 14. Careful *Form* readers would also have noticed that Sisterhood had been nominated to Delaware Park's Open Fire Stakes, a grass event for three-year-old fillies run on July 15. That July 4 race obviously had been meant as a prep for the stakes race.

Sisterhood — B. f. 3, by Exclusive Native—Lost Horizon II, by Court Harwell
Own.—Harbor View Farm — Br.—Newstead Farm (Va) — Tr.—Barrera Lazaro S — **114**

Turf Record						St.	1st	2nd	3rd	Amt.
St.	1st	2nd	3rd		1978	7	2	0	0	$16,275
1	1	0	0		1977	0	M	0	0	

14Jly78-	5Bel	fm	1	Ⓣ:46⅗	1:10⅘	1:35⅕	3↑ⒻAllowance	2	1	1^{hd}	1^{hd}	$1\frac{1}{2}$	$1^{2\frac{1}{2}}$	Cordero A Jr	113	13.50	94-11	Sisterhood $113^{2\frac{1}{2}}$WorthyMelody$111^{2\frac{3}{4}}$QuidProGal$113^{4\frac{1}{2}}$	Ridden out	7
4Jly78-	5Bel	sly	$1\frac{1}{16}$	:46⅗	1:11	1:45⅘	3↑ⒻAllowance	6	7	$7^{6\frac{1}{2}}$	8^{12}	8^{20}	8^{24}	Cordero A Jr	113	12.50	49-13	Miss Ivor 111^{nc} Linda Maureen 117^{4} Aces Full 116^{4}	No threat	8
22Jun78-	7Bel	fst	6f	:22⅘	:45⅗	1:10⅖	3↑ⒻAllowance	1	6	$7^{6\frac{3}{4}}$	$5^{3\frac{1}{2}}$	6^{6}	7^{10}	Cordero A Jr	114	16.10	80-12	EveningBooBoo$112^{1\frac{1}{2}}$BetterTurn112^{3}WatangMiss$112^{1\frac{1}{2}}$	No factor	10
5Jun78-	7Bel	fst	6f	:23	:45⅘	1:09⅘	3↑ⒻAllowance	5	6	8^{5}	8^{10}	8^{15}	7^{17}	Cordero A Jr	113	6.20	77-21	Decorator $112^{4\frac{3}{4}}$ Ice Skater $114^{3\frac{3}{4}}$ Better Turn $112^{4\frac{1}{2}}$	Outrun	8
1Feb78-	7SA	fst	1	:46⅗	1:11⅗	1:37⅘	ⒻAllowance	8	6	6^{5}	$5^{4\frac{1}{2}}$	5^{8}	5^{7}	Cauthen S	113	4.60	73-20	ⒹEquanimity 116^{2} Mint Castle 115^{1} My Buck $113^{3\frac{1}{2}}$	No mishap	9
13Jan78-	3SA	fst	6f	:22⅘	:45⅗	1:10⅗	ⒻMd Sp Wt	7	4	$4^{2\frac{1}{2}}$	4^{1}	3^{2}	$1^{1\frac{1}{2}}$	Cauthen S	117	1.50	87-12	Sisterhood $117^{1\frac{1}{2}}$ Gay Juliet $117^{2\frac{1}{2}}$ Julie's Intent 117^{3}	Easily	8
6Jan78-	4SA	sly	6f	:22⅕	:45⅘	1:12⅘	ⒻMd Sp Wt	2	7	7^{7}	5^{5}	$5^{5\frac{1}{2}}$	$4^{3\frac{1}{2}}$	Cauthen S	117	3.40	71-24	ⒹPrincess Khalie 117^{hd} Mint Castle $117^{2\frac{1}{2}}$ Gay Juliet117^{1}	Rallied	7

LATEST WORKOUTS   Jun 17 Bel 5f fst 1:02 h   Jun 2 Bel 5f fst :59⅗ hg

○ POST POSITION ○

The unusual geometry of some turf courses increases the fascination of the infield sport. At Belmont Park, grass races at $1\frac{1}{16}$ miles on the Widener course are launched from a short chute in the middle of the clubhouse turn. Belmont's inner turf course now sports a chute almost perpendicular to the backstretch from which races at the $1\frac{1}{16}$ mile distance begin.

The seven-furlong grass courses at Aqueduct, Monmouth, Garden State, Calder, and Del Mar, and the $\frac{9}{10}$-miler at Hollywood all feature diagonal chutes cut into the infield, from which horses run onto the grassy oval for races at $1\frac{1}{16}$ and $1\frac{1}{8}$ miles. Each of these chutes involves a different angle of entry to the main part of the course, and each deposits the horses at a different distance from the first full turn.

Santa Anita's hillside chute starts behind the main track, running downhill into a conventional infield oval. It is used for sprints at six and a half furlongs and routes at $1\frac{1}{4}$ miles and longer. The sprints involve the only clockwise change of direction in American racing.

And Woodbine embellishes its main turf track with the Marshall course, on which races at $1\frac{1}{4}$ miles require only one turn.

Before investigating the effects of these various track designs on the outcome of races, we discuss the more usual situation—a turf race of one mile to 1⅛ miles, starting in front of the stands, and proceeding around two turns.

A survey of 2,270 such races produced the following information about post positions:

Posts	Starters	Winners	I.V.
1–3	6810	909	1.20
4–6	6789	728	0.97
7–9	5276	528	0.90
10–12	1582	105	0.60

Since these courses lie within the infield perimeters of dirt tracks, their turns are sharper. This would seem to provide an advantage to horses with inside post positions—an opportunity to save ground along the hedge on the first turn. The statistics bear this out. However, a closer look at a 487 race sample shows that racetrack crowds are well aware of this advantage. They bet the inside horses more heavily than others. Low odds cancel the effect of the higher I.V. Nobody can expect to show a long-range profit by betting on post positions alone.

Posts	NH	NW	WPCT	MPCT	$NET	%W	Ave. Odds
1–3	1461	226*	15.5%	40.3%	$1.88	46.4%	5.40–1
4–6	1450	150	10.3%	35.5%	$1.37	30.8%	5.90–1
7–9	1043	98	9.4%	28.7%	$1.35	20.1%	6.90–1
10–12	278	13	4.7%	16.9%	$0.62	2.7%	9.00–1

Returning to the full sample of 2,270 races, we find the following I.V.'s for post position on North American grass courses.

Post Positions: I.V.'s

Course	1–3	4–6	7–9	10–12
Saratoga	1.39	0.83	0.76	0.85
Meadowlands	0.95	1.21	0.94	0.60
Atlantic City	1.41	0.95	0.69	0.55
Pimlico	0.83	1.32	1.06	0.55
Laurel	1.54	0.99	0.75	0.48
Delaware	1.27	0.97	0.73	0.82
Suffolk Downs	1.06	1.18	0.74	0.49
Hialeah	1.08	0.97	1.13	0.63
Gulfstream	1.15	1.14	0.80	0.68
Arlington (both)	1.25	0.86	0.93	0.59
Hawthorne	1.20	0.86	1.00	0.78
River Downs	1.04	1.09	0.92	0.45
Beulah	1.31	0.58	1.11	——
Waterford	1.19	0.83	1.01	0.78
Santa Anita	1.21	0.63	1.37	0.38
Hollywood	1.57	0.68	0.73	0.00
Del Mar	1.09	1.19	0.62	0.00
Golden Gate	1.06	1.01	1.04	0.86
Fort Erie	1.10	1.07	0.78	0.87

Note: *The statistics for Santa Anita, Hollywood, and Del Mar refer only to races run on the main grass ovals, around two turns.*

The advantage of inner posts is evident to some extent at most tracks. However, it seems plain that at some courses, including Pimlico, Meadowlands, Hialeah, Santa Anita, Golden Gate, and Fort Erie, outer post positions are not as disadvantageous as at other tracks.

○ BELMONT'S TURF COURSES ○

On Belmont's main grass course (the Widener course), races at one mile and $1\frac{1}{16}$ miles begin on the clubhouse turn. A post position survey of 325 such races offers interesting results:

Posts	NH	NW	WPCT	MPCT	$NET	%W	I.V.
1	325	49	15.1%	38.8%	$1.86	15.1%	1.30
2–5	1300	150	11.5%	36.5%	$1.35	46.2%	1.00
6–7	609	75	12.3%	34.2%	$1.92	23.1%	1.06
8–12	572	52	9.1%	28.3%	$1.11	16.0%	0.79

The enormous dollar losses sustained by anyone betting uncritically on horses breaking from the inner posts should not be interpreted as proof that these posts are unfavorable. The figures show that horses breaking from the inside (especially post 1) win their share of the races, but are overbet. They are underlays. The crowd goes overboard on their chances, betting inside posts as if the race were around two turns. At the same time, the crowd fears that horses in posts 6 and 7 are at a serious disadvantage. Such horses are underbet, are at no disadvantage, win more than their share—and at good odds.

It should be pointed out that only 31 of the surveyed races were at the shorter distance of one mile. Because the starting gate is then placed a half-furlong closer to the backstretch turn, the inside posts are a great help, as the statistics proved.

Prior to the 1977 season, Belmont's inner turf course was given a chute, almost perpendicular to the backstretch, to be used for races of $1\frac{1}{16}$ miles. This chute forces the field to run a considerable distance before reaching the inner hedge, and this seems to work to the disadvantage of horses breaking from the inside, as the following small sample of 123 races suggests:

Posts	NH	NW	WPCT	MPCT	$NET	%W	I.V.
1–2	246	26	10.6%	33.6%	$1.00	21.1%	0.88
3–4	246	33	13.4%	44.5%	$1.96	26.8%	1.12
5–10	531	64	12.1%	37.6%	$1.58	52.0%	1.00

When it comes to predicting the outcome of a grass race, speed figures must take a back seat. The scarcity of grass races prevents the calculation of accurate daily variants. But variants are needed, because weather conditions often have a dramatic effect on the times in which grass races are run. Overnight rains can slow a course down by two or three seconds. A prolonged heat spell can dry a course out, allowing cheap claiming horses to run in times usually reserved for top-class stock.

But when two grass courses lie as close together as do Belmont's pair, comparisons of running times are frequently helpful. Statistics for 1977–1978 indicate that the Widener course tends to run one full second faster than the Inner course at the $1\frac{1}{16}$ mile distance. (Statistics from the 1978 meeting indicate that the new inner turf course at Saratoga averages two fifths of a second slower than that track's main turf course.)

INNER

WIDENER

○ DIAGONAL CHUTES ○

Here is a post-position study of 805 races at $1\frac{1}{16}$ and $1\frac{1}{8}$ miles on the grass courses at Aqueduct, Monmouth, Garden State, Calder, Hollywood, and Del Mar, all of which started from infield chutes.

Posts	NH	NW	WPCT	MPCT	$NET	%W	I.V.
1–3	2415	335	13.9%	38.5%	$1.67	41.6%	1.22
4–6	2411	252	10.5%	36.3%	$1.36	31.3%	0.92
7–9	1792	182	10.2%	29.9%	$1.59	22.6%	0.89
10–12	459	36	7.8%	23.2%	$1.88	4.5%	0.69

The statistics are not radically different from Belmont Park's Widener course. Interestingly, the audiences at these tracks seem to avoid overbetting inside post positions as stubbornly as those at Belmont do. But they make the usual mistake of underbetting horses from the outer part of the field.

Indeed, a separate part of this survey demonstrates that horses breaking from the far outside post in fields of eight or fewer starters are at no disadvantage whatsoever on these particular tracks. It can be stated with assurance that posts 1 through 8 are essentially equal, making post position a negligible factor.

The following table offers Impact Values for various combinations of post positions at individual tracks with infield chutes:

Aqueduct

Posts	I.V.
1–3	1.17
4–7	0.91
8–12	0.86

Garden State

Posts	I.V.
1–2	0.84
3–4	1.55
5–8	0.93
9–12	0.60

Monmouth

Posts	I.V.
1–2	1.18
3–6	0.95
7–8	1.34
9–12	0.72

Calder

Posts	I.V.
1–3	1.48
4–8	0.82
9–12	0.54

Hollywood

Posts	I.V.
1	1.50
2–4	0.90
5–8	1.08
9–12	0.59

Del Mar

Posts	I.V.
1	2.09
2–6	0.97
7–12	0.61

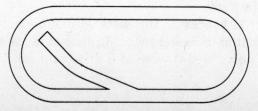

○ SANTA ANITA ○

In addition to the conventional infield oval used for turf races at 1⅛ miles, Santa Anita boasts a downhill chute (reminiscent of Epsom Downs), which extends beyond the backstretch of the main track. The downhill chute is used for sprints at six and a half furlongs and longer races at 1¼ to 1½ miles.

A study of 157 races out of the chute seems to indicate that the middle post positions are most advantageous:

Posts	NH	NW	WPCT	MPCT	$NET	%W	I.V.
1–3	471	44	9.3%	35.0%	$1.37	28.0%	0.86
4–6	470	66	14.0%	34.7%	$2.27	42.0%	1.30
7–9	362	33	9.1%	29.3%	$1.02	21.0%	0.84
10–12	148	14	9.5%	25.0%	$1.53	8.9%	0.87

Of the 157 races surveyed, 73 were sprints and 84 were routes. The statistical patterns were virtually identical in each category.

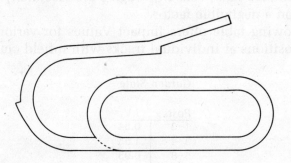

○ WOODBINE ○

Like Santa Anita, Woodbine supplements its infield grass oval with an enormous chute—this one long, straight, and outside the backstretch of the main track.

A survey of 191 races on the Marshall course indicates that post positions do not matter in longer races. In shorter races, horses breaking from the outside posts (9–14) were at a disadvantage.

Posts	NH	NW	WPCT	MPCT	$NET	%W	I.V.
1–3	543	70	12.9%	33.7%	$1.73	36.6%	1.03
4–6	535	71	13.3%	39.3%	$1.57	37.2%	1.06
7–9	353	45	12.7%	30.0%	$1.50	23.6%	1.02
10–14	99	5	5.1%	20.2%	$0.64	2.6%	0.40

This statistical pattern applies to all distances. Of the 191 races, 85 were at seven furlongs or one mile. These shorter races accounted for almost all the horses in posts 10 through 14.

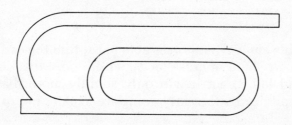

○ MARATHONS ○

A majority of North American races at 1¼ miles or farther are run on grass. Some involve only one turn (the Marshall course), some two turns (Belmont), while others require three turns (Aqueduct, Hollywood, Arlington, etc.), and still others begin with a downhill charge (Santa Anita). As might be expected, post position is meaningless in races of this length. Here is a survey of 209 such races.

Posts	NH	NW	WPCT	MPCT	$NET	%W	I.V.
1–3	627	72	11.5%	38.6%	$1.36	34.4%	0.99
4–6	621	76	12.2%	36.2%	$1.72	36.4%	1.06
7–9	434	50	11.5%	31.6%	$1.68	23.9%	1.00
10–12	126	11	8.7%	18.3%	$1.03	5.3%	0.75

○ EARLY SPEED ○

If grass racing were like dirt racing, early speed would be a tremendous asset on most grass courses. The shorter stretch runs would improve a speedster's chances of hanging on to the finish. The sharper turns would worsen the come-from-behinder's prospects, forcing him to begin his rally prematurely before reaching the turn, or tardily after entering the stretch.

But grass is unlike dirt. Statistics show that early speed does not fare quite as well on turf as on the main track. Horses who spend the early stages in the middle of the pack do better on grass than on dirt.

Here is a survey of 2,455 grass races, showing how horses finished after having been in one or another position early in the going.

FCP	NH	NW	WPCT	%W	I.V.
1	2455	472	19.2%	19.2%	1.90
2–3	4910	610	12.4%	24.8%	1.23
4–7	9549	1076	11.3%	43.8%	1.12
8–12	4946	297	6.0%	12.1%	0.59

The table shows that horses able to capture the early lead win almost twice their share of grass races, while those that contend for the early lead and fail to get it win only slightly more than their share. Horses that trail during the early going are usually not in contention at the end.

Before deciding whether to dismiss or embrace early speed on grass, it will be worthwhile to study 1,660 of our turf races in more detail.

FCP	NH	NW	WPCT	MPCT	$NET	%W	I.V.
1	1660	329*	19.8%	45.8%	$2.40	19.8%	1.73
2–3	3320	433	13.0%	39.2%	$1.65	26.1%	1.14
4–7	6427	725	11.3%	35.8%	$0.89	43.7%	0.98
8–12	3082	173**	5.6%	20.0%	$0.89	10.4%	0.49

The pattern is a replica of that in the complete sample of 2,455 races. And it points out quite clearly the difference between grass and dirt racing—pace prompters give up the chase much more frequently on grass than on dirt. On dirt, horses running second or third at the first call combine for a net profit. On grass, they break even with the pari-mutuel takeout, costing their backers 17.5 cents of every dollar bet.

Moreover, our study indicates that horses running first, second, or third at the first call were able to win "only" 1,082 of the 2,455 races surveyed. This works out to 44.1 percent, or about 11 percent below the corresponding figure for dirt.

However, on occasions when the handicapper can tell with some assurance that a particular horse is likely to get the early lead, the situation brightens greatly. Such a horse wins one race in five (as the statistics show), which is much more than a fair statistical share. And he pays good prices—high enough to return a 20 percent profit.

○ EXCEPTIONAL SITUATIONS ○

The study of early speed was subdivided to permit detailed scrutiny of grass races at all distances, on all tracks. Patterns previously noted held up with few exceptions. The most interesting were these:

1. In races at $1\frac{1}{4}$ miles or longer, the horse with the lead at the first call earned a large I.V. of 1.79 and a $NET of $2.67 Horses able to run first, second, or third at the first call in these long routes combined for an I.V. of 1.30 but averaged a considerable loss with a $NET of $1.82. Horses far off the early pace won only half their share of the races and accounted for an average loss of 44 cents per dollar.

2. Among turf courses with infield chutes, only Aqueduct, Monmouth, Garden State, and Del Mar were reasonably hospitable to early speed. At Del Mar, horses first, second, or third at the first call produced a $NET of $2.21, although those first at that call were overbet and averaged a slight loss. At Garden State, the horse with the early lead won more than twice its share of the races (an I.V. of 2.32) and awarded its backers a profit of 6.5 cents per dollar. At Monmouth, the leader at the first call made a profit of 11.5 cents per dollar with a moderate I.V. of 1.07. And those first, second, or third at the first call yielded a profit of 31.5 cents per dollar with an I.V. of 1.12. A small sample of 117 races over Aqueduct's newly renovated (inner) turf course showed the early leader returning a profit of 18 cents per dollar with an I. V. of 1.73.

3. Hollywood Park, widely reputed to be a death trap for grass runners with early lick, was even less hospitable than that to horses running eighth or worse at the first call. These come-from-behinders seldom arrived in time, and produced an I.V. of 0.49. Horses that raced from first to as far back as seventh in the early going all seemed to win their fair share. But as advertised, early speed was no advantage at Hollywood Park.

4. Early speed was quite effective on Belmont's Widener course. Leaders at the first call earned an I.V. of 1.83 with a $NET of $2.53. Pace prompters (FCP 2-3) did not do as well, producing an I.V. of 1.29 together with a $NET of only $1.80. At the same time, Belmont's inner turf course was an enigma. During 1977, only eight of the 64 races run out of the new $1\frac{1}{16}$ mile chute resulted in a front-running victory, just enough to produce a $NET of $2.02. Only 14 other races resulted in a pace-prompter going on to victory. In fact, horses running second or third at the first call produced a dollar net of only $1.41. But during 1978, with the grass cut somewhat shorter, early speed types had a picnic. Horses running first, second, or third at the first call accounted for 31 of the 59 races run out of the chute, ac-

cumulating a profit of almost 24% for their backers. At the longer 1¼ mile distance, front-runners were victorious in 9 of 33 races while producing an incredible $5.00 average payoff.

5. Coming off the hillside at Santa Anita, the horses with the most early speed had the highest I.V. (1.77) and returned a tidy profit of 19 cents per $2 bet. When horses second or third at the first call were combined with leaders, the I.V. dropped to 1.49 (not bad), but the profit per $2 bet was reduced to a mere 2 cents. Horses in the second flight (fourth to seventh) at the first call won almost exactly their share of the races (I.V. = 0.96), but at a slight loss to their backers.

6. At Woodbine's Marshall course, where some bettors expect early speed to excel, it does nothing of the kind. Horses first, second, third, and fourth at the first call had a combined I.V. of 0.95 and returned their backers a paltry $1.23 per $2 bet. On the other hand, horses fifth, sixth, seventh, and eighth at the first call combined for an I.V. of 1.15 and cost their supporters only 6 cents per $2 bet.

7. At the inaugural (1977) Meadowlands meeting, early speed types dominated for the first four nights—and then the rains came. A damp Meadowlands course proved highly unfavorable to front-runners. The weather during the first two months of the 1978 meeting was much better, but the results were pretty much the same. Overall, early leaders won only seven of 60 races run at the standard 1 mile to 1$\frac{1}{16}$ mile distances, costing their backers an enormous 41 percent loss. Horses running second or third at the first call fared just as poorly— only 14 of 120 won, resulting in a 42% loss for their followers. Horses running from the middle of the pack (sixth or seventh at the first call) had the most success.

○ CLEAR LEADS, SPEED DUELS ○

We have already seen that profits await the handicapper able to predict that a horse will get the early lead in a grass race. The profits increase if the horse is in front by at least a length at the first call. Such front-runners produce an I.V. of 2.24 and a $NET of $3.28. Apparently not many situations of this kind are easily foreseen, else the speedsters would be bet more heavily than they are.

In our study of dirt racing (Chapter 1), we found that when two horses duel for the early lead and reach the first call at least a length ahead of the third horse, it would be profitable to have a bet on both. But this does not work on grass. Such speed duels produce a comfortable I.V. of 1.38, but the $NET is only $1.77.

Speed duels become potentially lucrative when the handicapper can foresee which two horses will be involved, can tell that they will be a length or more in front of the pack at the first call, and uses his knowledge of turf course geometry. A study of 250 speed duels on grass shows that the sharper turns give a pronounced advantage to the speedster with the inner post position.

	NH	NW	WPCT	MPCT	$NET	I.V.
Inside	250	50*	20.0%	47.2%	$2.39	1.79
Outside	250	27	10.8%	34.4%	$1.14	0.96

The differences between these winning percentages and in-the-money percentages are statistically significant. The inside speed horse is better situated than his outside rival in a speed duel on grass.

○ SOFT FOOTING ○

When the turf course is dry, it is called firm or hard. When it is damp, the designation is usually good, yielding, or soft. The effects on early speed are noteworthy:

	Dry		Wet	
FCP	I.V.	$NET	I.V.	$NET
1	1.71	$2.36	1.34	$1.76
2–3	1.16	$1.73	1.14	$1.52
4–7	0.99	$1.53	1.04	$1.79
8–12	0.46	$0.81	0.61	$1.42

Although front-runners win more than their share of races under either dry or wet conditions, they are no longer overlays on good, yielding, or soft turf. The racetrack crowds seem to bet on racing style without proper concern for track conditions.

Here, broken down according to the kind of footing, is how 462 speed horses fared after gaining early leads of at least one length:

	NH	NW	WPCT	MPCT	$NET	I.V.
Dry	382	101*	26.4%	51.6%	$3.85	2.36
Wet	80	15	18.8%	53.8%	$2.13	1.68

And the 500 horses that engaged in our 250 speed duels:

	NH	NW	WPCT	MPCT	$NET	I.V.
Dry	404	66	16.3%	59.4%	$1.90	1.46
Wet	96	11	11.5%	31.3%	$1.18	1.03

All of which should be conclusive evidence that a wet turf course is hardly favorable to speed horses, especially those facing competition for the early lead.

○ TURF FAVORITES ○

In spite of upsets attributable to breeding, the sometimes surprising effect of post position, and the lessened effectiveness of early speed, favorites in grass races still manage to win almost as often as their counterparts on the main track.

NH	NW	WPCT	MPCT	$NET	I.V.
1660	524	31.6%	65.0%	$1.71	2.75

JOCKEYS
AND
TRAINERS

Thus far, we have had little to say about the two people who have the most influence on Thoroughbred performance: the jockey and the trainer.

Certain jockeys and trainers win more frequently than others, and the racing audience knows it. Lists of leading jockeys and trainers appear in the daily racetrack program and frequently in the *Daily Racing Form*. How does this affect the odds? How should the player approach the jockey and trainer factors? Those are the central questions in this chapter.

○ THE LEADING JOCKEYS ○

Some jockeys obviously are better than others. The jockey colony at any track contains some riders who are relatively inexperienced, others who are past their prime, still others with only marginal talent, and a few leaders who stand above the rest.

Riding a Thoroughbred requires split-second timing and split-second judgment, a sense of pace, and some knowledge of the horse's capabilities. Each rider has strengths and weaknesses. Some are better with speed horses, others prefer to come from behind. Some prefer routes to sprints, others have a knack for winning on grass. Some have an especially good touch with fillies, others help inexperienced two-year-olds.

But they all make mistakes. Tactical mistakes are bound to happen, even to the best riders. Strategic mistakes are another matter. It is a particularly bitter pill for the bettor to swallow when his selection runs well enough to win, but loses because a supposedly competent jockey made a strategic blunder. But it happens every day.

What most jockeys lack is consistent intelligence. How many times have you seen a rider come charging down the middle of a wet racetrack after cleverly avoiding the deeper going along the rail to win going away on a longshot, only to come out for the next race and try to barge through along the inside with the favorite?

Do horses run better for the leading riders? Probably not. Only a select few have that "magic touch," that way of communicating with a horse that makes the animal give a little extra, a little more than it would give another rider.

Actually, it is the horse that makes the rider, rather than vice versa. The leading riders are the leaders because they ride the better horses, and they ride the better horses because they are more talented than the other riders, and make fewer mistakes. Consequently, they have better agents, who find it easier to place them on mounts that are ready to win.

Many jockeys ride on a "first call" basis for certain trainers. That is, the jockey has agreed to ride all of that trainer's horses, unless given special permission to ride for a competitor.

Actually, a large percentage of a jockey's rides are of the "free agent" variety, riding for different trainers as the opportunities arise. It is the agent's job to search out these opportunities so that his rider gets on his share of "hot" horses. To be effective, an agent must know the condition and capability of every horse on the grounds.

When a leading rider suddenly turns up on a horse, and the horse wins, it was because the trainer had the horse ready to win, and sought out a leading jockey to increase the chances of victory. The jockey gave the horse a winning ride, but had little to do with making the horse run well.

A study of an entire New York racing season (1973) produced some interesting results concerning the dominant position of leading riders. The ten leading riders (in total number of winners) combined for the following statistics:

	NH	NW	WPCT	MPCT	$NET	%W	I.V.
Top Ten	10770	1547	14.4%	41.4%	$1.77	67.1%	1.23
Others	8921	760	8.5%	27.7%	$1.35	32.9%	0.73

Almost 55 percent of the starters in these races were ridden by one of the top ten jockeys, yet these same horses accounted for better than two of every three winners. Unfortunately, the presence of a leading jockey in the saddle attracted too much support at the mutuel windows, producing a net loss of 23 cents per $2 bet.

On the other hand, horses ridden by jockeys not among the top ten failed to win even 75 percent of their share of the races, and cost their backers 65 cents per $2 bet. This is a strong negative sign, since it involves almost half the starters in each race.

The statistics for the top five jockeys combined (Turcotte, Cordero, Velasquez, Maple, and Vasquez) were only slightly better:

	NH	NW	WPCT	MPCT	$NET	%W	I.V.
Top Five	6528	1002	15.3%	42.9%	$1.80	43.4%	1.31
Others	13163	1305	9.9%	31.3%	$1.47	56.6%	0.85

But we have lost the strong negative factor.

Interestingly, the 1,368 horses ridden by Jorge Velasquez in New York during 1973 produced a small profit of four cents per $2 bet. So it is possible to come out ahead betting on just one jockey. But not very likely.

Both the tabulations above suggest that leading riders are "winners" rather than "bridesmaids." Their number of winners was significantly larger than their number of places or shows (compare the WPCT and MPCT figures). A logical conclusion is that these leading riders were able to win more than their share of the tight finishes. When they find themselves in a tight race, they are able more often than not to outmaneuver less talented rivals and bring their horses home on top.

Moving away from New York, we now study 946 races at other major Eastern tracks. In the following tabulation, each horse has been placed into one of three categories:

Top 5: The horse was ridden by one of the top five riders at the meeting, according to the list published in the Form on the day of the race.
Good: The horse was ridden by a jockey who was not among the top five, but had previously ridden the horse in one of its "good" races.
Others: The horse was ridden by a non-top-five jockey who either had never ridden the horse or had been unsuccessful in all previous attempts on the horse.

Here is how the figures worked out for these three categories:

	NH	NW	WPCT	MPCT	$NET	%W	I.V.
Top 5	2540	427	16.8%	44.4%	$1.70	45.1%	1.46
Good	2060	271	13.2%	38.5%	$1.63	28.6%	1.14
Others	3619	248**	6.9%	25.3%	$1.34	26.2%	0.60

The fact that the top five riders at these tracks won more frequently than their counterparts in New York simply reflects the unusual talents of secondary New York jockeys. The fans at these tracks, however, concentrate their betting on top-five riders more heavily than New Yorkers do.

Surprisingly, this study revealed that switches to or from a top-five rider were insignificant. Horses switching to a top-five rider fared no better (actually, slightly worse) than horses also ridden by a top-five rider in their most recent start. Horses switching from a top-five rider to one that had been successful on the horse in the past seemed to run better than the typical horse in the GOOD category. Likewise, horses switching from a top-five rider to one with no record of success on the horse outperformed the average horse in the OTHERS category.

Although leading riders tend to get better mounts, their reputation, plus the animal's good or improving form, produces underlays. When you consider the additional fact that most races feature not one, but several leading jockeys, the conclusion becomes obvious: The horse's record, and not the jockey, is the most important factor in handicapping.

○ APPRENTICE JOCKEYS ○

One particularly interesting type of jockey is the apprentice, the inexperienced youngster with dreams of someday becoming a top rider. The weight allowance makes the apprentice an interesting proposition to many trainers. But lack of riding experience creates a problem for the bettor, who naturally is wary of paying for the youngster's education with his losing bets.

During the 1973 New York season, five apprentices "caught on" sufficiently to obtain mounts on a regular basis and win at least ten races each. The five combined for the following figures:

NH	NW	WPCT	MPCT	$NET	%W	I.V.
2208	220	10.0%	31.6%	$1.77	9.5%	0.85

Although they failed to win their share of races, these active apprentices did not do all that badly, considering their inexperience. Their dollar net was identical to that of the top ten riders combined, indicating that they brought in a considerable number of longshot winners.

Other apprentices rode infrequently and unsuccessfully, each failing to win even ten races during the year. Had their figures been added, the total, especially the impact value, would have been much less impressive.

A winning apprentice is much in demand. He (or she) often has the choice of two or three horses per race, and with the help of a good agent, ends up riding many "live" horses.

The sensational Steve Cauthen is the most recent example. Here are the figures for his first four months in New York (November 29, 1976 through March 31, 1977):

NH	NW	WPCT	$NET	I.V.
730	202	27.7%	$2.14	2.28

These figures are all the more remarkable when you consider how dramatically Cauthen caught on with New York bettors. At one point during January and February, Cauthen's horses were all bet well below what their past performances suggested their true odds should have been. The mere fact that Cauthen was riding made many a horse the betting favorite. But in spite of so many gross underlays, Cauthen's horses won often enough to return his followers an average profit of 7 percent.

It is not unusual for a hot apprentice rider to produce a profit. When Tommy Wallis was the "hot" apprentice during 1973, his horses yielded a $NET of $2.10 despite a low 0.88 impact value.

So any horse with the "hot" apprentice up must be respected, in spite of what its record may look like. The trainer thought enough of the horse's chances to go after the apprentice, and the rider's agent saw enough to choose the horse over others in the same race.

○ **LEADING TRAINERS** ○

We come now to the trainers. Not only are they responsible for the physical condition of their horses, but also for choosing the proper races in which to enter them and the best jockeys available to ride them.

The sole interest of the bettor is in how their horses perform on the racetrack. A study of the ten leading trainers during the 1973 New

York season turned up the following information:

	NH	NW	WPCT	MPCT	$NET	%W	I.V.
Top Ten	4402	751	17.1%	46.1%	$1.79	32.6%	1.46
Others	15289	1556	10.2%	32.0%	$1.52	67.4%	0.87

Although these ten leading trainers manage to win far more than their share of races, they do not dominate their colleagues as do the ten leading jockeys. Whereas the ten leading jockeys win slightly more than two thirds of the races, the ten leading trainers account for slightly less than one third. Of course, the number of trainers at a given track far exceeds the number of jockeys.

The unique situation on the New York racing circuit is partially responsible for the fact that the ten leading trainers account for so small a share of all the winners. Many of the well-known "establishment" stables race in New York, and many have trainers at least as competent as those in the top ten. Many of the trainers in the top ten handle claiming stock. The "establishment" trainers, on the other hand, deal mostly with stakes and allowance horses. Claiming trainers run their horses more frequently, and consequently win more races. The "establishment" trainers do just as well, if not better, but on a more modest scale.

A study of the combined records of ten leading "establishment" trainers (Basile, Burch, Cornell, L. Laurin, Miller, Nerud, Rondinello, Russell, Watters, and F. Whiteley) produced figures very similar to those for the ten leading trainers (who included "establishment" trainers Jerkins and L. Barrera):

NH	NW	WPCT	MPCT	$NET	%W	I.V.
1334	227	17.0%	43.1%	$1.78	9.8%	1.45

Obviously, horses from the barns of leading trainers have an advantage. But these trainers are well known, and their horses tend to be underlays.

The two big names among the claiming trainers in New York during 1973 were Pancho Martin and Johnny Campo. Combining their efforts, we found the following sad story:

NH	NW	WPCT	MPCT	$NET	%W	I.V.
1170	196	16.8%	49.4%	$1.51	8.5%	1.43

The New York betting public had gone overboard on Martin and Campo, so that the average $2 bet on their horses suffered almost a 50 cents loss.

○ CONCLUSION ○

Horses should be evaluated as possible contenders strictly on the basis of their records. If a logical contender is to be ridden by a leading jockey, or is trained by a leading trainer, it is all the more attractive and likely to win.

The serious reader is advised to study his local trainers individually, looking for winning patterns in their horses' performances. In other words, determine each trainer's "modus operandi." What does a drop or rise in class, or a switch in distance, or a return from a layoff, etc., mean for *that* trainer?

Such a study, unfortunately, would involve many different trainers at many different tracks, and is well beyond the scope of this book.

The reader is also advised to treat the jockey factor solely as a signal of the trainer's intentions. When a leading rider suddenly turns up on a horse, it usually means that the trainer has the horse fit and placed where it can win.

COMPUTER
GENERATED
SYSTEMS:
SPOT
PLAYS

On several occasions thus far we have mentioned handicapping "angles" that had proven profitable, or almost profitable. Most of these were based on just one handicapping factor, possibly embellished by a restriction such as "last race good." None came close to being a complete handicapping procedure.

In this chapter, we will discuss handicapping systems based on six of these "angles." These systems were produced by the computer, which was asked to find conditions that best supplemented the basic "angle"—conditions that would eliminate horses with glaring weaknesses likely to prevent them from winning, in spite of other positive signs in their records, and conditions that would improve the statistics for the "angle" standing alone, particularly the dollar net, and hopefully also the percentage of winners.

The computer was given its choice of two or three conditions in each of the following categories: class, speed figures, early speed, distance, consistency, recent form, and recent action, together with the option of including a jockey condition and (for routes) a post-position restriction. It was asked to determine which condition, if any, in each category, either alone or in conjunction with conditions from other categories, best improved the figures for the "angle" being studied. The computer made two interesting discoveries of a general nature.

First, it found three conditions that acted, in combination, as universal catalysts, improving any factor or combination of factors to which they were supplemented. Those conditions were:

1. At least one win in last ten starts.
2. At least one speed point.
3. Last race within ten days.

The consistency requirement guarantees that the horse knows how to win, the early speed condition that it is still capable of getting into position to win, and the strong recent action restriction that the trainer has good intentions.

On the other hand, the computer found that the jockey and both speed and class "figures" were of little, if any, help in improving dollar net figures. And for a good reason.

Jockeys and "figures" are probably the two most popular betting tools available to the public. Many bettors follow one particular jockey, betting only his (or her) horses. Others are fascinated by numbers, and like to manipulate the speed ratings and earnings figures into a numerical rating for each horse. Many of these bettors pay little (if any) attention to the other pieces of the handicapping puzzle.

The net result is that the horses ridden by the popular jockeys, and the horses with the better "figures," tend to be overbet. Apparently, good profits can be made by looking elsewhere.

Our studies suggest that when two positive signs combine—the original angle and the three catalysts—the horse is sharp and entered where its trainer thinks it can win. When these positive signs are present, the speed and class needed to win will also be there, often enough, at least, to make the horse a profitable betting proposition.

And now, here are the spot-play systems the computer devised. These systems apply only to non-maiden races run on the main track for horses at least three years of age. Unless noted to the contrary, the system works equally well for both sprints and routes.

○ SYSTEM #1: THE EARLY SPEED ANGLE ○

The tactical and psychological advantage of setting an uncontested early pace is often invincible. Any horse alone on the lead is dangerous. If in shape, it is all the more a threat to go all the way. If a horse is able to relax while setting an uncontested pace, its recent form may be of little significance. Most horses are in good enough shape to handle a two-furlong sprint through the stretch.

In Chapter 2 we saw that the speed points could be used to predict, with reasonable accuracy, those horses most likely to be among the leaders at the first call. And that the simple "angle" of having the highest speed-point total in the field proved slightly profitable. Add a few well-chosen conditions, and the profits become more significant.

SPEED POINT LEADER
LAST RACE WITHIN 30 DAYS
AT LEAST ONE WIN LAST TEN RACES
POST POSITION 1–8 (IF A ROUTE)

Here is how this system did over a sample of 1,549 races:

Lead	NH	NW	WPCT	MPCT	$NET	I.V.
1+ points	827	177*	21.4%	49.9%	$2.23	1.95
2+ points	457	98	21.4%	49.7%	$2.30	1.95

In this tabulation, all speed-point leaders are included on the first line, while the second line studies only those whose advantage was two points or higher. At this stage, little difference separates the two groups. Many of these speed-point leaders will, in fact, set an uncontested pace. Others, however, will have to fight for the lead, or rate slightly off the lead.

Consequently, some suggestion of sharpness would seem appropriate. According to the computer, the best way to accomplish this is by tightening the recent action requirement to ten days, rather than the 30 days previously suggested. This sharply reduces the number of plays, but increases both the percentage of winners and the percentage of profit.

Lead	NH	NW	WPCT	MPCT	$NET	I.V.
1+ points	363	87*	24.0%	55.6%	$2.38	2.18
2+ points	192	53*	27.6%	56.3%	$2.78	2.51

○ SYSTEM #2: THE TEN DAYS ANGLE FOR SPRINTS ○

Good form is fleeting, especially among cheaper horses. When a trainer has his horse at its peak, he wants to run it as soon as possible. A horse earns nothing while standing in its stall.

Consequently, it is a strong sign of a trainer's good intentions when a horse returns to action soon after a sharp performance. Surprisingly, such horses are not overbet.

TODAY'S RACE IS A SPRINT
LAST RACE WAS GOOD
LAST RACE WITHIN TEN DAYS
AT LEAST ONE WIN LAST TEN STARTS
AT LEAST ONE SPEED POINT

This system produces considerable action, approximately five plays every six races. Here are its results in 1,249 sprints:

NH	NW	WPCT	MPCT	$NET	I.V.
1069	223*	20.9%	51.8%	$2.11	1.92

Although this system makes no explicit requirement concerning the distance of the horse's most recent start, the speed-point requirement compensates. It demands that the horse have shown at least a modicum of early speed in a recent sprint.

The same type of system does not work in route races. As we mentioned in Chapter 7, many horses appreciate additional time (15–30 days) to prepare for a route engagement.

○ SYSTEM #3: THE FRESHENED-UP ANGLE ○

At the beginning of its seasonal campaign, a horse has an advantage over rivals that may be weary from the rigors of too many recent races. A horse generally performs at its peak when fresh and in form. The odds are often surprisingly high, perhaps because the horse did not run well immediately before or after its recent layoff.

Routers generally are able to return to top form after two races (preferably sprints). Sprinters, on the other hand, often return to top form after just one race.

Our first system (of this type) focuses on sprinters in their second starts after layoffs.

TODAY'S RACE A SPRINT
SECOND RACE AFTER A LAYOFF
LAST RACE A SPRINT
FINISHED IN FRONT HALF OF FIELD LAST RACE
NOT SEVERELY TESTED IN STRETCH RUN LAST RACE (see page 86)
AT LEAST ONE WIN LAST TEN STARTS
AT LEAST ONE SPEED POINT

Here is how this system worked out for a sample of 1,249 sprints:

NH	NW	WPCT	MPCT	$NET	I.V.
366	66	18.0%	44.5%	$2.18	1.68

We have not explicitly required recent action here, although the fact that the horse is making its second start after an absence implies that it has raced within the past 30 days. Some horses are able to come back quickly (ten to fourteen days), while others benefit more if rested two to three weeks, giving them a chance to recover and profit from that first all-out effort after a period of relative relaxation.

Even greater profits derive from bets on horses in their third and fourth starts after a layoff.

THIRD OR FOURTH START AFTER A LAYOFF
LAST RACE WAS GOOD
LAST RACE WITHIN TEN DAYS
AT LEAST ONE WIN LAST TEN STARTS
AT LEAST ONE SPEED POINT
POST POSITION 1–8 (IF A ROUTE)

The following tabulation discloses the results this system is capable of producing:

NH	NW	WPCT	MPCT	$NET	I.V.
288	65*	22.6%	50.3%	$2.74	2.05

Regardless of the distance of the third or fourth start after the layoff, this system was most effective when the horse's first and second starts back both were sprints.

The absence of a class requirement in either of these two systems raises an interesting point. Horses do not lay off from racing to go to college. Some rest because they have suffered injury. Injured horses may never return to action. Many that do are never able to approach their previous form. Others rest because they are exhausted. And theirs is a different story. Many trainers fail to recognize (or do not want to recognize) that a horse is tuckered out and needs a rest. Hoping to squeeze one more purse out of the poor animal, they interpret its deteriorating form as an indication of declining class. So they enter the animal in races of lower class, and then still lower, until they either ruin it or finally recognize that it is in desperate need of a rest.

When such an animal returns to the races and rounds into shape, it usually is able to climb back up the class ladder, sometimes all the way back to its former level. It provides a few good bets along the way. Never underestimate the sharp horse moving back up, especially if this happens early in its campaign, after a rest.

○ SYSTEM #4: THE BID-HUNG ANGLE ○

The ability to make a sharp move in the middle stages of a race is often a dependable omen of success, even if the horse was unable to prolong that move to the finish.

BID, BUT HUNG, LAST RACE
FINISHED IN FRONT HALF OF FIELD LAST RACE
LAST RACE WITHIN TEN DAYS
NO FAILURES
AT LEAST ONE WIN LAST TEN STARTS
POST POSITION 1-8 (IF A ROUTE)

BID and HUNG were both defined in Chapter 9. Part of the combined definition was the requirement that the horse's last race was at the same distance (sprint or route) as today's race.

The early move—at the second or third call—guarantees that the horse has the early speed to get into position to win. Consequently, no speed-point requirement is needed.

There is a need, however, to determine if the HUNG is a bad sign, negating the BID which otherwise would be a positive sign. Did the horse hang in its last race because it was going off form, because it ran out of gas? Was the BID the horse's last hurrah? The "no failures" requirement seems to provide the correct answer to these questions. If a horse has failures on its record, it most likely is not on the improve. The BID, HUNG "angle" is supposed to be a sign of improvement.

Here are the statistics for this system, based on 946 races:

NH	NW	WPCT	MPCT	$NET	I.V.
140	42*	30.0%	60.0%	$3.32	2.61

Our study indicated that a horse should capitalize on such a move immediately—within ten days. Horses waiting eleven to thirty days won only half as frequently, and returned their backers a net payoff of just $1.25.

○ SYSTEM #5: THE CONSISTENCY ANGLE ○

Consistency does not mean as much nowadays as it did twenty to thirty years ago. With so many tracks running concurrent dates, especially in the Northeast, racing secretaries often have difficulty filling races. Trainers are often asked to enter unready horses, just to give the public something else to bet on.

The horse that can win three (or more) races in ten is much more consistent and reliable than a 30 percent win percentage might suggest, provided that it is entered in the right race, of course.

When a consistent winner comes right back after a good race, it often is a solid bet. The fact that the trainer wheels the horse back so quickly is a good sign that he, rather than the racing secretary, has chosen the spot for the horse. Consequently, the horse probably will be competitive. Often enough, the result is victory.

AT LEAST THREE WINS LAST TEN STARTS
LAST RACE WAS GOOD
LAST RACE WITHIN TEN DAYS
POST POSITION 1—8 (IF A ROUTE)

Here are the results for this seemingly "obvious" system, after 1,549 races:

NH	NW	WPCT	MPCT	$NET	I.V.
368	105*	28.5%	58.7%	$2.50	2.59

○ SYSTEM #6: THE FIGURES ANGLE ○

When a horse is the "class" of its field, simply better than those it is facing, it has a powerful advantage and should win. The trick, of course, comes in identifying such horses.

Figures can be used for this purpose. Rank the contestants according to their average earnings per start during the past year (use two years if the horse has not started six times during the current year). Also rank the contestants according to their speed figures—use the "failures" method explained in Chapter 18.

The two figures obtained complement each other. The speed figures are closely related to current form, while the earnings figures combine both class and consistency.

According to the computer, the horses to watch are the ones ranked either first or second in *both* categories.

RANKED 1–2 IN SPEED FIGURES
RANKED 1–2 IN EARNINGS FIGURES
LAST RACE WITHIN TEN DAYS
AT LEAST ONE SPEED POINT
LAST RACE A SPRINT (IF A SPRINT)
POST POSITION 1–8 (IF A ROUTE)

Here is how these "class" horses performed in a sample of 700 races:

NH	NW	WPCT	MPCT	$NET	I.V.
193	61*	31.6%	67.4%	$2.36	2.87

The figures were almost identical for the 400 sprints and 300 routes in the sample. The fact that this system finds plays in approximately two of every seven races suggests that it will very seldom pick out two horses in the same race as the "class" of that race.

○ CHECKLIST SYSTEMS ○

The computer was also asked to try a different approach, one that would produce a checklist of conditions, each of which a horse must satisfy to qualify as a possible bet. Checklist conditions were defined in such a way so as to eliminate horses that failed to meet just minimum requirements in any one handicapping category.

Although the computer made an exhaustive search, choosing from among several conditions within each of the major areas of the total handicapping picture, it found no interesting checklist systems. Apparently, most of the horses selected by such a system are "too perfect," with no glaring holes in their records, and consequently are over-bet.

COMPUTER GENERATED SYSTEMS: MULTIPLE REGRESSION FORMULAS

The statistical technique called multiple regression is a second approach to computer-generated systems. It produces what some might scorn as "magic formulas." After you learn about multiple regression,[1] however, you may begin to accept the possibility that "magic formulas" actually do beat the races. Including the two formulas in this chapter.

Multiple regression assigns values to the various handicapping factors, reflecting their importance in the total handicapping picture. The player then multiplies a horse's "score" for each factor by the corresponding weighted value. Simple addition produces the horse's final rating. The horse with the *lowest* rating becomes the selection in the race.

Of course, the computer must be guided in selecting the factors for a potential multiple regression formula. The factors used must strike a reasonable balance among the major handicapping categories.

To insure this, the computer was given its choice of two or three different factors in each of the seven major handicapping categories

---

[1] More details about multiple regression, and the other regression techniques mentioned in this book, can be found in Appendix B.

(class, speed figures, consistency, distance, early speed, recent form, and recent action), together with the option of including or excluding jockey and post position factors. The computer was then asked to try all possible combinations of one factor from each category.

The two formulas below are the best the computer produced. The sprint formula is based on an analysis of the records of 5,800 horses entered in 646 sprint races. The route formula is based on 2,419 horses entered in 300 routes from one mile to one and an eighth miles.

○ THE SPRINT FORMULA ○

Horses entered in a sprint race must be rated in seven categories. Each horse begins with 2,000 points. That score is then modified according to the following set of factors and weights:

1. *DAYS SINCE LAST RACE*   Weight: +2
Multiply "days away" by 2, and *add* to the total.

2. *NUMBER OF GOOD RACES IN LAST TEN STARTS* Weight: −40
Multiply "good races" by 40, and *subtract*.

3. *NUMBER OF FAILURES*   Weight: +37
Multiply "failures" by 37, and *add*.

4. *SPEED POINT PERCENTAGE*   Weight: −14
Multiply "percentage points" by 14, and *subtract*.

5. *RANK: AVERAGE EARNINGS PER START*   Weight: +93
Multiply place in rank by 93, and *add*.

6. *RANK: AVERAGE SPEED RATING LAST TWO*
    GOOD RACES   Weight: +116
Multiply place in rank by 116, and *add*.

7. *JOCKEY RATING*   Weight: +250
Multiply the jockey's rating by 250, and *add*.

Horses are ranked (factors 5 and 6) as follows:

1 point—if first in field.
2 points—if second in field.
3 points—if third in field.
4 points—if otherwise in front half of field.
5 points—if in rear half of field.

In factor 6, the modified *Form SR+TV* is used.

Jockeys are rated as follows:

1 point—a top-five jockey.
2 points—a jockey who has been successful on the horse.
3 points—any other jockey.

Notice that horses with better rankings in earnings or speed figures, or with better jockeys, or with more recent races, or with fewer failures, have *fewer* points *added* to their ratings. And horses with more good races in their last ten starts, or with a higher percentage of the race's speed-point total, have *more* points *subtracted* from their ratings. That is why the horse with the *lowest* final rating is the selection for the race.

By way of example, take a look at the past performances for the first race at Aqueduct on Saturday, February 19, 1977. Ten horses went to the post for this six-furlong claiming event over the Big A's (then) new inner course.

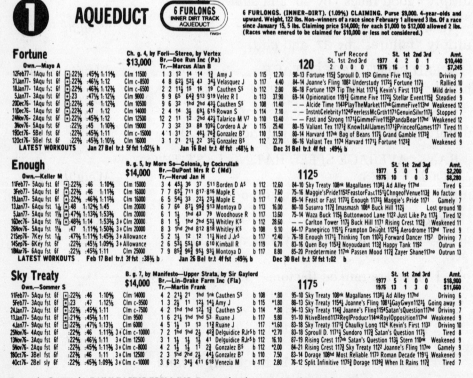

Court Reporter

Dk. b. or br. g. 5, by Reviewer—Table, by Round Table
$13,000 Br.—Linder B N (Ky)
Own.—King Ranch Tr.—Hirsch William J

115

Turf Record	St.	1st	2nd	3rd		St.	1st	2nd	3rd	Amt.
	1	0	0	0	1977	1	1	0	0	$4,800
					1976	3	M	0	0	$600

4Feb77- 2Aqu	fst	6f	⊡:23⅕	:48	1:14⅕	Md 10000	9	1	11	2hd	1hd	1nk	Santiago A	b	122	3.00	78–16	Court Reporter 122nk Runs Harder1156¾FootsieKing1134½	Driving	9
12Mar76- 5Aqu	fst	6f	:22⅘	:46⅕	1:11⅕	3↑Md Sp Wt	6	4	89½	86¼	65	57¾	Whitley K7		116	5.50	80–18	Judging Man 1121¼ Bally Hoop 1141¼ Open Plains1151¾	No factor	8
26Feb76- 6Aqu	fst	6f	:23⅕	:46⅗	1:12	3↑Md Sp Wt	2	3	31½	42	41½	41¾	Whitley K7		116	15.50	81–16	RegalProducer1131LastIntrigue114nkRomnConsul112½	Weakened	6
19Feb76- 9Aqu	fst	6f	:22⅖	:45⅖	1:10⅗	3↑Md Sp Wt	3	3	53½	612	615	914	Whitley K7		116	9.60	76–18	Missing Marbles 1145½ Irish Sentry 1122¼ Robert's Bay1132	Tired	9
20Nov75- 5Aqu	fst	6f	:23	:46⅕	1:11	3↑Md Sp Wt	11	1	1½	66¼	79½	811	Turcotte R		121	4.30	77–13	Boy Emperor 1212 Chief's Holiday 1213½ Trail Signs 121¾	Tired	11
10Nov75- 4Aqu	sly	6f	:22⅖	:45⅘	1:12	3↑Md Sp Wt	8	2	32	32½	31½	2¾	Turcotte R		121	2.80	82–18	OurDoctor121¾CourtRportr121hdSomthingGold1215¾	Carried wide	8
27Oct75- 9Key	fst	6½f	:23	:46⅖	1:17⅗	3↑Md Sp Wt	9	4	2hd	21½	23	28	Whitley K10		109	12.50	81–23	PrincelySong1198CourtReporter1093YoungFredrick1194	2nd best	10
6Oct75- 1Bel	fm	7f	Ⓣ:23⅕	:45⅘	1:23⅗	3↑Md Sp Wt	2	12	96½	811	711	57½	Whitley K7		109	17.00	78–15	Windhover 1192 Axe to Grind 119no Pumpkin Pie1192¾	No factor	12
30Jly75- 1Sar	fst	6f	:22⅘	:46⅕	1:12⅕	3↑Md Sp Wt	1	14	53	63¼	1410	1411	Bracciale V Jr	b	118	30.00	68–14	Napier 118¾ Yu Wipi 118hd Bad Talk 118½	Tired	14
26Sep74- 5Bel	sly	6f	:22⅘	:46⅖	1:11⅗	Md Sp Wt	5	5	42	813	1021	1127	Marquez C H	b	121	12.30	58–14	Bravest Roman 1215LineOfficer1214½MongoLeader121nk	Checked	11

LATEST WORKOUTS Feb 15 Aqu ⊡ 4f fst :51⅗ b Feb 11 Bel tr.t 3f fst :38 b Jan 23 Bel tr.t 6f fst 1:15⅗ h Jan 19 Bel tr.t 6f fst 1:18 b

Coronation Day

B. g. 5, by Prince John—Prime Time, by Eight Thirty
$12,000 Br.—Vanderbilt A G (Md)
Own.—Garren M M Tr.—Puentes Gilbert

108⁵

Turf Record	St.	1st	2nd	3rd		St.	1st	2nd	3rd	Amt.
	10	2	0	4	1977	1	0	0	0	$600
					1976	29	4	2	6	$37,210

11Feb77- 5Aqu	fst	6f	⊡:22⅖	:46	1:10⅘	Clm 14000	1	6	68	58	58¾	48½	Gonzalez B5		108	11.90	86–10	Sky Treaty 108nk Magallanes 1138¼ Ad Alley 117hd	No mishap	6
27Nov76- 6Aqu	fm	1 1/16	Ⓣ:49	1:12⅗	1:44⅖	3↑Allowance	2	4	35½	38	412	510	Cruguet J		117	5.70	74–16	Con Neddy 117nk Notably Different 1153 Volney 1176½	No excuse	6
20Nov76- 5Aqu	fm	1 1/16	Ⓣ:48	1:12⅕	1:43⅘	3↑Allowance	1	4	48½	46	35½	32	Gonzalez B5		112	12.70	85–11	Quick Decision 117nk Heliologist 1151¾CoronationDay112½	Rallied	7
11Nov76- 5Aqu	fst	1⅛	:47⅕	1:12⅖	1:50⅗	3↑Clm 25000	1	6	68½	95½	816	718	Vasquez J		117	3.70	64–20	Rastaferian1195¾FrmptonDelight1171½RestlessRuler120no	Outrun	9
2Nov76- 3Aqu	fst	1⅛	:46⅖	1:12⅖	1:51⅖	3↑Hcp 10000s	2	2	27	2hd	32	34¼	Woodhouse R		117	5.60	74–19	RstlssRlr114noCompnyCommndr1174¼CorntnDy1175¼	Speed, tired	8
30Oct76- 6Aqu	gd	1 1/16	Ⓣ:48⅖	1:13⅗	1:45⅘	3↑Allowance	9	8	75½	42	73¾	64¾	Woodhouse R		117	9.00	72–26	Practitioner1141½QuickDecision1221¾NotblyDifferent114¾	Outrun	10
20Oct76- 5Bel	fst	1⅛	:46⅗	1:10⅖	1:48⅘	3↑Hcp 10000s	1	1	1½	2hd	2½	2½	Woodhouse R		118	11.30	82–12	CompnyCommnder113½CorontionDy1183½LowRturn111hd	Gamely	8
11Oct76- 4Bel	sf	1¼	[T]:50	1:16⅕	2:06⅘	3↑Hcp 12500s	4	6	32½	31½	33½	35½	Rodriguez J A		120	10.30	60–33	Silver Prince 122½ Roam Free 1175 Coronation Day 120¾	Evenly	8
2Oct76- 7Bel	sly	1 1/16	:46⅘	1:11⅕	1:43	3↑Allowance	8	7	64	44½	68½	611	Hernandez R		117	14.50	76–11	Fabulous Father 114¾ Kalong 117no Magnetizer 1167½	Tired	8
21Sep76- 6Bel	fm	1¼	[T]:50⅘	1:13⅗	2:03⅖	3↑Clm 35000	5	2	2½	2hd	1hd	3¾	Rodriguez J A		113	7.30	82–14	Megalomania 115¾ Volney 117hd Coronation Day 113¾	Weakened	6

LATEST WORKOUTS Feb 4 Bel tr.t 4f fst :49⅖ bg ●Jan 28 Bel tr.t 3f fst :35⅗ h

Awayfromitall

B. g. 5, by Your Alibhai—Waikiki, by Devil Diver
$14,000 Br.—Kinship Syndicate (Fla)
Own.—Ge-Joy Stable Tr.—Martin Jose

119

Turf Record	St.	1st	2nd	3rd		St.	1st	2nd	3rd	Amt.
	2	0	0	0	1977	5	3	1	0	$20,120
					1976	21	1	2	2	$11,135

8Feb77- 7Aqu	fst	1⅛	⊡:48	1:13	1:52⅖	Clm 15000	4	4	46	44½	56½	610	Gonzalez B5	b	117	4.00	80–15	Pepysian 1122 Restless Ruler 115¾ Above the Belt 1152½	Tired	8
28Jan77- 6Aqu	fst	1 1/16	⊡:49⅘	1:14⅗	1:48⅗	Hcp 5000s	3	2	22½	21½	1½	12¼	Gonzalez B	b	124	*1.40	75–18	Awayfromitall 1242¼ Final Offer 112¾ Mountbatten 115nk	Driving	5
18Jan77- 4Aqu	fst	1⅛	⊡:48⅗	1:13⅘	1:54⅘	Hcp 5000s	4	1	11½	12½	14	14	Gonzalez B	b	122	*.80	78–18	Awayfromitall 1224 Lanvin's Toy 111¾ Mountbatten 1154	Driving	6
11Jan77- 6Aqu	gd	1⅛	⊡:48⅘	1:13⅘	1:54⅗	Clm 11500	10	2	11	1½	12	2hd	Gonzalez B5	b	109	*3.50	79–21	Grey Royalty111hdAwayfromitall109¾TropicMonkey1164½	Bumped	11
6Jan77- 5Aqu	fst	1 1/16	⊡:48⅕	1:13⅘	1:48	Hcp 5000s	5	1	14	14	15	1½	Gonzalez B	b	111	3.10	78–16	Awayfromitall 111½ Wave The Flag 1227 Nativetivo 120no	Driving	8
17Dec76- 2Aqu	fst	1⅛	⊡:48⅗	1:13⅘	1:54⅗	3↑Clm 9000	9	4	32½	31½	21	22	Velasquez J	b	115	3.80	— —	Nite Port 1122 Awayfromitall 1151¾ Loyal Haven 1171¾	Lugged in	9
2Dec76- 1Aqu	fst	1 1/16	⊡:48⅖	1:13	1:47⅖	3↑Clm c-6500	4	5	44½	34½	44	66¾	Cruguet J	b	122	*1.50	— —	Handsome Ghost 1072¼ Flight of Apollo 1171 Resident 115½	Tired	10
24Nov76- 1Aqu	fst	170	⊡:48	1:13⅖	1:44⅖	3↑Clm c-5000	1	5	42	31	15	17¾	Velasquez J	b	117	3.70	— —	Awyfromitll1177¾MsterRight117nkPrincePretense1173½	Mild drive	10
8Nov76- 2Aqu	fst	7f	:23⅗	:47⅗	1:26⅕	3↑Clm 9000	6	1	65½	66	86	76½	Hawley S	b	113	5.60	63–27	Cardinal George 117hd [D]One's Too Many 1121 Stern1081¼	Outrun	9
25Oct76- 1Aqu	fst	7f	:23	:45⅘	1:23⅖	3↑Clm 10500	4	10	94¾	76½	67½	47¼	Delguidice RJr5	b	108	13.60	77–13	CannelCoal1106TrainerMickey1171¼CardinlGeorge117hd	No threat	11

LATEST WORKOUTS Jan 26 Bel tr.t 4f fst :49⅕ h Dec 30 Bel tr.t 4f fst :48 h

Magallanes

B. g. 6, by Fathers Image—Close Play, by Shut Out
$14,000 Br.—Karsner A B (Ky)
Own.—Al-Frank Stable Tr.—Parisella John

117

Turf Record	St.	1st	2nd	3rd		St.	1st	2nd	3rd	Amt.
	3	0	0	0	1977	2	1	1	0	$6,100
					1976	6	0	1	0	$1,430

11Feb77- 5Aqu	fst	6f	⊡:22⅖	:46	1:10⅘	Clm 14000	5	1	11½	11	2hd	2nk	Amy J		113	1.70	95–10	Sky Treaty 108nk Magallanes 1138¼ Ad Alley 117hd	Sharp	6
5Feb77- 1Aqu	fst	6f	⊡:22⅗	:46	1:11⅕	Clm c-6250	6	1	11	15	12½	12¾	Amy J		115	3.10	93–13	Magallanes 1152¾ Little Miracle 1135PurchaseStreet1174¾	Driving	8
21Dec76- 9Aqu	fst	6f	⊡:23	:47⅘	1:13⅖	3↑Clm 6250	5	6	23	1½	1hd	23½	Santiago A		115	10.90	— —	Challenge 1143½ Magallanes 1153½ Nu Dunce 113nk	Gamely	11
12Nov76- 7Mth	fst	6f	:22	:45⅕	1:11⅖	3↑Clm 6500	12	9	87¾	79¼	913	914	Solomone M		116	14.30	69–22	RestlessTerresto115noGreyRoyalty1193BuddyBoots1143	No factor	12
7May76- 5GS	fst	6f	:23	:46⅗	1:12⅗	Clm 10000	4	4	53	79½	87½	77¾	Castaneda K		116	5.80	72–27	TudorNugget116noReblRoch119hdBlzinWondr1163½	Through early	10
24Feb76- 5GS	gd	6f	:22⅗	:46⅖	1:13⅖	Clm 15000	6	2	21	55	66¾	67¼	Castaneda K		116	15.60	69–33	Weehawken 106¾ Pembles 1161¼ Stook 106¾	Early speed	7
16Feb76- 6GS	fst	6f	:22⅗	:46⅗	1:12⅗	Clm 15000	5	1	2½	63¼	64¾	913	Castaneda K		116	10.30	67–34	Big City Blues 114hd Wenceslas 1147 Pembles 116no	Tired	10
6Feb76- 9GS	my	6f	:23	:47⅖	1:14⅕	Clm 15000	2	4	73	72¼	55	99¼	Castaneda K		116	10.70	63–42	Blue Barbizon 1162 Lester Gem 116¾ Winning Point 116¾	Outrun	9
19May75- 5Aqu	fst	6f	:22⅖	:45	1:10	Clm 27500	4	8	43	33½	36	68½	Turcotte R		116	6.10	85–12	Smoked Salmon 114nk Dorage 1144 Passen Mood 113½	Tired	9
1May75- 9Aqu	fst	6f	:22⅕	:45	1:10⅕	Clm 30500	1	7	55	45½	54	72½	Turcotte R		114	5.20	89–13	The Twenties116¾PassenMood112¾SmokedSalmon112½	No excuse	9

LATEST WORKOUTS Feb 1 Aqu ⊡ 5f fst 1:03 b Jan 20 Aqu ⊡ 5f fst 1:03 b

Amberdias

B. g. 4, by Madias—Ambergold, by Amerigo
$14,000 Br.—Sarival Farm (Ariz)
Own.—Reiner H Tr.—LaBoccetta Frank

117

	St.	1st	2nd	3rd	Amt.
1977	4	0	1	1	$3,640
1976	19	2	3	3	$9,239

7Feb77- 7Aqu	fst	1⅛	⊡:48	1:12⅘	1:52⅗	Clm 19000	4	2	22½	21½	31½	59	Montoya D	b	115	10.30	80–18	MonetaryPrinciple112noSturdyUnion1152¾SavgeMoon1171¾	Tired	8
28Jan77- 3Aqu	fst	170	⊡:49	1:14⅖	1:44⅗	Clm 16000	1	1	1½	11½	1hd	33¾	Montoya D	b	117	5.40	79–18	HawinGulf1123¾GenuineSilver117hdAmberdis1173¾	Weakened late	7
18Jan77- 2Aqu	fst	6f	⊡:22⅗	:46⅗	1:12⅕	Clm 12500	7	4	43	32½	22	2¾	Montoya D	b	117	79.00	87–18	PrinceofGmes117¾Amberdis1171¾PeerlssMcGrth117nk	Alt. course	12
11Jan77- 3Aqu	gd	6f	⊡:22⅖	:46⅕	1:12⅕	Clm 15000	9	1	62¾	64¾	712	1115	Montoya D	b	117	39.10	73–21	SplitInfinitive112½InstntCelebrity1191¾Lrry'sDogoon1142½	Outrun	12
26Sep76- 9Suf	fst	6f	:22⅖	:46	1:12⅕	3↑Allowance	7	1	76¼	78¼	712	79¼	Swatman W	b	110	36.70	71–27	Official Record 1142 Black Kitchen 111nk Bevron 1053	Trailed	7
6Sep76- 8Rkm	fst	170	:46⅖	1:11⅘	1:42	L Smith H	5	4	31	53	612	718	Smith B	b	106	71.00	68–23	On The Sly 1204½ In a Trance 1221¼ Mr. PittyPat1185¾	Weakened	8
6Sep76-Evening Program																				
22Aug76- 8Rkm	fst	6f	:22⅕	:45⅖	1:11⅖	3↑Allowance	6	6	64¾	55	54¼	57¼	Smith B	b	109	14.60	80–21	Northern Image 114no Jet Fiaca 1141 Grand Gamble1124¼	Outrun	7
14Aug76- 8Rkm	sly	140	:46⅕	1:12⅕	1:42⅘	De Spirito H	9	7	79	77½	58	34½	Smith B	b	106	52.90	73–24	Bennino 1143 Sittin Chilly 1101½ Amberdias 106no	Stride late	10
19Jly76- 8Rkm	fst	140	:46⅖	1:10⅘	1:39⅖	3↑Allowance	3	3	31½	33	36½	312	Smith B	b	108	11.60	83–16	Punchout Cowboy 1192½ He Man Jr.1129½Amberdias108hd	Rallied	6
4Jly76- 9Suf	fst	1 1/16	:46⅗	1:11⅗	1:44⅖	Bicentennial	2	9	107¾	106½	72¾	57½	Smith B	b	112	119.60	79–18	Troll By 1224½ Sea Ice 1171 Eager Red 1171½	Late bid	12

LATEST WORKOUTS Feb 14 Aqu ⊡ 4f fst :49 h ●Jan 24 Aqu ⊡ 3f fst :36 h Jan 9 Aqu ⊡ 4f fst :49⅗ h Jan 4 Aqu ⊡ 5f fst 1:03 b

Ad Alley

Ch. c. 4, by Copy Chief—Fabled Queen, by Amarullah
$14,000 Br.—Martin J V (Ky)
Own.—Verde V Farm Tr.—Deliso Genaro J

117

Turf Record	St.	1st	2nd	3rd		St.	1st	2nd	3rd	Amt.
	1	0	0	1	1977	5	0	0	1	$1,860
					1976	21	5	1	3	$39,260

11Feb77- 5Aqu	fst	6f	⊡:22⅖	:46	1:10⅘	Clm 15000	2	5	35½	46½	47¼	38½	Venezia M		117	6.80	86–10	Sky Treaty 108nk Magallanes 1138¼ Ad Alley 117hd	No mishap	6
23Jan77- 5Aqu	fst	6f	⊡:22⅘	:45⅗	1:11⅖	Clm 20000	8	8	31½	25	39	67	Venezia M	b	117	25.50	85–12	Elena'sBoy1103BoldandStormy1171¾MonetryPrinciple114hd	Tired	9
21Jan77- 6Aqu	fst	1 1/16	⊡:48	1:14	1:47	Clm 20000	7	2	69¾	45½	58½	515	Martens G	b	117	10.70	68–19	MonetaryPrinciple1122SavageMoon1171ImperialBomb1154½	Tired	7
15Jan77- 5Aqu	my	6f	⊡:22⅖	:45⅘	1:11	Clm 20000	9	4	33	46	36½	411	Martens G	b	117	22.90	83–10	Pres De Tu 1195½ Paul's Hero 1173½ Sail On Top 1121¾	Weakened	10
11Jan77- 3Aqu	gd	6f	⊡:22⅖	:46⅕	1:12⅕	Clm c-15000	11	8	86	811	812	811	Vasquez J	b	117	*3.10	77–21	SplitInfinitive112½InstntCelebrity1191¾Lrry'sDogoon1142½	Outrun	12
22Dec76- 5Aqu	fst	6f	⊡:22⅕	:45⅖	1:11⅖	Clm 20000	2	8	43¼	47	46½	3¾	Velasquez J	b	117	7.40	— —	Elena's Boy 115½ Instant Celebrity 112nk Ad Alley 117no	Rallied	10
8Dec76- 7Aqu	my	6f	⊡:23⅕	:47⅗	1:12⅖	Clm 25000	6	4	43¼	31	67½	611	Vasquez J	b	117	9.00	— —	Sunderance 1143½ Mighty Strong 117¾ Howies Heat 1172	Tired	8
11Nov76- 1Aqu	fst	7f	:22⅗	:45⅗	1:24⅗	Clm 25000	3	5	65¾	712	79	67¼	Velasquez J	b	122	3.60	71–20	VlintTex1201¾WhiskeyChrley1171¼ImpressivCount1154	No factor	8
28Oct76- 5Aqu	fst	7f	:23⅕	:46⅕	1:23⅘	Clm 35000	7	6	85½	74½	57	55½	Hernandez R	b	114	6.40	76–21	Full Catch 115hd Gaitor Ratten 1123½ Salim Alicum 1221	Outrun	9
22Oct76- 2Bel	fst	6f	:23⅖	:46⅗	1:11	Clm 25000	2	3	22	33	21½	1no	Velasquez J	b	117	18.60	87–21	Ad Alley 117no Bright Discovery117¾PrinceofGames1191½	Driving	12

LATEST WORKOUTS Dec 31 Aqu ⊡ 5f fst 1:02⅖ h

The table below contains all the vital information for each horse. Check it over. Make sure that you understand such new handicapping concepts as speed points, failures, and good races.

Horse	DAYS AWAY	GOOD RACES	FAILURES	SPEED PTS	SPEED %	AVERAGE EARNINGS	BY RANK	SPEED FIGURES	BY RANK	JOCKEY	RATING
Fortune	7	4	0	5	17%	$884	5	101 96	5	1	2911
Enough	8	2	2	0	0%	$699	5	101 96	5	3	3805
Sky Treaty	8	6	0	7	23%	$1698	2	103 99	4	1	2354
Court Reporter	15	4	0	5	17%	$1350	4	92 94	5	1	2834
Coronation Day	8	5	0	0	0%	$1260	4	100 103	3	2	3036
Awayfromitall	11	6	0	0	0%	$1202	5	98 99	5	3	3577
Magallanes	8	3	0	6	20%	$941	5	103 104	1	1	2447
Amberdias	12	4	0	1	3%	$560	5	101 103	2	2	3019
Ad Alley	8	3	0	4	13%	$1582	3	94 106	4	1	2707
Forest Stream	229	5	0	2	7%	$3233	1	95 101	5	3	3583

30

30

Note: *All route speed figures have been scaled by one third towards 100. Also, SR + TV adjustments in effect at the beginning of the Winter 1977 meeting have been used. They are: at six furlongs, −2; at one mile, 70 yards, +4; at $1\frac{1}{16}$ miles, +4; and at $1\frac{1}{8}$ miles, +3.*

Each horse's final rating is listed in the last column of the table. Sky Treaty has the *lowest* rating, and therefore is the selection in the race. Here, in more detail, is how his final rating total was calculated:

	2000 points
$+2 \times 8$ days away	+16
-40×6 good races last ten starts	−240
$+37 \times 0$ failures	0
$-14 \times 23\%$ of speed point total	−322
$+93 \times$ rank 2 in average earnings per start	+186
$+116 \times$ rank 4 in speed figures	+464
$+250 \times$ jockey rating 1	+250
	2354 points

Needless to say (as always happens in handicapping books), Sky Treaty won, and returned \$8.20. It was his fourth in a streak of seven consecutive wins.

FIRST RACE
Aqueduct
FEBRUARY 19, 1977

6 FURLONGS.(INNER DIRT). (1.09⅗) CLAIMING. Purse \$9,000. 4-year-olds and upward. Weight, 122 lbs. Non-winners of a race since February 1 allowed 3 lbs. Of a race since January 15, 5 lbs. Claiming price \$14,000; for each \$1,000 to \$12,000 allowed 2 lbs. (Races when enered to be claimed for \$10,000 or less not considered.)

Value of race \$9,000, value to winner \$5,400, second \$1,980, third \$1,080, fourth \$540. Mutuel pool \$157,219, OTB pool \$105,942.

Last Raced	Horse	Eqt.	A.	Wt	PP	St	¼	½	Str	Fin	Jockey	Cl'g Pr	Odds \$1
11Feb77 ^{5}Aqu^{1}	Sky Treaty	b	7	117	3	5	2^{2}	$2^{1\frac{1}{2}}$	$1^{\frac{1}{2}}$	$1^{\frac{1}{2}}$	Cauthen S^{5}	14000	3.10
11Feb77 ^{5}Aqu^{2}	Magallanes		6	117	7	2	3^{1}	3^{4}	2^{2}	2^{8}	Velasquez J	14000	2.00
12Feb77 ^{1}Aqu^{1}	Fortune	b	4	120	1	6	1^{3}	1^{2}	3^{5}	3^{nk}	Graell A	13000	5.80
7Feb77 ^{7}Aqu^{5}	Amberdias	b	4	117	8	1	$5^{\frac{1}{2}}$	$4^{\frac{1}{2}}$	$4^{\frac{1}{2}}$	$4^{\frac{3}{4}}$	Montoya D	14000	5.30
11Feb77 ^{5}Aqu^{4}	Coronation Day		5	108	5	7	$8^{\frac{1}{2}}$	7^{1}	6^{1}	$5^{1\frac{1}{4}}$	Gonzalez B^{5}	12000	14.50
11Feb77 ^{5}Aqu^{3}	Ad Alley		4	117	9	3	$7^{1\frac{1}{2}}$	8^{1}	7^{hd}	$6^{\frac{3}{4}}$	Venezia M	14000	13.10
11Feb77 ^{5}Aqu^{5}	Enough	b	5	112	2	10	$4^{\frac{1}{2}}$	5^{4}	5^{2}	$7^{\frac{3}{4}}$	Shepherd D R^{5}	14000	32.40
4Feb77 ^{2}Aqu^{1}	Court Reporter		5	115	4	9	$6^{\frac{1}{2}}$	$6^{\frac{1}{2}}$	8^{2}	$8^{1\frac{1}{2}}$	Santiago A	13000	28.70
8Feb77 ^{7}Aqu^{6}	Awayfromitall	b	5	119	6	8	10	10	9^{3}	9^{6}	Bacon M	14000	27.70
4Jly76 ^{2}Aqu^{6}	Forest Stream		4	110	10	4	$9^{1\frac{1}{2}}$	$9^{\frac{1}{2}}$	10	10	Borden D A^{5}	13000	9.40

OFF AT 12:30 EST. Start good, Won driving. Time, :22⅕, :45⅖, 1:10⅘ Track fast.

Official Program Numbers↘

\$2 Mutuel Prices:			
3–(C)–SKY TREATY	8.20	3.40	2.60
7–(G)–MAGALLANES		3.00	2.60
1–(A)–FORTUNE			3.60

B. g, by Manifesto—Upper Strata, by Sir Gaylord. Trainer Martin Frank. Bred by Lin-Drake Farm Inc (Fla).

SKY TREATY raced in closest attendance to FORTUNE, took over soon after entering the stretch and turned back MAGALLANES under strong handling. The latter, reserved early, loomed boldly from the outside after entering the stretch but wasn't good enough. FORTUNE tired badly from his early efforts. AMBERDIAS lacked a rally. AD ALLEY was always outrun. ENOUGH was finished early. FOREST STREAM showed nothing.

Owners— 1, Sommer S; 2, Al-Frank Stable; 3, Mayo A; 4, Reiner H; 5, Garren M M; 6, Verde V Farm; 7, Keller M; 8, King Ranch; 9, Ge-Joy Stable; 10, Rosenthal Frances.

Trainers— 1, Martin Frank; 2, Parisella John; 3, Marcus Alan B; 4, LaBoccetta Frank; 5, Puentes Gilbert; 6, Deliso Genaro J; 7, Nerud Jan H; 8, Hirsch William J; 9, Martin Jose; 10, King Everett W.

Fortune was claimed by Sheena K; trainer, Hirsch Jerome; Coronation Day was claimed by Top the Marc; trainer, Tufariello Frank; Forest Stream was claimed by Castle Jerome; trainer, Martin Jose.

Interestingly, Sky Treaty was not the favorite in this race, even with the sensational Steve Cauthen riding. Instead, Magallanes, who had just been beaten by Sky Treaty, was the favorite. Why did the formula pick Sky Treaty to repeat his narrow victory over Magallanes? Consistency is the answer—it allowed Sky Treaty to overcome Magallanes's number-one ranking in the speed figures category. Looking at Magallanes's "shady" past, one would have to be a little dubious of his ability to come back after a tough race.

Now that we have explained how to use the formula, all that remains is the proof that it can pick the winner of more than just one race. The study below shows how the system performed over a sample of 646 sprint races:

NH	NW	NP	NS	WPCT	MPCT	$NET	I.V.
646	186*	114	99	28.8%	61.8%	$2.16	2.59

Almost 29 percent winners producing an 8 percent profit, with a play in every race, is an excellent showing. The potential investor is advised, however, to test this system further on paper before risking real money on its selections. Although it has proven itself on one "paper" sample of 646 races, and statistical tests suggest continued success, there is the chance that it will not do as well on future samples.

○ THE ROUTE FORMULA ○

After studying the records of 2,419 horses entered in 300 route races, the computer concluded that some of the traditional "major" handicapping categories were superfluous and should not be included in multiple regression formulas (for routes). Not surprisingly, in light of statistics presented in earlier chapters, distance and recent action both can be ignored. In addition, a factor revealing current form need not be included.

The computer produced the following set of factors and weights for routes:

a
1. *POST POSITION*   Weight: +74
Multiply the post position by 74, and *add*.

b
2. *NUMBER OF WINS IN LAST TEN STARTS*   Weight: −11
Multiply wins by 11, and *subtract*.

c
3. *JOCKEY RATING*   Weight: +228
Multiply the jockey's rating by 228, and *add*.

de

4. RANK: AVERAGE EARNINGS PER START — Weight: +115
Multiply place in rank by 115, and *add*.

+9

5. RANK: AVERAGE SPEED RATING LAST TWO GOOD RACES — Weight: +110
Multiply place in rank by 110, and *add*.

Notice that the second factor has a very small weight. This factor, therefore, will usually have little to say about the ultimate selection in a race, but rather will play the role of tie breaker.

As an example of this formula, take a look at the field for the 1977 Ruthless Stakes, a mile-and-a-sixteenth test for three-year-old fillies which was run at Aqueduct February 19.

 AQUEDUCT 1 1/16 MILES INNER DIRT TRACK AQUEDUCT START FINISH

1 1/16 MILES, (INNER-DIRT). (1.43%) 4th Running THE RUTHLESS. $50,000 added. Fillies, 3-year-olds. Weight, 121 lbs. By subscription of $100 each, which shall accompany the nomination; $250 to start, with $50,000 added. The added money and all fees to be divided 60% to the winner, 22% to second, 12% to third and 6% to fourth. Non-winners of two races of $25,000 at a mile or over in 1976-77 allowed 3 lbs. Of a race of $15,000 at a mile or over in 1976-77, 6 lbs. Of a race of $35,000 at any distance in 1976-77, 9 lbs. Starters to be named at the closing time of entries. Trophies will be presented to the winning owner, trainer and jockey. Closed with 19 nominations Saturday, February 5, 1977.

Road Princess
118
Own.—Elmendorf
B. f. 3, by Gallant Man—One Lane, by Prince John
Br.—Elmendorf Farm (Ky)
Tr.—Campo John P

	St.	1st	2nd	3rd	Amt.
1977	2	1	0	1	$26,343
1976	5	M	3	2	$20,536

LATEST WORKOUTS Feb 14 Aqu 5f fst 1:00½ h   Jan 27 Bel tr.t 5f fst 1:01½ h   Jan 14 Bel 5f fst 1:02 b   Jan 8 Aqu 6f fst 1:13½ b

Sweet Alliance
118
Own.—Windfields Farm
B. f. 3, by Sir Ivor—Mrs Peterkin, by Tom Fool
Br.—Newstead Farm (Va)
Tr.—Delp Grover G

	St.	1st	2nd	3rd	Amt.
1977	3	3	0	0	$31,218
1976	2	2	0	0	$17,649

25Nov76-irst Division
LATEST WORKOUTS Feb 17 Bow 4f fst :50 b   Feb 10 Bow 4f fst :48 h   Feb 3 Bow 7f fst 1:26⅜ h   Jan 23 Bow 4f fst :48 h

Someday Queen
112
Own.—Keewaydin Stable
Dk. b. or br. f. 3, by His Majesty—Three Red Bells, by Third Martini
Br.—Bryan Mr-Mrs H L & Yowell Renee (Fla)
Tr.—Veitch Sylvester E

	St.	1st	2nd	3rd	Amt.
1977	1	1	0	0	$9,000
1976	9	1	0	2	$7,920

LATEST WORKOUTS Feb 16 Bel tr.t 4f fst :50 b   Feb 4 Bel tr.t 3f fst :36½ b   Jan 31 Bel tr.t 6f fst 1:18 b   Jan 26 Bel tr.t 4f fst :50½ b

Meteor Dancer
112
Own.—Buckland Farm
B. f. 3, by Northern Dancer—Solometeor, by Victoria Park
Br.—Taylor E P (Md)
Tr.—Campo John P

	St.	1st	2nd	3rd	Amt.
1977	3	0	2	0	$16,110
1976	8	2	0	1	$13,070

26Nov76-Placed first through disqualification
LATEST WORKOUTS Feb 14 Aqu 5f fst 1:00½ h   Dec 29 Bel tr.t 6f fst 1:15 b

Maria's Baby B. f. 3, by Quadrangle—Round Figures, by Round Table
Br.—Kay A (Va)
Tr.—Zito Nicholas P
Own.—Tedmar Stable
112

	St.	1st	2nd	3rd	Amt.
1977	3	2	0	0	$26,194
1976	6	1	2	0	$13,680

2Feb77- 8Aqu fst 1 1/16 ⊡:49⅘ 1:15⅖ 1:46⅘ ⒻSearching 2 1 1hd 2hd 22½ 48 Santiago A b 115 2.20 76-19 RodPrincess1126¼MeteorDncer114noOneNightAffir1121¾ Bore out 7
25Jan77- 8Aqu my 6f ⊡:22⅘ :47⅖ 1:13 ⒻAllowance 1 2 22 54½ 2hd 11¾ Cauthen S5 b 116 *.80 84-20 Maria's Baby 1161¾ Bold Bow 114¾ Comical Passtime121½ Driving 6
14Jan77- 4Aqu fst 6f ⊡:22⅘ :46 1:10⅘ ⒻAllowance 4 2 53¾ 46½ 31 12 Cauthen S5 b 109 *1.00 95-12 Maria's Baby 1092 Shufleur 115nk Fashion Ruler 1148½ Driving 6
22Dec76- 7Aqu fst 6f ⊡:22⅕ :45⅘ 1:11⅕ ⒻAllowance 8 2 21½ 31½ 44½ 23½ Cordero A Jr 114 *1.20 — — When And If 1143½ Maria's Baby 114no FashionRuler114½ Gamely 12
15Dec76- 4Aqu fst 6f ⊡:22⅘ :46⅗ 1:11⅖ ⒻAllowance 3 3 42½ 64¾ 35 23¼ Maple E 114 4.20 — — Ring O' Bells 1193¼ Maria's Baby 114½ Fashion Ruler 1143¼ Wide 7
4Dec76- 5Aqu fst 6f :22⅕ :45⅖ 1:11 ⒻAllowance 2 2 31½ 52½ 54 54 Cordero A Jr 113 5.30 84-14 Ring O' Bells 1131 Shufleur 113¾ Voddi Dottie 1191¼ Tired 7
27Aug76- 8Sar fst 6f :22 :45 1:10⅖ ⒻSpinaway 10 1 75¾ 99½ 911 813 Martens G 119 10.80 75-10 Mrs. Warren 1193 Exerene 119½ Sensational 1192 Outrun 10
16Aug76- 8Sar fst 6f :22⅕ :45⅗ 1:11 ⒻAdirondack 4 3 — — — — Martens G 114 2.70 — — Harvest Girl 1142BonnieEmpress114½DramaCritic1191¼ Lost rider 7
6Aug76- 3Sar fst 5½f :22⅘ :46⅘ 1:05⅕ ⒻMd 55000 2 9 2½ 41½ 1½ 15¼ Martens G 115 3.20 91-16 Maria'sBaby1155¼WantonWomn115¾Spontneous1152¼ Ridden out 10
LATEST WORKOUTS ●Feb 15 Aqu ⊡ 4f fst :46⅖ h Feb 11 Bel tr.t 4f fst :51 b Jan 22 Bel tr.t 4f fst :47 h ●Jan 9 Bel tr.t 4f fst :47⅕ h

Indian Bend B. f. 3, by Triple Bend—Need E Indian, by Needles
Br.—Parisi J (Ky)
Tr.—Martin Jose
Own.—Camijo Stable
112

	St.	1st	2nd	3rd	Amt.
1977	4	1	1	0	$9,680
1976	3	1	0	0	$5,700

1Feb77- 2Aqu fst 1 1/16 ⊡:48⅕ 1:13⅘ 1:46⅘ ⒻClm 20000 5 1 15 14 110 116 Cauthen S5 b 113 *.90 84-18 Indian Bend 11316 Polara1093½FourthDimension1092½ Easy score 7
26Jan77- 4Aqu gd 6f ⊡:22⅘ :47 1:13 ⒻClm 22500 4 3 2hd 1hd 21 44½ Gonzalez B5 b 109 9.50 80-17 Telly's Aunt 1161½ Lace Pillow 1112½Model'sSeat113nk Weakened 7
12Jan77- 2Aqu fst 6f ⊡:22⅘ :46⅗ 1:12 ⒻClm 20000 4 5 2½ 23 25 25 Gonzalez B5 b 113 *1.70 84-13 Model's Seat 1115 Indian Bend 1133¼ Johnna Mae 116hd 2nd best 7
4Jan77- 7Aqu fst 6f ⊡:22⅘ :47⅕ 1:12⅖ ⒻClm 30000 8 4 1hd 21 68½ 712 Gonzalez B5 b 116 5.90 75-18 Breach Of Faith 116nkWincomaLass1162½LittleCannes118no Tired 8
17Dec76- 4Aqu fst 6f ⊡:22⅘ :46⅘ 1:13 ⒻMd 27500 2 3 12 13 14 12¾ Gonzalez B5 b 112 *.80 — — Indian Bend 1122¾PassageWay1191¼WordToTheWise1196 Driving 7
27Oct76- 4Aqu fst 6f :22⅘ :46⅖ 1:11 ⒻMd Sp Wt 5 1 2½ 31½ 34 811 Amy J 119 5.70 77-18 Fashion Ruler 1195¼ Kennelot 1191¼ Clover Bloom 119¾ Tired 10
20Oct76- 6Bel fst 6f :22⅘ :46 1:11⅕ ⒻMd Sp Wt 4 2 1½ 32 31½ 52¾ Amy J 119 45.60 83-12 Straight Street 119hd Road Princess1192½DearColleen119hd Tired 11
LATEST WORKOUTS ●Feb 17 Bel tr.t 5f fst 1:04 b Feb 11 Bel tr.t 5f fst 1:02⅖ b Dec 31 Bel tr.t 4f fst :49 hg Dec 25 Bel tr.t 4f fst :51 b

Home by Sunset B. f. 3, by The Axe II—Home by Dark, by Hill Prince
Br.—Mangurian H T Jr (Ky)
Tr.—Root Thomas F Jr
Own.—Mangurian H T Jr
112

	St.	1st	2nd	3rd	Amt.
1977	5	M	0	1	$1,920
1976	5	M	1	0	$2,200

16Feb77- 4Aqu fst 6f ⊡:23⅖ :48⅖ 1:13⅖ ⒻMd Sp Wt 4 7 79 77½ 64 54¾ Velasquez J b 121 15.90 77-10 Old Hag 116½ Dream O' Loot 116nk Milina 1212 Wide 7
9Feb77- 1Aqu fst 6f ⊡:23⅕ :47⅕ 1:13 3↑ⒻMd Sp Wt 1 4 65 52¼ 42 44¾ Velasquez J b 114 4.10e 79-16 One Sum 1142½ Snared 1142 Dream O' Loot 115nk No rally 8
27Jan77- 4Aqu gd 170 ⊡:49⅗ 1:15 1:46⅗ ⒻMd Sp Wt 1 5 46½ 34 51¼ 52¾ Vasquez J b 121 3.10 70-16 Variety Show 121nk Milina 116¾ Dream O' Loot 116nk Tired 6
13Jan77- 4Aqu fst 6f ⊡:22⅗ :46⅖ 1:11⅗ ⒻMd Sp Wt 3 8 1013 912 57 57¼ Vasquez J b 121 2.50e 84-10 Equal Honor 1162 East of Paris 121nk Old Hag 1211 No mishap 10
5Jan77- 4Aqu fst 6f ⊡:23⅕ :47⅘ 1:13⅕ ⒻMd Sp Wt 5 2 58 47½ 43½ 33½ Vasquez J b 121 4.00 79-14 Mary Bryant 1211½ Passage Way 1212HomebySunset1212½ Rallied 11
23Dec76- 3Aqu fst 6f ⊡:22⅖ :46⅘ 1:12⅗ ⒻMd Sp Wt 2 10 1013 108¾ 66½ 25 Vasquez J b 119 31.10 — — Casquette1145HomebySunset119¾PrincessRaindrop119½ Steadied 11
15Dec76- 5Aqu fst 6f ⊡:22⅘ :46⅘ 1:12⅗ ⒻMd Sp Wt 4 10 912 912 613 67¾ Vasquez J b 119 38.10 — — Done Good 119no Road Princess 1193 Box Supper1191½ No factor 11
7Dec76- 6Aqu sly 6f :22⅖ :47⅕ 1:13⅗ ⒻMd Sp Wt 4 8 78 34½ 79½ 78¾ Vasquez J b 119 12.10 66-22 Your Nuts 119½ Box Supper 1191 Dorriea 119nk Bid, tired 12
29Nov76- 4Aqu sly 6f :22⅘ :46⅗ 1:12⅕ ⒻMd Sp Wt 4 2 51½ 53½ 67 67 Velasquez J 119 5.40 75-19 Impartiality 1192¼ Miz Lizann 119½ Outward Sunshine 1192 Tired 8
19Nov76- 6Aqu fst 6f :22⅖ :45⅖ 1:10⅗ ⒻMd Sp Wt 2 10 78¾ 513 922 1022 Cruguet J 119 *2.00 68-14 VoddiDotti1199¾Distinctv'sGrl114¾OutwrdSunshn1191¼ Off slowly 10
LATEST WORKOUTS Jan 23 Bel tr.t 5f fst 1:05 b

Jacinto Rose Dk. b. or br. f. 3, by Jacinto—Sun Rose II, by Mossborough
Br.—Casse N E (Fla)
Tr.—Sazer David
Own.—Schuetz J L
112

	St.	1st	2nd	3rd	Amt.
1977	2	0	0	2	$3,480
1976	10	1	1	3	$11,050

5Feb77- 7Aqu fst 170 ⊡:48⅖ 1:14⅖ 1:45⅗ ⒻAllowance 3 1 1½ 1hd 21 33 Graell A b 114 3.40 75-13 SomedayQueen1091¼EastofParis1141¾JcintoRose114nk Weakened 6
11Jan77- 4Aqu gd 6f ⊡:22⅗ :46⅕ 1:12⅕ ⒻClm 35000 2 6 55¼ 55 55¼ 34½ Graell A b 116 11.30 83-21 Clever Miss 1111½ Wincoma Lass 1123 Jacinto Rose 116½ Evenly 6
22Dec76- 7Aqu fst 6f ⊡:22⅕ :45⅘ 1:11⅕ ⒻAllowance 2 10 75¾ 84¾ 1115 1113 Graell A b 114 28.20 — — When And If 1143½ Maria's Baby 114no Fashion Ruler 114½ Tired 12
10Nov76- 7Aqu fst 7f :22⅗ :45⅘ 1:25⅗ ⒻAllowance 7 4 45½ 43½ 51¾ 66¾ Vasquez J 114 25.90 66-23 Brookward 114¾SplendidSize1141¾Mariner'sMate1141¾ No mishap 10
22Oct76- 4Bel fst 7f :23⅗ :47⅖ 1:25⅗ ⒻAllowance 7 4 52¾ 64¼ 68 58¾ Cordero A Jr 114 3.40 65-21 YourPlaceorMine1123½TumbleAlong1143½LittleCannes1141¼ Tired 7
13Oct76- 6Bel fst 6f :22⅗ :46⅕ 1:11⅗ ⒻAllowance 1 6 64 43 32½ 33¾ Cordero A Jr 112 5.40 80-16 Penny Catcher 1123 Little Cannes 112¾ JacintoRose1121¼ Rallied 7
22Sep76- 7Bel fst 7f :23⅗ :47⅖ 1:24⅗ ⒻAllowance 6 2 33 31 47½ 411 Turcotte R 114 6.30 68-17 Pearl Handle 119hdSplendidSize1196EasternRuler1194½ Weakened 8
14Sep76- 3Bel fst 6f :23⅕ :46⅗ 1:11 ⒻMd 45000 2 2 2hd 11 11½ 12 Cordero A Jr 119 *2.10 87-11 Jacinto Rose 1192 Done Good 119¾ Disturber 1082¾ Driving 8
24Aug76- 1Sar fst 6f :22⅖ :46⅕ 1:12 ⒻMd 50000 2 7 31 45 48 411 Cordero A Jr 119 2.90 69-16 ⒹSplendidSize1172½DlphicOrcl115nkRomnGroundr1198 Stumbled 8
24Aug76-Placed third through disqualification
16Aug76- 1Sar fst 6f :22⅕ :46 1:12⅕ ⒻMd 40000 8 2 11½ 2½ 2½ 21¼ Vasquez J 119 6.50 78-18 Go BackLand1191¼JacintoRose1192¾WantonWoman119nk Gamely 8
LATEST WORKOUTS Feb 17 Aqu ⊡ 4f fst :49⅗ b Feb 12 Aqu ⊡ 7f fst 1:28 h ●Feb 3 Aqu ⊡ 5f fst 1:01⅗ h ●Jan 26 Aqu ⊡ 5f gd 1:04 b

Once again, we have included all the pertinent information about each horse in one table.

Horse	POST POSITION	WINS LAST TEN	JOCKEY	AVERAGE EARNINGS	BY RANK	SPEED FIGURES	BY RANK	RATING
Road Princess	1	1	1	$6697	2	107 102	2	2741
Sweet Alliance	2	4	2	$9773	1	95 97	5	3225

Horse	Post Position	Wins Last Ten	Jockey	Average Earnings	By Rank	Speed Figures	By Rank	Rating
Someday Queen	3	2	3	$1692	5	95 101	4	3899
Meteor Dancer	4	0	1	$2653	4	101 104	3	3314
Maria's Baby	5	3	1	$4430	3	103 107	1	3020
Home By Sunset	6	0	1	$412	5	90 87	5	3797
Jacinto Rose	7	1	1	$1211	5	92 103	5	3860

Note: *All sprint speed figures have been increased by 50 percent away from 100 for comparison with route figures.*

The bettors at Aqueduct thought the Ruthless to be a two-filly race between Road Princess and Sweet Alliance. According to our figures, Road Princess was the clear choice. She won, catching the pacesetting Sweet Alliance in the final eighth, and paid $5.20.

EIGHTH RACE
Aqueduct
FEBRUARY 19, 1977

1 $\frac{1}{16}$ MILES.(INNER DIRT). (1.43$\frac{3}{5}$) 4th Running THE RUTHLESS. $50,000 added. Fillies, 3-year-olds. Weight, 121 lbs. By subscription of $100 each, which shall accompany the nomination; $250 to start, with $50,000 added. The added money and all fees to be divided 60% to the winner, 22% to second, 12% to third and 6% to fourth. Non-winners of two races of $25,000 at a mile or over in 1976-77 allowed 3 lbs. Of a race of $15,000 at a mile or over in 1976-77, 6 lbs. Of a race of $35,000 at any distance in 1976-77, 9 lbs. Starters to be named at the closing time of entries. Trophies will be presented to the winning owner, trainer and jockey. Closed with 19 nominations Saturday, February 5, 1977.

Value of race $53,650, value to winner $32,190, second $11,803, third $6,438, fourth $3,219. Mutuel pool $426,995, OTB pool $242,487.

Last Raced	Horse	Eqt.	A.	Wt	PP	St	¼	½	¾	Str	Fin	Jockey	Odds $1
2Feb77 ^{8}Aqu^{1}	Road Princess		3	118	1	1	3^{1}	$3^{1\frac{1}{2}}$	2^{hd}	2^{hd}	$1^{1\frac{1}{4}}$	Velasquez J	1.60
12Feb77 ^{8}GS^{1}	Sweet Alliance	b	3	118	2	2	1^{hd}	$1^{\frac{1}{2}}$	$1^{\frac{1}{2}}$	3^{2}	$2^{\frac{1}{2}}$	McCarron C J	1.70
2Feb77 ^{8}Aqu^{4}	Maria's Baby	b	3	112	5	3	2^{2}	$2^{1\frac{1}{2}}$	3^{2}	1^{hd}	$3^{1\frac{3}{4}}$	Cauthen S	3.70
2Feb77 ^{8}Aqu^{2}	Meteor Dancer		3	114	4	5	6^{4}	4^{hd}	4^{6}	4^{10}	$4^{7\frac{3}{4}}$	Turcotte R	4.70
5Feb77 ^{7}Aqu^{1}	Someday Queen	b	3	112	3	4	4^{1}	$6^{\frac{1}{2}}$	7	5^{3}	5^{7}	Venezia M	32.70
16Feb77 ^{4}Aqu^{5}	Home by Sunset	b	3	114	6	6	7	7	5^{2}	6^{6}	$6^{7\frac{1}{2}}$	Santiago A	71.50
5Feb77 ^{7}Aqu^{3}	Jacinto Rose	b	3	112	7	7	5^{hd}	5^{3}	$6^{\frac{1}{2}}$	7	7	Graell A	35.40

OFF AT 4:15, EST. Start good, Won driving. Time, :23$\frac{1}{5}$, :47$\frac{4}{5}$, 1:12$\frac{4}{5}$, 1:38$\frac{4}{5}$, 1:45$\frac{2}{5}$ Track fast.

Our route formula performs almost as well as its sprint counterpart—not quite as many winners, but the same net profit. Here are the results for 300 routes:

NH	NW	NP	NS	WPCT	MPCT	$NET	I.V.
300	77*	62	42	25.7%	60.0%	$2.16	2.07

○ CREATING AN ODDS LINE ○

What do these multiple regression ratings mean in terms of a horse's chances of winning? Can they be used to create an odds line for a race?

A regression analysis of the results of 646 sprint races and 300 route races produced formulas that predict a horse's chances of winning as a function of its regression rating.

For sprints, use the formula

$$PCT = 1.54 - .07 \times RATING + .0008 \times RATING \times RATING.$$

And for routes, the formula:

$$PCT = 1.46 - .06 \times RATING + .0006 \times RATING \times RATING.$$

Here, PCT represents the horse's probability of winning—that is, its expected winning percentage. And the RATING used is the multiple regression rating divided by 100.

For example, if a horse entered in a sprint had a multiple regression rating of 3000, its probability of winning would be

$$1.54 - .07 \times 30.0 + .0008 \times 30.0 \times 30.0 = .16.$$

That is, such a horse has a 16 percent chance of winning.

In other words, horses with multiple regression ratings of approximately 3000 won approximately 16 percent of the time over our 646 race sprint sample.

Since a horse's chances of winning must be viewed in light of the chances of each of its opponents, these probabilities are only the first step in determining a horse's likelihood of winning. Individual probabilities must be added to determine the total for the race. And then each horse's probability must be divided by this total to determine the horse's true probability of winning.

Once a horse's true probability of winning is known, its fair odds (0 percent pari-mutuel take) can be calculated from the formula

$$\text{ODDS} = \frac{1.0}{\text{PROB}} - 1.0.$$

The table below shows these calculations for the Sky Treaty race. The RATING column contains the horses' multiple regression ratings divided by 100, the PCT column the horses' expected winning percentages (according to the formula above), the PROB column the horses' probabilities of winning (calculated as described above), and the ODDS column the horses' fair odds assuming 0 percent takeout.

Horse	Rating	PCT	Prob	Odds
Fortune	29.11	.180	.105	8.50 − 1
Enough	38.05	.035	.020	48.00 − 1
Sky Treaty	23.54	.336	.196	4.10 − 1
Court Reporter	28.34	.199	.116	7.60 − 1
Coronation Day	30.36	.152	.089	10.20 − 1
Awayfromitall	35.77	.060	.035	27.60 − 1
Magallanes	24.47	.306	.179	4.60 − 1
Amberdias	30.19	.156	.091	10.00 − 1
Ad Alley	27.07	.231	.135	6.40 − 1
Forest Stream	35.83	.059	.034	28.00 − 1
		1.714	1.000	

Here, in more detail, is how Sky Treaty's $4.10 to $1 odds were calculated. First, his multiple regression rating of 2354 was divided by 100, giving 23.54. Then his PCT was calculated according to the formula:

$$\text{PCT} = 1.54 - .07 \times 23.54 + .0008 \times 23.54 \times 23.54 = .336.$$

Sky Treaty's PCT was then divided by 1.714, the total PCT for the field, to determine that his true probability of winning was .196, or 19.6 percent. His odds were then calculated according to the formula

$$\text{ODDS} = \frac{1.0}{.196} - 1.0 = 4.10 \text{ to } 1.$$

The odds-line calculations for the Ruthless Stakes are contained in the table below:

Horse	Rating	PCT	Prob	Odds
Road Princess	27.41	.266	.310	2.20 — 1
Sweet Alliance	32.25	.149	.173	4.80 — 1
Someday Queen	38.99	.033	.038	25.30 — 1
Meteor Dancer	33.14	.131	.153	5.50 — 1
Maria's Baby	30.20	.195	.227	3.40 — 1
Home By Sunset	37.97	.047	.055	17.20 — 1
Jacinto Rose	38.60	.038	.044	21.70 — 1
		.859	1.000	

The selections in both of these races were underlays—both Sky Treaty and Road Princess went off at odds lower than their estimated fair odds.

Our statistics indicate, however, that almost one half of all multiple regression selections are betting overlays, starting at odds higher than their estimated fair odds. The statistics also reveal that these overlays are by far the better betting propositions. Here, first, is how the overlays in our sample of 646 sprints and 300 routes performed:

	NH	NW	WPCT	$NET	I.V.
Sprints	291	55	18.9%	$2.36	1.70
Routes	156	26	16.7%	$2.24	1.34
Totals	447	81	18.1%	$2.32	1.57

And then, the underlays:

	NH	NW	WPCT	$NET	I.V.
Sprints	355	131	36.9%	$1.99	3.31
Routes	144	51	35.4%	$2.07	2.86
Totals	499	182	36.5%	$2.02	3.17

Of course, the underlays win far more frequently than the overlays. But the underlays are far more heavily bet than are the overlays, and consequently should win more often. The important fact is that the overlays win far more often than their actual odds suggest they should, actually more in accordance with their estimated odds. That is what makes them such good bets.

And that is why it is desirable to create an accurate odds line—so that potential overlays can be identified.

○ **CONCLUSION** ○

What are the advantages and disadvantages of the multiple regression approach? Obviously, any system that turns an 8 percent profit playing every race is preferable to one that yields the same percentage but plays fewer races. But then, not every race should be played. Not every race is playable. Nevertheless, the multiple regression formula will make its selection, and it will win its share of these "unplayable" races.

Needless to say, these formulas demand a considerable amount of handicapping time. But, in an age of the 48-hour entry rule and advance editions of the *Daily Racing Form*, the serious handicapper finds more time to dope out the next day's races. And, with the electronic calculator becoming a familiar household item, the drudgery of the arithmetic can be eliminated.

MONEY
MANAGEMENT

A computer technique called "simulation" can be used to determine how to get the most out of a winning system. The computer must be given an imaginary bankroll plus two important facts about the system: the expected winning percentage and the expected rate of profit, based on previous flat-betting results.

Given this information, the computer can answer the following two questions:

1. How much should be bet on each horse? That is, what percentage of bankroll should be risked on any one bet? Of course, the larger the bet, the greater the potential profits, and the higher the risk of ruination.

2. Is a flat-bet scheme (all bets in the same amount, regardless of the size of the bankroll) preferable to progressive betting, in which a certain percentage of the bankroll is bet on each race (and consequently, the bets enlarge as the bankroll grows)?

Before proceeding any further, a few words are in order about progressive betting formulas. There are a few such money-management systems on the market. Most of them are totally fraudulent. They may look good on paper, but they are not sound. Their success is usually based on one key high-priced winner occurring at just the right time in the sequence. The following trivial example provides a good example of this type of deception.

The betting scheme works as follows: Bet $2 on the first horse. After each loss, add $2 to the bet. After a win, begin again with a $2 bet.

Imagine a ten-race card on which you pick one winner, that paying $20.00. With flat $2 bets, you break even for the day. But suppose that winner had come in the last race of the day, and you had used the betting scheme described above. Here is how your day would have gone:

Race 1:	bet	$2	lose	minus	$2
Race 2:	bet	$4	lose	minus	$6
Race 3:	bet	$6	lose	minus	$12
Race 4:	bet	$8	lose	minus	$20
Race 5:	bet	$10	lose	minus	$30
Race 6:	bet	$12	lose	minus	$42
Race 7:	bet	$14	lose	minus	$56
Race 8:	bet	$16	lose	minus	$72
Race 9:	bet	$18	lose	minus	$90
Race 10:	bet	$20	win	plus	$90

That $20 bet in the tenth race was made on a 9-1 shot that won, resulting in a $180 profit for that race, and a total profit of $90 for the day. Makes the betting system look ingenious.

But if that one winner had come in the first race instead, look at how the day would have turned out:

Race 1:	bet	$2	win	plus	$18
Race 2:	bet	$2	lose	plus	$16
Race 3:	bet	$4	lose	plus	$12
Race 4:	bet	$6	lose	plus	$6
Race 5:	bet	$8	lose	minus	$2
Race 6:	bet	$10	lose	minus	$12
Race 7:	bet	$12	lose	minus	$24
Race 8:	bet	$14	lose	minus	$38
Race 9:	bet	$16	lose	minus	$54
Race 10:	bet	$18	lose	minus	$72

So much for "ingenious" betting schemes.

The computer can be programmed to avoid such problems, to give a completely fair picture of how well a particular money-management system works.

Our computer simulation procedure consists of 100 experiments of 1,000 bets each—certainly a large enough number of bets to determine how well the money-management system being tested works.

As mentioned earlier, the computer knows how frequently the

betting system is supposed to produce winners. The simulation process assumes (or "simulates") that percentage. The betting system may have hot streaks and cold spells during the process, but in the long run, it will tally about as many winners as expected.

The computer also was told what the betting system's average winner pays, and it assumes that every winner pays exactly that much. This circumvents the problem of one big winner popping up at the wrong time and distorting the final results.

Now, let us see what happened when our multiple regression sprint system was subjected to this computer simulation experiment. Recall that this system produced an 8 percent profit together with a winning percentage of 28.8. Its average winner returned $7.50.

○ FLAT BETS ○

Here are the results of a flat-betting simulation in which the size of the bets ranged from (a flat) $10 (1 percent of the original $1,000 bankroll) up to $100 (10 percent):

Bet	NW	NL	Tapouts	Average	Median	Maximum	Average Profit
$10	96	4	0	$1802	$1763	$3000	8.0%
$20	96	4	2	$2599	$2525	$5000	8.0%
$30	86	14	12	$3142	$3231	$7000	7.1%
$40	81	19	18	$3721	$3750	$9000	6.8%
$50	76	24	24	$4248	$4438	$10966	6.5%
$60	71	29	29	$4655	$4900	$10975	6.1%
$70	61	39	39	$4703	$5288	$12638	5.3%
$80	53	47	47	$4629	$3050	$14300	4.5%
$90	49	51	51	$4799	$0	$15963	4.2%
$100	45	55	55	$4886	$0	$17625	3.9%

Here is an explanation of the column headings:

BET: the amount bet per race.

NW: the number of 1,000-bet runs that produced a profit.

NL: the number of 1,000-bet runs that produced a loss.

TAPOUTS: the number of times the 1,000-bet procedure succeeded in wiping out the entire $1,000 bankroll.

AVERAGE: the average number of dollars in the final bankroll, after 1,000 bets.

MEDIAN: if the bankrolls for the 100 different runs of 1,000 bets each were arranged in increasing order, the median bankroll is the one in the middle.

MAXIMUM: the largest bankroll produced in the 100 runs.

AVERAGE PROFIT: divide the gross profit on the 1,000 bets by the total amount of money bet (1,000 times the average bet), then average over the 100 runs.

Before you can evaluate the results of this experiment, you must decide what is more important to you: the percentage of profit, the size of the final bankroll, or the risk of losing the original bankroll. Here are a few observations that may help you decide.

The system produces its expected 8 percent profit only when the bets are kept low—either $10 or $20 (1 or 2 percent of the bankroll). Larger bets sharply increase the chances of ruination, and this reduces the average profit. But larger bets also increase the chances of making a significant profit.

When the bets are high ($80 to $100, or 8 to 10 percent of the bankroll), the chances of tapping out are about the same as the chances of showing a profit. But the profits, if realized, are much higher than they would be had the bets been kept smaller. The average bankrolls on the last three lines of the table do not reflect this, because the profitable runs have been averaged with the tap-out runs. To get a better idea of the potential profits, double the average that appears on these lines.

It seems fair to say that if you bet $80 to $100 (8 to 10 percent) per race on this system, you stand a 50-50 chance of increasing your original $1,000 bankroll to $10,000. And a 50-50 chance of losing it completely. That is 9-1 odds on an even-money proposition.

○ PROGRESSIVE BETS ○

If you were to bet a certain percentage of your bankroll rather than a fixed amount of money on each race, you can imagine what might happen. With a successful system, the size of your bets would increase in proportion to the growing bankroll. This means larger potential profits than in flat betting, with greater risk of tapping out.

Here are the results of a progressive betting simulation in which the size of the bet was allowed to range from 1 percent up to 5 percent of the current bankroll. (Anything higher than 5 percent resulted in disaster with this particular betting system—our multiple regression sprint system.)

%	NW	NL	Tapouts	Average	Median	Maximum
1%	95	5	0	$2184	$1923	$6448
2%	91	9	2	$4495	$3075	$31,903
3%	77	23	16	$7970	$2899	$122,338
4%	70	30	26	$13,738	$2665	$367,150
5%	55	45	41	$20,105	$1195	$867,596

Once again, small bets proved safest. Bets of 1 or 2 percent produced more than 90 winning runs in the 100-run experiment.

But with bets of "just" 5 percent, the bettor stands a better than 50-50 chance of turning $1,000 into approximately $40,000. In fact, during one of the 100 runs of 1,000 bets, the system got so hot that the original $1,000 bankroll grew to an incredible $867,596.

○ WHAT PERCENTAGE SHOULD BE BET? ○

The multiple regression sprint system was not the only one tested in this manner. In fact, the computer tested theoretical systems that produced varying percentages of winners in combination with differing percentages of profit. The table below gives the percentage of one's bankroll that might safely be bet to guarantee at least a 90 percent chance of coming out ahead after making 1000 bets under a progressive-betting plan.

Percentage Profit For System

WPCT	10%	15%	20%	25%
10%	x	x	1%	1%
15%	x	1%	2%	2%
20%	1%	2%	2%	3%
25%	2%	3%	4%	4%
30%	2%	4%	5%	6%

Obviously, certain systems are not worth considering, even though they may produce a profit on paper. Any system expected to produce approximately 10 percent winners that does not promise more than a 15 percent profit leaves its followers open to a serious risk of tapping out, even if they bet just 1 percent of their bankroll per race. The same can be said for any system expected to produce approximately 15 percent winners if its expected profit rate does not exceed 10 percent.

On the other hand, a system expected to produce a higher percentage of winners together with a greater rate of profit allows the player to bet a larger percentage of his bankroll per race, with little chance of tapping out after 1,000 bets. Of course, the more that can be bet safely, the higher the expected profits will be.

We have seen that flat-betting systems are safer, although less rewarding over the long run, than are progressive-betting systems. The following table is the flat-bet counterpart of the table above.

	Percentage Profit For System			
WPCT	10%	15%	20%	25%
10%	x	x	1%	1%
15%	x	1%	2%	2%
20%	1%	2%	3%	3%
25%	2%	4%	4%	6%
30%	3%	5%	6%	8%

So, with a system expected to produce 30 percent winners together with a 25 percent rate of profit, flat bets of up to 8 percent of the player's original bankroll can be made with little risk of tapping out. Using a progressive betting scheme with the same selections, the player could safely bet only 6 percent of his bankroll.

○ CONCLUSION ○

For the player willing to follow religiously the selections of a good system, the discussion above should prove helpful. But for those of us who prefer to "wing it," to make our own selections after careful scrutiny of the past performances, a different manner of betting is more appealing. And that simply is to bet more on the horses we like best—make the big bets on the horses we really like, and small "fun" bets on the other races.

This leaves one serious problem concerning the "serious" bets—is the horse worth its price? Are the odds commensurate with the horse's chances of winning?

The answer to this question is probably an individual matter. Each of us must learn, through experience, how to place a price on a horse's head, and how "not to bet" when we fail to get that price.

A horse's chances of winning depend on a number of things in combination, not the least of which are its opponents' chances of winning. That is why the multiple regression formulas are so attractive. They carefully balance the various aspects of a horse's past performances, and allow the handicapper to compare the different horses in a race—to create an odds line, if desired.

But multiple regression odds lines tend to be conservative. Better than 50% of all regression selections will be underlays. And very few horses will be rated as "worth a bet" when their toteboard odds are below 2-1. This is the computer's way of telling us that very few horses are worth low odds.

Racing is a game of percentages, and not many horses are capable of winning even one of every three races. Especially with claiming horses, it would seem wise to demand odds of at least 2-1 before making a bet.

The table below shows how the systems discussed in Chapter 24 performed when restricted to horses whose odds were below 2-1 (systems appear in the order presented in Chapter 24):

	NH	NW	WPCT	$NET
System #1 (A)	65	29	44.6%	$1.94
System #1 (B)	40	19	47.5%	$2.16
System #1 (C)	35	17	48.6%	$2.16
System #1 (D)	23	13	56.5%	$2.28
System #2	169	64	37.9%	$1.77
System #3 (A)	54	20	37.0%	$1.67
System #3 (B)	47	18	38.3%	$1.83
System #4	27	15	55.6%	$2.61
System #5	88	37	42.0%	$1.92
System #6	59	31	52.5%	$2.32

With the exception of System #6, all of these systems prove better betting tools when restricted to horses sent to the post at odds of 2-1 or higher.

Surprisingly, the two multiple regression systems of Chapter 25 produced their 8 percent profit regardless of whether or not their selections ran at odds of 2-1 or higher.

Appendix A
THE
ODDS

This appendix is written for the mathematically inclined reader who would like more detail about odds and how and why they can be used to calculate the expected number of winners in a sample of horses.

We begin by explaining how racetracks calculate the odds that flash on the toteboard. As you probably know, these odds are determined by the percentage of the total pari-mutuel pool bet on each horse.

By way of example, suppose that $100,000 has been bet on a race, $25,000 of which has been bet on a horse named Lower The Take. So 25 percent of the pool has been bet on this horse, making Lower The Take a natural 3-1 shot. But no racetrack in this country will pay at odds anywhere near 3-1.

The reason is the "take." A certain percentage of the pari-mutuel pool is deducted in the form of a pari-mutuel tax, which is divided among the state, the track, and the horsemen. In New York, 17 percent is deducted for this purpose; in other states, this tax ranges from as low as 14 percent to as high as 20 percent. On some forms of exotic wagering (exactas, triples) the tax may be as high as 25 percent.

In our example, $17,000 (17 percent of $100,000) in tax money is taken off the top of the pari-mutuel pool, leaving only $83,000 for redistribution among the supporters of the winning horse. But some of this $83,000 already belongs to these people. If Lower The Take were to win, $25,000 (the amount bet on the horse) must be subtracted from the $83,000, leaving only $58,000 in profits for the backers of Lower The Take.

The odds are then calculated as the ratio of this profit—the money contributed by the losing bettors—to the amount of money bet on the winning horse. Should Lower The Take win, this ratio would be $58,000/$25,000 = 2.32, which means the odds on Lower The Take should be 2.32-1.

At this stage of the game, the winning bettor is hit with another tax—breakage. Most American tracks use what is called dime breakage, meaning that all odds are rounded down to the nearest dime. So odds of 2.32 to the dollar are reduced to 2.30 to the dollar. The payoff on Lower The Take will be $6.60—the original $2 bet plus a profit of $2.30 for each dollar bet.

Dime breakage accounts for an average of about 1 percent of the pari-mutuel win pool, and almost $1\frac{1}{2}$ percent of the place and show pools. Together with the 17 percent pari-mutuel tax, this means that the racetrack audience loses more than 18 percent of every dollar it bets. A $2 win ticket suffers instantaneous depreciation once it is purchased —it is worth approximately $1.64 before the race is run. That's the price for playing the game.

Let us now derive a more general formula for calculating a horse's odds. Suppose that the pari-mutuel win pool contains N dollars, of which M dollars were bet on a particular horse. Therefore, M/N percent of the pool has been bet on this horse. We will call this percentage PCT.

After a 17 percent pari-mutuel tax has been deducted, the pool contains $.83 \times N$ dollars, leaving $.83 \times N - M$ dollars profit for the backers of the given horse, should it win. The ratio of profit to amount bet is

$$\frac{.83 \times N - M}{M} = .83 \times (N/M) - (M/M) = .83/PCT - 1.$$

or odds of $.83/PCT - 1$ to the dollar. In other words, the formula for the odds, prior to breakage, is

$$ODDS = .83/PCT - 1.$$

Consequently, if 25 percent of the betting is on a particular horse, as in our example, the odds on that horse will be

$$ODDS = .83/.25 - 1 = 2.32,$$

or $2.30 to $1, after breakage.

If 40 percent of the betting is on a particular horse, the track will pay at odds of

$$\text{ODDS} = .83/.40 - 1 = 1.08,$$

which, because of breakage, reduces to 1.00, even money.

The natural even-money horse, one that has cornered half the pari-mutuel pool, will be sent off at odds of

$$\text{ODDS} = .83/.50 - 1 = 0.66,$$

which, after breakage, reduces to 60 cents on the dollar, 3-5 on the odds board.

You can see from these examples how the pari-mutuel tax has stacked the odds against the bettor.

The formula for the odds can be solved instead for PCT:

$$\text{PCT} = \frac{.83}{\text{ODDS} + 1}.$$

Since this formula fails to take breakage into account, we prefer to use instead the formula

$$\text{PCT} = \frac{.83}{\text{ODDS} + 1.05}$$

which does. (This formula adds a nickel to the odds to counter the average amount lost from the odds because of dime breakage.)

If the odds are indeed a true reflection of the horse's chances of winning, this formula can be used to determine exactly what that chance is. For example, corresponding to odds of 4-1, we have

$$\text{PCT} = \frac{.83}{4.00 + 1.05} = .164.$$

This means that 4-1 shots should win approximately 16.4 percent of their races. Looking at it another way, in a large sample of 4-1 shots, approximately 16.4 percent should be winners.

We are now in a position to determine if a horse's odds really are a true reflection of its chances of winning. Table 1 on page 296 contains the results of a study of the odds of every horse that started during an entire New York racing season (1971). Each line of the table studies all horses that started at the odds listed, or at odds higher than the listed odds, but lower than the odds listed on the following line.

For example, the 4-1 line refers to all horses whose odds were $4.00, $4.10, $4.20, $4.30, or $4.40 to the dollar.

If our hypothesis concerning the odds is true, we could use the formula above to determine the expected number of winners for each line. We have done this, multiplying the number of starters by the corresponding PCT for each odds value possible on the line, then adding to determine the expected number of winners for the line.

Table 1

Odds	NH	NW	WPCT	EW
1-5	15	13*	86.7%	9.7
2-5	8	6	75.0%	4.7
1-2	18	12	66.7%	9.9
3-5	86	43	50.0%	42.5
4-5	132	59	44.7%	58.7
Even	188	88*	46.8%	75.1
6-5	234	88	37.6%	85.3
7-5	111	43	38.7%	37.9
3-2	104	32	30.8%	34.1
8-5	235	72	30.6%	72.8
9-5	237	75	31.7%	67.3
2-1	795	216	27.2%	204.4
5-2	765	193*	25.2%	170.5
3-1	821	137**	16.7%	161.0
7-2	759	126	16.6%	132.6
4-1	722	113	15.7%	114.2
9-2	604	73	12.1%	86.9
5-1	1147	149	13.0%	146.3
6-1	1058	138*	13.0%	116.6
7-1	964	93	9.7%	93.7
8-1	833	70	8.4%	72.5
9-1	715	49	6.9%	56.2
10-1	2530	146	5.8%	158.8
15-1	1567	69	4.4%	70.6
20-1	1850	52	2.8%	60.2
30-1	1614	34	2.1%	34.4
50-1	963	7	0.7%	11.8
	19075	2196		

Notice that in most cases the values NW and EW are quite close. But there are a few cases where the discrepancy appears large. For example, 193 5-2 shots won, but only 170.5 were expected to win. And only 137 3-1 shots won, well below the 161.0 that were expected to win. Notice that the actual number of winners more likely than not will exceed the expected number of winners towards the top of the table, while the opposite tends to be true towards the bottom of the table.

The differences we have just mentioned, and all the others you see in the table, are real. But are they solid evidence that horses in certain odds ranges win (significantly) more or less frequently than expected? Let us now discuss two statistical tests that can be used to answer this question.

First, we have subjected the entire table to the "chi-squared" test, to determine if the overall discrepancy between expected and actual numbers of winners is excessively large. This is done by adding the values

$$\frac{(NW - EW)^2}{EW}$$

for each line of the table. In our case, the sum was 24.9, which passed the chi-squared test. It was not large enough to cast doubt on the hypothesis that horses win in accordance with their odds.

Each line of the table was then subjected to the "standard normal" test to determine if there was a significant difference between the NW and EW on that line. This is done by evaluating

$$\frac{NW - EW}{\sqrt{EW\left(1 - \frac{EW}{NH}\right)}}$$

Usually—99 percent of the time—this number will be somewhere between $+2\frac{1}{2}$ and $-2\frac{1}{2}$. When it is not, we have found something unusual and significant—a group of horses that, by their very nature, win more (a value larger than $+2\frac{1}{2}$) or less (a value smaller than $-2\frac{1}{2}$) than expected, *and figure to continue doing so.*

We will indicate finding such a group of horses by an asterisk (*) or a double asterisk (**), as explained in the Introduction. Notice that we have found five such groups in our study of the odds. Two of these, the 5-2 and 3-1 categories, seem to compensate for each other. The other three are sufficiently isolated to suggest that there is no overall pattern of deviation present.

So it would seem a valid conclusion that horses win about as often as their odds suggest they should. This conclusion, in turn, justifies our method for calculating expected numbers of winners.

Thus far, we have applied this method only to the odds categories in Table 1. The horses in each odds category all had approximately the same odds. But what happens when we study a group of horses with more disparate odds? This will certainly be the case when we classify horses in terms of different handicapping characteristics. Each horse in such a sample will count as a fraction of an expected winner. For example, a 4-1 shot will count as .164 of an expected winner, since 16.4 percent (the percentage of 4-1 shots that should win) of 1 is .164. The expected number of winners for the sample will be the sum of these fractions, one for each horse in the sample.

Additional information from our odds study appears in Table 2 on this page. Each line in this table combines the corresponding line from Table 1 with all preceding lines. The information in this table is in cumulative form. For example, the 3-2 category includes all horses whose odds were 3-2 or less. And the 5-1 category includes all horses whose odds were 5-1 (actually 5.90-1) or less. For each category, we

Table 2

Odds	NW	EW	$NET	%H	%W	I.V.
1-5	13	9.7	$2.20	0.1%	0.6%	7.38
2-5	19*	14.4	$2.17	0.1%	0.9%	7.25
1-2	31*	24.3	$2.09	0.2%	1.4%	6.71
3-5	74	66.8	$1.79	0.7%	3.4%	5.03
4-5	133	125.5	$1.72	1.4%	6.1%	4.46
Even	221	200.6	$1.81	2.3%	10.1%	4.30
6-5	309	285.8	$1.77	3.6%	14.1%	3.94
7-5	352*	323.7	$1.78	4.2%	16.0%	3.86
3-2	384	357.8	$1.75	4.7%	17.5%	3.72
8-5	456	430.6	$1.72	5.9%	20.8%	3.50
9-5	531	498.9	$1.74	7.2%	24.2%	3.37
2-1	747*	703.3	$1.73	11.3%	34.0%	3.00
5-2	940*	873.9	$1.77	15.4%	42.8%	2.79
3-1	1077	1034.4	$1.69	19.7%	49.0%	2.50
7-2	1203	1167.0	$1.66	23.6%	54.8%	2.32
4-1	1316	1281.2	$1.66	27.4%	59.9%	2.19
9-2	1389	1368.1	$1.63	30.6%	63.3%	2.07
5-1	1538	1514.4	$1.63	36.6%	70.0%	1.91
6-1	1676	1631.0	$1.67	42.1%	76.3%	1.81
7-1	1769	1724.6	$1.67	47.2%	80.6%	1.71
8-1	1839	1797.2	$1.66	51.6%	83.7%	1.62
9-1	1888	1853.4	$1.64	55.3%	86.0%	1.55
10-1	2034	2012.2	$1.62	68.6%	92.6%	1.35
15-1	2103	2089.8	$1.61	76.8%	95.8%	1.25
20-1	2155	2143.0	$1.59	86.5%	98.1%	1.13
30-1	2189	2177.5	$1.59	95.0%	99.7%	1.05
50-1	2196	2189.0	$1.56	100.0%	100.0%	1.00

Note: *Seven dead-heats account for the fact that there were seven more actual than expected winners.*

have given the number of winners, the expected number of winners, the dollar net, and the impact value. In addition, we have indicated the percentage of the total number of starters that fell into each category (%H), and the percentage of the total number of winners that fell into each category (%W). Remember, the impact value is calculated by dividing the latter percentage by the former.

Notice that the cumulative number of winners always exceeds the cumulative expected number of winners. The difference starts out small at the top of the table, quickly builds up, reaches its peak with the addition of the 5-2 group, then gradually diminishes. Why? Simply because horses at low odds win more frequently than expected, and horses at high odds win less frequently than expected. The group of horses that were sent to the post at odds less than 3-1 won significantly more often than expected.

Had we presented this cumulative study of odds from higher odds to lower odds, you would have seen that the cumulative number of winners lagged behind all the way, with the peak occurring at the 10-1 category. The group of horses that were sent to the post at odds of 10-1 or higher won significantly less often than expected.

This seems to be a direct contradiction of the conclusion we reached above—namely, that horses win in accordance with their odds. There is room, however, for both conclusions.

The key to this seeming paradox is the size of the samples involved. The larger the size of a sample, the more solid the information contained therein. Differences or trends that appear in small samples may be canceled or reversed when a larger sample is obtained. Fortunately, statistical tests such as the ones we are using demand more from smaller samples before jumping to conclusions.

If you will look at Table 1 again, you will notice that in most of the lower odds categories, the actual number of winners slightly, although not significantly, exceeds the expected number of winners. But these small differences add up, so that when we consider the much larger sample of horses that started at odds less than 3-1, the difference between NW and EW has now grown to be statistically significant.

The impact value column presents a similar picture. Reading between the 9-2 and 5-1 lines, we see that approximately one third of the horses—those bet at 5-1 or lower—account for approximately two thirds of the winners. And only 14 percent of the winners were longshots—winning at odds of 10-1 or higher—although 45 percent of the starters were in this longshot category. This indeed makes picking longshot winners a very difficult business.

Longshot players may claim that, even though only a small percentage of their selections win, the size of the winning payoffs more than makes up for their infrequent visits to the cashiers' windows. The dollar net column of Table 2 refutes this claim.

Notice that the cumulative dollar net drops below the $2 break-even point rather quickly. Horses that ran at odds of 1-2 or lower returned a small profit of nine cents per $2 bet. But once the 3-5 shots were included, this profit was turned into a considerable loss. By the time the 5-2 shots had been added, the average payoff had dropped to $1.77—this for a group of horses that won significantly more often than expected.

And the average payoff continues to drop as the odds grow longer. This means that longshots are failing to match even the after-taxes average of $1.64. As a matter of fact, the group of horses that raced at odds of 10-1 or higher returned an average payoff of just $1.45. So it would seem that selecting a longshot winner is as difficult as finding a needle in a haystack, and not nearly as rewarding.

The $1.56 figure at the bottom of the $NET column may surprise you. It is the average payoff for all 19,075 horses in the study. Theoretically, this figure should be $1.64—$2 minus the effect of the pari-mutuel tax and breakage. If horses won exactly in accordance with their odds, the $1.64 figure would have been realized. But, as we have seen, there is a slight imbalance. A few more low-priced horses won, and a few less longshots won than expected, causing the average payoff to fall somewhat short of the $1.64 expected.

Appendix B
REGRESSION

A major objective of many statistical investigations is to establish relationships which make it possible to predict one variable in terms of others. Thus, studies are made to predict the average income of a college graduate in terms of the number of years he has been out of college, the potential sales of a new product in terms of its price and the amount of money spent advertising on television, the average performance of students starting college in terms of their I.Q.'s, their high school rankings, and their scores on a college entrance examination, and the overall performance of the stock market in terms of the performances of several key stocks.

And handicappers are interested in estimating the number of lengths a horse will lose because of a poor post position. Or in predicting the finish of a race in terms of how well the contenders shape up in several different handicapping categories.

Each of these studies would make use of a statistical technique called regression. Regardless of which of its many forms is used, the goal of regression is the same: to produce an equation that expresses one variable (the predicted variable) in terms of one or several others (the predictor variables).

The regression is termed "simple" if just one predictor variable is used. If, for example, we wished to predict "lengths behind at the first call" as a function of "post position," we would use one of the many forms of simple regression—linear regression, polynomial regression, or exponential regression, to mention just three.

Multiple regression, on the other hand, expresses the predicted variable as a function of several predictor variables. If we wished to predict a horse's finish position in terms of days away, speed points, number of wins last ten starts, earnings, and speed figures, we would use some form of multiple regression.

The regression equation is obtained after a detailed analysis of past data, usually carried out on a computer. Of course, the more data used, the better the resulting equation, both as a tool for predicting future results and as an accurate reflection of past history.

For example, if we wished to predict finish position in terms of the five factors listed above, we could feed the computer the results of (say) 500 races. We would tell the computer the finish position of each horse entered in these races, together with that horse's pre-race "scores" on each of the five factors. The regression analysis would then produce the appropriate regression equation.

What does the regression analysis do? Most of the calculations are concerned with determining the strengths of the relationships between the variables, and in particular between each individual predictor variable and the predicted variable. Relationships between variables are measured by numbers called correlations.

Do high scores on one variable tend to correspond to high (or low) scores on another variable? In particular, do high (or low) scores on a predictor variable tend to correspond to good finishes, while low (or high) scores are usually matched with poor finishes? Correlations are the numerical answers to questions like these, based on the information contained in the data.

Once the correlations have been calculated, they are used to determine the weights (coefficients) of the predictor variables in the final regression equation. Naturally, those variables more highly correlated with the predicted variable receive the higher weights.

The regression equation is an attempt at balancing the contributions of the different predictor variables. As such, it is sensitive to each individual data case. However, when a large number of data cases are used, unusual patterns in a few cases tend to be "averaged out," and the resulting equation reflects trends apparent in the data as a whole.

In addition to the regression equation itself, the regression analysis produces two numbers—the correlation coefficient and the standard error of the estimate—that indicate how well the regression equation explains the relationship between the predicted variable and the predictor variables.

These two numbers are especially useful in determining the set of predictor variables that does the best job. Starting with an especially productive variable, one that is highly correlated with the predicted variable, one could search for a second predictor variable by trying several possibilities in combination with the first variable. That variable which, in combination with the first variable, produced the highest correlation, or the lowest standard error, would be chosen as the second element of the predictor-variable set.

Several variables could then be tried in combination with the first two variables. The one which, in combination, produced the highest correlation, or the lowest standard error, would be chosen as the third predictor variable. This process would continue until the addition of further variables failed to significantly improve the standard error or the correlation. Once the set of predictor variables is complete, multiple regression can be used to produce the equation that best expresses the predicted variable as a function of the predictor variables.

The remainder of this appendix is written for the mathematically inclined reader who is interested in the arithmetic details of the regression procedure. To demonstrate how the regression process works, we present the details of one fully worked out example. For the sake of simplicity, our example uses linear regression, the simplest form of regression.

Suppose that we wish to find an equation that expresses beaten lengths as a function of post position at the $1\frac{1}{16}$-mile distance at Belmont Park. Linear regression would produce an equation of the form $y = a + bx$, where y, the predicted variable, represents beaten lengths, and x, the predictor variable, represents post position. The goal of the linear regression procedure is to determine the proper values for a and b.

For data, we use the results of the ninth race at Belmont on July 6, 1977. (Of course, a valid equation of this type would be based on the results of several hundred races, not just one race.)

NINTH RACE
Belmont
JULY 6, 1977

$1\frac{1}{16}$ MILES. (1.40⅘) CLAIMING. Purse $11,000. 3-year-olds and upward. Weights, 3-year-olds, 115 lbs. Older, 122 lbs. Non-winners of two races at a mile or over since June 15, allowed 3 lbs. Of such a race since then, 5 lbs. Claiming Price $25,000; for each $2,500 to $20,000, 2 lbs. (Races when entered to be claimed for $18,000 or less not considered.)

Value of race $11,000, value to winner $6,600, second $2,420, third $1,320, fourth $660. Mutuel pool $131,290, OTB pool $168,912. Triple Pool $149,220. OTB Triplė Pool $323,696.

Last Raced	Horse	Eqt.	A.	Wt	PP	St	¼	½	¾	Str	Fin	Jockey	Cl'g Pr	Odds $1
29Jun77 ^{6}Mth^{9}	Tropic Monkey	b	4	113	3	5	7^{4}	7^{6}	$5\frac{1}{2}$	$2\frac{1}{2}$	1no	Trosclair A J	20000	11.60
23Jun77 ^{7}Bel^{5}	Silver Bullet		4	117	5	3	4^{1}	6^{3}	$4^{1\frac{1}{2}}$	$1\frac{1}{2}$	$2^{1\frac{1}{2}}$	Gustines H	25000	2.40
25Jun77 ^{5}Bel^{8}	Company Commander	b	6	117	7	2	3^{hd}	$3\frac{1}{2}$	$3\frac{1}{2}$	5^{4}	$3\frac{1}{2}$	Cordero A Jr	25000	3.00
27Jun77 ^{5}Bel^{5}	Rastaterian		8	113	6	1	1^{1}	1^{3}	1^{hd}	3^{hd}	$4^{1\frac{1}{2}}$	Hernandez R	20000	12.80
27Jun77 ^{5}Bel^{4}	Buttonbuck	b	4	117	4	7	6^{4}	4^{1}	2^{1}	4^{hd}	5^{nk}	Maple E	25000	3.30
28Jun77 ^{9}Bel^{1}	Surf		5	114	8	4	8	8	8	6^{6}	6^{14}	Rosado O	20000	21.40
5Jun77 ^{5}Hol^{3}	Dance D'Espoir		5	117	2	8	5^{1}	$5\frac{1}{2}$	6^{2}	7^{2}	7^{nk}	Vasquez J	25000	6.30
13Jun77 ^{3}Bel^{1}	Good Beau	b	4	113	1	6	2^{2}	2^{hd}	$7^{1\frac{1}{2}}$	8	8	Gonzalez B	20000	9.50

OFF AT 5:30, EDT. Start good, Won driving. Time, :24, :47, 1:11⅘, 1:37, 1:43⅕ Track fast.

$2 Mutuel Prices:			
3-(E)-TROPIC MONKEY	25.20	8.40	3.80
5-(G)-SILVER BULLET		4.80	3.00
7-(I)-COMPANY COMMANDER			3.00

$2 TRIPLE 3-5-7 PAID $282.00.

dk b or br. c, by Tropical Breeze—Monkey Doodle, by Petare. Trainer DeBonis Robert. Bred by Stavola M J (NJ).

TROPIC MONKEY, void of early foot, loomed boldly from the extreme outside leaving the turn and prevailed over SILVER BULLET in a stiff drive.The latter, reserved early, made a run while racing well out in the track nearing the stretch and just missed in a sharp effort. COMPANY COMMANDER, always close up, ducked to the inside of the leaders entering the stretch and continued with good energy. RASTAFERIAN weakened after showing speed to midstretch. BUTTONBUCK went up after RASTAFERIAN on the turn, remained prominent to midstretch and tired. SURF lacked the needed response. DANCE D'ESPOIR moved up along the inside at the turn but was finished after going six furlongs. GOOD BEAU tired badly from his early efforts.

Owners— 1, Harmonay R M; 2, Blum P E; 3, Barrera O S; 4, Tesher R C; 5, Meadowhill; 6, Cuitino W I; 7, Miron Julie; 8, Willowbay Stable.

Trainers— 1, DeBonis Robert; 2, Jerkens Steven T; 3, Barrera Oscar S; 4, Tesher Howard M; 5, Johnson Philip G; 6, Cuitino Walter I; 7, Fernandez Floreano; 8, Tufariello Frank.

Overweight: Surf 1 pound.

Scratched—Pepysian (27Jun77 5Bel6); Handsome Tod (1Jly77 6Bel4); Don't Believe It (1Jly77 6Bel6); Oil Crisis (28Mar77 6Aqu5).

This race contributes eight data points, one for each horse in the race:

(3, 0.0)
(5, 0.0)
(7, 1.5)
(6, 2.0)
(4, 3.5)
(8, 3.7)
(2, 17.7)
(1, 17.9)

Each data point (data pair) contains two numbers, the first being the horse's post position, and the second the same horse's number of beaten lengths. (Note that we have treated a one-neck margin as 0.2 lengths. Likewise, a head would be 0.1 lengths, and a nose 0 lengths.)

The objective of linear regression is to find the straight line that best "fits" the eight data points. The linear regression line is sensitive to each of the eight points, in the sense that each point "tilts" the line slightly in its direction.

For visual purposes, a graph called a "scattergram" is popular. The straight line drawn on our scattergram provides a reasonable fit for our eight data points, which apparently defy a really tight fit.

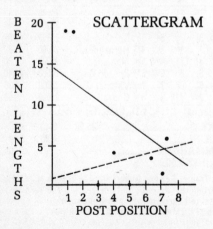

SCATTERGRAM

A quick glance at the scattergram reveals a potential problem. Two of the eight horses—those breaking from posts 1 and 2—were beaten by considerable margins. Over a large sample of races, their contribution would probably be "averaged out," unless they were part of a trend favoring outside horses at the expense of inside horses.

In a small sample like ours, however, a few extreme (and possibly meaningless) data points can completely change the complexion of the regression equation. A regression line based just on posts 3 to 8 would have looked completely different from the line based on all eight posts—as the dashed line on the scattergram suggests. A regression line based on posts 3 to 8 gives an advantage to the inside horses, while a regression line based on all eight posts indicates exactly the opposite.

When using a small sample, therefore, it is wise to carefully scrutinize the data, eliminating extreme data points that can only serve to distort by introducing meaningless data into the calculations.

But how do we determine which line best fits our observed data? That is where the linear regression formulas come in. They determine the coefficients a and b of the straight line $y = a + bx$ that best fits the data.

According to the regression equations, these two coefficients should be calculated according to the following formulas:

$$a = \frac{(\Sigma y)(\Sigma x^2) - (\Sigma x)(\Sigma xy)}{n(\Sigma x^2) - (\Sigma x)^2}$$

$$b = \frac{n(\Sigma xy) - (\Sigma x)(\Sigma y)}{n(\Sigma x^2) - (\Sigma x)^2}$$

Here, the notation Σy, for example, means the sum of the y-values (beaten lengths, in our example) of all the data points. The notation Σxy represents the sum of the products of the x- and y-values of all the data points. And n is the total number of data points (in our example, $n=8$).

The table below contains all the needed calculations for our example:

x	y	x²	xy
1	17.9	1	17.9
2	17.7	4	35.4
3	0.0	9	0.0
4	3.5	16	14.0
5	0.0	25	0.0
6	2.0	36	12.0
7	1.5	49	10.5
8	3.7	64	29.6
36	46.3	204	119.4

Consequently, $\Sigma x = 36$, $\Sigma y = 46.3$, $\Sigma x^2 = 204$, and $\Sigma xy = 119.4$. Therefore,

$$a = \frac{46.3 \times 204 - 36 \times 119.4}{8 \times 204 - 36 \times 36} = 15.3$$

and

$$b = \frac{8 \times 119.4 - 36 \times 46.3}{8 \times 204 - 36 \times 36} = -2.1$$

So the linear regression line expressing beaten lengths as a function of post position (at $1\frac{1}{16}$ miles at Belmont) is $y = 15.3 - 2.1x$; that is,

BEATEN LENGTHS $= 15.3 - 2.1 \times$ POST POSITION

Multiple regression is far more complex. The typical multiple regression equation takes the form

$$y = a_1 x_1 + a_2 x_2 + \cdots + a_n x_n$$

where y is the predicted variable and x_1, x_2, through x_n are the predictor variables. The object of the multiple regression calculations is to determine the values of the coefficients a_1, a_2, through a_n that define the equation that best fits the observed data. Equations for these coefficients are far more complex than those for a and b in the linear regression case, and the calculations are usually done by computer.